D1488222

MAGILL'S
SURVEY
OF
CINEMA

MAGILL'S SURVEY OF CINEMA

English Language Films

SECOND SERIES
VOLUME 6
THE-Z

Edited by

FRANK N. MAGILL

Associate Editors

STEPHEN L. HANSON

PATRICIA KING HANSON

SALEM PRESS
Englewood Cliffs, N.J.

LIBRARY OF CONGRESS CATALOG CARD NUMBER: 81-84330

Complete Set: ISBN 0-89356-230-0
Volume 6:   ISBN-0-89356-236-X

PRINTED IN THE UNITED STATES OF AMERICA

LIST OF TITLES IN VOLUME SIX

MAGILL'S SURVEY OF CINEMA

THERE'S ALWAYS TOMORROW

Released: 1956
Production: Ross Hunter for Universal
Direction: Douglas Sirk
Screenplay: Bernard C. Schoenfeld; based on an original story by Ursula Parrott
Cinematography: Russell Metty
Editing: William Morgan
Running time: 84 minutes

Principal characters:
Norma Miller Vale	Barbara Stanwyck
Clifford Groves	Fred MacMurray
Marion Groves	Joan Bennett
Ann	Pat Crowley
Mrs. Rogers	Jane Darwell
Vinnie	William Reynolds

Douglas Sirk was a German filmmaker who fled to Hollywood in the 1930's after Hitler came to power. Like many such artists, he brought with him a rich background in theater and film direction that enriched the American commercial film industry for decades. Coming from a tradition in cinema that was known for its visual qualities, Sirk put a great deal of the real meaning, especially meaning critical of dominant ideology, in the visual style of his films. He directed primarily for Universal in the 1950's, before retiring to Switzerland in 1959 after his enormously successful remake of *Imitation of Life* that same year. He made melodramas almost exclusively, in which the values of love, family, and, above all, emotion, figure most importantly. In this genre, the narrative tells a story which values home, family, and marriage—the status quo. Its required ideological operation is to pose a threat to these "fundamental" values and then to vanquish that threat, reinstating the primacy of the stable nuclear family.

Sirk made many films which, at some level, challenged this operation. *Written on the Wind* (1956), *Imitation of Life*, *All I Desire* (1953), *All That Heaven Allows* (1955), and *There's Always Tomorrow* are films which subvert the genre and its ideological function. *There's Always Tomorrow* is the least recognized and written-about film in the recent resurgence of interest in Sirk, but it is the most single-minded and effective critique of the bourgeois family in his entire canon.

Clifford Groves (Fred MacMurray) is a successful toy manufacturer with a lovely wife named Marion (Joan Bennett), three lovely children, and a beautiful house—all the trappings of a comfortable, happy, middle-class dream. Norma Vale (Barbara Stanwyck), a dress designer who used to work for Cliff when he was beginning his toy company and who left for New York because she was in love with him and realized he did not love her, returns to town on a temporary job and renews her friendship with Cliff. Norma's presence awakens in him a sense of excitement and life that has been numbed by years of living in a rut, and he falls in love with her. They plan to run off together, but his children come to see Norma and she realizes that he belongs with his family. She leaves him and returns to New York.

From the description of the plot, one would assume that *There's Always Tomorrow* carries out the operation of the genre very well. A threat is posed to the family, then vanquished (with the complicity of the threat itself), leaving the family intact and presumably even stronger for its fresh view of itself. Nothing could be further from the truth about this film. Sirk is a master of critiquing narrative with visuals. *There's Always Tomorrow* opens with a title card reading, "In Sunny California," then dissolves through to a dark rainy day, making explicit the obvious discrepancy between what is asserted and what is shown, a gap between what the narrative tells us and what is actually happening on the screen.

This discrepancy is carried out through the entire film. The beautiful house in which the Groves live is actually a nightmare of dark, oppressive shadows which swallow up Cliff. Bars of shadow thrown from chairs, and a bannister make the interior resemble a cage or prison. Compositions force foreground objects to loom threateningly over characters, dominating and sucking the life from them. Cliff is especially unwelcome in this suburban prison: he is often left standing alone in a shadow while another character walks away from him, pulling the camera away and forcing him to follow, half in and half out of the shot. The children interrupt Cliff's birthday wishes to his wife, claiming her attention in the most trivial of matters, crossing between husband and wife and pulling their mother away with them, leaving Cliff trailing along, ignored flowers in his hands, unsuccessful in his attempts to take Marion out for her birthday. Cliff is often shot outside the house, looking in like a stranger at his wife and children who have no time or attention for him. The low ceilings and dark shadows crowd him out, even as the characters are talking about what a wonderful home it is.

Sirk uses the device of a family portrait to show further Cliff's status as outsider. It is a picture of Marion and the three children; Cliff has no place in it just as he has none in the house itself. The film's "happy" ending, with the family reunited and Norma flying off to New York alone, is one of the bleakest in all cinema. Cliff closes the window after seeing the airplane in which Norma is flying disappear in the distance and turns back to his family like a zombie. The connection with his latest toy, "Rex, the Walky, Talky Robot Man," is complete as Marion takes his arm and leads him into the center of the room, where shadows block his face and shadow bars cross his path. He looks like a man who has been beaten as he tells Marion, "You know me better than I know myself," and lets her walk him past the watching children. They are behind the bars of the bannister, an ominous symbol of their own futures, and in the false perception of all of Sirk's characters, they comment on what a handsome couple their parents are.

Norma, on the other hand, is light and movement itself. She stands out from the darkness during our first view of her on Cliff's porch, turning and radiating a glow. Onscreen she attracts the eye instantly because her light coat and her quick, impulsive movements contrast with the lethargy of Marion. Indeed, Marion, in her all-consuming role of mother, takes on a frightening calmness in the face of any emergency. She is plastic perfection as she glides through her role as comforter and soother, serenity itself. Norma excites Cliff, challenging him to swim, ride, and be active, while Marion shakes her head over his certain stiffness the next day and draws him a bath he does not want. She takes him back into the smothering house when he wants to get a little fresh air, and tells him that if life were always exciting it would also be exhausting.

The truly radical element of Sirk's indictment of the bourgeois family is that he makes it clear that it is neither lack of love nor individual failure that makes the Groves's home so oppressive and Norma's representation of escape so liberating. It is not the people themselves, but rather the very structure of their roles in relation to one another that dooms them. This is evident in the illusions each has about the others and what would make their own lives happy. Norma sincerely believes that Cliff's home and family are perfect. She agrees with Marion's private assessment to Cliff of her successful career, "Poor Norma—she's missed what every woman really wants—a home and family." Cliff does not fall in love with Norma any more than he did twenty years ago; she just represents excitement and escape from his deadly rut. Not one character is aware of the truth Sirk makes so visually clear to his audience—that the roles of mother, father-provider, and lonely career woman are in themselves confining traps. Marion is so much a mother to her children that she ignores Cliff, except when she mothers him as well. She tries to keep her bratty children dependent on her in the name of nurturing, and becomes dull to her husband for the same reason.

Children, generally viewed as a woman's true meaning in life in the melodrama genre, the element of woman's life she must put before all others, are actually a conservative, negative force in Sirk's films. They are the most insensitive to Cliff, dominating the telephone and their mother and then begging for the return of their father's affections from Norma. Sirk has stated that "Children are usually put into pictures right at the end to show that a new generation is coming up. In my films I want to show exactly the opposite: I think it is the tragedies which are starting over again, always and always." Vinnie (William Reynolds) and Ann (Pat Crowley), Cliff's oldest child and his girl friend, respectively, are not the "hope for the future" they might be in an ordinary melodrama. Instead, they represent the irony of the title in that they will follow exactly in the Groves's numb footsteps.

The film shows a cycle: Norma goes off to New York just as she did twenty years ago; Vinnie and Ann watch from behind bars as Cliff and Marion walk into the dark, oppressive interior of their house. Sirk presents a world in which men's and women's options are limited and bleak and their view of their possibilities distorted and destructive. Instead of showing their unhappiness as the result of their individual failure, he shows that the social prisons and false values which trap people are structural, and that change must be radical if it is going to have a real effect on people's lives. Sirk raised the level of consciousness of the genre by relocating the source of people's emotional pain from personal failure to the structure and ideology of American bourgeois society and its values.

Janey Place

THEY DIED WITH THEIR BOOTS ON

Released: 1941
Production: Hal B. Wallis for Warner Bros.
Direction: Raoul Walsh
Screenplay: Wally Kline and Aeneas MacKenzie
Cinematography: Bert Glennon
Editing: William Holmes
Art direction: John Hughes
Makeup: Perc Westmore
Costume design: Milo Anderson
Music: Max Steiner
Running time: 140 minutes

Principal characters:
George Armstrong Custer	Errol Flynn
Elizabeth Bacon Custer	Olivia de Havilland
Ned Sharp	Arthur Kennedy
William Sharp	Walter Hampden
General Winfield Scott	Sydney Greenstreet
Samuel Bacon	Gene Lockhart
Crazy Horse	Anthony Quinn
California Joe	Charley Grapewin
Major Romulus Taipe	Stanley Ridges
General Philip Sheridan	John Litel
Callie	Hattie McDaniel

George Armstrong Custer (1839-1876) was an ambiguous figure in American history. Graduating from West Point in 1861, he fought in the first Battle of Bull Run, served on General McClellan's staff in the Peninsular campaign, became the youngest general in the Union Army, and served with distinction at Gettysburg and in the Shenandoah Valley. He received the Confederate flag of truce and was present at Lee's surrender at Appomattox. He ended the war as a major-general with one of the most impressive records in the Union Army. In the peacetime army, he was reduced in rank to lieutenant-colonel and put in command of the Seventh Cavalry. For leaving his command without permission, he was court-martialed in 1867 but was reinstated by General Sheridan. In November, 1868, he massacred a band of peaceful Cheyenne Indians and their allies at a reservation on the Washita; but later, he was a spokesman for Indian rights and against the incursion of gold-hunters into Sioux lands in the Dakotas. In 1876, under the command of General Alfred H. Terry, he encountered the Sioux on the Little Bighorn in Montana, divided his command, and attacked with one third of them (about two hundred men). Blundering into a vast horde of concealed Indians, he and his entire command were killed. It is ironic that for this overwhelming defeat Custer became a national hero. His wife, Elizabeth Bacon Custer (1842-1933), championed his reputation with numerous books about army life in the West.

Inevitably, Custer came to figure in Western films. In 1926, Dustin Farnum played him in *Flaming Frontier*. Frank McGlynn portrayed him in 1936 in *Custer's Last Stand*, and in the same year he appeared in Cecil B. De Mille's epic *The Plainsman*, in which he plays a rather rigid martinet. Ronald Reagan played Custer in *The Santa Fe Trail* (1940), as a sidekick to J. E. B. Stuart (Errol Flynn) pursuing John Brown in Kansas in the 1850's. The real Custer never saw service at that time and place and had not yet been through West Point. Later, Custer made brief appearances in *Warpath* (1951), *Bugles in the Afternoon* (1952), *The Great Sioux Massacre* (1965), and *Little Big Man* (1970), a satiric revisionist Western in which Richard Mulligan portrayed Custer as a demented megalomaniac. Robert Shaw played a more traditional version in *Custer of the West* (1968).

The largest-scale treatment of Custer is *They Died with Their Boots On*, starring Errol Flynn under the direction of Raoul Walsh. Walsh, a veteran actor and director from the days of early silent films, had made a number of earlier Westerns, including a semidocumentary on Pancho Villa filmed with the real Villa during the actual Mexican revolution. He was directing and starring in *In Old Arizona* (1929), the first sound Western, when he lost an eye in a car accident and was replaced in the lead by Warner Baxter, who won the Academy Award as best actor in the role. The next year, Walsh discovered John Wayne and starred him in *The Big Trail*. In 1939, Walsh went to work for Warner Bros., where he made some outstanding films starring James Cagney and Humphrey Bogart and directed seven films with Flynn. The first of these was *They Died with Their Boots On*, and it is one of the best. Although he was Tasmanian and seemed rather British, Flynn had made three successful Westerns in 1939 and 1940. As Warners' most dashing male star, he was the inevitable choice for Custer.

They Died with Their Boots On, epic in scale although it is, is not wholly authentic. Walsh called it "a romanticized version of George Custer's life," and as such he and Flynn presented Custer with great panache as a dashing and ultimately noble hero. Yet the film does not present simpleminded heroics but gives Custer considerable complexity as well as colorfulness. Inspired perhaps by Flynn's earlier *The Charge of the Light Brigade* (1936), with the tragic inevitability of its final battle, *They Died with Their Boots On* also leads to the tragic climax that audiences would expect, yet it has a great deal of fun along the way.

The film begins with Custer's arrival at West Point as a cadet from Michigan. Like a naïve young D'Artagnan, he arrives full of braggadocio, the country bumpkin come to town. Entering the academy on horseback, followed by a pack of hunting hounds, he is wearing a plumed hat and a homemade uniform that seems to belong to the Napoleonic wars. He instantly arouses the sardonic disdain of Ned Sharp (Arthur Kennedy), who directs him to his "quarters," actually the quarters of the commanding officer. Custer makes himself at home, sprawling on the bed with his hounds, until the commander enters and reacts with stunned outrage. Thus Custer begins his career as a cadet by being put on report. Throughout his years at West Point, he gets into trouble through his irrepressible high spirits, as he jumps a horse over cannon, violates discipline, is insubordinate to the ever-hostile Sharp, and is indifferent to his studies. He excels only in horsemanship and use of the sabre. Once when he is walking guard on punishment detail and is forbidden to speak to anyone, he is approached by Elizabeth Bacon (Olivia de Havilland), who asks him for directions and is offended when he keeps marching and will not answer her. As soon as his punishment is up, he pursues her and explains the reason for his offense. They soon fall in love, but her crusty father (Gene Lockhart) disapproves of her romance with a ne'er-do-well cadet.

Ned Sharp and the other upperclassmen graduate and are commissioned, while Custer continues in disgrace at West Point, where he is called the worst student since Ulysses S. Grant. When the Civil War breaks out, however, the remaining cadets are commissioned and sent off to war. Eager to get to the front, Custer finds himself stranded in Washington, entangled by military red tape. As he is dining one day at an officers' club, about to enjoy a plate of creamed Bermuda onions, he overhears a portly, elderly officer request creamed Bermuda onions, only to be told that Custer received the last dish. Gallantly, Custer offers the officer his own serving. He turns out to be General Winfield Scott (Sydney Greenstreet), then commander-in-chief of the army. When Scott thanks him and offers him a favor in return, Custer requests an order to the front. Dispensing with protocol, Scott writes him one on the spot. On leaving the club, Custer sees a horse being held for another officer, commandeers it, and is off to the war.

To their mutual chagrin, he finds himself in the same regiment with Ned Sharp. Custer distinguishes himself in a few skirmishes and at the battle of Bull Run, and his name is sent to Washington for commendation. By sheer accident, a bureaucrat handling promotions gets Custer's name by mistake and promotes him to brigadier general. Custer is the last person to learn this, and he shoos away a haberdasher who tries to sell him a general's uniform. When Sharp grudgingly calls him "General," Custer snaps; the joke has gone too far, and he is about to throttle Sharp when the latter informs him that, crazy though it may seem, he is indeed a general. Custer then runs after the uniform salesman, who, thinking him demented, takes to his heels. Custer's response to the promotion is that someone must have made a mistake, but if the army wants a general, by thunder he will be a general. He takes the initiative, and in a series of brilliant operations becomes a dashing commander. In the process, he breaks orders, but since he has succeeded, he is decorated instead of being court-martialed. At the end of the war, he returns home a hero. Elizabeth's father now cannot properly object and gives his grudging consent for her to marry Custer.

Civilian life bores Custer with its inactivity; he needs adventure, and without it he turns to drink. In some desperation, his wife appeals to General Philip Sheridan (John Litel), who arranges for Custer to be restored to active duty in command of the Seventh Cavalry. In the Dakota Territory, he finds that his command, under Major Romulus Taipe (Stanley Ridges), the officer whose horse he had commandeered, has become slack. On his way to the post, he has captured an Indian warrior, who turns out to be Crazy Horse (Anthony Quinn). Thanks to the careless discipline of the post, Crazy Horse breaks out of the guard house, seizes a mount, and escapes in a spectacular display of horsemanship. Custer states that Crazy Horse is the only real cavalryman around. The formerly scapegrace Custer, now a professional soldier, insists on discipline but finds that his efforts are being undermined by Taipe in collaboration with Ned Sharp and his father William (Walter Hampden), who are now Indian traders. When Custer orders the men to fall out for parade, they do so crazy drunk from the Sharps' whiskey. Custer then orders the post saloon shut down; he admits that he likes a drink as well as the next man, maybe better, so he knows what the men must endure, but the Seventh Cavalry must become professional again.

In a short time Custer restores both discipline and morale and turns the Seventh Cavalry into a crack regiment, respected throughout the West. For a regimental marching tune, he picks "Garry Owen," a spirited reel that he heard an Irish officer, Lieutenant Butler, play on the piano. Soon the sound of it played by the Seventh's fifers is the symbol of Custer's command.

Meanwhile, the Sharps, following the tradition of innumerable villains in frontier fiction and films, are trading guns to the Indians and selling them liquor. Custer is portrayed as a friend and supporter of the Indians (the film makes no mention of the massacre at the Washita), and he goes to Washington to use his influence on their behalf. Walsh observed that "Most Westerns had depicted the Indian as a painted, vicious savage. In *They Died with Their Boots On*, I tried to show him as an individual who only turned vindictive when his rights as defined by treaty were violated by white men." The violators in this case are the Sharps, who get Custer temporarily disgraced and relieved of command by manipulating the failure of his agreement with the Cheyenne and Sioux. Custer has promised to keep the white men out of the Black Hills, but the Sharps spread a false rumor that gold is in the area. When greedy prospectors pour in, the Sioux retaliate, and Custer is disgraced. President Grant restores his command, however, and sends him to subdue the now warlike Indians in the Dakota territory.

As the campaign develops, Custer realizes that Sheridan's command is in danger of being ambushed and destroyed. To prevent this from happening, he decides to sacrifice the regiment, to send the Seventh Cavalry on a virtual suicide mission. He informs Lieutenant Butler of his plan and offers to leave him—an Irishman—out of it, but Butler determines to go along with his comrades. Custer then takes Ned Sharp prisoner and makes him ride with the regiment. When Sharp asks where they are on the morning of the battle, Custer tells him that they are at the Little Big Horn in Montana and that ahead of them lies hell—or glory. When the Seventh Cavalry encounter the Sioux, Custer orders the charge and seems to be defeating the enemy, but the Indians draw them into a trap, and the soldiers find themselves surrounded by a vast horde of Indians. They fight to the last man; even Sharp dies bravely. Finally, only Custer is left alive, standing by the flag, armed with a sabre. The Indians shoot him down, and Crazy Horse's braves sweep over the battlefield of corpses.

The film ends with Elizabeth Custer testifying in Washington on her husband's behalf. She reads his final letter, which she interprets as the death wish of a man about to die. Thanks to it and to her, the government agrees to deal justly with the Indians. Thus, despite the Little Big Horn, *They Died with Their Boots On* takes the side of the Indians and presents Custer as their defender. This was in part true, but his defense of them was more than counteracted by his infamous massacre of the reservation on the Washita. In the film, however, Custer does indeed die for our sins.

Despite its historical inaccuracies, *They Died with Their Boots On* has much to commend it. Flynn gives a bravura performance that even Jack Warner called one of his best. He develops from a reckless young daredevil who seeks adventure for the pure excitement of it to a responsible, concerned commander and finally to a man who gives himself as a tragic sacrifice. The opening episodes have a great deal of humor, which Flynn handles with engaging panache. The supporting cast are first-rate, with Kennedy and Hampton as a fine pair of villains, Greenstreet as an affable Winfield Scott, Hattie McDaniel doing a reprise of her role from *Gone with the Wind* (1939), Quinn as a virile Crazy Horse, and Charley Grapewin as a grizzled frontier scout. *They Died with Their Boots On* was the eighth and last film in which Flynn was teamed with de Havilland, and they played particularly well together in a relationship more mature than in their previous motion pictures. The scene of his final leavetaking, when he knows but she does not that he will never see her again, has a richness unmatched in their films. Custer makes some attempts at humor that are pathetic under the circumstances and pretends to be an old man with a paunch settling into senile retirement, but he captures a sense of their entire marriage with the line, "Walking through life with you, ma'am, has been a very gracious thing indeed." It is as if he is pronouncing his own elegy, and after he leaves, she falls in a faint, as if she, too, foresees his death.

Warners mounted the film on an epic scale, and Max Steiner provided a fine score that blends in "Boots and Saddles," other cavalry bugle calls, and

"Garry Owen" with his own rich romanticism. Walsh's direction has a flair that matches Flynn's bravado. Although the film runs 140 minutes, its excitement never flags, and it moves with a mounting sense of tragedy to its inevitable climax. It remains one of the most impressive epic Westerns.

Robert E. Morsberger

THEY LIVE BY NIGHT

Released: 1948
Production: John Houseman for RKO/Radio
Direction: Nicholas Ray
Screenplay: Charles Schnee; based on Nicholas Ray's adaptation of the novel
   Thieves Like Us by Edward Anderson
Cinematography: George E. Diskant
Editing: Sherman Todd
Running time: 95 minutes

Principal characters:
Keechie	Cathy O'Donnell
Bowie	Farley Granger
Chicamaw	Howard da Silva
T-Dub	Jay C. Flippen
Mattie	Helen Craig
Mobley	Will Wright

They Live by Night is a tragic story adapted from Edward Anderson's 1937 novel *Thieves Like Us*. A moody, sensitive melodrama, it is set during the Depression and displays many of the characteristics of the *film noir* genre. In addition to being a gripping gangster/crime drama, it is also a delicate love story about two young people whose love cannot surmount the unfortunate circumstances which surround them.

The film centers on Bowie (Farley Granger), a twenty-three-year-old convict who has spent the last seven years in prison for accidentally killing a man. After escaping from jail in the company of two older, hardened criminals, Chicamaw (Howard da Silva) and T-Dub (Jay C. Flippen), Bowie meets Keechie (Cathy O'Donnell), a young, naïve, waifish girl who is the daughter of the escapees' outside accomplice. Although the girl has never known boys, she finds herself falling in love with the essentially good-hearted and decent Bowie. She sees in him a sensitivity which is not usually evident in someone who has been imprisoned from adolescence. In one touching moment, Bowie reveals some of his dreams to Keechie when he tells her "I've always wanted to hold hands with a girl in a movie." Despite the fact that their relationship seems predestined for tragedy, they marry in a rather shoddy civil ceremony.

Because of his connections to Chicamaw and T-Dub, Bowie is pressed by them into helping to commit some bank robberies. He consents to these robberies almost passively because he naïvely believes that the money he steals can be used to hire a lawyer to clear his name of the original crime. Instead of bringing him an opportunity for freedom, however, his crimes eventually force Bowie and Keechie to flee across country. Fearful of being recognized during the day, the ill-fated lovers are forced to "live by night,"

moving between dismal motor courts and cheap diners. During their wanderings Keechie becomes pregnant, but because Bowie wants his unborn child
to have a better chance at life than he had, he decides to leave his wife.
Before he can get away, however, Mattie (Helen Craig), the wife of one of
the gunmen who is involved in the robberies, betrays Bowie to the police in
order to gain a pardon for her own husband. In the end, the confused, unhappy
Bowie is machine-gunned to death.

Granger is very sympathetic as Bowie, the bewildered, desperate, yet
almost noble fugitive. O'Donnell, who possesses a certain gentle, unglamorous beauty, is equally believable as the girl who naïvely follows him. The
audience has great sympathy for the two because neither has had the chance
to lead a decent life, and therefore had no other paths to follow. The film
presents them as pawns of forces beyond their control. No amount of hope
or vindication will allow them a more rewarding life. The others in the cast
are competent character actors, although Silva, as usual, gives a fine performance which equals that of the two young stars. Silva made a career out of
playing antagonists in gangster films, but he did not reduce his roles to mere
thugs. In *They Live by Night* he deftly portrays the aggressive alcoholic Chicamaw as a proud, publicity-hungry crook who constantly checks the newspapers for accounts of the robberies. He is the antithesis of the shy, naïve
Bowie.

Although unglamorous and unsentimental, *They Live by Night* is nevertheless moving and lyrical in its compelling, romantic story, its dreamlike
atmosphere, and its impressionistic style. Cinematographer George E. Diskant captures the bleak highways, motels, and tourist camps which the young
couple inhabit with his expressive camera, and director Nicholas Ray fills the
somber film with suspense and understanding. It would have been easy for
a director to succumb to the many maudlin elements of the story, but Ray
instead has created a sensitive, understated film free of artifice.

Ray was thirty-six when he made *They Live by Night*, his first feature film.
Previously he had been a student of eminent architect Frank Lloyd Wright,
an actor, and a stage writer and director. His work with Wright seemed to
influence his style of filmmaking, as evidenced by this and many of his later
films. His works have often dealt with themes such as the loneliness of man,
his maladjustment to society, his alienation, dislocation, and disharmony.
Two of his most famous films, *In a Lonely Place* (1950) and *Rebel Without
a Cause* (1956), reflect these themes. Often Ray's characters are isolationists
who are suspected wrongly (or without sufficient evidence) of crimes. They
tend to become involved in anguished relationships, and they suffer from
inner turmoils which are seemingly unresolvable. To reinforce the turbulence
of his characters' lives, Ray creates cinematic turbulence within the frames
of his scenes with a kinetic visual style that makes use of cutting on movement,
rather than simply cutting on static shots.

In 1974 Robert Altman made his own film version of Anderson's novel, retaining the book's original title, *Thieves Like Us*. This film was a depressing, almost nightmarish story with Keith Carradine and Shelley Duvall as Bowie and Keechie. The Altman film (which is not a remake of the Ray film) focuses upon the sociological aspects of the poverty-stricken rural Depression areas used as locations for the film. A director of a very different style, Ray filmed the story in a way that emphasizes the tender love story between Bowie and Keechie and their relationships to other members of the gang, rather than concentrating on exterior circumstances. Both films, however, fit into the "doomed lovers on the run" offshoot of the gangster genre film. Two other noteworthy examples of this type of film are Fritz Lang's *You Only Live Once* (1937) and Arthur Penn's *Bonnie and Clyde* (1967).

Leslie Taubman

THEY SHOOT HORSES DON'T THEY?

Released: 1969
Production: Irwin Winkler, Robert Chartoff, and Sydney Pollack for ABC
Direction: Sydney Pollack
Screenplay: James Poe and Robert E. Thompson; based on the novel of the same name by Horace McCoy
Cinematography: Philip H. Lathrop
Editing: Fredric Steinkamp
Running time: 120 minutes

Principal characters:
Gloria Beatty	Jane Fonda
Robert Syverton	Michael Sarrazin
Alice	Susannah York
Rocky	Gig Young (AA)
Sailor	Red Buttons
Ruby	Bonnie Bedelia
Rollo	Michael Conrad
James	Bruce Dern
Turkey	Al Lewis
Joel	Robert Fields

They Shoot Horses Don't They? is an attempt to depict on screen the stark reality of depression—not only the economic depression of the 1930's, but also the personal depression that engulfs all of those who fit into the category of "losers." Placing the action of this 1969 film in the Depression-era setting helps to compel the viewer to appreciate fully and feel the despair of the contestants in the marathon. In this marathon, intended to be a microcosm of life, the dancers are all put into a no-win situation, the rules are set, and basic needs are provided, but "acts of God are not covered." The ballroom's location at the end of a pier overlooking the Pacific Ocean also symbolizes that from this world, there is nowhere else to go.

The original short novel, written by Horace McCoy in 1935, is a bleak story of Depression-era losers trying through competition in the marathon to become winners. It is an existential story, praised by Albert Camus and Jean-Paul Sartre, which presents life, including the struggles of the contestants, as meaningless. In the novel it is inevitable that Gloria will seek death when she accepts the only option really left to her. In the film version, however, major changes in the characters and the plot, mainly at the hands of the second screenwriter, Robert E. Thompson, changed the story from its existential comment about life in general to the tragic story of a determined woman's defeat. The resulting film is a flawed but compelling rendition of the original classic.

Gloria Beatty (Jane Fonda) and Robert Syverton (Michael Sarrazin) are the lead characters in this drama, and it is their struggle—really Gloria's—that we care about. Fonda plays a determined, streetwise actress trying to survive despite her secret fear that the deck is really stacked against her. She displays a hard, cynical attitude throughout, quipping about buying rat poison with the winnings. She is also vulnerable, as director Sydney Pollack establishes in several ways, most particularly through her response to Robert's innocuous and unfruitful meeting with Alice (Susannah York). She, too, can be faithless as she nurses her hurt feelings by coldly seeking out Rocky (Gig Young), the MC, and ordering him to comply on her terms. We see in her a woman at the end of her resources trying desperately to be a winner for a change, hanging on by sheer willpower. In the end she is again defeated, receiving no breaks from Rocky and no support from Robert.

Robert is a less well developed and more enigmatic character. Sarrazin plays the wide-eyed innocent who gives the impression of having "checked-out" long ago—the ultimate passive character. He is going nowhere , apparently having no will at all. He is a bystander at the beginning when he is talked into being Gloria's partner, and throughout the entire film he is the quintessential dreamer. During the marathon he seems to pick up at least a direction toward a goal from Gloria and partly from Alice, but it is all second-hand. The opening scene and interjected vignettes from his childhood and the arrest tease the audience into an expectation that his character or his past is somehow significant; but the truth is less fulfilling than the promise.

The other contestants all represent struggling losers too, out to win the prize of fifteen hundred dollars while getting room and board for their effort. James (Bruce Dern) and Ruby (Bonnie Bedelia) are expecting a child and have been marathoning across the country, somewhat reminiscent of migrant workers going from crop to crop. Bedelia is perfect as a fragile scrapper who can resist Gloria's nasty remarks about abortion as well as put on a pathetic performance for the audience's entertainment. Dern is also convincing, showing both pride and determination to survive as he angrily picks up the coins thrown to his wife. Red Buttons plays the sailor who has blatantly lied about his age in order to compete. As a veteran of other marathons and campaigns, he is worldly wise and generously tries to help out the younger folk. He alone of all the contestants maintains an optimistic attitude. Knowing the game and the possible outcome as well, he is still a survivor, although he, too, is obviously going nowhere. Ironically, it is Gloria's determination to be a survivor that finishes him off as she drags his body across the finish line of the second derby.

The slick couple, Alice (Susannah York) and Rollo (Michael Conrad), typify those in the contest seeking stardom. Their dream is to be discovered by a big producer and taken off to nearby Hollywood—a dream exploited by the marathon promoters who have decorated the hall with movie posters and have Rocky introduce any person in the film industry who enters the ballroom. Alice and Rollo are too naïve to realize the true nature of the marathon. It is not run for the contestants, but instead is a show for the audience, as Rocky points out to Robert. It is necessary for the contestants to appear worse off than the audience, and it is necessary for Rocky to destroy Alice's Jean Harlow act to help make the marathon a financial success. Rollo does quit the marathon when offered another bit part in a movie, but it is clear that his success is not only random, but also minimal.

Although this movie earned nine nominations for Academy Awards, Young was the only winner for his portrayal of the sophisticated, cynical MC, Rocky. Young's portrayal is a subtle blend of varying aspects of manipulation, at which Rocky excels. He is a smooth crowd-pleaser and huckster, keeping up a steady patter punctuated by his boisterous "yowza, yowza, yowza"; a kind of natural-born psychiatrist, able to encourage the contestants to keep going as well as to calm them down when they finally crack like Alice; and a shrewd, hard-nosed manager who, failing in his initial marriage pitch to Gloria and Robert, fills her in on the harsh realities of the marathon game. He pulls no punches in his effort to win her cooperation. Seen between stints as MC, he appears tired and unshaven, and it is clear that the event takes its toll on him as well. But he has learned that to survive, he must sell out. He is a master at survival, however bleak that survival may seem.

They Shoot Horses Don't They? succeeds because of its ability to draw the audience into the action. The movie is structured and paced very carefully from the beginning confusion of registration through the excitement, tension, and anguish of the last derby. It is a long movie whose pace mirrors the more than forty-two days of the marathon. The audience feels as if they too, are in a marathon, a feeling which is heightened by the steeplechase segments of the derbys which are run whenever the marathon action seems a little dull. During this ten-minute race, the contestants must perform in track suits, not needing to be first, but needing not to be last to stay in the contest. These sequences are very powerfully portrayed and conveyed on film. During these segments, Gloria's determination and strength really show as she first pounds out a cramp from Robert's leg, and later drags Sailor through to the end. It is impossible not to care for these characters, although the only noncontestant who seems to share this feeling is an old lady who cheers on Gloria and Robert. As time passes through days and weeks, the contestants are slowly eliminated to a fraction of the original mob. For those who remain, there is no relief.

Throughout this relentlessly long marathon there is little character development or interaction. Aside from the initial introductions and some partner changes, the progress is all in one direction—downhill. The competition prevents more than superficial relationships. At varying speeds, the hopes and façades accompanying each contestant are stripped, stolen, or worn down until each is left with only a grim determination to survive until he collapses or cracks under the pressure of weeks of almost constant motion.

Gloria's breaking point comes when Rocky finally lets her know that winning the marathon is useless, since she will have to pay the cost of her room and board. Symbolically, we are to believe that this is true of life in general: there is no use in winning, since there is nothing to win. In McCoy's original story, this was the central theme, and although the marathon also works as a microcosm of life in the film, Pollack's life is different, in more ways than merely the difference caused by our distance from the era when dance marathons flourished. Pollack shows us a world, seen in the more political terms of the 1960's, in which there are those who have power—Rocky, the promoters, Central Casting—and those who do not—the contestants. The change of Gloria's character, from a despairing actress dragged through the dancing by Robert into a tough fighter, changes the story irrevocably. Keeping the ending intact, however, is where the film fails. Gloria's decision to die after struggling so hard fails to satisfy. It is hard to believe that once the decision is made, she cannot pull the trigger. It is also incredibly ironic that here, at last, someone as ineffective as Robert will finally come through and help her. At this point, we suddenly make sense of the flash-forwards that were so confusing throughout. The "punch line" of the title and final line of dialogue hits the audience before Gloria hits the ground. This feeling of a contrived, heavy-handed climax makes the film a failure as an existential comment and finally unsatisfying as an artistic statement about life.

Christine Gladish

THEY WON'T FORGET

Released: 1937
Production: Mervyn LeRoy for Warner Bros.
Direction: Mervyn LeRoy
Screenplay: Aben Handel and Robert Rossen; based on the novel *Death in the Deep South* by Ward Greene
Cinematography: Arthur Edeson and Warren Lynch
Editing: Thomas Richards
Running time: 94 minutes

Principal characters:

Andy Griffin	Claude Rains
Robert Hale	Edward Norris
Bill Brock	Allyn Joslyn
Imogene Mayfield	Linda Perry
Detective Laneart	Cy Kendall
Carlysle P. Buxton	E. Alyn Warren
Jim Timberlake	Clifford Soubier
Mrs. Mountford	Ann Shoemaker
Governor Mountford	Paul Everton
Sybil Hale	Gloria Dickson
Tump Redwine	Clinton Rosemond
Joe Turner	Elisha Cook, Jr.
Gleason	Otto Kruger
Mary Clay	Lana Turner

During the 1930's, Warner Bros. produced a series of liberal, reform-oriented "social message" features. All were pungent, hard-hitting critiques of contemporary society and focused on such controversial subjects as the lack of justice in the American penal system (*I Am a Fugitive from a Chain Gang*, 1932), the racist activities of the Ku Klux Klan (*Black Legion*, 1936), and the unsafe conditions in coal mines (*Black Fury*, 1935). One of their finest films of the era is a savage, scorching condemnation of mob violence, yellow journalism, and racial prejudice and intolerance, *They Won't Forget*. The film spotlights the issue of injustice in the South at a time when most Hollywood products were escapist entertainments.

In the story, Andy Griffin (Claude Rains), the district attorney in Flodden, a small Southern town, is anxious for election to higher office. His opportunity to elicit support from the voters arrives when Mary Clay (Lana Turner), a young student in a local business college, is murdered in the basement of the school building. The police "interrogate" Tump Redwine (Clinton Rosemond), the black janitor who discovers the body. One of the visual highlights of *They Won't Forget* is an overhead shot of the terrified Tump lying on a cot as he is grilled by police.

Griffin believes that Tump's conviction will not be politically expedient because he is black. The lynching of a black will hardly be sensational enough to gain the prosecutor the political spotlight. The indictment of two other suspects, a mill hand who was Mary's boyfriend and a highly respected colonel who is the school's principal, would alienate specific segments of the community on which Griffin relies for support. The lawyer therefore decides that the guilty party will be Robert Hale (Edward Norris), a new teacher at the school, a Northerner who has just settled in town with his wife (Gloria Dickson). The attorney can profit politically only if this "outsider" is convicted. A case is not difficult to build: the teacher was in the building at the time of the crime; a blood stain is discovered on a jacket he had sent to the cleaners (Hale claims a barber had cut him); the murdered girl had a crush on him; and he was thinking of leaving town, allegedly because of a new teaching position.

There is no concrete evidence that Hale is the killer, but he is convicted by the local press before the commencement of the trial. The actual proceedings are conducted like a circus, and the result is a fight between North and South. A mob beats up a detective sent to the scene by a Northern newspaper, Hale's New York attorney is stoned, and Tump is frightened into giving false testimony against Hale, who is, of course, found guilty. When his death sentence is commuted to life in prison by the governor, however, he is lynched. The hanging party boards the train in which Hale is a passenger, his guards are overpowered, and he is removed by the mob. As the train pulls away, the roar overcomes Hale's screams. His actual hanging is suggested in a memorable shot: another train rumbles toward the camera, and a mail bag that dangles from a crosstree nearby the tracks is abruptly snatched up by a hook as the train passes. At the film's finale, Hale's widow has accused Griffin and Brock (Allyn Joslyn), a newspaper reporter, of complicity in her husband's death. After she leaves, the newspaperman muses to the prosecutor that perhaps Hale had committed the crime after all. Griffin, with his career and upward mobility foremost in his mind, absentmindedly responds: "I wonder."

They Won't Forget was adapted from Ward Greene's novel *Death in the Deep South*, which was based on an actual incident which occurred two decades earlier in Georgia. In 1913, Leo Frank, a Jew, was convicted of murdering a fourteen-year-old white girl. The damning evidence was offered by a black who had himself been a suspect in the case, and his testimony was contradicted by other witnesses. Frank was found guilty, and his religion had as much to do with his conviction as any fact or testimony. Two years later, the governor of the state commuted Frank's sentence from death to life in prison on the grounds that he had not been given a fair trial. He was lynched soon afterward. The interlude with Tump Redwine is also reminiscent of the case of the Scottsboro Boys. In 1931, nine poor young black men were tried for the alleged rape of two promiscuous white girls. Despite evidence proving their innocence, they were convicted by all-white juries, and some remained incarcerated for almost twenty years. The Scottsboro trials were in active phases when *They Won't Forget* premiered.

Mervyn LeRoy's direction of the film is simple and direct. He unravels the narrative with no frills, in a polished, fast-paced manner not unlike a newsreel and characteristic of the Warner Bros.' style of filmmaking. Despite the striking camera angles and visual effects, narrative is LeRoy's primary concern. The director is no great stylist, but is more of a competent film technician with as much a feeling for musicals and comedies such as *Tugboat Annie* (1933) and *Gold Diggers of 1933* (1933) as for gangster and adventure films such as *Little Caesar* (1931) and *Oil for the Lamps of China* (1935) and social consciousness features such as *They Won't Forget* and *I Am a Fugitive from a Chain Gang*. In fact, Rains's casual response at the film's conclusion is similar in effect to Paul Muni's hissing of "I steal" at the finale of *I Am a Fugitive from a Chain Gang*. (Muni portrayed an innocent man sent to rot away on a Southern chain gang, where he becomes a hardened criminal.)

All of the performances in *They Won't Forget* are excellent. Rains, the only screen veteran in the cast, is appropriately callous and contemptible as Griffin, and this was his best role up to that time. Dickson, Joslyn, and all the rest offer incisive portrayals, but the film is most memorable for the appearance of the seventeen-year-old who played the ill-fated Mary Clay: Lana Turner. She attracted notice as, garbed in a tight sweater and skirt, she sits at a drugstore counter, and then saunters down the street. Audience reaction, notably among the male viewers, and the ensuing Sweater Girl publicity, launched her on a successful film career.

It is not surprising that *They Won't Forget* was banned throughout the South, but it is surprising that the film, despite phenomenal reviews, did not win a single Academy Award nomination. The National Board of Review and *The New York Times*, however, selected it as among the ten best films of the year. One of the screenwriters of *They Won't Forget* is Robert Rossen, and Andy Griffin may be compared to Willie Stark, the central character in *All the King's Men*, the Oscar-winning 1949 film produced, directed, and written by Rossen. Although Stark is honest at the start of his political career, he is transformed into an Andy Griffin as he rises to the governorship of his state. Both men are equally and frighteningly demagogical in their quest for power.

Historically, *They Won't Forget* is exemplary in its portrayal of the black janitor. Tump Redwine is one of the first black characters in the American cinema ever to be victimized by social injustice, although he is not the focus of the film, and any overt commentary about racism is avoided. Sadly, Rosemond plays the part in the stereotyped, eye-popping style characteristic of the era, but his identity as a black man who has been exploited still looms within the framework of the story. If Hale had not been a Northerner—a politically viable label for Griffin to exploit—Tump would have been the next likely suspect because of the color of his skin. It is unclear and irrelevant whether Hale is guilty or innocent—indeed, he even may have murdered Mary Clay after all—because Hale is simply a substitute for Tump Redwine. Hollywood would not portray as a protagonist a black man falsely accused of murder for another twelve years, with the release of *Intruder in the Dust* (1949).

Rob Edelman

THIEVES LIKE US

Released: 1974
Production: Jerry Bick for Jerry Bick-George Litto; released by United Artists
Direction: Robert Altman
Screenplay: Calder Willingham, Joan Tewkesbury, and Robert Altman; based
  on the novel of the same name by Edward Anderson
Cinematography: Jean Boffety
Editing: Louis Lombardo
Running time: 123 minutes

Principal characters:
> Bowie .... Keith Carradine
> Keechie Mobley .... Shelley Duvall
> Elmo (Chicamaw) Mobley .... John Schuck
> T-Dub Masefield .... Bert Remsen
> Mattie .... Louise Fletcher
> Dee Mobley .... Tom Skerritt
> Lula .... Ann Latham

Although it is essentially a "gangster" film, *Thieves Like Us* typifies Robert
Altman's repeated attempts to go beyond the traditional codes and conven-
tions of the particular genre within which he has chosen to work. In the
present instance, this is most clearly exemplified by his refusal to romanticize
either his heroes or their exploits. While this refusal undoubtedly goes a long
way toward explaining the film's disappointing reception at the box office, it
also helps to make *Thieves Like Us* a refreshingly original depiction of its
subject matter. Moreover, because *Thieves Like Us* is based on the same
Edward Anderson novel that served as the source for Nicholas Ray's *They
Live by Night* (1949), the originality of Altman's version is all the more
remarkable. It is not, as some people believe, a remake of the earlier film.

In addition to its unconventional narrative strategy of downplaying action
in favor of a series of unexpected domestic scenes, the originality of *Thieves
Like Us* is the result of a wide range of stylistic techniques. The most important
of these include Altman's use of naturalistic details, the impression of improv-
isation created by his performers, and the innovative use of sound. The
subdued colors and tones of Jean Boffety's beautiful cinematography also
provide a striking contrast when compared to the dramatic lighting used in
many films of the *film noir* genre. Finally, Altman's penchant for using moving-
camera shots instead of direct cuts represents the antithesis of the normal
Hollywood visual style.

Like many of Altman's other films, such as *Brewster McCloud* (1970),
McCabe and Mrs. Miller (1971), and *The Long Goodbye* (1973), *Thieves Like
Us* chronicles the eventual destruction of the hopes and aspirations of its

principal characters. Structurally, each of these films focuses on a protagonist who embarks on an adventure which he assumes he can control. Gradually, this sense of control is proved to be illusory and results in the protagonist's death or ultimate disillusionment. The three bank robbers in *Thieves Like Us* all fit this pattern. Among these, Bowie (Keith Carradine) is the most pivotal because his youthful innocence would seem to afford him the greatest chance to survive. In the end, however, even Bowie is defeated because he cannot adjust to the realities of the system.

Quite often in Altman's films, "dreamers" such as Bowie and the other thieves are played off against more realistic types whose lack of self-delusions insure that they will survive. In *Thieves Like Us*, Mattie (Louise Fletcher) is particularly representative of this other type, while Keechie (Shelley Duvall) is a somewhat more pathetic version. Thus, although Keechie makes the mistake of falling in love with Bowie, her awareness of her own limitations prevents her from sharing in his fate. Keechie also contributes to the anti-romantic tone of *Thieves Like Us* by demonstrating the failure of love to overcome the insurmountable web of circumstances which ensnare the hero.

Thieves Like Us opens just after Bowie, Chickamaw (John Shuck), and T-Dub (Bert Remsen) have escaped from the Mississippi State Prison. Although T-Dub and Chickamaw are both hardened criminals, Bowie's basic innocence is underscored by the fact that he has been in prison since the age of sixteen. Their first real hideaway is Dee Mobley's (Tom Skerritt) ramshackle service station. It is here that Bowie meets Keechie, and the two young people begin to fall in love. The couple's courtship is marked by their tender naïveté, neither of them having ever been involved in a mature relationship before.

Having no other viable alternative, Bowie helps T-Dub and Chickamaw rob several banks, after which the threesome regroups at the home of Mattie, T-Dub's cousin. In the ensuing scenes, Mattie's authoritarian middle-class ways contrast sharply with the behavior of the thieves. Deciding to split up for a month before pulling their next robbery, Chickamaw and Bowie head up towards Hermanville. Along the way, Bowie gets involved in a car accident which results in Chickamaw's having to kill two lawmen in order to facilitate their escape. After Chickamaw drops the injured Bowie off at Dee's, Altman now concentrates on expanding the relationship between Keechie and Bowie.

Keechie nurses him back to health, and shortly thereafter the young couple consummate their romantic union. These scenes are also marked by the film's most conspicuous device, as Altman uses the omnipresent chatter of a radio announcer to comment upon the action. Consequently, by punctuating Bowie and Keechie's lovemaking with the radio's vulgarization of *Romeo and Juliet*, Altman actually succeeds in undercutting the poignancy of their relationship. Similarly, by contrasting the thieves' aimless actions with a series of dramatic myths perpetrated by the media (*Gangbusters*, *Heart of Gold*, *The Shadow*, and others), Altman points out the absurdity of their existence.

Meanwhile, after telling Keechie that he has nineteen thousand dollars, a major change in Bowie's character is brought out by his subsequent statement that his only regret is that he did not get any more. The couple still entertain the hope that they may someday be able to settle down in Mexico, a fantasy that Bowie's increasing involvement with the robbers would seem to negate. Thus, when he refuses to promise Keechie that he will quit working with T-Dub and Chickamaw, Bowie actually seals his own fate. This change in Bowie's character is also reflected in the way that Altman handles the robbers' next bank job. Whereas their previous robberies were all shot from outside the banks, Altman now moves his camera inside and covers their actions in much greater detail.

The intensification of Bowie's culpability is also conveyed by the fact that this robbery is the first one in which Bowie works on the inside. No longer an innocent novice, he is rapidly becoming more and more like Chickamaw and T-Dub, who murder one of the bankers as the trio make their getaway. Realizing that his actions have put an end to their hopes, Keechie threatens to leave Bowie, just after her lover has heard (on the radio) that T-Dub has been shot and that Chickamaw is in jail, but she does not.

On the run again, Bowie takes Keechie to The Grapes Motor Hotel, which T-Dub had previously bought for Mattie. Since T-Dub is now dead, however, Mattie does not want to have anything more to do with the couple. Ever the realist, it is only after Bowie threatens her that she agrees to put them up. From here, Bowie leaves Keechie in order to spring Chickamaw from jail. Although his daring escape plan is successful, Chickamaw has become so psychotic that Bowie is forced to turn him out on the road. Returning to the hotel, the film reaches its climax when Bowie is gunned down by a group of state troopers who have been alerted by Mattie.

As she and Mattie watch, Keechie's sense of agony and loss is emphasized by Altman's use of slow motion. Moreover, because the police shoot at Bowie through the walls of his cottage, most of our attention is focused on Keechie and Mattie. Mattie holds Keechie back once the shooting starts. Following this, Altman tacks on a brief epilogue which serves to deflate any intimations of romanticism the previous scenes may have contained. This is accomplished by cutting directly to a railroad station where Keechie is seemingly prepared to board whatever train is leaving next. After lying to a fellow passenger about the cause of Bowie's death, Keechie displays her ultimate lack of illusion by adding that she is not going to name her soon-to-be-born child after its father. Finally, *Thieves Like Us* ends with the lonely image of an empty staircase, as if to reiterate the isolated quality of Keechie's survival.

Alan Karp

THIS GUN FOR HIRE

Released: 1942
Production: Richard M. Blumenthal for Paramount
Direction: Frank Tuttle
Screenplay: Albert Maltz and W. R. Burnett; based on the novel of the same
  name by Grahame Green
Cinematography: John F. Seitz
Editing: Archie Marshak
Running time: 80 minutes

Principal characters:
Phil Raven .... Alan Ladd
Ellen Graham .... Veronica Lake
Michael Crane .... Robert Preston
Alvin Brewster .... Tully Marshall

This Gun for Hire, Graham Greene's novel about hired killers and corruption, was turned into a curious film of ultrapatriotic ideals and hard-boiled cynicism by screenwriters Albert Maltz and W. R. Burnett. The story concerns a hit man, Raven (Alan Ladd), who becomes a pawn in a game of political assassination. He is befriended by Ellen Graham (Veronica Lake), a young nightclub singer who tries to keep him from murdering an important political figure. The conflict arises when the higher virtue of democracy is transposed into terms the killer can understand; and after a period of flight from the police, Raven resigns himself to the task of destroying the man who set him up. He enters the industrial fortress of this fifth columnist and eventually destroys him, but in the process he is also gunned down.

This Gun for Hire was one of the vanguard of what was later to be called the *film noir* genre. It also brought its antihero star, Alan Ladd, almost instant stardom. His portrayal of Raven, with all his psychological quirks brought about by his savage beatings as a child, is superb. Ladd is able to create a believable hero who functions outside the law. His attractiveness is offset by his occasional weirdness. Ladd is contrasted to Veronica Lake, an actress who also leaped to stardom only a year earlier; she was a mysterious figure whose talent lay not in her ability to act but rather in her ability to function as an icon or image of the hard-boiled woman of the 1940's. Lake's career underwent serious changes. From the vamp in *I Wanted Wings* (1941) to the bitchy woman in *Roughshod* (1949), Lake acted in a variety of roles that were not always the best showcases for her talent. With Ladd there was a certain spark that allowed her own personality to blend with the characterization. Their relationship in this film was the beginning of an onscreen romance which lasted through several films, including *The Glass Key* (1942) and *The Blue Dahlia* (1946). Ladd and Lake were an attractive and effective team.

The theme of the fugitive couple (a favorite of *film noir*) found in *This Gun for Hire* was never developed fully in their other films. In Ladd's later films, he was never granted the freedom to create a character with the psychological depth of Raven.

Beyond the charisma of Ladd and Lake, *This Gun for Hire* is distinguished by its visual intensity and portrayal of violence. The cinematography by John F. Seitz captures an expressionistic tone in many scenes, generating a dream-like quality in the outrageous conclusion that has Raven in a chauffeur's uniform wearing a gas mask, walking through smoke-filled rooms with a drawn gun, looking for "Mr. Big." This bizarre imagery is contrasted with the gritty realism of the railyard in which Raven hides in order to avoid capture by the police. Throughout the film the level of violence is powerful yet subdued, quite unlike the typical machine-gun antics of most crime films of the period. Raven delights in constructing extravagant murders and extracting information with mild forms of torture (sticking a fork into the hand of his former employer, for example). Pain goes beyond physical boundaries in the film, giving *This Gun for Hire* a very distinctive flavor.

Screenwriters Maltz and Burnett manipulated Greene's original novel to such a degree that it transcends its simple philosophy of vengeance and retribution to become an unnatural political statement. Maltz was, in much of his film writing, concerned with social problems. His embracing of liberal ideas eventually led to his blacklisting as one of the notorious "Hollywood Ten" in the late 1940's. Burnett, who started as a writer of such books as *Little Caesar*, eventually became involved in screenwriting. Both writers were able to instill a certain cynicism into Ladd's characterization of Raven. The dialogue is raw, and the implication of past activities creates a *persona* for Raven that owes more to the gangster tradition than to Greene's original loner.

This Gun for Hire stands at the transition between the crime-melodrama and *film noir*, successfully presenting criminal pathology, ritualized violence, and a fatalistic antihero; it thus set the standard for many films which followed in the turbulent 1940's. The use of Robert Preston to serve as a real romantic interest for Lake shows that in 1942, Hollywood was still not ready to accept the antihero completely; his personality could be captivating, but the morality of loving a murderer was not justifiable.

Carl F. Macek

THIS HAPPY BREED

Released: 1947
Production: Noel Coward for Cineguild/Two Cities/J. Arthur Rank
Direction: David Lean
Screenplay: David Lean, Ronald Neame, and Anthony Havelock-Allan; based
  on the play of the same name by Noel Coward
Cinematography: Ronald Neame
Editing: Jack Harris
Running time: 107 minutes

Principal characters:
Frank Gibbons	Robert Newton
Ethel Gibbons	Celia Johnson
Billy Mitchell	John Mills
Queenie Gibbons	Kay Walsh
Bob Mitchell	Stanley Holloway
Reg	John Blythe

This Happy Breed was the first production of a company formed by director David Lean, cinematographer Ronald Neame, and producer Anthony Havelock-Allan. This independent production unit, named Cineguild, was established with the assistance of Noel Coward after Lean, Neame, and Havelock-Allan had collaborated with him on *In Which We Serve* (1942). Cineguild's initial production schedule was not speculative: it called for three adaptations of Coward's stage plays. Coward was also to be producer of these films; and although Lean, Neame, and Havelock-Allan would relieve him of various day-to-day production chores, the emphasis remained firmly on him.

The filming of *This Happy Breed* was begun just months after the London opening of the stage production. The play had an immediate impact as a companion piece to Coward's classic, *Cavalcade*. It spans the years betweeen 1919 and 1939, and again concentrates on the personal history of an English family. *This Happy Breed*'s middle-class, ostensibly "democratic" members, however, do not follow in the Victorian, support-the-empire tradition of Coward's previous success. Beyond that, *This Happy Breed*, focuses on a past too immediate, too full of the bitter memories of Depression and Red Scare, and too flavored by the hindsight ironies of appeasement to give rise to nostalgia, as did *Cavalcade* (1933), which ended its action in 1931. Much more distinguished the reign of George V from that of Victoria than an added half-century on a throne. There was also the difference between tea in the dining room and a chaw in the parlor, between the florid manners of Victorian gentility and the boisterousness of the working class at home. *This Happy Breed* does bear some resemblance to *In Which We Serve*, specifically to the domestic scenes of the Hardys and the Blakes. The inhabitants of Number

Seventeen Sycamore Road, Clapham Common, are much the same people, with their irritable in-laws, their just-plain-folks camaraderie, and their unshakable belief that, no matter how hard the times, Mother England is forged of good stock, and common sense will somehow prevail. "The people themselves, the ordinary people like you and me," Frank Gibbons (Robert Newton) tells his infant grandson, "we know what we belong to, where we come from, and where we're going. We may not know it with our brains, but we know it with our roots."

The entire play is fashioned from a simple conceit: within the context of naturalistic dialogue and decor, it proceeds to pick out the nine key scenes, the climactic or transcendent moments of a half-dozen lives over a span of twenty years. The classic problem in transposing material of this variety to the screen is how to treat the episodic structure—whether to fill it in with other scenes and transitional montages or leave it precisely as written, enforcing the sensation of a photographed stage play. In addition, a host of secondary considerations, such as dialogue style, had to be dealt with. While Coward makes sure that all the correct "h's" are dropped, the demands of the narrative necessitate a good many blatantly expository remarks and exchanges primarily designed to inform the audience of certain events. Andre Bazin wrote in his essay "Theater and Cinema" that "however one approaches it, a play whether classic or modern is unassailably protected by its text. There is no way of adapting the text without disposing of it and substituting something else, which may be better, but is not the play." Clearly, the aim of the adapters of both *This Happy Breed* and *Blithe Spirit* (1946) was not to supersede the text. The essential issue becomes not how to deal with actual lines and scenes, but with basic qualities, and how to show what the play has that the film can render better.

The results, in *This Happy Breed*, are not wholly satisfactory. The film itself emerges as episodic without effect, calculatedly detailed under a semblance of accidental observation, a narrative of fits and starts as characters try to become people and people never succeed in becoming characters. The primary reason for this, aside from the aforementioned conventional problems, is the handicap of realism. What the adapters try to give the film and what ultimately causes it to fail is more "credibility," more documentary reality than it can support. Under the camera eye and in three-strip Technicolor, the Gibbons family ceases to be an assemblage of stage figures seen at a distance; they become graphically real. The aging that takes place between acts is a simple illusion on stage. On film, in close-up, the faces of Frank and Ethel Gibbons (Celia Johnson) have the authenticity of well-defined wrinkles framed by hair with subtler streaks of grey. The gradual stoop of Ethel's shoulders under the weight of passing years is as noticeable as the changing style of her dresses, which always retain the dowdiness befitting her station. Yet all this and a few shots of the "row" houses on Sycamore Road, giving the fictional Number 17 a physical presence it could never have on stage, still do not make those who dwell there more real.

Much of the difficulty lies with the original script, which is full of sterile half-truths and rigid slice-of-life posings. Its supporting characters are hopelessly one-dimensional. Here the film is an improvement, particularly in the case of Bob Mitchell (Stanley Holloway), making the "chum from the war" less of a drinking partner and convenient foil and more of an individual resident of Sycamore Road. The film also adds some wry touches either by shifting a scene (for example, Frank's premarital lecture to Reg, played by John Blythe, in the parlor now takes place in the lavatory, which makes their figures seem somewhat incongruous in their formal clothes and comically underscores the pompous aspects of his advice) or by inventing a new one (the trip to the cinema to see the incomprehensible American motion picture suggesting the intolerant remnants of Victorian xenophobia). It can even make a small detail such as Ethel's taking down Edward VIII's calendar after his abdication, which may have seemed too contrived in the play, a more spontaneous and acceptable action.

The major action, however, must continue to center on characters who do not speak words but utter lines of dialogue. Bazin's dictum holds true: the text cannot be merely appended with film effects or partially displaced by movie reality. The opening shots of the city and the traveling into the house establish one reality; then the "play" begins and asserts another. A view of the mob of people greeting Prime Minister Neville Chamberlain at 10 Downing Street compounds the irony of Frank's remark—"It's exciting all right, if you like to see a lot of people yelling themselves hoarse without the faintest idea what they're yelling about"—but subverts its drama. For Coward's personages are not merely any inhabitants of Clapham Common, they are *the* inhabitants of Clapham Common. They are nothing more or less than lumps of observed traits, everymen and women mouthing uncertain epithets of earthly wisdom and, as such, not meant to venture out of the dramatic insulation of three walls of a parlor. They are, like Frank Gibbons, framed in medium shot between his sister and daughter as they roll up yarn, trapped by a graphically mundane reality that is not inherently theirs.

For many critics and filmgoers alike, however, the charm of *This Happy Breed* is the very ordinariness of its characters and situations. The subdued use of color, the settings, and the wonderfully understated acting of the excellent cast make the film. If the situations and the progression of the plot lack real drama, these faults are more than compensated for by the other merits of the film. It was well received both by critics and the public and was a top moneymaking film when it was released.

Alain J. Silver

THE THOMAS CROWN AFFAIR

Released: 1968
Production: Norman Jewison for United Artists
Direction: Norman Jewison
Screenplay: Alan R. Trustman
Cinematography: Haskell Wexler
Editing: Hal Ashby, Ralph E. Winters, and Byron Brandt
Music: Michel Legrand
Running time: 102 minutes

Principal characters:

Thomas Crown	Steve McQueen
Vickie Anderson	Faye Dunaway
Lieutenant Eddie Malone	Paul Burke
Carl	Yaphet Kotto
Benjy	Todd Martin
Dave	Sam Melville
Abe	Addison Powell
Arnie	Sidney Armus
Erwin Weaver	Jack Weston

The Thomas Crown Affair, considered in the context of its time period, contains a curious mixture of anti-Establishment philosophy and upper-class chic. Norman Jewison's lavish crime thriller concerns an impressively successful Boston Back Bay investment banker, Thomas Crown (Steve McQueen), who wears three-hundred-dollar conservative business suits, a two-thousand-dollar Patek Phillipe watch, and a Phi Beta Kappa key. Despite his wealth and power, the polo-playing, hard-driving millionaire is bored and looking for new excitement.

The film opens with a slickly carried out bank robbery in which five accomplices, none of whom knows or has ever seen the others before, successfully steal several million dollars from a downtown Boston bank. It is revealed to the audience that Crown, who has more than enough money to support his lavish life style, has carried out the robbery as an exercise to test his own intelligence and to prove his mental superiority. The police are baffled by the robbery, which has no clues or suspects, and so Lieutenant Eddie Malone (Paul Burke), who is in charge of the investigation, grudgingly calls for the assistance of the insurance company which will have to make good on the bank's losses. The investigator for the company turns out to be beautiful Vickie Anderson (Faye Dunaway), a chicly dressed free-lance investigator who commands high prices for her work.

Vickie comes up with the idea that eventually unravels the crime when she suspects that perhaps someone who is a frequent traveler to Switzerland on business might be the suspect, since she reasons that the money could only be useful in a numbered Swiss bank account, and that the money would have to be transported gradually by someone who is not a known criminal. She also discovers that the robbers had never seen one another before and were contacted by the mastermind of the crime himself. Because of the small number of people who fall into the category established by Vickie, Crown is one of the pool of suspects. Vickie immediately feels that Crown is the likely person, and she decides that two courses of action should be taken to entrap him and thus prove that even he cannot commit a "perfect crime."

For the first part of her plan, Vickie goes to meet Crown on a polo field, then at an art auction, where she boldly tells him that she knows he committed the crime. Crown is intrigued both by her beauty and by her intelligence, and they begin an affair, with each playing a cat-and-mouse game about the robbery. For the second part of her plan, Vickie places an ad in a newspaper reading "Be a Fink for $25,000," hoping to lure one of the robbers into admitting something about the crime. This works up to a point, when Erwin Weaver (Jack Weston) comes forward. He at first resisted the money offer, but yields to pressure when Vickie and some of her colleagues stage a bogus "kidnaping" of Erwin's child. Erwin, however, knows no details of the crime and has never actually seen Crown. Up to this point Eddie has been infatuated with Vickie and admiring of her talents as an investigator, but when he learns that she is having an affair with Crown and has staged the kidnaping, he becomes angry with her. He righteously criticizes her, saying "You know what you are?" but she only answers "I know what I am," then leaves him with a gift, a sign that reads "Think dirty."

Events leave the cat-and-mouse stage about two-thirds of the way through the film. Up to this point the relationships between Vickie and Crown and Vickie and Eddie have been flip and sophisticated. Now, however, Vickie and Crown begin to fall in love, and they realize that there is no way that Crown can be free of the police hounding him. Vickie tries to make a deal with Eddie to return the money in exchange for amnesty, but Eddie adamantly refuses. Crown now feels that the only way out is to plan another robbery of the same style, only this time telling Vickie about it. He tests her love by telling her that he will meet her in a particular drop-off place, a cemetery, and she can come with him to Switzerland if she loves him. In the last sequence Vickie is waiting in a police car with Eddie as Crown's familiar Rolls Royce drives up the hill to the meeting place. When the car stops, the police surround it, but the chauffeur instead of Crown steps out and hands Vickie a note from Crown, who says to meet him with the money in Switzerland; if not, keep the car. Vickie starts to cry as a jet flies overhead bearing Crown, presumably on his way to Switzerland.

The use of split-screen optical effects is very effectively utilized in the film to present two segments of action simultaneously. In the initial robbery, for example, the convergence of various members of the robbers is shown side by side with a polo match in which Crown is playing. The juxtaposition of realism with impressionism in this way makes the film different from any film before it; it not only has the two-screen effect, but in other places the screen also becomes a checkerboard of tiny images, each showing the same action. The use of the double and multiple images proves particularly effective when seen against the background theme, "Windmills of Your Mind," one of the most effective film themes ever written. Michel Legrand, who wrote the beautiful score for the film, also wrote the music for the song, with the lyrics provided by the husband-and-wife lyricist team Alan and Marilyn Bergman. According to the Bergmans, in fact, after several days of not finding the right melody to fit the lyrics which they had written for the film (the opposite of the usual practice of music first, then lyrics), Legrand sat down at the piano and composed the music in a matter of minutes. Although there are a number of excellently filmed scenes in *The Thomas Crown Affair*, perhaps the best, and certainly the best remembered, is the scene in which Crown and Vickie play a game of chess which begins slowly; then the camera cuts rapidly back and forth between the characters and the chess board, and finally the scene dissolves into a long embrace of the two as they kiss while turning around and around. It was a highly erotic scene that was parodied in Ashby's 1979 film *Being There*. In the latter film, Peter Sellers and Shirley MacLaine whirl around in an embrace as Sellers tries to emulate the scene from *The Thomas Crown Affair* which is being shown on television.

In addition to the music and the cinematography by Haskell Wexler, the film editing deserves special note. The effects of the multiple screen images as well as the overall smooth flow of the film is due to a large extent to the fine work of supervising film editor Hal Ashby (who would later go on to become an important director in his own right, directing such successful films as *Coming Home*, 1978) and editors Ralph Winters and Byron Brandt. Actually, as the associate producer to Jewison, Ashby had as much to do with the overall success of the film as Jewison.

The acting of the film is good, although perhaps not equal to the magnificent technical properties. Dunaway, appearing in her first film since *Bonnie and Clyde* (1967), shows that she can play a sophisticated woman as easily as she can the more earthy type of woman that Bonnie Parker was. McQueen, slightly out of character in expensive suits and a Rolls Royce, nevertheless exhibits a versatility here which did not often come through on the screen. In a sense, he is playing the same cocky kid that he played in Jewison's earlier film, *The Cincinnati Kid* (1965), and most of his other screen roles. The difference here is that his character has more polish and sophistication than it does in *The Great Escape* (1963) or *Papillon* (1973). In McQueen's films he always seemed to "buck the system," and his image of a youthful, cocky, yet basically good person remained with him throughout his career. Although he was fifty when he died, McQueen had made few films in the last years of his life out of choice, and because of this, all of his films show him at roughly the same age. Although Thomas Crown is not thought by some to be one of his better roles, it at least proved that he could move into something different and do so quite successfully.

Jewison is not what film critics would term an *auteur*, but over the years he has produced a number of very good films. Beginning with several mild comedies for Universal, such as *Send Me No Flowers* (1964), Jewison went on to direct the multiple-Oscar-winning 1969 film *In the Heat of the Night*. In recent years his films have not been particularly successful, although his most recent film *And Justice for All* (1979) was highly acclaimed by critics. His best films have utilized location shooting, such as in *The Thomas Crown Affair*, to best advantage.

Janet St. Clair

THOSE MAGNIFICENT MEN IN THEIR FLYING MACHINES, OR: HOW I FLEW FROM LONDON TO PARIS IN 25 HOURS AND 11 MINUTES

Released: 1965
Production: Stan Margulies for Twentieth Century-Fox
Direction: Ken Annakin
Screenplay: Jack Davies and Ken Annakin
Cinematography: Christopher Challis
Editing: Gordon Star
Running time: 152 minutes

Principal characters:

Orvil Newton	Stuart Whitman
Patricia Rawnsley	Sarah Miles
Richard Mays	James Fox
Count Emilio Ponticelli	Alberto Sordi
Lord Rawnsley	Robert Morley
Sir Percy Ware-Armitage	Terry-Thomas
Colonel Manfried Von Holstein	Gert Frobe
Pierre Dubois	Jean-Pierre Cassel
Brigitte/ Ingrid/ Marlene/ Francois/ Yvette/ Betty	Irina Derwick
Yamamoto	Yujiro Ishihara
Neanderthal Man	Red Skelton
Countess Sophia Ponticelli	Zena Marshall

The genesis of *Those Magnificent Men in Their Flying Machines* was research done by director Ken Annakin for a documentary on the early days of flying. The film deals with a fictional race between London and Paris sponsored by a London newspaper publisher in 1910. The probable inspiration was the first flight across the English Channel in 1909 accomplished by Louis Bleriot for a one-thousand-pound prize offered by the London *Daily Mail*. The film newspaper publisher Lord Rawnsley, played by Robert Morley, offers a prize of ten thousand pounds for the winner. The plot of this film is of minor significance, however, just as the plots of silent film producer/director Mack Sennet's films of an earlier era were unimportant. Although the film boasts a large international cast, the real stars are the reconstructed pioneer airplanes as they maneuver on the widescreen of the Todd-AO process.

The film opens as a pseudodocumentary illustrating man's early attempts at flying in which Red Skelton portrays various early dreamers from Neanderthal times onward who risked their lives attempting to imitate the flight of birds. Interspersed with Skelton's antics are authentic black-and-white shots of the various contraptions man has used in his desire to leave the earth.

Skelton reappears in the epilogue of the film as a modern-day harried airline passenger who has just been notified of the cancellation of his jet flight. His eyes light up as he reverts to the primitive behavior he had displayed in the beginning, flapping his arms imitating the birds.

The film's contest is suggested to publisher Lord Rawnsley by his progressive-minded daughter Patricia (Sarah Miles), who hides her motorcycle in a shed on which she has a poster advocating women's suffrage posted on the inner side of the door. Patricia is all but engaged to Richard Mays (James Fox), whose spare time is taken up in flying, and who, of course, figures prominently in the race.

The actual race takes up only a minor part of this long film, with the main part of the action devoted to the flyers from different nations preparing for the contest. The humor is broad, relying primarily on the single-dimensional caricatures of the nationalities presented. The hero is Orvil Newton (Stuart Whitman), a free-wheeling, carefree barnstormer from Arizona trying to win the race to pay his debts. Richard Mays, on the other hand, is the typical stiff-upper-lip, fair-play Britisher. Count Emilio Ponticelli (Alberto Sordi), is the Italian patriarch, ever accompanied by his fearful wife, who is not above reminding the mother superior of a convent where he has crash-landed that without the help of the nuns a Protestant will win the race. There is a running joke throughout the movie about the Frenchman, Pierre Dubois (Jean-Pierre Cassel) constantly meeting what appears to be the same girl (all played by Irina Derwick) who invariably turns out to be someone else, but no less resistant to his amorous designs.

Most of the film's satire and fun is directed at the strictly regimented, Prussian-style German contingent led by Colonel Manfried Von Holstein, broadly played by Gert Frobe. The Colonel believes in doing everything by the book—literally. When he is required to replace the pilot in the race, he flies with the book in his hand, reading step by step as he performs the maneuvers. His hanging onto the upside-down plane running with his feet over the surface of the water is one of the highlights of the film. In the byplay among the various nationalities, the Germans again supply the most humor. At one time the French dupe the Colonel into diving into waist-deep water with the expected results, and a subsequent duel between him and Dubois with blunderbusses in balloons over the sewage pond often requisitioned to soften the many air crashes, is another hilarious sequence. Of the other characters, the Japanese flyer, Yamamoto (Yujiro Ishihara), is a virtual throwaway. After being built up as a major threat in the race with his intricate, delicate-looking, kitelike plane, which he claims to have flown all the way (four miles) to Dover (after shipping it by mule train, train, and ship), his part in the race is short-lived.

The villain for the piece is the Englishman Sir Percy Ware-Armitage (Terry-Thomas). Sir Percy is underhanded, but rather subdued in his villainy. He drugs the German pilot by mistake when the pilot drinks the wine prepared for Yamamoto, he sabotages the American and Japanese planes, and he hires a ship to ferry his plane across the channel. All this villainy comes to naught, however, when he crash-lands on a train which destroys his plane when it enters a tunnel.

Of the fourteen starters, two crash on take-off, three crash on the way, eight make the first checkpoint, and one is last heard to be on his way to Scotland. It is in the flights of the authentically reconstructed planes that the picture also soars. There are six flyable models of the actual planes, including the one flown by Louis Bleriot in 1909 and a modification of that of the Wright brothers, besides the many others used for ground shots. As would be expected, many of the planes experience difficulties and crash-land during the trip. The director has wisely refrained from embellishing the flying scenes with slapstick humor so prevalent elsewhere in the film, realizing that the fragile aircraft need no help in sustaining their visual charm and humor.

There are few surprises at the end of the film. The American wins the girl as expected, but he does not win the race—partly because of his heroic rescue of the Italian in midair. The viewer has little interest in the plot anyway, as the entire point of the picture consists of the sight gags of a daring, romantic era. The dialogue is of little consequence except that the trouble with international affairs is that they attract foreigners.

One more noteworthy attraction is the animation of famous British cartoonist Ronald Searle at the beginning and end of the film. One would almost wish the entire film were animated by his drawings rather than acted live. Searle's style perfectly evokes the atmosphere of the early twentieth century and is possibly the only thing which could be better than the planes themselves.

Those Magnificent Men in Their Flying Machines is not a classic film in the usual sense. Although it was nominated for an Academy Award for best story and screenplay written directly for the screen, the script is not outstanding. The characters are all stereotypes, the plot inconsequential and predictable. The picture is patterned after the slapstick antics of the old silent comedies. In fact, the fire department at the London airport is a direct imitation of the Keystone Kops. If one were to delete sound and color and substitute antique cars for the planes, the film would be indistinguishable from the comedies of Mack Sennet. This idea undoubtedly occurred to the producers, who subsequently filmed a sequel entitled *Those Daring Young Men in Their Jaunty Jalopies* (known as *Monte Carlo or Bust* in Britain) in 1969. Unfortunately, the successful fragile blend of slapstick and authenticity in the earlier film was not repeated, mainly because the later film relied less upon the visual humor of the machines and overdid attempts at humor of the characters, especially the machinations of the repeat villain, Terry-Thomas.

While the film has never been among the top moneymakers in any given year, by 1979 it had grossed enough to earn a tie for the 116th top moneymaker of all time, at fourteen million dollars. This statistic tells the story of the film's popularity. It may not stand up to the real film "greats," but it will probably always remain popular with the general public for its evocation of an earlier era of history and moviemaking and its mentally unchallenging entertainment value.

Roger Geimer

THREE DAYS OF THE CONDOR

Released: 1975
Production: Stanley Schneider for Paramount
Direction: Sydney Pollack
Screenplay: Lorenzo Semple, Jr., and David Rayfiel; based on the novel *Six Days of the Condor* by James Grady
Cinematography: Owen Roizman
Editing: Frederic Steinkamp and Don Guidice
Running time: 117 minutes

Principal characters:
Turner	Robert Redford
Kathy	Faye Dunaway
Higgins	Cliff Robertson
Joubert	Max von Sydow
Mr. Wabash	John Houseman
Atwood	Addison Powell
Barber	Walter McGinn
Janice	Tina Chen

Robert Redford, the 1970's answer to the charismatic stars of Hollywood's Golden Age, made his film debut in *War Hunt*, a well-made low-budget Korean War drama released in 1962. During the next seven years, he appeared in comedies such as *Barefoot in the Park* (1967), dramas such as *Tell Them Willie Boy Is Here* (1969), soap operas, character studies, and Hollywood exposés. Although his performances were adequate and he was matinee-idol handsome, he was hardly deemed worthy of film fan idolatry or massive coverage in the media. He was not big box-office.

A film role opposite Paul Newman in 1969 changed all that. When he costarred with Newman in *Butch Cassidy and the Sundance Kid*, he reached superstardom. The film earned a fortune—it took in more than forty-six million dollars in receipts in its first twelve years—and Redford's popularity has not waned since that time. As of 1981, *The Sting*, which won an Academy Award in 1973, had grossed almost seventy-nine million dollars, and is among the top moneymaking films of all time; *All the President's Men* (1976) had earned thirty million dollars and was the second biggest rental film of the year; and *The Way We Were* (1973) had taken in twenty-five million dollars. The actor's presence in even such an average drama as *Three Days of the Condor* is enough to guarantee a profit: as of 1981, it has earned a tremendous twenty million dollars, an extraordinary amount for such unassuming entertainment.

Three Days of the Condor is a fascinating if not consistently original spy-versus-spy mystery with much of its interest arising from the antistereotypical character portrayed by Redford. His Turner is no Howard Hunt involved in surrealistic plots. With a code name of Condor, Turner is what can best be described as a humanist employed by the Central Intelligence Agency. He is, in fact, a super bookworm devouring novels and magazines as part of a CIA New York front, The American Literary Historical Society, which computerizes popular literature in its endless search for patterns of intrigue. Turner rides a motor scooter to work, ignores agency codes and jargon, and resents that he cannot tell his friends his true profession. As he explains, he "trusts few people," which makes him somewhat of a rebel and differentiates him from his coworkers.

One rainy afternoon as he returns from a trip to the local deli via a hidden route from the office, Turner discovers that all of his workmates have been systematically executed. He phones an emergency CIA number, wanders through the city streets, and soon realizes that he has become a nonentity within the system. His newly acquired gun and his wits are all he has for his defense, which may not be quite enough in his one-against-the-system effort at survival. Yet he is an amateur who reads books. This makes him an intellectual, an unpredictable quarry for the CIA.

Until this point, *Three Days of the Condor* works as a crisply directed, edited, and photographed thriller. The film is particularly chilling when Turner discovers the bodies of his colleagues one by one, with not a sentence spoken, accompanied by the monotonous rhythm of operating computers. Next, Turner, in an effort to secure a place to hide out, kidnaps Kathy (Faye Dunaway), a photographer shopping in a small boutique.

Kathy is appropriately alarmed as she is forced to drive Turner to her Brooklyn Heights brownstone, but she has been accosted by a blonde, WASP-ish mystery man and not by a shivering black junkie or overweight Italian hit man, and it seems obvious from the outset that her fears will soon dissolve into a fascination with him. Redford and Dunaway verbally wrangle as they blurt out rather heavy dialogue that attempts to be profound. It is this relationship between Turner and Kathy that causes the film to falter a bit. As a character, Kathy is essential for plot development and to give Turner a chance to verbalize his thoughts for the benefit of the audience, which would be thoroughly confused had Redford pantomimed his way through this part of the film. Yet the relationship between the two is unnecessarily pretentious and superficial since it tries to create artificially some magnetism between the two. Kathy has deep but inarticulate feelings about life that come through in the photographs she takes, particularly those with eloquently empty spaces. In the love scene between Turner and Kathy, however, director Sydney Pollack pretentiously intersperses the scene with samples of Kathy's pseudoexistential photographs. This heavy-handed sexual relationship does nothing significant to affect the development of the characters; maintaining Kathy as a hostage would probably have better served the film's sense of realism.

Turner soon learns that he has inadvertently uncovered a counteragency within the CIA—a sort of spy agency within a spy agency—and, in a James Bondish effort, he manages to rewire part of the New York City telephone system and unmask several of his faceless superiors. That this scene is believable or at least encourages the audience to suspend its disbelief is caused by the carefully established image of Turner as a man who reads books. This is hammered home through several scenes containing statements to that effect made by Mr. Wabash (John Houseman), who is directing the CIA's efforts to capture Turner. Turner is dangerous because he reads. He probably read a book at one time dealing with the subject of rewiring New York telephone exchanges.

At the conclusion, a revealing and expertly staged encounter between Turner and his CIA department head, Higgins (Cliff Robertson), causes the film to return full cycle to the intensity of the first scenes. Turner has taken his information concerning a CIA-within-a-CIA to *The New York Times*. "But will they print it?" asks Higgins as the film ends. Director Pollack obviously wants to raise the bigger specter of war and apocalypse with this last scene, but the film clouds the issue with its two CIAs, one black and one white, when the issue is in reality the one, dangerously gray CIA.

As a thriller, *Three Days of the Condor* boils down to thrills that work and thrills that do not. Happily, there are more of the former. The violent scenes are crisp and creatively portrayed, particularly the initial massacre with its velvety explosion of muffled machine guns and the scene of the duel between Turner and the mailman assassin in Kathy's apartment. Heading a smaller list of thrills that fail is, of course, the heavy-handed love scene between Turner and Kathy. The characters who come closest to working perfectly are the sinister international gunman, played with a dapper deadliness by Max von Sydow, and the enigmatic Mr. Wabash of the CIA, played by Houseman. Houseman personifies the ambiguity of the CIA that other parts of the film dilute; he is superb in the part, conveying an intimidating civility and a total cynicism. His lightning-speed mind incarnates the intelligence profession as, perhaps, a superintelligence that knows so much that it can do almost anything with what it knows.

Redford gives his usual type of performance as Turner. While he certainly is not a bad actor, he somehow is never able to *become* the characters he acts. Whether he is playing a sheriff or skier, a reporter or a con man, one is always aware that one is watching a star, while many of Redford's contemporaries, including Dustin Hoffman, Al Pacino, Robert De Niro, and his two-time costar Newman, are all able to transform themselves into the characters they portray as well as retain their identities as celluloid names. Redford is rendered fine support by Robertson, and particularly by Sydow as the erudite hired killer Joubert. The latter's role is strikingly similar to his part in the recent *Brass Target* (1979). Dunaway, with her one-dimensional character, walks through the film, proving that her best acting—in *Bonnie and Clyde* (1967), *Chinatown* (1974), and *Network* (1976)—has been achieved when her parts are of substance.

Three Days of the Condor is full of arty, attractive, angular shots and makes better than average use of New York City locations. In addition, sounds and images signifying good against evil or innocence in the midst of terror are effectively pitted against each other. Christmas carols and Salvation Army singers fill the sound track as Turner roams the streets; the terror-stricken Kathy is ordered to turn on a television set, and is greeted with an innocuous commerical jingle; a wife is gaily preparing dinner, unaware that her husband has been killed; and a landlady cheerfully informs Turner that two of his "friends" are waiting for him upstairs.

Despite these touches, *Three Days of the Condor* is laden with a Muzak-like score which detracts from the suspense, as does the ill-conceived Redford-Dunaway encounter. The film certainly did not hinder Redford's career and is much better than some critics would have us believe, but it would have been a far better effort if its creators—notably screenwriters Lorenzo Semple, Jr., and David Rayfiel and director Pollack (who had acted with Redford in *War Hunt* and directed him previously in *This Property Is Condemned* (1966), *Jeremiah Johnson* (1972), and *The Way We Were*—had simply been more creative and explored in more detail the possibilities inherent in a character as unusual as Turner. Still, the film is interesting and worth seeing because it presents a refreshingly different secret agent—one who reads.

Rob Edelman

THE THREE FACES OF EVE

Released: 1957
Production: Nunnally Johnson for Twentieth Century-Fox
Direction: Nunnally Johnson
Screenplay: Nunnally Johnson; based on the book of the same name by Corbett Thigpen and Hervey M. Cleckley
Cinematography: Stanley Cortez
Editing: Marge Fowler
Running time: 91 minutes

Principal characters:
Eve ....Joanne Woodward (AA)
Ralph White ....David Wayne
Doctor Luther ....Lee J. Cobb
Doctor Day ....Edwin Jerome
Narrator ....Alistair Cooke
Bonnie ....Terry Ann Ross
Earl ....Ken Scott
Soldier ....Vince Edwards

The Three Faces of Eve is probably most easily labeled as a "psychological melodrama," a label which gives some indication of the film's premises. The 1957 production immediately establishes its credentials to the viewer as a "docudrama," a dramatization of an actual case history of mental illness. Eve (Joanne Woodward), the film's subject, suffers from multiple personalities. To use a psychological phrase, her "character disorder" is plural. The implicit idea in this psychological melodrama is that psychology is a medical routine and a privileged ritual into which the viewer can be initiated only through the help of a professional. In this film, the professional is actually two people. One is the narrator, Alistair Cooke, who introduces the action of the film and supplies background material as well. The other is the character of Eve's doctor, the wise unflappable Doctor Luther (Lee J. Cobb). Between the narrator and doctor, the mysteries and incongruities of Eve's behavior are explained, and through them, the psychological melodrama takes on a pronounced clinical tone of voice. In a literal as well as a practical sense, all melodramas are of course psychological. They tell the story of characters' lives with some idea that they can be told from the inside out. With the introduction of the narrator/doctor, however, who frames the events of Eve's life within a factual medical history, the film subtly suggests that viewer empathy is not enough to understand a character's life; it helps to have a professional.

The Three Faces of Eve begins not with Eve (Joanne Woodward) but with the narrator, who introduces the characters and their "credentials." The screenplay, Cooke explains, is based on a book by two doctors, Corbett H. Thigpen and Hervey M. Cleckley. In that book they present a medical case history which *The Three Faces of Eve* is about to present in condensed, dramatized form. The case involves a young woman with multiple personalities, who first came to the attention of doctors in 1951. As Cooke puts it, a little simply, "In 1951 a Georgia housewife startled her husband by behaving strangely." The following events may have been telescoped for the sake of the film but Cooke stresses that they are true; they actually happened. Thus, this melodrama carries an extra emotional impact drawn from its authenticity, although clearly any dramatization treads carefully between re-creation and embellishment.

The facts that Eve's doctors gradually discover about her are things which she cannot know about herself because she has several selves, none of which is on speaking terms with the others. As the character that her doctors have dubbed "Eve White," she is married, has a daughter, and lives a quiet life, as a housewife in a small town. Eve White, drab, repressed, and not too bright, suffers from blackouts during which another, separate personality, "Eve Black," emerges. Eve Black takes her cue from everything that Eve White is afraid to do; she is loud and flippant, eager to flirt, dance, and tease the male population of Georgia out of their minds. Eve Black is a harmless, amusing vamp; Eve White is a mousy, eager-to-please housewife. Somewhere in the crossover between the finger-snapping bad girl and the dull good girl, however, Eve has a very destructive shadow.

One day Eve buys several fancy dresses and has them delivered to her home. It was Eve Black who bought the dresses, however, and Eve White who is at home when they are delivered. Her husband (David Wayne) is outraged when the clothes, which they cannot afford, arrive. Eve, upset, wanders out of the room. Suddenly her husband hears their small daughter, Bonnie, scream: Eve is trying to strangle Bonnie with the cord from the window shade. Her husband pulls her away and throws her to the floor. "Don't get up," he says. "I'll kill you if you get up." He does not understand his wife's reply, "I didn't do it." After this blackout, Eve begins seeing a doctor regularly. He is Doctor Luther who will eventually introduce the two Eves to each other, and witness the arrival of a third personality, "Jane."

From the beginning of her treatment, Eve's husband is excluded from any explanation of his wife's illness or participation in her therapy. He sits, mystified, in the waiting room as Eve's doctors excitedly discuss their "find": a woman with multiple personalities. They assume that her husband is too dull to understand this medical problem. Throughout the film Eve's husband is used as comic relief and is depicted as a slow-witted, easily angered Southern cracker. Part of Eve's treatment hinges on getting rid of this husband. First she withdraws to an institution, then to an apartment in her doctor's town. Finally, as "Jane," she gets a new boyfriend, Earl (Ken Scott), a man much more intelligent and well mannered than Eve White's husband.

There is little doubt that the filmmakers demonstrate a fondness for some of Eve's personalities over others. Eve White, the good girl, is listless and guilt-ridden. She dresses badly and looks worse. Eve Black is a good deal more fun. With her, the film acquires some interesting action. She literally lets down her hair, loosens her clothes, dances a little, and flirts alluringly; she is a caricature of a Southern vamp and is totally free of any soul-searching. Her most penetrating comment about her alter ego, Eve White, whom she knows, is, "She crazy?" It is an offhand question which resolutely avoids facing the implication of the answer.

Because the crucial difference between Eve Black and Eve White is a sexual one, a key question for the film is just how far Eve Black will go to show the far side of Eve White's repression. A soldier, played by Vince Edwards, tries to make good on Eve Black's advances one night in a bar. After a few drinks, he is ready to have Eve do more than sing "Hold Me." When his hustling becomes oppressive, however, Eve White emerges, starts to cry, and gets rid of the soldier quickly. Later Eve Black goes to see Eve White's husband in his hotel room. Her husband, of course, sees only that his wife seems unusually sexy. He cannot wait to take her to bed, but Eve will not let him touch her, since she is not his wife—Eve White is. As Eve Black she is not responsible for teasing him; she can have fun without making good on the promise. Ultimately, Eve Black is not going to compromise Eve White's sexual integrity.

Dr. Luther treats the sexy Eve Black with amused detachment, but trying to cure either Eve White or Eve Black with reason and patience seems fairly hopeless. Eve White tries to slit her wrist; Eve Black has to take over and bandage it up. Hearing that story from Eve Black, Dr. Luther decides to hypnotize Eve White. Under hypnosis the doctor has the power to summon Eve's personalities at will, like changing channels on a television set; he has only to say, "May I speak with Eve White?" She agrees to be hypnotized, and while Luther's back is turned, a third personality emerges. This one is "Jane," a well-behaved, poised, and more intelligent woman. Of the three, she is clearly the most well balanced, respectable, and reasonable. Because she is reasonable, Dr. Luther's reasonable therapy now has a chance of success.

Now that all three faces have appeared, quick scenes of each establish their characters succinctly. Jane, in demure white, dances at the country club; Eve Black, the irresponsible playgirl, can be heard squealing "cut that out" from the back of a parked car; Eve White is a drudge working for the phone company, failing to make proper connections on calls at her switchboard. Clearly, both in terms of social position and ability to respond to her doctor's treatment, Jane is the face to be preferred.

In a climactic scene in Dr. Luther's office, Jane does emerge the victor.

Under hypnosis, Eve Black and Eve White replay a traumatic childhood event, each filling in parts of the story. As a little girl, Eve was asked to kiss her dead grandmother as she lay in an open coffin. Once Black and White remember "kissing granma goodbye," each "dies." Eve White simply disappears in midrecollection, while Eve Black has a touching farewell scene with the doctor who was the first to let her speak her name. Just as Eve White never knew what Eve Black did, so Eve Black does not know anything about Jane; she is dependent upon her doctor for information about the other personality. Both White and Black wistfully ask their doctor what he thinks of this third personality and whether she should be the most desirable. Dr. Luther is reassuring in his portrayal of Jane. Finally, Jane emerges and talks to her doctor. She realizes that the other two are gone completely, unsummonable, and that she has inherited their memories of childhood. All the faces now belong to Jane.

In an epilogue, Jane writes to her doctor two years later to say that she, Earl, and her daughter Bonnie are now a happy family. Just as the film began with a narrator, it closes with Eve's doctor giving the viewer the news of the heroine's happy ending. The epilogue, although true at the time when the film was released, has eventually proven to be overly optimistic. The woman upon whom the film's plot is based has had various new personalities emerge over the years and had been undergoing therapy extensively into the 1980's.

For the star of the film, however, the story did indeed have a happy ending. Critically acclaimed as an actress of great promise, Woodward won an Academy Award as Best Actress for her performance in *The Three Faces of Eve*, her first starring role. In the twenty-five years since that film's release, she has starred in many films, frequently with her husband, actor/director Paul Newman, and has received consistently high praise from critics. She is an actress of versatility and integrity who has often stayed away from inferior roles which other, more commercially successful actresses might have taken.

Leslie Donaldson

THREE LITTLE WORDS

Released: 1950
Production: Jack Cummings for Metro-Goldwyn-Mayer
Direction: Richard Thorpe
Screenplay: George Wells; based on the lives of Bert Kalmar and Harry Ruby
Cinematography: Harry Jackson
Editing: Ben Lewis
Music: Bert Kalmar and Harry Ruby
Running time: 103 minutes

Principal characters:
Bert Kalmar .... Fred Astaire
Harry Ruby .... Red Skelton
Jessie Brown Kalmar .... Vera-Ellen
(sung by Anita Ellis)
Eileen Percy Ruby .... Arlene Dahl
Helen Kane .... Debbie Reynolds
(sung by Helen Kane)

Hollywood has made so many musicals based on the lives of songwriters that the form is practically a subgenre of the film musical. The films themselves are usually sedate, reverential treatments of their subjects that tend to dehumanize them. Films such as *Night and Day* (1945, Cole Porter), *Deep in My Heart* (1954, Sigmund Romberg), *Till the Clouds Roll By* (1946, Jerome Kern), and *Words and Music* (1948, Richard Rodgers and Lorenz Hart) are memorable chiefly for their musical numbers. Unlike most other films in this category, *Three Little Words* presents a warm, intimate, and very human picture of two songwriters, Bert Kalmar and Harry Ruby, even though the plot is largely fictionalized. Besides several charming dance sequences performed by Fred Astaire and Vera-Ellen, the film also has engaging performances by Astaire and Red Skelton, whose screen *personae* complement each other surprisingly well.

In the film Bert Kalmar (Fred Astaire) is a vaudeville dancer with a passion for magic who becomes a lyricist after a knee injury cuts short his dancing career. He meets Harry Ruby (Red Skelton), a composer and song plugger with a passion for baseball, when Ruby disrupts Kalmar's magic act. Soon, they are writing songs together and go on to compose the music for many successful Broadway shows, including *The Ramblers*, *Five O'Clock Girl*, and *Animal Crackers* (starring the Marx Brothers).

Three Little Words depicts the struggles as well as the triumphs and successes of Kalmar and Ruby. Kalmar is quickly established as the dominant partner in the professional relationship. It is also quite clear that the diverse personalities of the two will present ample opportunities for friction during the course of their relationship. Kalmar is suave, domineering, and condescending toward Ruby, who in turn is bumbling, happy-go-lucky, and inept. Kalmar makes the decisions and Ruby acquiesces. Kalmar protects and rescues the naïve Ruby from several entanglements with predatory females, usually by sending him away to work out with his favorite baseball team, the Washington Senators. Finally, he settles down and marries a film star, Eileen Percy (Arlene Dahl). Kalmar's wife and former dancing partner, Jessie Brown (Vera-Ellen), besides providing some of the inspiration for his songs essential to this type of film, also dispenses the calm understanding and wise advice that are equally important for the wife of a famous songwriter.

Because it is the story of two songwriters, *Three Little Words* necessarily devotes several scenes to showing how Kalmar and Ruby composed some of their songs. Creativity is always difficult to present visually, especially when it involves a well-known song immediately recognizable by the film audience while the composers are struggling to get through the first bar, which they play over and over while waiting for inspiration to strike. The most memorable inspiration scene occurs near the end of the film. After Kalmar and Ruby have quarreled, their wives plot to reunite them by arranging for them to appear on a radio program featuring their songs. The two realize they must prepare a new routine and a new song for the program and arrange to meet beforehand at Kalmar's house. At the end of the meeting the two quarrel again and Kalmar tells Ruby what he thinks of him "in just three little words. You're a dope!" Ruby realizes those are the very words that fit a tune he has been working on for years; and thus the popular song "Three Little Words" is born. After the radio program is over the happy reunion is symbolized by an enormous cake that bears the legend "Three Little Words" and the figures of a baseball player and a magician.

Kalmar and Ruby's discovery of the famous show business personality, the "boop-boop-a-doop" girl, Helen Kane (Debbie Reynolds), is imaginatively depicted in the film. The two are strolling along a city street when inspiration strikes yet again. Fortunately, furniture movers happen to put down a piano practically in their path. They begin singing and playing their latest creation, "I Wanna Be Loved by You," and are joined by a passing youngster who inserts "boop-boop-a-doop" at appropriate moments. A star is born. In real life, however, Helen Kane (who did the singing for Debbie Reynolds in the film) was already an established Broadway star when she appeared in the Kalmar and Ruby show in which she introduced the song.

The most imaginative and memorable dance routine in the film is "Mr. and Mrs. Hoofer at Home." In it Astaire and Vera-Ellen, through dance and pantomime, depict the home life of two dancers, from her dusting the room before his arrival, to his exuberant greeting, to a rhythmical meal, and some syncopated bouncing of the baby. The number ends as the two whirl right through the living room wall on their way to an evening on the town.

Three Little Words is a competent rather than innovative film that presents a warm, intimate picture of a songwriting team, with the performances of Astaire and Vera-Ellen particularly warm and believable. In addition to the sprightly dancing of these two, the often amusing interaction between Astaire and Skelton gives an added dimension to the film, lifting it above the average musical biography.

Julia Johnson

THE THREE MUSKETEERS

Released: 1948
Production: Pandro S. Berman for Metro-Goldwyn-Mayer
Direction: George Sidney
Screenplay: Robert Ardrey; based on the novel of the same name by Alexandre Dumas
Cinematography: Robert Planck
Editing: Robert J. Kern
Running time: 125 minutes

Principal characters:

D'Artagnan	Gene Kelly
Milady de Winter	Lana Turner
Constance Bonacieux	June Allyson
Athos	Van Heflin
Richelieu	Vincent Price
Queen Anne	Angela Lansbury
King Louis XIII	Frank Morgan
Planchet	Keenan Wynn
Duke of Buckingham	John Sutton
Porthos	Gig Young
Aramis	Robert Coote
Treville	Reginald Owen
Rochefort	Ian Keith
Kitty	Patricia Medina
Jussac	Sol Gorss
Bonacieux	Byron Foulger
Felton	Gil Perkins

Although Sir Walter Scott can be credited with inventing the swashbuckling historical novel with *Ivanhoe*, the first full-fledged cape-and-sword swashbuckler is Alexandre Dumas' *The Three Musketeers* (1844). In turn, it became the second motion picture swashbuckler to be made when Douglas Fairbanks filmed it in 1921, the year after he created that movie genre with *The Mark of Zorro*. Both were directed with considerable flair by Fred Niblo, who went on to make the silent *Ben-Hur* (1925). In 1929, Fairbanks played D'Artagnan again in a sequel, *The Iron Mask*, directed by Allan Dwan; then in 1935, a talking version of *The Three Musketeers* was directed by Rowland V. Lee. A lackluster production, it was particularly handicapped by the miscasting of gruff-looking Walter Abel as a very undashing D'Artagnan. It was Abel's film debut and later he settled more congenially into a stereotyped role as a nervous, modern-day harassed husband or businessman. Despite good support by Paul Lukas and Ralph Forbes, the film is dull and undistinguished. A mere four years later, in 1939, Dwan returned to the story of D'Artagnan with a spirited musical spoof of *The Three Musketeers*, in which the real musketeers are impersonated by the three Ritz Brothers, who turn their adventures into slapstick. Don Ameche is a singing D'Artagnan, Binnie Barnes a striking Lady de Winter, and there is good support by Joseph Schildkraut, Lionel Atwill, and John Carradine. Although the general treatment was a travesty, the plot revolving around the Queen's diamond studs was kept intact, there was some lively swordplay, and the production was a good-humored romp.

Up to this point, none of these versions told the entire story. All stopped with D'Artagnan's saving the Queen from Cardinal Richelieu's dastardly plot to discredit her with the King by revealing that she had given his gift of diamond studs to her lover the Duke of Buckingham. This takes us through only twenty-two of the novel's sixty-seven chapters and constitutes only about one-third of the book. Accordingly, in 1948, M-G-M decided to film the entire story and to do it for the first time in color. During World War II, the swashbuckler had been discontinued in favor of contemporary war films, but afterwards the genre again became popular as war-weary audiences turned to escapist costume adventure set in earlier eras. M-G-M had never made a swashbuckler before, but the success of films such as *The Spanish Main* (1945), *The Bandit of Sherwood Forest* (1946), *Captain from Castile* (1947), and *Sinbad the Sailor* (1947) at other studios in the postwar years encouraged the studio to take on the most enduring swashbuckler of them all.

Unfortunately, there was no established swashbuckling star at the studio. Errol Flynn was at Warner Bros., Tyrone Power at Fox, Cornel Wilde at Fox and Columbia, and Douglas Fairbanks, Jr., was freelancing. Accordingly, M-G-M turned to dancer Gene Kelly. Kelly's favorite star during his boyhood had been Douglas Fairbanks, and his favorite film *The Three Musketeers*, so he was eager to take on the role. In part to prepare audiences for this transformation of Kelly from the brash American hoofer to a seventeenth century swordsman, M-G-M put a moustache on him and cast him in *The Pirate* (1948), a Cole Porter musical comedy that allowed him to do some swashbuckling without departing entirely from his image. Lana Turner, the studio's chief *femme fatale*, became Milady de Winter, and June Allyson, M-G-M's leading sweet ingenue, was cast as Constance Bonacieux.

For the three musketeers of the title, Van Heflin was cast somewhat incongruously as Athos, Gig Young as Porthos, and Robert Coote as a somewhat overage and effeminate Aramis. Frank Morgan was definitely overage and miscast as King Louis XIII, whom he portrayed as a royal French Wizard of Oz. As his adulterous Queen, Angela Lansbury was suitably erotic; John Sutton played her noble lover the Duke of Buckingham. Keenan Wynn was Planchet, D'Artagnan's lackey, and Vincent Price played a sinister and oily Richelieu. Most of this was casting against the grain; only Sutton and Price had any experience in this sort of period playing, and most of the others seemed painfully American. The director was George Sidney, whose previous work had been almost entirely with musical comedies, such as *Bathing Beauty* (1944), *The Harvey Girls* (1946), and *Anchors Aweigh* (1945); later he would direct *Annie Get Your Gun* (1950), *Kiss Me Kate* (1953), and *Pal Joey* (1957). (Interestingly, he would also do *Scaramouche*, 1952, and *Young Bess*, 1953.) Thus it is not surprising that the film has something of the quality of a musical comedy, although the background music is mostly from Tchaikovsky's *Romeo and Juliet Overture*.

The screenplay by Robert Ardrey necessarily condenses Dumas' novel somewhat but is generally faithful to the story and does cover the entire plot. The story begins with a young and impoverished D'Artagnan, leaving home to seek his fortune in Paris. All he has is a large yellow plow horse, his father's sword, and a letter of introduction to the commander of the King's musketeers. Entering the town of Meung, he encounters the sinister Comte de Rochefort (Ian Keith) and Milady de Winter. When the count mocks his horse, D'Artagnan demands satisfaction and draws his sword, but the Comte does not wish to duel with a man he considers a yokel. He therefore has his servants brain D'Artagnan from behind. When D'Artagnan recovers his senses, he is alone. Vowing revenge on de Rochefort, he proceeds to Paris.

During his interview with Monsieur de Treville (Reginald Owen), commander of the musketeers, three musketeers—Athos, Porthos, and Aramis—are ushered in so that the captain can dress them down for brawling with the Cardinal's guards. Athos has been wounded in the right arm. After they leave, when the interview resumes, D'Artagnan sees outside below the window the Comte de Rochefort. Impulsively, he dashes out in pursuit, only to collide with Athos and bump his injured arm. When Athos calls him a bumpkin, D'Artagnan challenges him to a duel at noon. He then continues his pursuit but becomes entangled in Porthos' new cloak; the encounter results in another duel—at one. By the time D'Artagnan dashes into the street, de Rochefort has disappeared. D'Artagnan then unintentionally insults Aramis, who asks him to adjudicate a dispute over a lady's handkerchief. They arrange for a duel at two.

When the musketeers arrive together at the dueling ground, they are amazed and amused to find that all three are to fight the same man. They feel an admiration for the brash courage of this newcomer who has challenged three of the best swordsmen in France. He and Athos are about to cross swords when they are interrupted by five of the Cardinal's guards, who try to arrest them for violating the ordinance against dueling. Although they are outnumbered and Athos is wounded, the three musketeers prepare to fight rather than surrender. D'Artagnan joins them, and they engage the guards. D'Artagnan finds himself pitted against Jussac (Sol Gorss), the best blade, but he attacks with such skill and vigor that he completely outfences Jussac and makes a mockery of him. When Athos, fencing left-handed, is hard-pressed, D'Artagnan comes to his rescue and defeats his opponent. The other guards are disabled or flee, and D'Artagnan and his three new friends remain in possession of the field, where they pledge the loyalty of "All for one, one for all." When they are summoned before King Louis XIII, he rewards them for embarrassing his rival, Cardinal Richelieu.

Now a cadet in the musketeers, D'Artagnan takes lodgings in the home of M. Bonacieux (Byron Foulger), an aged man with a pretty young wife, Constance (June Allyson), who is lady-in-waiting to the Queen, Anne of Austria. D'Artagnan discovers a knothole in the floor, through which he peeps at Constance, while she is undressing, when suddenly a band of men hired by the Cardinal break in and try to abduct her. D'Artagnan dashes downstairs, fights off the entire gang, and rescues Constance, who asks him to escort her to the palace. When she meets a gentleman, D'Artagnan thinks it is for an amorous rendezvous. He prepares to fight, but Constance informs him that the man is the Queen's lover, the English Duke of Buckingham. Chastened, D'Artagnan guards them the rest of the way.

Cardinal Richelieu, a Machiavellian schemer, is the gray eminence behind the throne. Competing for power with the weak king, he tries to obtain proof of the Queen's infidelity. She has given Buckingham a set of diamond studs that were a gift from the King. Through his agent Milady de Winter, Richelieu learns of this and persuades the King to ask the Queen to wear the studs at an approaching ball. To save herself, the Queen must get the studs back from England. Constance persuades D'Artagnan to go to England and bring back the studs. The three musketeers insist on accompanying him, and it is well that they do, for Richelieu's men have set a series of ambushes that take out Athos, Porthos, and Aramis. D'Artagnan alone escapes. He reaches Buckingham, but the latter is dismayed to find that someone has stolen two diamonds out of the set. He is sure Milady de Winter is guilty. Meanwhile, with no time to lose, Buckingham has the missing gems duplicated, and D'Artagnan arrives in Paris with them in the nick of time. Richelieu has shown the two stolen studs to the King, with the implication that the Queen has betrayed him, but when Anne appears with all twelve, the embarrassed Cardinal has to pretend the other two are a gift to their majesties.

That night D'Artagnan is to be rewarded with a tryst with Constance, but when he arrives, he finds that their meeting place is a shambles and that she has been abducted by the Comte de Rochefort, acting for Milady and the Cardinal. Unable to find Constance, D'Artagnan then retraces his steps on the route to England and is happy to discover the three musketeers alive and recovered. Athos, maudlinly drunk, tells him of the Comte de la Fère, who as a young man married a beautiful girl, only to discover that she had been branded on the shoulder with the *fleur-de-lis* of a convict for having stolen the sacred vessels from a church. The Comte was actually Athos, and the bride became Milady de Winter. Not knowing this yet, however, D'Artagnan returns to Paris and begins courting Milady de Winter in hopes of learning the whereabouts of Constance. He finds himself becoming enamored of Milady despite himself, but she loves the Comte de Wardes and despises D'Artagnan. Her maid Kitty (Patricia Medina), herself enamored of D'Artagnan, helps him to Milady's bedroom in the dark, wherein he pretends to be de Wardes. When Milady discovers the masquerade, she tries to kill D'Artagnan. In defending himself, he tears the gown from her shoulder and discovers the branded *fleur-de-lis*. She then rouses the house to capture him, but he manages to outfight the lot of them and escape.

The musketeers then go to the siege of La Rochelle, under attack by the English. There, Athos seizes from Milady a *carte blanche* that Richelieu has given her to go to England and murder the English commander, the Duke of Buckingham. Athos arranges for her honorable brother-in-law, Lord de Winter, to arrest and imprison her upon her arrival. He does so, but she manages to seduce her jailer, a Puritan fanatic named Felton (Gil Perkins), persuading him that she has been traduced by Buckingham. Felton then enables her to escape and murders Buckingham as he is about to embark for France.

Having arrived safely back in France, Milady goes to a Carmelite convent, where Constance has been kept a prisoner and dressed as a novice. Learning that Constance loves D'Artagnan, Milady poisons her just as D'Artagnan and the musketeers arrive. They pursue Milady, and after capturing her she is tried and condemned for her crimes. She is finally beheaded by the executioner of Lille, who had branded her years ago when she corrupted his brother, a young priest.

Back in Paris, D'Artagnan is summoned to Richelieu, who intends to punish him for the death of Milady, but when he presents the *carte blanche* signed by the Cardinal himself, Richelieu pardons him and makes him an officer in the musketeers.

Under Sidney's direction, these events move at a spirited pace, but the tone and casting are uncertain. Kelly is an extremely agile fencer and a most acrobatic D'Artagnan, but at times he clowns so broadly that it is hard to take him seriously. He nevertheless carries off the acting honors of the film. As Milady de Winter, Turner is voluptuous, but as Bosley Crowther observed, "she walks through the palaces and salons with the air of a company-mannered Mae West. And she makes ardent love to her victims with elegant high-school hauteur." Heflin is too heavy-handed and maudlin as Athos, and Young and Coote are little more than clothes-horses as Porthos and Aramis. Allyson's Constance is an all-American nice girl who seems lost in seventeenth century France. As Richelieu, always dressed as a cavalier and never in his Cardinal's robes, Price is an unctuous villain. All in all, like Sidney's later *Scaramouche*, the film seems almost a spoof of costume swashbucklers, and its slapstick manner becomes increasingly out of place as the film moves into its tragic climaxes. The film's assets are a genial and light-hearted if sometimes hammed-up performance by Kelly, its almost breakneck pace, and some of the most spectacular swordplay and assorted acrobatics ever screened.

Hollywood was not yet finished with D'Artagnan and the three musketeers. In 1952, Louis Hayward played D'Artagnan in a "B"-class cape-and-sword opera called *The Lady in the Iron Mask*, and in the same year Cornel Wilde played the son of D'Artagnan in a second-generation swashbuckler called *At Sword's Point*. In 1974, Richard Lester directed a memorable remake of *The Three Musketeers*, which, despite the miscasting of Michael York as a yokelish, clean-shaven D'Artagnan, spectacularly inaccurate swordplay (with more kicking than fencing), and a good deal of slapstick throughout, was in some ways the best version yet because of its European locations, elaborate and often amusing use of period detail, and good performances by all the rest of the cast, including Charlton Heston as a wily Cardinal Richelieu (properly robed this time). The next year, Lester followed it with the second half of the story, *The Four Musketeers*. In the late 1970's, Louis Jourdan played D'Artagnan in a television version of *The Man in the Iron Mask*, and in 1979, Wilde graduated from playing the son of D'Artagnan to playing the older D'Artagnan himself in another version of *The Man in the Iron Mask*, called *The Fifth Musketeer*. Wilde's performance in it was probably closer to the spirit of Dumas than that of any other actor. It is unfortunate that the young D'Artagnan was never played by Flynn or Douglas Fairbanks, Jr., in their primes. Kelly's performance is flawed by the broad clowning; but even so, his is the best we have so far of the young D 'Artagnan. Kelly has said it is his favorite role.

Robert E. Morsberger

3:10 TO YUMA

Released: 1957
Production: David Heilwell for Columbia
Direction: Delmer Daves
Screenplay: Halsted Welles; based on an original story of the same name by Elmore Leonard
Cinematography: Charles Lawton, Jr.
Editing: Al Clark
Music: George Duning
Song: Ned Washington and George Duning
Running time: 92 minutes

Principal characters:
Ben Wade	Glenn Ford
Dan Evans	Van Heflin
Emmy (barmaid)	Felicia Farr
Alice Evans	Leora Dana
Alex Potter (town drunk)	Henry Jones
Charlie Prince	Richard Jaeckel
Butterfield	Robert Emhardt

3:10 to Yuma is a Western in a tradition of which *High Noon* (1952) and *Last Train from Gun Hill* (1959) are also famous examples. In each of these films, the hero faces a test of courage which ultimately reveals something about his values, and in each story, an element of tension is introduced by having the resolution of conflict dependent on the arrival or departure of a train at a given hour. Suspense is common to most Westerns, but generally it plays a part only in certain key sequences, such as climactic gunfights or last-minute rescues by the cavalry. The "train" Westerns stand out as a group because the climactic moment is anticipated so early in the film—often in the title itself—and everything leads to that moment. The virtues of this structure are immediately apparent. Once the story has aroused the interest of the audience, there are no slow passages, and dramatic momentum is certain.

This structure can be a heavy burden, however; if the screenplay does not allow the characters to develop naturally within the course of the action, the result can be a work which seems irritatingly contrived. This fault explains the relative failure for some critics of *High Noon*, once the most celebrated of all Westerns and an undeniable influence on all of the "train" Westerns which followed it. The courage and integrity of Will Kane in that film exist not to be explored but as a foil for the story to demonstrate the shabby lack of civic responsibility of his fellow citizens. His increasing isolation is not altogether unmoving, but once the audience understands that the central conflict is not between one man and another, or inside the protagonist, but between misplaced virtue and the society in which it has no place, the elaborate editing techniques for which the film has won praise seem unduly calculating and emphasize the lack of spontaneous feeling in the film's design.

By contrast, *3:10 to Yuma* does not depend on aggressive formal devices and is more subtly stylized. It takes its theme not from the sociology of the 1950's but from a struggle with nature true to its historical setting. Dan Evans (Van Heflin), a small rancher with a wife, Alice (Leora Dana), and two sons, is suffering a feeling of physical and moral defeat because of a drought which threatens the survival of his way of life. In this situation, his failure to intervene in the robbery of a stage by Ben Wade (Glenn Ford) and his gang, while practical and motivated by protectiveness toward the two sons who are with him, acts as a catalyst to bring into the open his dispirited attitude, which is even affecting his essentially stable relationship with his wife. When Butterfield (Robert Emhardt), the manager of the stage line, offers a reward to help capture Wade and take him to prison, the opportunity of subduing Wade having presented itself because of his brief romantic alliance with a town barmaid, Evans volunteers for the chance of earning enough money to buy water rights. Although neither a brave nor a cowardly man, Evans, with the help of the town drunk (Henry Jones) who is the only other volunteer, takes Wade to a nearby town to wait in a hotel room for the arrival of the train which will take them to the prison at Yuma. Taunted by the mocking threats of the cheerful Wade and menaced by the presence outside of Wade's men, who succeed in killing the drunk, Evans discovers reserves of strength and self-possession that he did not know he had. Although even his wife begs him to relent and let Wade go, and Butterfield offers to pay him even if he does, Evans sees his job through, catching the train at the last moment as Wade's men attempt to shoot him, and killing Wade's murderous henchman, Charlie Prince (Richard Jaeckel).

The film's climax includes a human miracle followed by a natural one. Giving up his chance for escape, Wade jumps on the train of his own volition, out of respect for Evans' determination. As the two men ride the train to Yuma, there is a crackle of thunder, and rain begins to pour down onto the parched land as Evans looks out to see his wife beside the train, the water pouring down her face as she gazes rapturously up at him. This metaphor of the human spirit rewarded by the blessing of nature is very moving, as its appearance seems in no way arbitrary but delicately articulated through the style and substance of the film as the conclusion of a progression which sees spiritual and material truths as coexisting.

The opening shot begins with a stretch of parched earth, and the camera then rises on its crane to present a long view of the stage racing across the landscape. An implicit feeling of destiny has been created visually, and the audience will soon make a natural connection between this desolate land and the crisis of Evans. This movement of the camera later links Evans and Wade as the outlaw is taken out of the first town while the barmaid, Emmy (Felicia Farr), stands alone in the street looking after him, the camera again rising to an overhead view which affirms the harmony of a natural order which understands and transcends the lives of people locked into existences of limited meaning. Finally, there is the view from the train in the last sequence, as Evans looks out at the receding image of his wife in the rain from a vantage point that is like that of a god, the magical image created by the camera transforming the vision of a simple man into a moment of new understanding.

A grasp of eternal values is central to Westerns, as is the true meaning of human liberty. Westerns are visually predisposed to examine these themes, blessed with archetypal conflicts and physically expressive landscapes; however, these conflicts and landscapes must be artistically shaped to create a work of stature. *3:10 to Yuma* is affecting and exciting because its director, Delmer Daves, and his screenwriter, Halsted Welles, have imbued it with a deep respect for the implicit promise of its story, and with a skill for invention at once simple and daring. Nothing could demonstrate this better than the interlude between Wade and the barmaid. The theme of an unromantic existence, elaborated in the presentation of Evans and his family, is explicitly developed in the character of the barmaid, who might otherwise be marginal in the story, and the sequence is realized with a lyricism and eroticism not often identified with the genre. In the few minutes in which she is alone on the screen with Ford, Farr creates a touching and singular portrait of a romantic sensibility seeking expression on the rugged frontier. This portrait deepens one's appreciation of Dana's Alice Evans, making her not merely a wife and mother but a woman of rich and often unexpressed feelings, and the link between the two women is heightened by their responses to Wade, who reveals a tender side early in the film in his sympathetic understanding of them.

Among a number of unjustly neglected Westerns—*Jubal* (1955), *Cowboy* (1957), *The Hanging Tree* (1959—*3:10 to Yuma* is the film to demonstrate most convincingly that Daves was an unusually gifted practitioner of the genre, capable of inspiring the best in his collaborators. The black-and-white cinematography of Charles Lawton, Jr., is very beautiful, striking a subtle balance between naturalism and artificiality which is perfectly attuned to the theme. Heflin and Ford are effectively contrasted, and Ford deserves credit in his own right for rejecting the role offered him, that of Evans, and suggesting himself for the role of Wade, counter to his accepted screen image. Finally, the ballad heard at the beginning and end of the film and sensitively referred to elsewhere in its score is one of the most haunting and evocative ever written for a Western, beginning quietly and building to a powerful refrain as the irreplaceable Frankie Laine sings out its last words: "Take that train! Take that train!"

Blake Lucas

3 WOMEN

Released: 1977
Production: Robert Altman for Twentieth Century-Fox
Direction: Robert Altman
Screenplay: Robert Altman
Cinematography: Charles Rosher
Editing: Dennis Hill
Music: Gerald Busby
Running time: 124 minutes

Principal characters:
Millie Lammoreaux .... Shelley Duvall
Pinky Rose .... Sissy Spacek
Willie Hart .... Janice Rule
Edgar Hart .... Robert Fortier
Mrs. Bunweil .... Sierra Pecheur
Doctor Maas .... Craig Richard Nelson
Mrs. Rose .... Ruth Nelson
Mr. Rose .... John Cromwell
Peggy .... Patricia Ann Hudson
Polly .... Leslie Ann Hudson

Robert Altman has written of a disturbing dream that came to him during the final weeks of shooting *Buffalo Bill and the Indians, or Sitting Bull's History Lesson* (1976), a commercial and artistic failure that may have marked one of the low points of his professional career. This dream of two girls from Texas who meet in the desert wasteland of California at a geriatric spa became the basis for one of the most profoundly adventurous and hypnotic films of recent decades and perhaps Altman's greatest achievement. *3 Women* begins in a vein of stylized realism but subtly builds, through a sequence of minimal events, repeated motifs, and carefully orchestrated polarities, into a frightening, surrealistic exploration of the fragility of identity. Eschewing the visual busy-ness, overlapping sound tracks, and the proliferating sets of characters of *Nashville* (1975), or *Buffalo Bill and the Indians*, the film is atypical for Altman; more than anything else, it invites comparison with Ingmar Bergman's *Persona* (1966), which it resembles in uncanny ways, and with the stark emptiness and deliberate palette of Michelangelo Antonioni's *Zabriskie Point* (1970) and *The Passenger* (1975). Altman here has reduced the elements of his art to an exhilarating minimum, constructing his vision out of a handful of characters in only three or four primary settings and animating it through dazzling juxtapositions of desert and water, pinks and blues, youth and age, overwhelming isolation and small moments of oblique connection. It is a film of bleakness and pervasive sorrow, growing, like a dream, by means of subtle echoes and abrupt metamorphoses whose implications are emphatically open-ended.

The film begins like a warm bath: Gerald Busby's haunting woodwind score ushers us through the wading pool of an expensive rehabilitation resort, Desert Springs, where Millie Lammoreaux (Shelley Duvall) and the other "girls" lead their charges slowly on constitutional walks. For several minutes we see only the foreshortened lower halves of bodies, young and lithe, beside the swollen and bent, stepping cautiously through the dreamy, primordial medium of water. This is a world of stunning regularity, of strictly maintained patterns, and only reluctantly does the camera rise to show us the warm cameo of Pinky Rose (Sissy Spacek), her rust-gold hair pulled back from her open face, standing behind an observation window in a pink dress. Millie ("one of our best girls") is assigned to break in the new girl, and in the next several scenes, a kind of fugue on the theme of alliance, we meet the various "pairs" who make up the human landscape of Desert Springs: the bossy, masculine Nurse Bunweil (Sierra Pecheur) and the irritable, oddly enervated Dr. Maas (Craig Richard Nelson); Doris and Alcira, of similar build and coloring, who work with Millie: and Peggy and Polly (Patricia Ann Hudson and Leslie Ann Hudson), the identical twins whom the confused Pinky meets one at a time before the small epiphany of seeing them whispering together across the pool. The "unpartnered" Millie unfolds her world for Pinky. It is the realm of ladies' magazines, of self-help and chic mottoes. Her monologue with the young doctors at the hospital across the street consists of recipes and ideas about home decorating. No one listens to her, but Pinky watches with admiration from a nearby table and takes down the card Millie has tacked to the bulletin board advertising her need for a roommate.

Millie takes Pinky to "Dodge City" in her "mustard"-colored Pinto with the hem of her skirt hanging out the door. This is one of the other major settings of Altman's film—a former amusement park, now a bar and hangout, with an abandoned miniature golf course out front and a shooting range in back where "the boys" drink and shoot and ride dirt bikes all day, everyday, it seems. Pinky's eye is arrested by odd murals on the patio behind the bar, enormous frescoes of scale-covered, quasihuman figures frozen in dramatic postures, the savage males in defiant macho stances, the females, often pregnant, holding their bellies in poses of despair, horror, or resignation. These are the work of Willie (Janice Rule), the third woman of the title, very pregnant herself, who lives with her husband Edgar (Robert Fortier) in the house out back. They run Dodge City and manage the Purple Sage Apartments where Millie lives. Willie does not speak as she serves beer to Millie and Pinky. As they leave, a truck pulls up and a seedy cowboy steps out and greets the two women by drawing his sixguns and "rescuing" them from a nearby "snake," a prop from his former days as Hugh O'Brian's stunt double on the *Wyatt Earp* show. To Edgar's question about her name, Pinky confesses that her real name is "Mildred." We shortly learn that Mildred is also Millie's real name.

Millie initiates Pinky into her life at the Purple Sage Apartments, a world of purples and yellows and of surfaces covered with flowers. "Decorated it myself," boasts Millie, with barely concealed pride. The garden apartments are a garish singles' complex spread out around a pool where idle young men and women congregate, rarely speaking as they lounge conspiratorially on deckchairs. They refer to Millie as "Thoroughly Modern Millie," often in her presence, with contemptuous smiles. So hermetic is her aura, however, that Millie manages to perceive none of this, and Pinky, a shy creature seemingly with no "history" of her own, is impressed with the style and self-sufficiency of her only companion.

At the spa, Pinky writes Millie's social security number on her work forms and later punches out on Millie's timecard, drawing the wrath of Nurse Bunweil and Dr. Maas. In the next days, she borrows a robe belonging to Millie and notices the locked diary where Millie records the "event" of her new roommate. She observes Willie tending the apartment pool, which also bears a mural like the one at Dodge City. The screen during this shot, and several other times later on, is bisected by a shifting wash, half pink, half blue, which rolls over Pinky's view of the pool.

When Millie throws one of her "famous" dinner parties for her ex-roommate Dierdre, the latter drops by early in a truck with two men and tells Pinky she cannot make it because she is going out drinking with the boys at Dodge City. Millie is crushed at the news and leaves to find them. She returns late at night and wakes up Pinky to move her to the cot in the outer room. Her "date" moves into the light and Pinky sees Edgar. "Not a word," threatens Millie, "what do you know anyway?"

Pinky walks out of the apartment to the second story railing and stares down into the pool. Then, in silence, she collapses and falls into her reflection, hanging in the water like a still ghost. Willie appears, screams for help—her first words in the film—and pulls her to safety. Millie comes down to identify her roommate, and Willie stares up in unvoiced rage at Millie's doorway where Edgar is standing.

So ends *3 Women*'s extended "first movement," but what follows forces a rethinking of all we have seen as the surrealistic undertones rise to the fore. While Pinky lies in the hospital in a coma, Millie manages to contact her parents, who arrive from Texas in Dust Bowl clothing. When Pinky awakens, she falls victim to an eerie kind of amnesia. With a new brashness, she denies the aged couple are her parents and insists her name is Millie, not Pinky. Moreover, when her parents leave and she returns to the apartment, she now believes herself to *be* Millie, making entries in Millie's diary, wearing makeup, and flirting and drinking with Edgar and the other tenants of the Purple Sage. Millie, for her part, is shocked into some deeper self-awareness by the sight of this parody of her former self and finds the strength not only to "mother" Pinky, but also to tell off Nurse Bunweil and Dr. Maas for their callow indifference to the girl's trauma. She quits her job, in fact, but after this show of bravado, she is unable to go home because her car has been stolen. With help from a pair of police officers, she finds the car parked at Dodge City, where Pinky is shooting and drinking out back with Edgar. Pinky insists she did not steal the car. "I just borrowed it," she states.

The two women co-exist in an uneasy truce until one night Pinky has a dark, troubling dream. This sequence forms a virtuoso piece of filmmaking, a fluid collage of overlaid images from the film up to that point blended with some new images that we have not yet seen, over a soundtrack of deepening, metronome-like chords. After these audacious minutes, Pinky awakens and opens the doors to the outer room where Millie is sleeping. Pinky speaks in a softer voice again as she tells Millie of her bad dream and asks if she can sleep with her. The two climb under the blanket together, but are soon disturbed when Edgar bursts in drunk and becomes excited at finding not one, but two women in bed.

When Millie and Pinky learn from Edgar that Willie is having her baby, they drive to the house behind Dodge City where Willie has gone into labor. Millie orders Pinky to go get a doctor and enters the house to help Willie. Pinky can not move, however, and stares in passive fascination as the women join hands and amid Willie's screams, Millie delivers a baby boy. The baby is stillborn. Millie walks from the house with blood on her hands to where Pinky has been standing and slaps her. Pinky, who does not seem to feel the slap, touches the blood on her hair.

The final sequence, or epilogue, begins with a lengthy shot of a yellow soda truck looming larger as it approaches Dodge City. The delivery boy finds Pinky, the simple Pinky of the film's opening, tending the counter. She calls in a tall, aproned figure with sweptback hair to sign the form. It is Millie, quieter now, and with an air of mystery. We learn that Edgar has had a shooting accident, strange for a man so adept with guns. The women stare and say nothing. Pinky and Millie then go back out to the house where Willie is sitting on the porch in a rocker. The three "generations" of women are now a community, or commune, without men. Willie remarks, her first full statement in the film "I just had the most wonderful dream. I tried to remember it, but I couldn't."

By reducing the number of moving parts in his story and placing it in a realistic landscape that is also, as Richard Schickel wrote in *Time* magazine, "a very persuasive analogue to a dream landscape—essentially empty, so that it throws its few symbolic structures into high relief," Altman has raised his film to the status of a modern myth. When a trio of women appeared in Greek mythology, they carried heightened, even magical significance, sometimes as arbiters of destiny, sometimes as instruments of divine retribution. What began as a "realistic" meeting in a remote desert community of two young women whose relationship is catalyzed by a silent, older artist and her philandering husband has been transformed into a suggestive poem about the mysteries of self-creation and the interdependence of human personalities. However open-ended, *3 Women* locates the stability and continuity of life in the person of women, a stability won, in this case, at the cost of excluding men altogether. Indeed, as embodied in the grotesque figure of Edgar, the male is seen as an irresponsible and disruptive force which women must become strong enough to survive.

The sense of timelessness that pervades *3 Women* is reinforced by its "negative" incorporation of archetypal processes: one woman's failure to die, at the center of the film, and another's failure to give birth at the end. Altman manages to wring from his contemplation of this bleak condition a work of tragic, delicate beauty. Working from his detailed outline, the cast contributed greatly to the definitive script during the shooting of the film. Duvall, who reportedly wrote eighty percent of her lines, has created in Millie Lammoreaux a truly haunting modern paradigm, and Spacek is scarcely less impressive as the highly malleable Pinky. It is hard to visualize either role apart from these actresses' flawless realizations. Rule and Fortier are also strong as a pair who represent perhaps the ultimate male-female schism, never addressing each other once during the entire film. The cinematography by Charles Rosher is probably his greatest work and contributes heavily to *3 Women*'s prismatic, mythical quality. Busby's score and Bodhi Wind's eerie murals also play integral roles in the success of a masterwork which the Academy largely ignored. Duvall, however, was voted Best Actress at the 1977 Cannes Film Festival; Spacek received the New York Film Critics Award for Best Supporting Actress.

Leslie Wolf

TIGER BAY

Released: 1959
Production: John Hawksworth for J. Arthur Rank
Direction: J. Lee Thompson
Screenplay: John Hawksworth and Shelley Smith; based on the novel
  Rodolphe et le Revolver by Noel Calef
Cinematography: Eric Cross
Editing: Sidney Hayers
Running time: 105 minutes

> *Principal characters:*
> Superintendent Graham .... John Mills
> Korchinsky .... Horst Buchholz
> Gillie .... Hayley Mills
> Anya .... Yvonne Mitchell
> Mrs. Phillips .... Megs Jenkins

Good child actors and actresses are rare. Even talented ones often betray a cloying cuteness, an awareness of being on camera that detracts from their performance and can throw an entire film off balance. There have been some gifted child stars, most of them, such as Jackie Coogan, the phenomenal Shirley Temple, Mickey Rooney, and Freddie Bartholomew, active during the 1930's. The supply seemed to dry up after World War II, with the exception perhaps of Margaret O'Brien and Natalie Wood in America. In 1959, however, Hayley Mills, the daughter of the respected British actor John Mills, made her film debut in *Tiger Bay*, and although only twelve years old at the time, she exhibited a naturalness and virtuosity not displayed on the screen by a child for many years. She had a good vehicle with which to work, it is true. *Tiger Bay* has all the ingredients of a successful thriller—a murder, a chase by the police, an appealing hero, and the charm of Mills as a lonely girl who prefers her exciting falsehoods to the grim reality around her. The film pits Mills against her own father, and in scene after scene, she outshines him, although the elder Mills does not seem to mind.

Directed by J. Lee Thompson, *Tiger Bay* is well paced and filled with edge-of-the-seat tension throughout. It is shot in the beautiful black-and-white cinematography of Eric Cross, and Thompson and Cross have found a rich poetry in the streets of Cardiff Bay, Wales, where Black Jamaican faces are as common as white ones. Although the film is essentially a two-character study, with John Mills as an important subsidiary third, the incidental people around Cardiff—sailors, shopkeepers, neighbors—give the film a feeling of ordinary life going on, which contrasts beautifully with the odd drama that is central to the story. There is the feeling of authenticity throughout, but it is not allowed to become obtrusive and be an end in itself.

The story concerns the mutual affection that grows between an anguished Polish sailor named Korchinsky (Horst Buchholz), who, in a moment of anger, kills someone, and a child named Gillie (Hayley Mills) who is given to telling lies and who joins the murderer on the run. The basis of their relationship is that they are both outsiders, not only in the real sense of running from the police, but in an emotional way as well. Korchinsky is already an alien as a Pole. He has been at sea for a long time and when he returns, things are not as he left them. Gillie is taunted by other children, probably because she is so much cleverer than they. She has a watchful eye for the goings-on of the adult world, which she finds as interesting as the games of her contemporaries. Both of these figures also share a loneliness that is temporarily alleviated by their adventure together. For Korchinsky, however, this friendship is destructive, since if he clings too hard to Gillie, his freedom is denied him. The film poses the classic dilemma of conflicting loyalties. It is an oft-repeated theme, but in *Tiger Bay*, the sailor's choices are heartrending, and the film packs quite an emotional wallop. This is due primarily to the acting of Hayley Mills, but Buchholz also gives a powerful performance. The popular German actor was on the verge of becoming an international star when he made *Tiger Bay*, and his boyish good looks and tragic intensity proved a perfect foil for Mills's streetwise Gillie.

The film opens as Korchinsky walks through a square in Tiger Bay, a section of Cardiff near the docks. He has been at sea and is now coming home to his Anya (Yvonne Mitchell), whom he expects to marry. At her flat, he finds a mulatto girl. Korchinsky puts his duffel bag in a cupboard in the corridor and goes to see the landlord, who tells him that Anya has moved to a nearby apartment building leaving unpaid rent behind her. At the building, Korchinsky finds Anya, but she tells him that she now has a new gentleman friend. A violent quarrel ensues, and Anya takes a gun from a drawer. Meanwhile, a lonely ten-year-old girl, Gillie, has heard the raised voices and watches the fight through a letter flap. Gillie desperately wants to join the local gang of boys and girls, but because she has no gun with which to play cowboys and Indians, they rebuff her. She has bought a toy bomb which she clutches as she listens to Korchinsky argue. Provoked into a blind rage, Korchinsky takes the gun from Anya and shoots her three times. Gillie, stunned by what she has just witnessed, lets her bomb fall, and there is yet another explosion in the hallway. When the neighbors come rushing, Gillie runs to hide while Korchinsky hides his gun in the hallway. As he waits until he can safely leave the building, he sees Gillie pick up the gun and put it in her pocket.

The police come to the building, led by Superintendent Graham, masterfully played by John Mills. Gillie, determined to keep the gun, gives a false description of Korchinsky in a beautiful scene in which the Superintendent *knows* she is lying, but because she is a child, he cannot prove it. The fact that an actual father and daughter are locked in a battle of wills makes the scene even more gripping. Later Korchinsky follows Gillie into a church where she sings in the choir. She hides, but after everyone has left, he confronts her. Gillie assures him that she has no intention of giving him up to the police, but will gladly submit to becoming a hostage. She hands over his gun and happily goes with him to a hideout. An odd rapport begins to grow between the distraught man and the child. Meanwhile, Graham has learned from a friend who sings in the choir with her that Gillie has the gun. The hunt is on, but so far only for Gillie. For the moment, Korchinsky is not connected with the crime. He goes to a dockland pub to buy food and learns that a ship is leaving for South America the next day. He also hears on the radio that the police are searching for Gillie, and he is tempted to kill the child to save himself, but knows he cannot; Gillie is passionately "on his side."

A plan comes to him, and he tells Gillie to stay hidden until seven o'clock the next evening, by which time Korchinsky will be safely aboard the ship. Meanwhile, the Mulatto girl from Anya's flat turns in the bag that Korchinsky left in the hall. Inside it is a photograph of the sailor and Anya. The evidence begins to mount up, for the police also find the gun, which Korchinsky had hidden in an outhouse near his hiding place. Tension rises as Graham traces Gillie and finds her. Despite her lies, Graham figures out that Korchinsky must be on the ship that is departing for South America. The police with Gillie board the ship just inside the three-mile limit. Gillie refuses to identify Korchinsky as the ship approaches the point of safety for the sailor. Suddenly, just as the three-mile limit is reached, Gillie falls overboard, and in a moving and dramatic climax, Korchinsky jumps in to save her, giving up his chance for freedom.

The tragic ending of the film is somewhat mitigated when Graham promises Gillie that he will try to go easy on Korchinsky in the light of his rescue and treatment of her, but still the audience is left gasping by the last five minutes of *Tiger Bay*. Hayley Mills was to continue to shine for a time as a child star in British films such as *Whistle Down the Wind* (1962) before the English lost her to Walt Disney Studios and the world lost her youthful charm to puberty. She made several films as an adult, and has appeared frequently on the London stage, but in *Tiger Bay* she proved that the rare phenomenon of a gifted but natural child actor does continue to occur.

Joan Cohen

TITANIC

Released: 1953
Production: Charles Brackett for Twentieth Century-Fox
Direction: Jean Negulesco
Screenplay: Charles Brackett, Walter Reisch, and Richard L. Breen; based on their original screen story (AA)
Cinematography: Joe MacDonald
Editing: Louis R. Loeffler
Running time: 98 minutes

Principal characters:

Richard Sturgess	Clifton Webb
Mrs. Sturgess	Barbara Stanwyck
Giff Rogers	Robert Wagner
Annette	Audrey Dalton
Mrs. Young	Thelma Ritter
Captain Smith	Brian Aherne
Healey	Richard Basehart
Earl Meeker	Allyn Joslyn
John Jacob Astor	William Johnstone
Norman	Harper Carter
Officer Lightoller	Edmund Purdom
Mr. Guggenheim	Camillo Guercio
Mrs. Straus	Helen Van Tuyl
Mr. Isidor Straus	Roy Gordon
Narrator	Michael Rennie

When the *S. S. Titanic* sank on April 14, 1912, on her maiden voyage, not only did it take hundreds of lives and cause the loss of millions of dollars, it also opened the way for endless speculation about the ship, its tragic end, and the lives of those on board. More than any other disaster in history, the story of the *Titanic* has led to countless stories, films, novels, and even a childhood jingle that summarizes the ship's fate: "The *Titanic* blew the whistle, the *Titanic* rang the bell, the *Titanic* hit an iceberg, the *Titanic* went to hell."

The San Francisco earthquake of 1906 has had numerous stories written about it, but the *Titanic*'s sinking is definitely the most popular subject. Not only has it provided a major setting for a wide variety of books and films, but its sinking is also a frequent subplot of other stories which take place in 1912. It can almost be assumed that if any portion of a film takes place in 1912, the *Titanic* disaster will somehow fit into the plot.

There were two films in the 1950's which featured the *Titanic*'s sinking as their central action. One, a 1958 British film titled *A Night to Remember*, is a straightforward, almost documentary approach to the incident with only minimal emphasis on the lives of various passengers. By contrast, the 1953

Hollywood-produced version, titled simply *Titanic*, is a star-studded, large-budget production which emphasizes the lives of various passengers. Not in any sense a documentary, this version is competently directed and acted, and it earned an Academy Award for its screenwriters.

There are a number of loosely entwined stories in the film, in the same vein as *Grand Hotel* (1932) and some of the later "disaster" films of the 1970's. The principal characters are Richard Sturgess (Clifton Webb) and his recently estranged wife (Barbara Stanwyck). Mrs. Sturgess has taken their children on the ship to return to their home in the United States after some years spent in Europe. Sturgess is not scheduled to go with them, but he pays for passage on the ship just before it sails, planning to stay in the salon for the duration of the voyage. Sturgess is a pompous American expatriate who condescendingly treats his wife like an inferior. Mrs. Sturgess does not want their children, Annette (Audrey Dalton) and Norman (Harper Carter), to become insufferable snobs like her husband, so she plans to take them back to the United States to finish their educations. When Sturgess tries to force his wife to let him take Norman, she admits that he is the product of a brief affair rather than her husband's son. When the ship sails, Sturgess decides that he will ignore Norman, even though he loves the boy very much. Mrs. Sturgess tries to convince her husband not to treat the boy so badly, but he coldly dismisses her and continues playing an endless bridge game.

While the main story is taking place, a love story between Annette and a young American college boy, Giff Rogers (Robert Wagner), develops. Annette is shy and self-conscious about the fact that she is not one of the carefree, dancing college girls that he usually dates, but she gradually loosens up and they begin a romance. Another subplot concerns Healey (Richard Basehart), an alcoholic, recently defrocked priest returning from Europe. Rather than blaming his drinking on his no longer being a priest, he admits to Mrs. Sturgess that he was forced to leave the priesthood because he drank. He does not blame anyone for the drinking, realizing that it is his own fault.

The other main characters of the film are Captain Smith (Brian Aherne), who is captain of the huge vessel, Mrs. Young (Thelma Ritter), a boisterous, rich American, and Earl Meeker (Allyn Joslyn), who plays cards with Sturgess. Smith (the actual name of the *Titanic*'s captain) is a charming man of impeccable manners with the passengers, but it is his lack of judgment as the ship's captain which eventually leads to the sinking. Mrs. Young is obviously patterned after Molly Brown, one of the real survivors of the *Titanic*, and the woman about whom another film, *The Unsinkable Molly Brown* (1964), was written. Meeker is a fictional character, but an incident in which he dresses in women's clothing in order to have a place in one of the lifeboats is based on fact. J. Bruce Ismay, chairman of the White Star Line which owned the *Titanic*, reportedly did almost the same thing during the actual disaster.

Some of the minor characters of the film add authenticity to the story as famous passengers on the ship: Benjamin Guggenheim (Camillo Guercio); Mr. and Mrs. Isador Straus (Roy Gordon and Helen Van Tuyl); Officer Lightoller (Edmund Purdom in one of his first films), who was the senior officer among the ship's survivors; and multimillionaire John Jacob Astor (William Johnstone), whose death was the lead story about the sinking in *The New York Times*, which carried the now-famous headline, "John Jacob Astor Dies at Sea." All of these names and bits of information about the way the passengers conducted themselves during the disaster have become legendary, and the film *Titanic* had to include them to add realism to the story.

The scenes of the ship's crashing into the iceberg and its subsequent sinking are the best sequences of the film. At first virtually none of the passengers seems to know anything. People are even playing with snow on the upper decks, not worried because they believe the publicity about the *Titanic* being unsinkable. Some of the crew members, however, including Lightoller (who is the central character in the 1958 film), who tells Sturgess straightforwardly that the ship is sinking, try to save as many people as they can. Sturgess, in his typical calm, pompous manner, goes to get his wife and children, jokingly warning them to put on life jackets, if only for the sake of appearance. His wife realizes immediately that they are in danger, and they have an emotional reconciliation as he confesses his deep love for her and his regrets over their years of estrangement.

The plot begins to move swiftly as some of the lower decks become flooded, and some panic sets in. The ship has an insufficient number of lifeboats to accommodate all of the passengers, and of the boats that there are, some are lowered half empty and others break upon impact with the icy waters of the North Atlantic. Giff's life is saved only because he falls as one of the boats is lowered. We see a number of tragic scenes, and some heroic ones as well. Healey, for example, goes into the exploding boiler room to comfort the men, and Sturgess takes charge of some foreigners to make certain that they get into lifeboats. While the upperdecks of the *Titanic* catered to the rich, the lower decks contained hundreds of immigrants crowded together, many of whom could not speak English and did not know what to do in the panic.

When almost all of the lifeboats are lowered, Norman suddenly gives up his seat to a frightened woman and goes in search of his father. His mother does not know this until her boat is already in the water, and by the time Norman finds Sturgess, all of the boats have gone and he must go down with the ship like his father. In the most touching moment of the film, Sturgess tells Norman how proud he is of him, and the two embrace as the ship's orchestra plays a Welsh hymn, while the remaining passengers and crew sing and the ship slips into the water. In the last scene, we see the survivors grouped in lifeboats, and the narrator (Michael Rennie) tells the audience the statistics about the number of people lost and saved.

Titanic is not a great film, but it is competently acted by the major stars, especially Stanwyck and Webb. *A Night to Remember* is probably more realistic than *Titanic* and is an interesting parallel to it. It is almost a law of filmmaking that if Hollywood were to make the same film as England, the Hollywood version would be lavish and filled with stars while the English production would be understated and would have more "actors" than "stars." *Titanic* still has something to offer, however, and has become something of a prototype for the television movies called "docudramas" which have enjoyed a wide popularity in the last few years. The combination of real and fictional characters in a dramatization of an important event has become a television staple whose origins can be traced back to lavish Hollywood productions such as *Titanic*.

Patricia King Hanson

TO EACH HIS OWN

Released: 1946
Production: Charles Brackett for Paramount
Direction: Mitchell Leisen
Screenplay: Charles Brackett and Jacques Thery; based on an original story
   by Charles Brackett
Cinematography: Daniel L. Fapp
Editing: Alma Macrorie
Running time: 122 minutes

Principal characters:
Josephine (Jody) Norris .... Olivia de Havilland (AA)
Captain Cosgrove/Gregory Piersen .... John Lund
Lord Desham .... Roland Culver
Corinne Piersen .... Mary Anderson
Alex Piersen ....Phillip Terry
Mac Tilton .... Bill Goodwin
Liz Lorimer .... Virginia Welles
Mr. Norris .... Griff Barnett
Gregory (younger) .... Bill Ward

To Each His Own is truly a film in which the acting, directing, and screen-writing make a superior work out of melodramatic and sentimental material. The plot is full of the usual elements of what is derogatorily called the "woman's picture" or "the soaper." It has a tragic love affair, an illegitimate child, unrequited mother love, and the sacrifices of a woman. In fact, it took quite a bit of persuasion and some rewriting of the script before Mitchell Leisen would agree to direct the film, and according to Olivia de Havilland, the star of the film, it was not until the third week of shooting that Leisen became enthusiastic about the project. In the finished film it is his enthusiasm that shows, not his initial hesitancy.

The basic story of *To Each His Own* concerns the adventures of Josephine Norris (Olivia de Havilland). As a young woman in the small town of Piersen Falls during World War I she hopes for a thrilling love, "upside down and sky-blue pink," as one of her suitors calls it. Because she does not feel that sort of love, she rejects the proposals of two perfectly acceptable beaux— Alex Piersen (Phillip Terry) and Mac Tilton (Bill Goodwin). Hurt by her rejection, Alex marries Corrine (Mary Anderson) almost immediately. Josephine (who is always called Jody) does find her true love; he is Captain Cosgrove (John Lund), a dashing pilot in town for a brief stop on a war bond drive. He and Jody have only a few hours together before he leaves, never to return; a short time later he is killed in France.

Jody is pregnant and hopes for some way that she can rear the child even in the small-town atmosphere of Piersen Falls. She can tell no one except her understanding father (Griff Barnett). She goes away to have the baby and devises an elaborate strategy to have it found on a doorstep and be given to her without anyone knowing it is hers. Fate, however, intervenes. The first child of Corinne and Alex dies soon after birth, so the baby is given to them. Jody is forced to watch from the sidelines as her child is brought up as Gregory Piersen. She puts her energy into a cosmetics business and becomes rich and successful. At one point, when Gregory is about five or six, she tries to reclaim him. She has told Corinne and Alex who he is, and she offers to give them the money to rescue their failing business if she can have Gregory (played by Bill Ward at this age). They reluctantly and bitterly accept her offer, but after two months, Jody sends Gregory back because he misses the only parents he has ever known. Then Jody goes to England to run the new London branch of her business. She does not see Gregory until he arrives there as a military pilot in World War II. She lavishes attention upon him, but does not tell him who she is. Finally, at the very end of the film, Gregory realizes that Jody is his mother.

This basic story, however, does not make *To Each His Own* the superior film that it is. The film's chief virtues are in the writing, acting, and directing, and the one word that could best describe all three is *subtlety*. Rather than emphasizing the melodramatic elements, the filmmakers concentrate upon the basic human feelings within each scene to make the audience feel the universal elements in the story as well as the abnormal ones.

The script was written by Charles Brackett and Jacques Thery from an original story by Brackett. Brackett was also the producer of the film and did some rewriting while the film was being shot. In addition, director Leisen contributed to the screenplay, apparently by making suggestions and demands rather than by actually writing any scenes. One of the best features of the script is that it begins with Jody as a middle-aged woman and presents most of the plot in a long flashback that is briefly interrupted once or twice.

At the beginning of the film, therefore, she is an American woman in London serving firewatch duty on New Year's Eve during World War II. Serving with her that night is Lord Desham (Roland Culver), a stickler for details and a very cold person. While he is inspecting the roof (and criticizing Jody, or "Miss Norris," as she is called now), he makes a stupid mistake and falls, and only Jody's quick response saves his life. The combination of the brush with death and the injury to his pride makes Desham begin to talk. He says that he and Jody are forlorn people who fill in on holidays while other people celebrate. Forlorn people, he says, are those who either cared too little or too much. He reveals that in his case it was the death of his wife in a flu epidemic during World War I that causes him to be the empty man he is today, but he is unable to induce Jody to respond with a confidence of her own. Then Jody learns that Gregory Piersen is arriving in London on a train, and she excitedly goes to meet it.

Thus we are aware of what will happen to Jody before we see her as a young woman. The exact moment that triggers the flashback is also revealing. A young woman who is also waiting for the train becomes exasperated when they find that it has been delayed. "You can't imagine," she tells the matronly Jody, "what it's like to be in love with a flier." Jody mumbles the words to herself and we are back in Piersen Falls at the beginning of the story.

Also powerful but understated are the scenes between Jody and Cosgrove, the flier who becomes the love of her life. Jody is looking for an exciting, romantic love, and when Cosgrove begins talking to her about flying, it becomes clear that it is the dangerous excitement that attracts him even though part of him would like to be able to turn away from it. Jody senses the same danger in her attraction for him. Once she even tries to stop, saying to herself "What's come over you, Jody Norris?" Ultimately she accepts the danger with the excitement.

De Havilland has given Leisen much of the credit for her magnificent acting performance, while he praised her ability to be flexible, to understand the character, and to use her acting talent to enhance the whole film, not just her own reputation. She could have overplayed the emotional scenes and insisted on being glamorous as the middle-aged Miss Norris, but instead her portrayal is controlled throughout, although it never hides the passions inside Jody, and in the "present day" sequences she shows all the years Jody has lived and what they have done to her. Her aging was accomplished by three main means: she gained more than twenty pounds during the filming; she received an expert makeup job based on a *Life* magazine feature showing the aging of Winston Churchill's face; and her face was lighted in a harsh, unflattering manner. The Academy recognized the quality of de Havilland's performance by awarding her an Oscar, just as Leisen had predicted during the filming that they would; the next year, 1947, in a *Saturday Evening Post* feature article, de Havilland chose Jody Norris as the role she liked best.

Brackett and Leisen both contributed a number of other subtle touches to the film. They portray small-town life without being condescending, and large events are often announced in small ways. For example, we first learn of Jody's pregnancy when she pours herself a glass of milk after hearing that milk is necessary for pregnant women, and we first learn of Cosgrove's death just as Jody does, by overhearing a conversation in her father's drugstore, where Jody works.

De Havilland's is the main performance, but she is well supported by virtually every member of the cast—from Alma Macrorie, who not only edited the film but also played the small part of a perennially pregnant woman of Piersen Falls, to Lund and Culver, who have the largest male roles. Lund, who was acting in his first film, plays both Captain Cosgrove and Gregory

Piersen, the son of Jody and Cosgrove. He is excellent in both roles, appearing both dashing and cynical in the first and rather naïve and open in the second. Culver plays Lord Desham superbly, showing both the stereotyped British reserve and the man beneath it.

The last segment of *To Each His Own* is the best and embodies most of the virtues of the entire film. Jody meets Gregory at the train, hoping to spend a week with him while presenting herself as merely someone from his home town, but she finds that he is interested only in seeing Liz Lorimer (Virginia Welles). In fact, the two spend most of one day trying to get married, but they are unable to overcome British red tape. Jody arranges theater tickets and dinner reservations for Gregory, and he is appreciative but naturally does not give them the weight that Jody does. When he gives her a hug, we see through her face that Jody is barely able to contain her emotion.

It seems that Gregory's leave will end early, and Jody will barely be able to see him. Then Lord Desham reenters the picture. When he finds Jody crying, she tells him that Gregory is her son but that he does not know and never will. Desham also finds that Gregory wants to marry Liz and that Jody is in favor of the marriage. He then uses his connections to prepare a surprise for all three. He takes Jody to the restaurant where he knows Liz and Gregory will be dining; then all four are ushered into an anteroom, where Liz and Gregory are married. Jody will not let Desham reveal that she is Gregory's mother, but he does give some hints. As they dance after the wedding, Liz says to her new husband that anyone would think he was Jody's own son. He then walks over to where Jody and Desham are dancing, says to her, "I think this is our dance, Mother," and the film ends.

Timothy W. Johnson

TO SIR WITH LOVE

Released: 1967
Production: James Clavell for Columbia
Direction: James Clavell
Screenplay: James Clavell; based on the book of the same name by E. R. Braithwaite
Cinematography: Paul Beeson
Editing: Peter Thornton
Running time: 105 minutes

Principal characters:

Mark Thackeray	Sidney Poitier
Gillian	Suzy Kendall
Barbara Pegg	Lulu
Pamela Dare	Judy Geeson
Mrs. Evans	Faith Brook
Denham	Christian Roberts
Rosie	Avis Bunnage
Moira	Adrienne Posta

To Sir with Love features Sidney Poitier in one of his best-known roles as a black super-gentleman. This time he is a teacher named Thackeray working in the slums of the East End of London and endeavoring to help the senior class of a large comprehensive school get through. The students are an unruly bunch who curse, smoke in class, and take little or no care of their appearance. By sheer virtue of his quiet strength and obviously superior character, Poitier wins them over in a glossy reworking of *Blackboard Jungle* (1955), English style. Although all of the performances in the film are good, the classroom scenes are unfortunately not convincing. Especially jarring are the efforts of "Sir" (as the students call Poitier) to show the students that he was once one of them, which does not ring true. This handsome, well-spoken man with the wisdom of Solomon seems to be worlds removed from his recalcitrant students. If Poitier had been allowed to be a little more human, to "lose his cool" even once, the whole pupil-teacher relationship may have seemed more honest.

Even with its glaring faults, however, the film does have its moments, and it was very successful at the box office. The interplay between the faculty, who represent every view from latent racism to progressive education, is interesting and realistic. The actors playing the students are fresh and winning, and if their cockney speech is not authentic, at least it is colorful. Finally, it is rewarding to see the children mature into adults. The issue of racism is skirted and only touched upon by the students when they appear at the funeral of a classmate's mother who was black. "Sir's" blackness is entirely beside the point, except that he is not allowed to become romantically involved, even though it is hinted that a fellow teacher named Gillian (Suzy Kendall) has more than a passing interest in him. One of his blonde and pony-tailed students, Pamela Dare (Judy Geeson), also gets a crush on "Sir," but he soon sets her straight. It was not until *Guess Who's Coming to Dinner*, made later in 1967, that Poitier was allowed to show his feelings overtly for a white girl.

As an example of a film about an inspiring teacher in a slum classroom, *To Sir with Love* falls somewhere between *Blackboard Jungle* and *Up the Down Staircase* (1967). In the other two films, the classroom chaos happens in Manhattan, which is always portrayed as more frightening than London. In this classroom, the children may be hard-to-handle smart-alecs, but one never has the feeling that they are dangerous. Their most alarming aspects seem to be their inability to learn very much and the dim prospects that await them when they do graduate. One of the senior teachers says to Thackeray that his job is just to get them through and out. Indeed, his goals seem to be limited to teaching them to dress neatly and to comport themselves with more dignity. Little is said about what kind of jobs are in store for them or what they can expect from the world, which is perhaps not much.

The film was produced, written, and directed by James Clavell, the author of *Shōgun*, who adapted E. R. Braithwaite's autobiographical book for the screen. It was filmed partly on location in and around London, and at Pinewood Studios. The film livens up when it manages to get out of the classroom and around the city, when "Sir" takes his class on school outings. The classroom scenes do take up most of the film, however, and they unfortunately look like they were shot in the studio.

The film opens as Thackeray, a qualified black engineer, takes up a post in a tough East End school in London after eighteen workless months. He is in charge of a group of rough, rowdy teenagers in their last term before going out into the world. The youngsters are basically all right; their swearing and crude behavior is explained by their poor upbringing. The veteran teachers all give Thackeray advice, ranging from telling him not to "take any crap from the little tykes" to trying patience. He is encouraged by Mrs. Evans (Faith Brook), the Deputy Head, and by Gillian Blanchard, who, like Thackeray, is a new teacher. Thackeray is soon shocked by the blatantly adult behavior of his students and finds them rather rebellious. He has a hard time reaching them, but finally decides to treat them like grown-ups and try to instill in them a sense of self-respect. His lessons with the class are very basic as they discuss feelings, sex, and other subjects which are meaningful to them.

At first the going is tough and the students are insolent, testing Thackeray every day. Gradually, however, his approach begins to pay off. They begin calling him "Sir" when he addresses the girls as Miss and the boys by their surnames. He gains their confidence even further when he tells them how he started from a neighborhood much like the one in which they live, and how he worked his way through engineering school by washing dishes. "Sir" soon starts taking the class to the theater and museums, usually accompanied by Gillian, with whom he has become quite friendly. There are setbacks, however, such as when one of the boys in his class is arrested for an attack on a fellow student and is placed on probation. When a particularly fat boy is treated unfairly by a Physical Education instructor, arousing his friend to attack the teacher, "Sir" insists that the aggressive student apologize to the teacher. This causes charges of unfairness to be leveled at "Sir" by his class. Another incident involves a boxing round in the gymnasium, where one of "Sir's" most difficult students challenges him to a round, hoping to humiliate him; but "Sir" knocks the boy down and thus gains his awed respect.

Things improve, but Thackeray is still far from happy and applies for an engineering job for the following summer. When an offer presents itself, "Sir" is elated, yet has mixed feelings toward the end of the year when he realizes that his students have indeed improved. They are dressing better and are acting with more maturity and with an increased sense of responsibility. At the end-of-term school dance, the students pay tribute to "Sir" by thanking him in front of the entire student body for what he has given them as a teacher. Visibly touched, one of "Sir's" favorite students, Pamela, hands him a beautifully gift-wrapped package. He looks at the card, and under the signatures of all of his students, he reads "To Sir, With Love."

The film enjoyed a good run, earning more than seven million dollars, but was not favorably received by the critics. It was one of Poitier's last roles as a "super black." After *Guess Who's Coming to Dinner*, the actor diversified and played a political extremist in *The Lost Man* (1969), a detective in *They Call Me Mr. Tibbs* (1970), and tried his hand at comedy in *Buck and the Preacher* (1972). Unfortunately, none of these vehicles was quite worthy of his talents, and he remains an actor capable of much more than he has given. In recent years Poitier has turned to directing; in 1980 he made the enormously popular although critically unsuccessful *Stir Crazy*, starring Richard Pryor and Gene Wilder.

Joan Cohen

TONIGHT AT EIGHT-THIRTY
(MEET ME TONIGHT)

Released: 1952
Production: Anthony Havelock-Allan for British Film Makers
Direction: Anthony Pelissier
Screenplay: Noel Coward; based on his series of one-act plays collectively
 known as *Tonight at Eight-Thirty*
Cinematography: Desmond Dickinson
Editing: no listing
Running time: 85 minutes

> *Principal characters:*
> **Red Peppers**
> Lily Pepper .... Kay Walsh
> George Pepper .... Ted Ray
> Mabel Grace .... Martita Hunt
> Mr. Edwards .... Frank Pettingell
> Bert Bentley .... Bill Fraser
> **Fumed Oak**
> Henry Gow .... Stanley Holloway
> Doris Gow .... Betty Ann Davies
> Grandma Rockett .... Mary Merrall
> Elsie .... Dorothy Gordon
> **Ways and Means**
> Stella Cartwright .... Valerie Hobson
> Toby Cartwright .... Nigel Patrick
> Murdoch .... Jack Warner
> Olive .... Jessie Royce Landis

Tonight at Eight-Thirty is the collective title for a series of nine one-act
plays—*Red Peppers*, *The Astonished Heart*, *We Were Dancing*, *Hands Across
the Sea*, *Fumed Oak*, *Shadow Play*, *Still Life*, *Family Album*, and *Ways and
Means*—written by Noel Coward, in the first six of which he and Gertrude
Lawrence successfully starred on the stage in London in 1935 and in New
York in 1936. The collective title was easily changed when necessary; for
example, if it was a matinee, the show was called *Today at Two-Thirty* .
Coward composed a number of songs for the plays, the most notable of which
are "Has Anybody Seen Our Ship?" and "Men About Town" from *Red
Peppers* and "Play, Orchestra, Play" and "You Were There" from *Shadow
Play*. *Tonight at Eight-Thirty* proved immensely popular in repertory, and has
been played by everyone from Mary Astor and Bramwell Fletcher to Beatrice
Lillie and Vic Oliver. *The Astonished Heart* was made into a fairly disappointing 1950 British film, while *Still Life* was the basis for what is perhaps
the finest of the Coward-scripted film productions, *Brief Encounter* (1946).

Despite the fact that the title *Tonight at Eight-Thirty* was such a familiar one, three of the most popular plays in the series, *Red Peppers*, *Fumed Oak*, and *Ways and Means*, were filmed in England in 1952 not under that title but as *Meet Me Tonight*. The production was mildly successful in Britain, although *The New Statesman* (September 20, 1952) thought it Coward at its worst and commented, "Heaven help those who queue ninety minutes in order to enjoy it." Happily, British films were enjoying something of a vogue in American art houses at that time, and thus *Meet Me Tonight* was picked up by an American distributor, Continental, and released in the United States as *Tonight at Eight-Thirty*. The three separate plays in the film are not linked together in any way, and one can only ponder why the producers went to the trouble of shooting the film in Technicolor, when at least two of the plays cry out for the quality which only black-and-white can provide.

The first play is *Red Peppers*, the most enduring and the most entertaining, which features two slightly decayed vaudeville or music-hall performers, Lily (Kay Walsh) and George Pepper (Ted Ray), who are still proud and haughty. While appearing at a suburban music hall, they get into an argument with the orchestra leader (Bill Fraser) as to the tempo of their music, an argument into which is drawn the house manager and an ancient dramatic actress named Mabel Grace (beautifully played by Martita Hunt), who, in a general state of alcoholic stupor, is reduced to playing the music halls. The argument climaxes on stage when the Peppers and the orchestra leader fight in front of the audience—what little of it there is—while a team of Oriental jugglers (the Young China Troupe) try to perform their act and sprinklers are accidentally set off, drenching the entire company. As in the rest of the film, it is the acting and the dialogue which matter most, and both are first-rate. In particular Ted Ray, himself a one-time music-hall artist and a popular British radio entertainer for years with his own show, *Rays a Laugh*, is perfectly cast as George Pepper, and he receives able support from Kay Walsh as his wife and Bill Fraser as the orchestra leader.

The dictionary definition of *Fumed Oak*, the title of the second story in the film, is "oak wood given a darker color and more distinct markings by exposure to ammonia fumes," a description which perhaps fits the hero of the play, with the ammonia fumes being the constant nagging and complaining from his family to which he has been exposed for years. Stanley Holloway plays Henry Gow, who is first seen at the breakfast table, saying not a word, while his wife (Betty Ann Davies), mother-in-law (Mary Merrall), and adenoidal daughter (Dorothy Gordon) whine, complain, and nag. His only comments are at the end of the scene as he prepares to leave for work, a brief explanation as to why he was late home the previous evening, comments which give no indication of the shock he is to deliver his family in the next scene, set in the same room that evening. Gow returns home and announces that he is leaving his family, all of whom he detests, and that he is sailing for South America and freedom. It is a classic tale of the worm that turns, which succeeds thanks to Stanley Holloway's gentle underplaying, never raising his voice and never allowing the anger that has built up within him through the years to overcome his desire to make the final farewell as painless as possible.

The final episode in the trilogy is the poorest, which is used by the director chiefly as an excuse for some pretty Technicolor shots of the French Riviera. Stella (Valerie Hobson) and Toby Cartwright (Nigel Patrick) are professional house guests. Their current hostess in the South of France, Olive (Jessie Royce Landis), is about to evict them gracefully, which will leave them without any immediate plans for a new house in which to guest, and, worse still, the couple lacks funds. Stella and Toby's philosophy is summed up by their desultory conversation over breakfast. She asks, "Why do other people's breakfasts always taste much nicer than one's own," and he replies, "Probably because they are." That night, while Olive is out and Stella and Toby are in bed, an intruder enters, an intruder who is to be the couple's salvation. They recognize him as a former servant, Murdoch (Jack Warner), and, in order to avoid their turning him in, he agrees to leave the cash he is stealing from their hostess in their possession, while at the same time tying the two up so there will be no hint of collusion.

Tonight at Eight-Thirty was to be the last film on which Noel Coward worked in any capacity other than as an actor, and it is certainly one of the least important of his ventures in the area of film (although in no way as poor as the film version of *The Astonished Heart*). Critical response to the American release of the film was mild, but appreciative. *Newsweek* described the trilogy as "agreeable playlets, funny without being uproarious, clever without being brilliant, and at times sharp without being especially searching." *Variety* thought the film "a better class, although somewhat dated entertainment."

The film succeeds because each of the plays has considerable charm, and, dated as they now quite definitely are, that charm still shines through. The three sets of characters seem as far removed from our present environment as it is possible to be, and, in a sense, it is that distance which appeals to the viewer and gives him a sense of nostalgia for the time in which these play actors are living. Music hall and vaudeville are dead. Lower-middle-class families of the Gow family type have been wiped out, and the impoverished upper classes no longer have the luxury of living as perpetual house guests.

Tonight at Eight-Thirty came at a time when this type of film with three or four distinct stories was fairly popular in British cinema. In particular, W. Somerset Maugham's stories had been filmed under the titles of *Quartet* (1948), *Trio* (1950) and *Encore* (1951). In his introduction to the published plays comprising *Tonight at Eight-Thirty*, Noel Coward wrote, "The primary object of the scheme is to provide a full and varied evening's entertainment for theatregoers, who, we hope, will try their best to overcome any latent prejudices they may have against short plays." As a film, *Tonight at Eight-*

Thirty certainly succeeds as the former, and, as far as the latter is concerned, it does remind one that there is something missing from a theater scene which has deliberately and firmly turned its back on the one-act play.

Anthony Slide

TOPAZE

Released: 1933
Production: RKO/Radio
Direction: Harry d'Abbabie d'Arrast
Screenplay: Benn W. Levy; based on the play of the same name by Marcel Pagnol
Cinematography: Lucien Andriot
Editing: William Hamilton
Running time: 80 minutes

Principal characters:
Topaze	John Barrymore
Coco	Myrna Loy
Henri	Albert Conti
Dr. Bomb	Luis Alberni
Baron	Reginald Mason
Baroness	Jobyna Howland
Charlemagne	Jackie Searl
Dr. Stegg	Frank Reicher

Marcel Pagnol originally had been a French schoolteacher, who started writing plays. He quickly became a very popular playwright in the French theater, and from there went on to become one of the best screenwriters in the profession. His screenplays based on his own well-beloved trilogy about a group of characters in Marseilles—*Marius* (1931), *Fanny* (1932), and *César* (1937), later reworked into Joshua Logan's *Fanny* (1960)—gave him an international audience, and he set up his own studio in Marseilles. The culmination of his efforts was the screen versions of his plays as written and supervised by him. In France, his play *Topaze* was very popular, and over the years three different French actors appeared as Professor Topaze in three different screen versions: Louis Jouvet (1935); Arnaudy (1936); and Fernandel (1952). In 1961 a version in English was filmed in London as *Mr. Topaze*, which Peter Sellers directed and in which he also played the title role. Released in America, it was known as *I Love Money.*

In 1933, however, RKO/Radio had acquired the rights to film *Topaze.* Benn W. Levy had translated the play into English, and it was performed to stunning effect on the New York stage by Frank Morgan. Once the property was brought to Hollywood, it was given to a very gifted director, Harry d'Abbabie d'Arrast, who looked upon it favorably as a dark farce, making it into a rare, beautifully cast picture. It opened in New York at Radio City Music Hall, and in spite of its being rather arty, the average filmgoer found it entertaining. The period from 1932 to 1934 was distinguished in Hollywood by some of the cinema's best acting as offered by John Barrymore, and

Barrymore was given the pleasant task of bringing Professor Topaze to life on the screen. He must have approached the role with delight, because only the roles of Professor Topaze and Rudolf, the Viennese taxi driver who had once been an archduke from Robert E. Sherwood's *Reunion in Vienna* (1933), gave him the chance to play droll comedy. As a comedian, on stage or film, Barrymore had no equal.

In the story, Professor Auguste Topaze is a shy, honest nitwit who teaches in a boys' school in France. His class is victimized by the young bully Charlemagne de Latour-Latour (Jackie Searl). Although Professor Topaze's report on this young potential gangster is completely honest, it angers the boy's parents, the Baron and Baroness de Latour-Latour (Reginald Mason and Jobyna Howland). They raise such a fuss that Professor Topaze is fired by the school. This turns out to be the best thing that ever happened to Topaze, for the Baron realizes that he can profitably use a fool of such impeccable honesty. At a ridiculously high salary, Topaze is hired to head the Baron's allegedly scientific laboratory. Topaze has always dreamed of wearing an academy decoration, and as an inducement, the Baron claims that this can easily be arranged.

The main product of the laboratory, and the thing from which the Baron derives his wealth, is a health-giving water, but Topaze, experimenting with it, finds it loaded with impurities and completely unfit to drink. To keep Topaze quietly cooperative, the Baron arranges for him to receive the academy decoration he has long dreamed of possessing. Topaze is so impressed that his whole character goes through a revolutionary change. He reasons that if the rewards of dishonesty are this overwhelming, then he might as well not only outwit the public, but turn the tables on those who employ him. Physically, he changes from the modest, retiring professor with an unclipped beard to an immaculately tailored rich man who has no qualms, in his position as head of the Baron's laboratory, about letting the end justify the means. He uses blackmail as a weapon, and is not beyond high thievery, particularly in the case of stealing the Baron's enchanting mistress Coco (Myrna Loy). They fall in love, and together become consummate cheaters, growing richer than they had ever dreamed of being.

Critics praised the picture, especially d'Abbabie d'Arrast's comedy touches as director, the great comedic skill of Barrymore in the title role, and the performances of the entire cast, particularly Loy and Albert Conti as Henri. Some of those critics, however, feared that the picture was possibly too "highbrow" for the average film fan. This fear was justified, but casting helped build the picture's business, for word of mouth on Barrymore's excellence brought in attendance as did reports about Loy, who, with every picture, was building increasingly devoted viewers from all backgrounds.

Interestingly, Paramount had bought the film rights to *Topaze* earlier when they filmed a French-language version, but they did not think it was appropriate American fare, so did not make an English-language version. RKO/ Radio thus acquired the English-speaking rights and made this film, which enjoyed considerable success in its day. Since it is one of the few d'Abbabie d'Arrast films in existence, younger film devotees have taken it over as a discovery, which fortunately has led to a revival in the popularity of the film.

DeWitt Bodeen

TOPKAPI

Released: 1964
Production: Jules Dassin for United Artists
Direction: Jules Dassin
Screenplay: Monja Danischewsky; based on the novel *The Light of Day* by
  Eric Ambler
Cinematography: Henri Alekan
Editing: Roger Dwyre
Running time: 120 minutes

> *Principal characters:*
> Elizabeth Lipp .... Melina Mercouri
> Arthur Simpson .... Peter Ustinov (AA)
> William Walter .... Maximilian Schell
> Cedric Page .... Robert Morley
> Geven .... Akim Tamiroff
> Giulio .... Gilles Segal
> Fischer .... Jess Hahn

"Heist" films have been a staple in the cinema ever since *The Great Train Robbery* in 1903. During the 1950's, however, filmmakers began to depict the detailed machinations of how the crimes were planned, as well as their execution. Among the earliest and most exciting are John Huston's *The Asphalt Jungle* (1950) and Stanley Kubrick's *The Killing* (1956), while others released over the years have included the appropriately named *Robbery* (1967), *Seven Thieves* (1960), and *The Day They Robbed the Bank of England* (1960). Tongue-in-cheek variations on the theme have included *The Lavender Hill Mob* (1951), *The Ladykillers* (1956), *The League of Gentlemen* (1960), *Ocean's Eleven* (1960), *The Hot Rock* (1972), and *The Bank Shot* (1974). Two of the best films of both genres were directed by Jules Dassin. *Rififi*, made in France (after Dassin had been blacklisted and he was living in exile) and originally released in 1954, is a straightforward suspense thriller which became an international hit. The highlight is a thirty-five-minute robbery sequence played without dialogue or background music. A decade later, Dassin directed *Topkapi*, a delightful spoof of his earlier film which won a deserved Best Supporting Actor Oscar for Peter Ustinov.

As in most films of the type, the participants in the proposed robbery are the heroes. They are dreamers who take action on their illusions, who risk their all for a shot at untold wealth and lifetime security. The viewer roots for them to elude the police and succeed at their nefarious task, even though they are breaking the law. Herein lies the appeal of *Rififi*, *Topkapi*, and the rest of the films in the genre. In *Topkapi*, the instigators are *femme fatale* Elizabeth Lipp (Melina Mercouri) and one of her lovers, master thief William

Walter (Maximilian Schell). Their goal is to purloin from an impregnable spot in the Topkapi Palace Museum in Istanbul a dagger encrusted with priceless emeralds. To avoid arousing the suspicion of the police, they decide to recruit a group of amateurs as their assistants: Cedric Page (Robert Morley), a zany inventor who provides some rather eccentric equipment to neutralize the museum's alarm system; Giulio (Gilles Segal), a mute acrobat; and Fischer (Jess Hahn), a strong man. Geven (Akim Tamiroff) is their drunken cook, and Arthur Simpson (Peter Ustinov), a shabby tourist guide, is duped into delivering to them a car that is loaded with grenades and a rifle.

The prerobbery activities are a complicated although delightfully nonsensical series of misunderstandings and misadventures. The impetus is the fumbling, pea-brained Simpson. The car is searched at the Turkish border, the ammunition is discovered, and Simpson is forced to spy on his employers to avoid going to prison. With the assistance of the irrational Geven, he manages to convince the police that the robbers are Russian spies.

Lipp and Walter's passion for the dagger is all-consuming. The most skilled larcenist would have to be insane to attempt such a caper as this. The knife is attached to a tunic-garbed model sultan who is locked inside a glass case, and the floor of the museum is rigged with an alarm system that will sound off when touched by the slightest weight—even a ping pong ball. Yet, in the spirit of good fun, they construct an elaborate, ingenious plan.

As the robbery is actually staged, *Topkapi* is as tense and thrilling a film as *Rififi*. Briefly, three of the thieves sneak into the museum as it is about to close. Eventually, Giulio is lowered down into the room in which the dagger is displayed, and hangs by his toes from the ceiling. The glass case is opened and the dagger removed via suction cups devised by Page from rubber plumber's suckers; the knife is then replaced with a copy. Outside, the guards are distracted by a tape recording of Elizabeth laughing, which has been installed in a toy parrot constructed by Page. All of this lasts slightly more than forty minutes, and is almost as silent as its sister sequence in *Rififi*. This lengthy, detailed account of the crime is a risky proposition for Dassin, as he is repeating—and conceivably attempting to top—his earlier, much-praised effort. It takes up more than one-third of the film's running time, and an unfavorable comparison to *Rififi* would have been devastating. The sequence, like the entire film, is masterfully crafted throughout. *Topkapi* is as spine-tingling as *Rififi*, with the addition of the comedic characters and complications.

Dassin's best films are taut, tough action dramas such as *The Naked City* (1948), *Brute Force* (1947), and *Rififi* or amusing entertainments such as this or *Never on Sunday* (1960), but when he focuses on human relationships, as in *Phaedra* (1962), the result is plodding. Dassin chooses not to pursue the romantic relationship between Elizabeth and Walter, but centers solely on the planning and execution of the robbery. In *Topkapi*, he is ably aided by

Henri Alekan's picture-postcard cinematography, a colorful travelogue of Istanbul and locations throughout Greece. The scenery is lush, but does not detract from the story.

All of the performances in *Topkapi* are charming, but most outstanding are Mercouri's and Ustinov's. Mercouri, Dassin's wife, is particularly alluring as Elizabeth. She rolls her eyes and lasciviously coos and licks her lips in anticipation of the larceny. She loves jewels as much, if not more, than she does men. Her performance almost rivals that of Ustinov, who attempts a belly dance while listening to Turkish music in his car. He puffs and huffs and sweats as he explains to Turkish police about the weapons. Ustinov's is a knowing portrayal of a little man, a loser, who is thrust without his consent into a situation that is far above him. He was awarded his second Oscar (his first was also a supporting performance award, for *Spartacus* in 1960) in competition with John Gielgud in *Becket*, Stanley Holloway in *My Fair Lady*, Edmond O'Brien in *Seven Days in May*, and Lee Tracy in *The Best Man*.

The major gaffe in *Topkapi* is a "cop-out" ending which is meant to be amusing and ironic but is only maddening. A bird flies through an open window in the museum, lands on the floor, and sets off the alarm—after the replacement of the dagger has been successfully completed. After all the elaborate planning, the evading of the authorities who believe they are far more dangerous than they actually are, and the finishing of the job, they are nabbed because of an errant bird.

Despite this disappointing denouement, *Topkapi* is a sparkling, enjoyable escapist film. It garnered excellent notices, but took in a paltry $1,100,000 at the box office. As an example of reality imitating art, several months after the film opened, three men broke into the American Museum of Natural History in New York and made off with the priceless Star of India, De Long Ruby, and other valuable pieces. Their elaborate plan was possibly pilfered from *Topkapi*, with the accused even admitting to seeing the film before they attempted their caper.

Rob Edelman

A TOUCH OF CLASS

Released: 1973
Production: Melvin Frank for Joseph E. Levine and Brut; released by Avco Embassy
Direction: Melvin Frank
Screenplay: Melvin Frank and Jack Rose
Cinematography: Austin Dempster
Editing: Bill Butler
Song: George Barrie and Sammy Cahn
Running time: 105 minutes

Principal characters:

Steve Blackburn	George Segal
Vicki Allessio	Glenda Jackson (AA)
Walter Menkes	Paul Sorvino
Patty Menkes	K. Callan
Gloria Blackburn	Hildegard Neil
Wendell Thompson	Cec Linder
Martha Thompson	Mary Barclay
Night Hotel Manager	Nadim Sawalha

A Touch of Class is a top-notch romantic comedy which compassionately examines the foibles, frustrations, and fun of an extramarital affair. Director Melvin Frank, in conjunction with writer Jack Rose, has struck a rare and heartwarming harmony between comedy and drama. The film is not vulgar, ribald, or exploitive; rather, it is a tender, compelling love story that gently pokes fun at the frailties in all of us and, in particular, in two decent people who naïvely expect to reap the pleasures of extramarital love without experiencing its pain. They find, however, before film's end, that adulterous love can never be simple. A PG rating for a film dealing with a story line such as this is a tribute to the taste and artistic sensitivity of the directon and the screenplay.

The film begins with the camera panning a hazy afternoon in a London park with horseback riding, picnics, and a softball game in full swing. Steve Blackburn, (George Segal), his eyes riveted on a ball in flight, accidentally knocks down a child belonging to Vicki Allessio (Glenda Jackson), a young Englishwoman who successfully maintains herself and her two children by pirating Paris fashions and reproducing them *en masse*. She is separated from her Italian husband who lives in Milan. She later confides to Segal: "He'd send me money for the children if I'd send him money for the cars." Their first meeting is only significant because it establishes the characters as complete opposites who do not seem to be attracted to each other.

They meet again, quite by accident, during a torrential rainstorm when both of them hail the same taxi and, recognizing each other, agree to share it. Steve, we learn, is an American insurance executive living in London with his wife and two children. Vicki, the cool, classy Englishwoman with her no-nonsense idea of what she expects from a man, and Steve, the high-powered young executive and typical modern American male, are drawn to each other. The casting is superb, for Jackson and Segal generate the type of screen chemistry that is needed to make this movie come alive.

Following a lunch during which they quite frankly discuss their mutual needs, a rendezvous at the Spanish resort of Marbella is planned. Here, within sight of the breathtaking Rock of Gibraltar, they feel that they can relax and enjoy a brief affair without distraction. The trip is fraught with roadblocks, however, as the Blackburn family decides at the last minute to accompany Steve, and a good deal of fast talking is needed to dissuade his wife and children. A chance meeting between Steve and an old friend further complicates the weekend. Then, when Steve throws his back out of place during the couple's first attempted encounter, it seems they will never consummate their relationship. This particular part of the film does stretch the limits of credibility a bit, and it is overly long. It is similar to the moralistic films of the 1940's and 1950's in which adultery was intimated but hardly ever consummated, and in which the characters in the illicit relationships were usually punished for daring to breach the sanctity of marriage.

As the frustration builds between Steve and Vicki, tempers reach the boiling point, and soon the would-be lovers are releasing tension by hurling lamps and insults at each other with obvious invective delight. Jackson, who had previously won an Academy Award for her performance in *Women in Love* (1970), is one of the few women on screen who can maintain a certain inherent, haughty dignity while lambasting the hapless victim of her wrath with the cruelest form of tongue lashing.

Segal, a versatile actor with great depth and range, who has played a poor, impotent fool and a rugged, virile leading man with equal proficiency, is perfectly cast as the vulnerable American male caught up in his own macho image. His fragile ego is crushed by Vicki's brutally honest tongue. His ability to laugh at his own frailties, however, adds an air of believability to the character of Steve Blackburn that invokes the audience's interest and concern. In one particularly hilarious scene, Blackburn throws Vicki on the bed and glowers threateningly over her cowed figure. He has been pushed too far, his manhood insulted beyond a point he can bear. Just as he is about to vent his rage and frustration by raping her, however, his zipper sticks and both parties dissolve into gales of laughter over the ludicrousness of the whole situation. It is gems like this scene that make *A Touch of Class* delightful.

Their affair is finally consummated, and over the course of the following week they have an idyllic time. Their fun is interrupted, however, by Steve's friend Walter Menkes (Paul Sorvino), who is residing in a nearby hotel with his wife Patty (K. Callen). He observes his friend's deepening involvement and, having gone through a similar situation, attempts to make Steve the beneficiary of some solid advice. Menkes himself had had a serious affair a few years before. He tells Steve that he must inevitably decide whether he loves Vicki enough to give her up. Sorvino as the caring friend adds dimension to a minor role, reinforcing the depth of emotion between the major characters.

The pace slows somewhat in the second half of the film. With the haunting, bittersweet refrain of the George Barrie and Sammy Cahn theme song to set the mood, the couple rents a flat in Chelsea and sets up a trysting place. The time they spend there together consists of moments stolen away from the merry-go-round of their daily lives. Cinematographer Austin Dempster creates the pefect backdrop, a colorful yet intimate side of London that beautifully reflects all the nuances of this full-blown romance.

Director Frank gives us an inside look at the ingenuity, complicity, and stamina required in living a dual existence. The danger of discovery seems to lurk in every doorway. In one humorous vignette, Steve, who supposedly is walking the dog, takes a cab to the apartment, steals a few moments in Vicki's arms, and returns home forgetting his dog. There follows a mad rush back to the apartment to fetch the poor, forgotten animal. Exhausted by the demands duplicity imposes and no longer content with the infrequent moments they share, Blackburn remembers the advice of his caring friend, and, to the eye-misting lyrics of the Sammy Cahn song "All That Love Went to Waste," he breaks off the relationship that is breaking their hearts.

Jackson received an Academy Award as Best Actress for her performance in *A Touch of Class*, reaffirming once again her well-deserved reputation as one of the great actresses of the 1970's. Segal breathes life into the character of Steve Blackburn, a role that could easily have become stereotyped in the hands of a less talented, less sensitive actor. On the technical side, cinematographer Austin Dempster and production designer Terry Marsh create a backdrop as rich and fulfilling as the dazzling performances of the two outstanding stars.

In addition to Jackson's success, *A Touch of Class* received four Academy Award nominations: as Best Picture; Best Story and Screenplay by Melvin Frank and Jack Rose; Best Original Dramatic Score by John Cameron; and best Song, "All That Love Went to Waste," music by George Barrie, lyrics by Sammy Cahn. This film is not without its flaws, however, for the pace through the first one-third of the picture is tiring and slightly erratic, and the comedy at times is strained. Overall, however, *A Touch of Class* most aptly lives up to its name.

D. Gail Huskins

TOUCH OF EVIL

Released: 1958
Production: Albert Zugsmith for Universal
Direction: Orson Welles
Screenplay: Orson Welles; based on the novel *Badge of Evil* by Whit Masterson and adapted from a screen story by Paul Monash
Cinematography: Russell Metty
Editing: Virgil W. Vogel and Aaron Stell
Music: Henry Mancini
Running time: 95 minutes

Principal characters:

Hank Quinlan	Orson Welles
Mike Vargas	Charlton Heston
Susan Vargas	Janet Leigh
Pete Menzies	Joseph Calleia
"Uncle Joe" Grandi	Akim Tamiroff

Orson Welles's *Touch of Evil* is a cult classic, discovered in retrospect rather than by contemporary acclaim, but it is doubtful, given its nature, that it will ever rank among the "official" classics of the screen. It is almost too obvious to say that a film must be seen to be appreciated, but in the case of *Touch of Evil*, that dictum requires extra emphasis. A written description cannot possibly do justice to the film's complex orchestration of sound and image, as fine in many ways as any of Orson Welles's work—*Citizen Kane* (1941) included.

Paradoxically, however, the film has often been called "trash," probably on the basis of its purely pulp-fiction plot: Mike Vargas (Charlton Heston), a Mexican narcotics agent, finds himself accidentally at the scene of a murder in the small border town of Los Robles. He becomes involved in the investigation and soon runs afoul of Hank Quinlan (Orson Welles), the local American official in charge of the case. Quinlan is obese, overbearing, and thoroughly corrupt; acting on a hunch (his "game leg"), he plants evidence implicting a Mexican shoe clerk in the murder. Vargas, who suspects the criminal Grandi family, gradually becomes aware of Quinlan's habitual framing of suspects, both past and present. Meanwhile, Vargas' wife Susan (Janet Leigh), who he thinks is safe at a remote desert motel, is harassed, drugged, and kidnaped by a band of Grandi hoodlums. This is revealed as part of a plot by Quinlan, in league with the family leader, "Uncle Joe" Grandi (Akim Tamiroff), to discredit Vargas by framing his wife on drug charges. Quinlan, fearing that Grandi may betray him, then murders him; Susan is found in the room with the body and is therefore implicated on murder as well as drug charges. Vargas realizes that his only hope for clearing his wife is to expose

Quinlan. Winning over to his side Pete Menzies (Joseph Calleia), Quinlan's long-time sidekick, he sets out to do so by wiring Menzies with a microphone and transmitter. The climax of the film has Vargas monitoring and recording the conversaton between Menzies and Quinlan, as Quinlan is maneuvered into admitting his guilt. Quinlan discovers the subterfuge and shoots Menzies. As he is about to kill Vargas, Menzies, for his final act, shoots Quinlan. Vargas and his wife are then reunited.

Welles's unlikely involvement with such "B"-grade material reflects his position in the American film industry at the time. Following his artistic triumph with *Citizen Kane*, the young maverick filmmaker had rapidly fallen out of favor in Hollywood; by 1957, he had not directed a film in his native country for nearly a decade. *Touch of Evil* marked his return from artistic exile, albeit through the back door at Universal. Gaining control over a project for which he had initially been contracted only as an actor (there are various versions of how his more extensive participation came about), he proceeded to make it his own. Rewriting the script, he introduced or emphasized themes which recur throughout his work—the law, morality, loyalty, and betrayal. By shooting largely on location in the run-down Los Angeles suburb of Venice, he managed to evoke not only a sleazy Mexican border town, but also a kind of nightmarish, otherworld locale reflecting the film's dark vision of moral decay. What would probably have become a routine potboiler in the hands of a lesser talent was transformed by Welles into one of the most astonishingly personal films in the history of the cinema.

Touch of Evil is unabashed melodrama, stylish, forceful, and exaggerated. All the characters are, in a sense, caricatures, and therein lies an important key to the film. Welles's typically full-blooded performance as Hank Quinlan dominates the film, his almost obscene appearance the result of heavy makeup and the exaggeration of his weight and bulk. Set against him is Heston as Mike Vargas; seldom have Heston's solidity and capacity for righteous anger been used to such excellent effect. Welles contrasts Heston's morally and physically upright image with the corruption and decay which permeate the film. Another vivid contrast with the film's dark mood is that of Vargas' blonde wife Susan, a part invested by Leigh with more strength that it would seem to call for. The other characters, major and minor alike, are a gallery of grotesques, quite unusual for an American film at that time, ranging from merely eccentric to downright bizarre. Tamiroff is memorable as "Uncle Joe" Grandi, who, whether fumbling with his unruly hairpiece or chomping on a cigar and effecting gangsterisms (at one point Susan calls him a "lop-sided Little Caesar"), is an unforgettable portrait of a slimy, cowardly, small-time hood with delusions of grandeur. Other standouts include Calleia as Quinlan's doggedly faithful, twitchy underling Pete Menzies; Marlene Dietrich as Tanya, madam of the local brothel to which Quinlan periodically retreats; and Dennis Weaver as an incredibly nervous and hyperkinetic motel attendant.

Under Welles's direction, Russell Metty's black-and-white cinematography is remarkable. The most notable example is the film's opening, one of the most audacious in the history of the cinema. Beginning with a close-up of a time bomb being placed in the trunk of a car, the camera, in a single, uninterrupted shot lasting over three minutes, follows the car and its occupants through the streets of Los Robles for several blocks, picking up and introducing the characters of Mike and Susan Vargas along the way, then following both them and the car across the border. As the camera moves in to the couple, they kiss; an explosion is heard, followed by the film's first cut—to the flaming body of the car in midair. This brilliant opening shot (which the above description greatly simplifies) is only one example of the directorial virtuosity which Welles brought to the film. (Sometimes he used this "long take" method for economy or to make a point; he filmed a lengthy interrogaton scene—ordinarily three shooting days—in a single shot on the first day of production to impress studio executives, who were nervous because of his reputaton for extravagance. "They left me alone after that," he says.) Throughout the film, the camera seems always to be on the move, almost as if it had developed a will of its own. The harsh lighting and frequent use of wide-angle lenses (with their distorting effect) and unusual camera angles also add to the grotesque overall look and feel of the film. The visual aspects, like the characters, are constantly exaggerated.

Welles's use of sound is equally bold; few films, even today, can match *Touch of Evil* for the inventive complexity of its visual and aural blending. The best example is the climactic sequence which has Vargas wading through the water of a canal as Menzies and Quinlan walk on the bridge above his head. At first we hear the conversation both from the characters and through the speaker on Vargas' receiver; then another dimension is added as the sound from the speaker begins to echo off the bridge. It is this echo which causes Quinlan to discover the hidden microphone (sound thus taking on something of the nature of an independent character in the scene), which in turn results in the shooting of Menzies. A few moments later, the tape recording which Vargas has made of the conversation is played back, and we hear Quinlan's admission of guilt again as we watch him dying. In addition to the sophisticated, multilayered use of sound, this sequence also features some of the film's most stylish camerawork and editing. It is reminiscent in many ways of the famous "house of mirrors" sequence in Welles's *The Lady from Shanghai* (1946). Another important element of the soundtrack is the music, a throbbing, restless, occasionally blaring mixture of brass and bongos that was one of Henry Mancini's early scores.

Those who believe that the best film direction is unobtrusive are likely to find *Touch of Evil* pretentious or simply detestable. Welles's style has never been that of the invisible craftsman, and the result is occasionally a bit too much; *Touch of Evil*, like Hank Quinlan, sometimes threatens to sink under its own weight. Like its creator, it is audacious and astonishing, often brilliant but hardly perfect.

Touch of Evil was from the beginning given short shrift in America. Universal removed the film from Welles's control in the editing stage, recut it, and added additional scenes shot by another director in an attempt to clarify what was felt to be its hopelessly muddled plot line. The effects of this tampering are evident (even to the untrained eye, a few scenes are blatantly at odds stylistically with the rest of the film), but for the most part it appears that Welles's conception has survived in the final product. Recently, an "uncut" version, some thirteen minutes longer, has been discovered which seems to approximate his original design more closely. It clears up a few of the ambiguities of the shorter version, but at some cost to the film's already sluggish pacing. (Curiously, the extra material includes both Welles and non-Welles footage.)

Although a critical success in France, where Welles was rightly praised for having made a film that could appeal to both the art-house and the drive-in crowds, in America the film came and went almost unnoticed, dumped on the market with very little publicity and no advance press screening. Its commercial failure added to Welles's already near-legendary reputation as a bad risk and returned him effectively to his former unemployable status as a film director (although he has always remained in demand as an actor). To date, Welles has not directed another film in America.

Howard H. Prouty

THE TOWERING INFERNO

Released: 1974
Production: Irwin Allen for Twentieth Century-Fox/Warner Bros.
Direction: John Guillermin and Irwin Allen
Screenplay: Stirling Silliphant; based on the novels *The Tower* by Richard Martin Stern and *The Glass Inferno* by Thomas M. Scotia and Frank M. Robinson
Cinematography: Fred Koenekamp (AA)
Editing: Harold F. Kress and Carl Kress (AA)
Special effects: Bill Abbot
Music: John Williams
Song: Al Kasha and Joel Hirschorn, "We May Never Love Like This Again" (AA)
Running time: 165 minutes

Principal characters:
Michael O'Halloran	Steve McQueen
Doug Roberts	Paul Newman
James Duncan	William Holden
Susan Franklin	Faye Dunaway
Harlee Claiborne	Fred Astaire
Patty Simmons	Susan Blakely
Roger Simmons	Richard Chamberlain
Lisolette Mueller	Jennifer Jones
Dan Bigelow	Robert Wagner
Lorrie	Susan Flannery
Senator Gary Parker	Robert Vaughn

It is difficult not to write about *The Towering Inferno* in terms of statistics, since this is very much the way it was conceived, marketed, and, to a considerable extent, received by the millions of people who viewed it. *The Towering Inferno* was made by two studios from a screenplay based on two almost identical novels, with two top stars each receiving a million dollars, filmed by two top cameramen, not to mention a special photography unit and an aerial unit, under the supervision of two directors. It cost more than fourteen million dollars to make, but grossed fifty-five million dollars in its first year of release on the domestic market of the United States and Canada, and enjoyed an estimated worldwide gross in excess of $150 million. It took four months to shoot, with fifty-seven separate sets, only nine of which were left standing by the end of the shooting. It won three Oscars, two of them the top technical awards, cinematography and film editing, which are traditionally the most venerated awards since they are made by professionals for professional skills. Put in simple terms, *The Towering Inferno* is a three-hour blockbuster which busted blocks. It also provided many people with a great deal of entertainment.

Not the least interesting aspect of the making of the film was its joint production. Warner Bros. had bought the rights to *The Tower* for $390,000, and some months later Fox had picked up the rights to the strikingly similar *The Glass Inferno* for $400,000. Rather than risk a box-office clash such as the one that had happened more than a decade earlier with the two Oscar Wilde biographies (*Oscar Wilde*, 1959, and *The Trials of Oscar Wilde* 1960), the studios decided to pool their resources for one super epic. This may seem a very sensible decision under the circumstances, but it is the kind of sanity that has not always been characteristic of Hollywood. The result was an attention to production detail which is one of the chief hallmarks of *The Towering Inferno*.

What was interesting about the novels was their basic idea, not their literary qualities. As one studio executive candidly admitted, "neither of them was great literature . . . neither of them was even as well written as *Airport*." Concern about what would happen if a 150-floor skyscraper caught fire, however, was a persistently nagging one. *The Towering Inferno* simply dramatized the idea in an imaginary building, the Glass Tower, eighty-three floors of offices, fifty floors of luxury apartments, topped by a penthouse restaurant and a roof-top heliport. The building is situated in downtown San Francisco, revealed at the movie's outset by a superb aerial matte shot which wobbles almost imperceptibly only once. Fire breaks out during the opening ceremony, when San Francisco's and Hollywood's luminaries are assembled in the restaurant. Through reluctance on the part of the developer to interrupt the festivities, the guests become stranded, and not all of them are saved by the combined efforts of architect Doug Robert (Paul Newman), fire chief Michael O'Halloran (Steve McQueen), the San Francisco Fire Department, and the United States Navy Air-Sea Rescue Unit. The story is really as simple as that. It is built around moments of protracted tension: climbing up a shattered stairwell, a descent in the building's outside scenic elevator which ends with a helicopter rescue, the transfer of certain guests by breeches buoy to a neighboring building, periodic looks at the reactions of the individuals trapped on the top floor. For the Glass Tower is, in this respect, a sort of up-ended ocean liner filled with slightly out-of-the-ordinary people with very ordinary problems—crumbling marriages, infidelities, and alcoholism—which the crisis forces them to handle.

On the assumption that *The Towering Inferno* is the "best" example of the 1970's cycle of disaster movies—the most expensive, most spectacular, most commercially successful, and, quite simply, the most exciting—there are a number of things about it which are worth examining in closer detail. In the first place, it plays on almost all of man's basic fears: fear of falling, fear of burning, fear of drowning. The trapped guests in the Glass Tower are threatened by all the basic "elements" of the medieval cosmology—falling through the air to the earth, burning in fire, and drowning in water—when, in an ingenious final attempt to put out the fire, the million-gallon water tanks on the roof are gelignited. In each case, the deaths are depicted in such a way as to play on the basic fear rather than wallow in the nastiness of the demise; *The Towering Inferno* is not *The Texas Chainsaw Massacre* (1974). In each climax, however, there are terrifying deaths. Robert Wagner and Susan Flannery are burned in an almost balletic dance of death in the former's apartment after turning off the telephones and locking the doors to make love; a man emerges blazing from the elevator which has been caught by a fireball on the eighty-second floor; Jennifer Jones falls out of the scenic elevator when one of its cables severs, and plunges down the seventy remaining floors; a burning fireman plummets like a meteorite past McQueen's group as they negotiate a 135-floor vertical elevator shaft.

The Towering Inferno, as its morality-play structure suggests, is very much of a lesson, explicitly voiced by O'Halloran when he meets Roberts on the building's piazza at the end. The bodycount, he says, was low, less than two hundred. One day, however, ten thousand people will die in a burning skyscraper. "And I'll go on eating smoke and carrying out the bodies until somebody comes to us and asks us how to build them." "OK," says Roberts: "I'm asking." "You know where to find me," is the inimitably laconic O'Halloran reply; "So long, architect." *The Towering Inferno* is concerned with more than simply the threat of fires in high buildings. It is about technology—about how we have become too dependent on it, how it is only as reliable as the people who operate it. We are immersed in a world of luxury, wealth, and electronics. The building by James Duncan (William Holden) is a masterpiece of modern technology, and he is inordinately proud of it. The interiors are the ultimate in modern luxury, they are the environment of people who "know how to live." Its destruction has a strong Sodom and Gomorrah feel to it. The guests are not particularly immoral, although there are illicit affairs going on, but they seem to be in need of a warning. They are in need, too, of a leader, someone who will tell them what to do when the crisis starts. Although the Senator (Robert Vaughn), and the Mayor of San Francisco (Jack Collins) acquit themselves admirably in keeping everyone calm and orderly—all except Roger Simmons (Richard Chamberlain) and his friend, who finally panic, jump the escape queue, and plummet to their deaths—the only one who can really save them is the uniformed professional, the man of action, aided by the technological expert, the architect.

The reason for stressing this underlying structure of this film is to provide some kind of suggestions for its phenomenal success. Not only is it brilliantly made and equipped with top-class special effects, but its appeal also lies in how it plays upon our fears and how it calms them. Much credit for this aspect must go to John Guillermin's frequently underrated direction of the main sequences, with their slightly solemn but precisely calculated crane movements at moments of building tension to take in the scope of the situation and the patterns of reaction to it. The film as a whole is constructed like a cross between a morality play and a melodrama, with carefully calculated build-ups, followed by flurries of lethal action, then lulls before the next storm devoted to brief scenes with the inactive characters.

In the final analysis, *The Towering Inferno* is the new Hollywood filmmaking behaving like the old. When the film's four production units started work in the same week in May, 1974, studio executives thought that perhaps this was a record, "certainly in recent years." The movie that came out of all the work was a package in the old tradition, a number of high-quality elements professionally put together into more than the sum of its parts. Under certain circumstances, Hollywood *does* still make them like that after all.

Nick Roddick

TRADER HORN

Released: 1931
Production: Metro-Goldwyn-Mayer
Direction: W. S. Van Dyke
Screenplay: Dale Van Every; based on the novel of the same name by Alfred Aloysius Horn and Ethelreda Lewis
Cinematography: Clyde DeVinna
Editing: Ben Lewis
Sound: Andrew Anderson
Running time: 119 minutes

> *Principal characters:*
> Trader Horn ....Harry Carey
> Nina .... Edwina Booth
> Peru .... Duncan Renaldo
> Rencharo ....Mutia Omoolu
> Edith Trend .... Olive Golden (Olive Carey)
> Witch doctor ....Riano Tindama

Trader Horn opened in early 1931 following much publicity about the film's unique production. It was the first feature film to be shot entirely on location in Africa, and one of only a small handful of films to be shot there until the early 1950's. The difficult production schedule began in March, 1929, and the entire company did not return to the United States until December of that year, a very long shooting schedule even by today's standards. Filming in such areas as the Belgian Congo, Nairobi, and Lake Victoria presented unique problems for the production crew, from the camera operator to the stars and director. The filmmakers had wanted to bring the settings described in the best-selling 1927 novel *Trader Horn* to light in a way which would enhance the story as well as capitalize on the public's recent interest in Africa. Contrary to popular belief, there had been previous films shot in Africa, of the documentary variety, and these had proven successful with the public. *Trader Horn* was thus an attempt to combine a documentary-style film on Africa with an adventure/love story.

The story seems rather hackneyed today. In fact, it was hackneyed in 1931, although most reviewers recognized the film's merits as an African travelogue and praised the technical aspects of the film rather than heavily scrutinizing the weak plot. The action centers around a famous African hunter, Trader Horn (Harry Carey), and his young companion Peru (Duncan Renaldo), who is new to the bush but has been taken under Horn's wing as a favor to the boy's father, who was an old friend. While traveling with their various pack bearers (all played by African natives), they encounter a white woman, Edith Trend (Olive Golden), who is also a friend of Horn. Mrs. Trend has been searching through the jungle for her lost daughter who has been missing since childhood. She feels certain that a young woman whom natives call a "white goddess" is her daughter, and she is determined to find her. Shortly after their encounter, however, she is killed, and in her memory, Horn decides to find the girl himself.

The remainder of the story concerns the attempt of Horn, Peru, and Rencharo (Mutia Omoolu), Horn's native guide and companion, to find the girl whom her mother named Nina. After traveling through various difficult areas of the jungle, the hunters find the white goddess (Edwina Booth), and they are convinced, because of her blond hair and physical resemblance to Edith Trend, that she is Nina. At first Nina is reluctant to go with the men, and they have a difficult time circumventing the tribe's witch doctor (Riano Tindama), but they finally make their way back to civilization. At the end of the journey, Peru, who has fallen in love with Nina, takes her away with him. Trader Horn remains behind in the jungle, somewhat sad to see Peru go, but happy that Nina, for whom he also had an affection, should be able to have a new life. Nina's feelings are left rather ambiguous. Because the character speaks no English dialogue, her emotions are conveyed almost entirely through eye expressions. The audience senses, however, that her parting with Trader Horn is bittersweet.

The reviews for the film were all in the same vein as one which appeared in *Variety*, stating that *Trader Horn* was a "good looking animal picture which will roll up a lot of coin." The acting, except for Carey's, is extremely wooden, and the plot, as mentioned, is very scant. The mainstay of the film's success rests on the marvelous locations, cinematography, and sound. Sprinkled throughout the plot are innumerable shots of African animals in their native habitats, many of them never before seen by the public. Indeed, many sections of the film are cinematic catalogues of wildlife rather than action drama. The cinematography, done principally by Clyde DeVinna, beautifully scans herds of animals grazing, playing, and stampeding in a very natural manner. The sound, by Andrew Anderson, also recorded the animals' natural noises, which makes the background to the film more realistic. The difficulties of working in the jungle, away from sound stages and under a blistering sun, undoubtedly caused the many months of shooting. It is ironic that the film's director, W. S. Van Dyke, whose nickname in Hollywood was "one take Woody" because of the speed with which he made movies, should have taken so long with *Trader Horn*.

Perhaps more important to journalists of the time than the location shooting, interesting cinematography, or story, however, was the drama surrounding the actors in the film. Although Carey, already an established actor, was the star, and his wife, Olive Golden (who later changed her name to Olive Carey), was also in the film, the two younger actors, Renaldo and Booth, were the subjects of the greatest publicity. It is not an exaggeration to say that they had their lives totally altered by the making of the film. Renaldo's and Booth's fortunes have been the subject of many magazine and newspaper articles over the last fifty years, and their personal histories have far outshone the film's merits in the minds of cinema historians.

Booth, who was born Josephine Woodruff in 1909, was the daughter of a Los Angeles physician. Her acting career had been very slight before *Trader Horn*, and at the age of nineteen, she was being groomed for stardom by M-G-M. Her blond hair, exotic features, and large eyes were frequent decorations on studio publicity releases for the new film. Even such magazines as *National Geographic*, which carried a feature on *Trader Horn*, had a prominent photograph of her among the others. While on location for the film, however, she contracted a rare tropical disease which began to affect her nervous system. Reportedly, one reason for many of the delays in the shooting of her scenes resulted from illness and the fact that her fair skin would not tan as it should. Additionally, rumors of an adulterous romance with Renaldo caused potentially unfavorable publicity which the studio wanted to suppress.

After returning to the United States, Booth appeared in minor parts in two other films, including one with Renaldo, but by 1932, her disease had so debilitated her that for the next six years she was confined to darkened rooms, unable even to hold a conversation. Eventually, after various trips to English and German hospitals specializing in tropical diseases, she recovered, although her career was never resumed. She is still alive, and after a marriage to a Mormon minister, she has been active in church work for a number of years. Rumors in the 1930's circulating around the time of the release of *Trader Horn* said that she had died from the disease contracted while on location, and even today many reference books falsely state that she died in the 1930's.

Renaldo, who had made several features in Hollywood before *Trader Horn*, was an actor who claimed to have been born in Camden, New Jersey, in 1904. His Hispanic good looks cast him as a Rudolph Valentino type, which was the type of image the studio wanted to be projected by the character Peru in *Trader Horn*. During the location shooting of that film, the reported liaison between Booth and himself caused publicity which eventually resulted in his wife's suing him and Booth for adultery. Booth was also married at the time, but her husband had their marriage annulled shortly after the end of filming. In the ensuing litigation, Renaldo and his wife, amidst charges and counter-charges of insanity, made headlines in the national newspapers which increased interest in *Trader Horn*. In the investigation during the divorce proceedings, however, it was discovered that Renaldo was an illegal alien in the United States, and therefore subject to deportation. For more than two years his case went unresolved until finally he was jailed. He was released from prison in 1936 after a special pardon from President Roosevelt and allowed to reenter the country legally at that time.

Renaldo began to make films again almost immediately after his release from prison and regained his popularity with little trouble. He was well known in the early 1940's for his role in a series of films starring "The Three Mesquiteers," and by the mid-1940's he began his very popular film series on "The Cisco Kid." This role stayed with him through the 1950's as he embarked on a successful television series of the same name. Renaldo died in 1980 after a lengthy retirement.

The Careys fortunately did not suffer the same rough times which Booth and Renaldo experienced. Harry Carey played a number of important featured roles throughout the 1930's, including that of the president pro tem of the United States Senate in Frank Capra's *Mr. Smith Goes to Washington* (1939). He had a status which was more common in the 1930's and 1940's than today, that of being a "star" character actor. There were many featured players at that time who were under contract to various studios who were as recognizable to the public as the lead actors and actresses, and Carey was one of the best-known of this type. He died in 1947, but his wife Olive and their son Harry Carey, Jr., have continued to act in supporting roles. The senior Carey was given a well-known tribute in John Ford's classic Western, *The Searchers* (1956), in which both Olive and Harry, Jr., had small parts. In the final famous scene which shows star John Wayne standing in the sunlight shot through the frame of a doorway of a darkened room, Wayne turns to the camera and assumes the recognizable Harry Carey stance: left arm at his side, with the other arm holding it. It was one of the few tributes ever to be given to another actor's screen *persona* in a serious film, and was a fitting gesture to one of the great character actors, given by his good friend.

Patricia King Hanson

THE TRAIN

Released: 1965
Production: Jules Bricken for United Artists
Direction: John Frankenheimer
Screenplay: Franklin Coen, Frank Davis, and Walter Bernstein; based on the
book *Le Front de l'Art* by Rose Valland
Cinematography: Jean Tournier
Editing: David Bretherton
Special effects: Lee Zavitz
Music: Maurice Jarre
Running time: 133 minutes

Principal characters:
Labiche .... Burt Lancaster
Colonel von Waldheim .... Paul Scofield
Christine .... Jeanne Moreau
Papa Boule .... Michel Simon
Miss Villard .... Suzanne Flon

The Train is an excellent example of the kind of exciting, rough-and-tumble
action filmmaking that has made war-themed motion pictures, particularly
those dealing with World War II, a popular staple of world cinema. Set in
the summer of 1944 in occupied Paris as the Allied troops are slowly working
their way to liberate the French capital, *The Train* is based on historical
reality, as related by Rose Valland, a curator at the famous Jeu de Paume
museum, in her book *Le Front de l'Art*. The book describes an attempt by
Nazi troops to take a trainload of the museum's art treasures, officially banned
as decadent by the Nazis but valuable on the world art market to help support
the floundering German war cause, back safely to Berlin.

In the film, a Wehrmacht officer named Colonel von Waldheim (Paul Scofield) is ordered by Goering to select the art and prepare the train. The
museum's curator, Miss Villard (Suzanne Flon), tells members of the Resistance about the plan and also attempts to persuade a railway inspector named
Labiche (Burt Lancaster) that he should stop the train and save the valuable
cargo. An accomplished Resistance fighter, Labiche refuses since it will, in
his opinion, cost senseless loss of lives in the name of mere art. He opts
instead for sabotaging a munitions train. Without Labiche's help, the train,
heavily armed, is damaged by the actions of an aged engineer, Papa Boule
(Michel Simon), who is killed for his effort by the Germans, and an angry
von Waldheim must make ready the train once more. He orders Labiche to
be its engineer. The train sets off for a second time, but with the cooperation
of various patriotic French station managers, the Nazis are led to believe that
the train is successfully on its way to Germany, when it is only circling through

the intricate network of French railroad yards, and indeed, winds up back at its departure point, where the Resistance again puts it out of commission.

Seeing the courage of the rail workers, Labiche is won over to the cause, additionally persuaded by Christine (Jeanne Moreau), a widowed hotel owner. Von Waldheim, now nearly driven insane by his obsession, takes over the engineer's position himself and sets off once more, impeded along the way by Labiche, who soon becomes almost equally obsessed, acting as a one-man sabotage force. As a final measure, von Waldheim fills the train with French hostages to insure safe passage, but Labiche succeeds in derailing it. As the retreating German army passes by, the train's soldiers panic and desert, killing all the hostages. Left alone, von Waldheim faces Labiche, who kills him. Surveying the wrecked train with its bloody corpses strewn among the crates of precious art, Labiche wanders off, his mission completed, but at a monstrous cost.

The Train was a French/Italian/United States coproduction (with Lancaster himself involved financially in it). The film's production was troubled. The initial script as well as the original director, Arthur Penn, were both discarded after three days of shooting (with Penn not receiving any screen credit), and Lancaster convinced his friend John Frankenheimer to take over as director. The pair had worked together previously on *The Birdman of Alcatraz* (1962) and *Seven Days in May* (1964). Much of the story was changed and characters thrown out. The shooting of the six-million-dollar film consumed six months, largely because of the elaborate special effects involved (devised by Lee Zavitz, who set Atlanta on fire in *Gone with the Wind*, 1939) and the sheer logistics of filming with real trains. Unlike most large-scale war films, no miniatures or optical effects were used, and during the filming some four locomotives and forty cars, as well as an entire station, were destroyed in carefully planned explosions and collisions.

Such authenticity, under Frankenheimer's energetic, brawny direction, gives a sheer physicality to the film that is awesome. Frankenheimer, trained as a director in the so-called "Golden Age" of live television drama, graduated to feature films with *The Young Stranger* (1957). *The Train* was his eighth film. Lancaster, a former acrobat who habitually performs his own film stunts, had hurt his leg during the filming of *The Leopard* (1963), and his resultant limp was built into his character in the film.

Such internationally casted epic war films as *The Train* are traditionally more popular in Europe than in the United States, with both critics and viewers. American reviewers faulted the rocky dubbing of the French actors, their clichéd characterizations (apart from Scofield and Lancaster, who was considered miscast as a Frenchman), and the film's length. Even so, the film had been cut some seven minutes for American release, having been first premiered, somewhat unusually, in Europe. Few could complain, however, about the film's spectacular action set-pieces. As a tribute to the French

Resistance fighters, a study of the nature of obsession (with von Waldheim and Labiche as parallel characters), and the final ironic questioning of the nature of art versus human life, *The Train* has never been surpassed. The National Board of Review voted the film one of the "Best English Language Films" of 1965, and the screenplay was nominated for an Oscar, losing to *Darling*.

David Bartholomew

A TREE GROWS IN BROOKLYN

Released: 1945
Production: Louis D. Lighton for Twentieth Century-Fox
Direction: Elia Kazan
Screenplay: Tess Slesinger and Frank Davis; based on the novel of the same name by Betty Smith
Cinematography: Leon Shamroy
Editing: Dorothy Spencer
Running time: 128 minutes

Principal characters:

Katie Nolan	Dorothy McGuire
Aunt Sissy	Joan Blondell
Johnny Nolan	James Dunn (AA)
Francie Nolan	Peggy Ann Garner
Neeley Nolan	Ted Donaldson
Officer McShane	Lloyd Nolan
McGarrity	James Gleason
Miss McDonough	Ruth Nelson

A Tree Grows in Brooklyn is, in effect, a filmed version of a Raphael Soyer painting, evoking images of pretty girls in their early twenties washing their hair out of tenement windows on a Saturday night, their arms dripping with soap suds; or perhaps of a thirteen-year old girl sitting and reading on the steps of a fire escape. It is the story of a poor but proud Brooklyn family in the early years of the twentieth century, showing how they live with poverty in a big city and how it affects their relationships with one another. Realistic subjects such as puberty and alcoholism are treated with honesty and without excessive sentimentality. The film does not moralize or pass judgment on the members of this family; it merely presents them.

When it first appeared as a novel, Betty Smith's *A Tree Grows in Brooklyn* was a phenomenal success. It was published in August of 1943, and the screen rights were purchased by Twentieth Century-Fox the following year. Elia Kazan, noted for his innovative work with the famed Group Theater in New York, was brought to Hollywood to direct the film. Kazan had received earlier offers from Fox and Warner Bros. to direct films, but only when he read *A Tree Grows in Brooklyn*, did he find one that was right for him. Here was material he knew something about: the streets of New York and the lives of the working class.

Tess Slesinger, a well-known novelist whose books always dealt with life in New York, coauthored the screenplay with Frank Davis. The story is seen through the eyes of Francie Nolan, a thirteen-year old girl with a great deal of sensitivity. Kazan had great difficulty finding someone who could play

Francie, but after testing many older actresses who could pass for thirteen, he selected Peggy Ann Garner, who was actually the right age. He felt that she had exactly the face and manner for the part—plain and rather withdrawn—and, because her father was overseas in the service and her mother was having problems, her face reflected real pain. Kazan has said of her performance, "she was not pretty at all, or cute or picturesque—only true." Dorothy McGuire, James Dunn, Joan Blondell, and Ted Donaldson play the other members of the Nolan family, with Ruth Nelson, Lloyd Nolan, and Mae Marsh in important supporting parts. The picture was shot on the studio lot at Fox, a decision that Kazan regretted, feeling that if it had been photographed on the streets of New York, it would have been more true to life.

The film opens in the living room of the Nolan tenement in Brooklyn at the turn of the century. Francie (Peggy Ann Garner) and Neeley (Ted Donaldson) are doing their household chores while their mother Katie (Dorothy McGuire) is scrubbing the staircase. It is soon established that the father of the children, Johnny Nolan (James Dunn), a part-time singing waiter, is a charming Irish alcoholic who brings very little money into the household, but who gives his children much-needed warmth and comfort. Francie worships her father and is constantly defending him against the taunts of her school friends. Johnny is always waiting for his ship to come in, and makes Francie believe that there is more to life than the four walls of their tenement.

Katie's sister Sissy (Joan Blondell) brings on a momentary family crisis by announcing that she has remarried even though her last divorce is not yet final. While Katie is scolding her for her unorthodox wedding, Sissy convinces Katie that she has hardened, lost faith in life, and that her attitude has brought trouble between her and Johnny. The children meanwhile are going about their daily activities, trying to circumvent their poverty by selling junk on a Saturday afternoon and going shopping for their mother at the very cheapest shops. It can be seen that if Katie is hard, it is because she is the one member of the family responsible for their survival because Johnny is the type of man on whom no one can depend. She tells Sissy not to come around anymore because her reputation with men might reflect on the Nolans. After a particularly hard day, Katie waits up for Johnny, wondering if, indeed, she has grown hard. That night the couple desperately try to recapture something of their former happiness with each other and make love. It does not work, and they end up facing the fact that Johnny is a failure in life and that their marriage is no longer the love idyll that it once was.

When Katie realizes that she is going to have a baby, the family moves to a cheaper apartment in the same building, but still cannot make ends meet. On Christmas Eve, Katie tells Johnny that Francie will have to drop out of school to work and help support the family. Johnny protests. He was determined that Francie have her heart's desire and finish high school. Katie remains firm, and Johnny leaves to search for work. Some days later, when

Johnny has still not returned home, officer McShane (Lloyd Nolan), the local policeman on the beat and a good friend to the family, tells Katie that Johnny has been found after walking the streets for three days in search of work. He is now in the hospital, critically ill with pneumonia. Three days later, he dies, his condition aggravated by acute alcoholism.

At his funeral, Katie is amazed to see so many mourners, but Francie is not surprised. She knew of the happiness this man brought to others and felt that her mother never appreciated Johnny. Francie manages to stay in school by working afternoons in a local saloon. She reads Katie a composition she has written about her father, and the two at last reach a complete understanding about this man that they both loved. Meanwhile, both Aunt Sissy and Katie have babies, effecting a reconciliation between the two sisters. Graduation time finally comes for Francie, and she is surprised by a gift of flowers that Johnny ordered long before Christmas to be given to her when she finished high school. Officer McShane proposes to Katie, who agrees to marry him "after a decent interval has elapsed." Up on the roof of the tenement, Francie and Neeley talk about their childhood. Francie feels very grown-up with her diploma. She asks Neeley if she is good-looking, and when he tells her that she will pass, her happiness is complete.

The critics were unanimous in their appreciation of the film when it opened in February of 1945. They especially praised the authenticity of the way in which city life was treated. Dunn won an Academy Award for Best Supporting Actor for his portrayal of Johnny Nolan, and Garner received a Special Award in which she was named Outstanding Child Actress of 1945. Kazan has said in interviews that the time was right for him to direct the film in the manner in which he did. He was separated from his wife, missed his children, and had a special feeling about a child's love for her father. He has said that he would not direct it in the same way now, but that he still has a special fondness for the film. Indeed, it is difficult not to be fond of it, for *A Tree Grows in Brooklyn* is a walk back through the years to everyone's old neighborhood, and there is a quality to the picture that will always appeal to both young people and adults, even if their own lives were in no way similar to the Nolans' in background. It is one of the few films ever made which, while extremely sentimental, was not maudlin, and evoked sympathy for its characters instead of pity for them.

Joan Cohen

THE TRESPASSER

Released: 1929
Production: Joseph P. Kennedy for Gloria Productions; released by United
    Artists
Direction: Edmund Goulding
Screenplay: Edmund Goulding
Cinematography: George Barnes
Editing: Cyril Gardner
Running time: 120 minutes

Principal characters:

Marion Donnell	Gloria Swanson
Jack Merrick	Robert Ames
Hector Ferguson	Purnell Pratt
John Merrick, Sr.	William Holden
Fuller	Henry B. Walthall
Jackie	Wally Albright
Catherine "Flip" Merrick	Kay Hammond
Miss Potter	Blanche Friderici

One by one, the big stars of the silent era made their debuts in talking
films, but the one who possibly came through the best in 1929 was Gloria
Swanson, starring in a modern drama of mother love, *The Trespasser*. In it
she proved beyond question that she not only had a speaking voice that was
a pleasure to hear, but also that she could sing. For her work in *The Trespasser*
she won a nomination as Best Actress of 1929-1930 from the Motion Picture
Academy (losing to Norma Shearer for *The Divorcee*); it was the second time
she was nominated, the first having been in the very first year Academy
Awards were given, 1927-1928, when she was nominated for her work in a
silent film *Sadie Thompson*.

Swanson must have filmed her first talking feature with a great sense of
relief, for she had spent more than a frustrating year working with Erich Von
Stroheim on a big special, *Queen Kelly*. It was two-thirds finished when, at
her instigation, her good friend and producer, Joseph P. Kennedy, halted
production and Von Stroheim was dismissed. It was a silent film, and at first
Edmund Goulding was engaged to remake it as an all-talking feature. There
was some discussion, until even that idea promised to be too expensive, of
releasing it as a part-talkie, but the plan fortunately was abandoned, and
eventually a new ending was devised and quickly filmed. *Queen Kelly* was
released in parts of Europe in the 1930's, and its production costs at least
were recouped.

Meanwhile, however, Goulding wrote and directed an original story for
Swanson, *The Trespasser*, and there is no doubt that in it she made the most

sensational talking film debut of any of the great silent stars. The leading role was written to order for her, and it offered her every opportunity to score on all counts.

The Trespasser tells the story of Marion Donnell (Gloria Swanson), who works as a stenographer to Hector Ferguson (Purnell Pratt), a rich corporation lawyer. She meets Jack Merrick (Robert Ames), a rich man's son, and the two fall in love and impulsively elope. John Merrick, Sr. (William Holden) has held great plans for a wealthy society marriage for his son, and when he learns of the elopement, he seeks out Jack and persuades him to have the marriage annulled, promising to build up Marion's importance through publicity so that they eventually can be remarried. Jack falls for the plan, but Marion will have nothing to do with it and angrily walks out on him and the whole Merrick family.

A year later Marion is the mother of a son; she has been working and lives in a cheap apartment, aided by a Cockney servant, Miss Potter (Blanche Friderici). She is heavily in debt, but refuses to go to the Merricks for aid. She has learned that Jack, having had his marriage to her annulled, has wed a society girl, "Flip" Carson (Kay Hammond). Jack and his new bride go to France on their honeymoon, and while there they are both injured in a train accident; the new Mrs. Merrick suffers permanent injuries and will be confined to a wheelchair for life.

Overcome and near a breakdown, Marion is persuaded by her former employer, Hector Ferguson, who has always secretly loved her, to take up residence in the country with her baby and Miss Potter. Ferguson sees to it that she has every luxury, but he is stricken by a sudden stroke and sends for her before he dies, assuring her that he has always loved her. Marion holds him in her arms until Ferguson's wife enters the room; Marion gives him up, placing him in his wife's arms, and he dies believing that he is in the arms of Marion. When Flip Carson sees Marion's son Jackie (Wally Albright), whom her husband fathered, she is greatly moved by the child, and, knowing she can never bear children, she entreats her husband to divorce her so that the boy and his mother can have Jack back as father and husband. Flip then dies, and Merrick, Sr., and Marion are reconciled, thus paving the way for Marion's remarriage to Jack, father of her son.

The Trespasser had its premiere in London just one week after it had scored a great hit at its New York opening. The London premiere was just as triumphant. Critics acknowledged that Swanson was the star of stars: she could act, she could talk, and she could sing. "Glorious Gloria" was the glamour star of all time. She sang two songs in the picture, and the theme song, "Love, Your Magic Spell Is Everywhere," written by Goulding and Elsie Janis for her, was an immediate hit. (Victor cut a record of the two songs, and they also became hits. The fact that a company such as Victor would press a record proved that no other singer had dubbed for Swanson.) All the players were praised; Goulding became the most sought-after director in Hollywood, and everyone agreed that no other actress had bridged the silents to sound with such stunning success as Swanson.

Unfortunately, Swanson could not find another property to follow *The Trespasser*. She scored as a comedienne in her next two, *What a Widow!* (1930) and *Indiscreet* (1931). She had a becoming vehicle in a onetime David Belasco hit, *Tonight or Never* (1931), but in Europe she made a stylish flop, *Perfect Understanding* (1933). She sang and played the diva role in a musical, *Music in the Air* (1934), but it was not popular. Irving Thalberg then signed her at Metro-Goldwyn-Mayer, dismayed that she no longer reigned as a top star and determined to restore her to her rightful place at the top. Thalberg planned possible remakes of Elinor Glyn's *Three Weeks* and Gertrude Atherton's *Black Oxen*, but he died quite young in 1936, and Swanson never made a film for M-G-M. She tried her luck in the theater, but did not then find the right vehicle.

Not until 1950, when Charles Brackett and Billy Wilder brought her back to Hollywood to play Norma Desmond in *Sunset Boulevard*, did she have a chance to top *The Trespasser*. *Sunset Boulevard* brought her a third nomination for the Academy Award for Best Actress of 1950, but she lost the Oscar to Judy Holliday for *Born Yesterday*. She returned to New York, where she costarred with José Ferrer on the stage in a revival of *Twentieth Century* that was tremendously popular. *The Trespasser* was remade in 1937 as *That Certain Woman*, starring Bette Davis and Henry Fonda; even though Goulding again directed, the film was certainly not in the same league with *The Trespasser*. The pictures Swanson has made following *Sunset Boulevard* have all been unworthy of her.

In 1981 the actress published her "tell-all" book, *Swanson on Swanson: An Autobiography*, which came on the heels of her acceptance of the D. W. Griffith Award presented by the National Board of Review and *Films in Review* in 1981. Because of the award and the book, she has enjoyed much publicity and admiration for her still-glamorous appearance at the age of eighty-four.

DeWitt Bodeen

TROUBLE IN PARADISE

Released: 1932
Production: Ernst Lubitsch for Paramount
Direction: Ernst Lubitsch
Screenplay: Grover Jones and Samson Raphaelson; based on the play *The Honest Finder* by Laszlo Aladar
Cinematography: Victor Milner
Editing: no listing
Interior decoration: Hans Dreier
Music: W. Frank Harling and Leo Robin
Running time: 83 minutes

Principal characters:
Lily Vautier	Miriam Hopkins
Mariette Colet	Kay Francis
Gaston Monescu (LaValle)	Herbert Marshall
François Filiba	Edward Everett Horton
The Major	Charles Ruggles
Adolph Giron	C. Aubrey Smith
Jacques, the butler	Robert Greig

The elegant world of the European upper crust in the early 1930's provides the "paradise" for this masterpiece of cinematic comedy. The "trouble" appears in the form of two attractive thieves, the famous Gaston Monescu (Herbert Marshall) and his nimble-fingered partner, Lily Vautier (Miriam Hopkins). Early in the film, a dinner for two in Gaston's suite at the Hotel Venezia provides the setting for the couple's first rendezvous. She, posing as a countess, thinks that she is dining with "the baron," until he bests her at a polite round of dinner-table pickpocketing: she gets a watch and a wallet; he gets a pin and one of her garters.

The scene then shifts to Paris and to Colet and Company by way of a comically exaggerated radio commercial for Colet perfume. Mariette Colet (Kay Francis), the attractive and eligible widow who runs the company, is spirited and independent. She says no to the board of directors, chaired by the archcapitalist, Adolph Giron (C. Aubrey Smith), with the same self-assurance with which she says no to her two suitors, François (Edward Everett Horton) and the Major (Charles Ruggles). Gaston contrives to get himself employed by Madame Colet. He returns a purse that she thought she had lost at the opera. She lost it, of course, because he stole it from her. After charming her with his wit and honesty, he agrees to become her secretary. Gaston and Lily, however, plan to rob Madame Colet as soon as she can be induced to keep one hundred thousand francs in her safe at home. A complication arises in the plan when Gaston finds himself lured, not unwillingly, into having discreet affair with his intended victim.

A subplot follows François and the Major as they observe the new developments, ever eager to regain Madame's affections. A complication arises in the subplot when François, who was robbed at the Hotel Venezia by a fine-looking man posing as a doctor, begins to think that he has seen Madame's secretary somewhere before. A flurry of accusations, denials, disclosures, and surprises concludes the film. Mariette and Gaston part sadly but amicably, Mariette having surrendered some of her wealth knowingly and some unknowingly. The two successful thieves hit the road, en route we presume, to their next conquest.

By the time Ernst Lubitsch came to the United States from Germany in 1922, he was already regarded as one of Europe's finest directors. His reputation was based on films such as *Madame DuBarry* (1919) and *Anne Boleyn* (1920), in which he re-created history on an epic scale but also managed to reveal the human imperfections that made his characters, Louis XV and Henry VIII, believable as real people. In later films he refined his use of irony and humor to reveal hidden human realities. In *Trouble in Paradise*, he displays this motif of hidden realities in several ways, but primarily through the placing of two charming impostors at the center of the action.

Sex is a major ingredient of the humor not only in *Trouble in Paradise* but also in several Lubitsch films preceding and following it, such as *The Love Parade* (1929). As a European newly introduced to the land of the Puritan ethic, Lubitsch was amused at Americans' reactions toward sex in his films, consisting of titters, blushes, raised eyebrows, and the like, so he had fun with sex, gently kidding his American audiences. For example, he had his female characters make sexual advances, as Mariette does toward Gaston: "Shut up! Kiss me!" He created charming, articulate pairs of lovers who entertained not the least thought of marriage; and he employed the famous "Lubitsch touch" to reveal the hidden truths about characters and their relationships.

Herman Weinberg in his book, *The Lubitsch Touch* (1971), traces both the style and humor of Lubitsch's American "sex comedies" of the 1920's to Charles Chaplin's *A Woman of Paris* (1923). Besides liking the sophisticated approach to sexual themes in the Chaplin film, Lubitsch admired Chaplin's economy of style, his ability to suggest, by subtle use of single details, the quality of a relationship between characters. Lubitsch's films of the 1920's and 1930's derive much of their charm and wit from this stylistic trait, which became known as the "Lubitsch touch." Most often it appears as a detail of action which crystallizes, with unexpected wit, brevity, and incisiveness, the import of an entire scene. Elements of satire, surprise, and sexual innuendo are often present. The effect is to give the scene an unexpected and memorable twist, a little extra sharpness, like the bubbles in a glass of champagne.

A few examples in *Trouble in Paradise* exemplify this elusive quality. Gaston and Lily are alone, having become acquainted over dinner and having also picked each other's pockets, when Gaston dramatically locks the doors, pulls the curtains, approaches Lily, and, tenderly taking her by the shoulders, suddenly shakes her like a rag doll. Next we see a close-up of her feet, and the wallet falls out of her evening gown. In a later scene, Gaston and Lily, both having been employed by Madame Colet, are plotting their next move when Madame Colet unexpectedly calls for Lily to come to her room. Lily begins to primp a bit, Gaston adds a touch or two—straightens her collar, perhaps, or pats a curl into place—and, as a last detail, he quickly and deftly zips up the front of her dress. In a memorable scene in Madame Colet's bedroom, we see her and Gaston embrace. The next shot frames their reflections in a large mirror, and the final shot shows their shadows on her bed.

Many Lubitsch touches take place in the dialogue. One example occurs when Lily asks Gaston where a lady should put her jewelry when she removes it in a gentleman's room. He lamely suggests the night table. She then adds, "But I don't want to be a lady." Another Lubitsch hallmark occurs in the music when Monescu whispers to François something about the girls in Constantinople. We hear no words, just music, a familiar and somewhat suggestive Eastern-sounding melody which calls up images of veiled harems and belly dancers.

The artistic felicities of *Trouble in Paradise* become even more remarkable in light of the technical obstacles facing Lubitsch and other filmmakers in the early 1930's. Sound films were still hampered by many of the technical difficulties brought on by the presence of microphones on the set. Dialogue scenes tended to be static and stiff, partly because the microphones picked up the extraneous noises associated with movement and partly because cameras were not easily or silently mobile. Postdubbing of the sound track was being done, however; music and sound effects could be recorded separately, apart from the picture, and added to the sound track later. Artistically, many films suffered from too much talking, singing, and dancing, as if the capability of sound had imposed an obligation to cram as much of it in as possible. Lubitsch, however, was among a group of innovators, including King Vidor and Lewis Milestone, who managed to bring movement back to the camera, to restore a sense of spontaneity to dialogue scenes, and to discover ways that the soundtrack, including music, could be used creatively and yet economically.

The rendezvous scene between Gaston and Lily near the beginning of the film provides a good example of how a little music, carefully applied, can increase camera mobility, thereby enhancing the viewers' feeling of fluidity and spontaneity in a dialogue scene. A clever use of alternating dialogue and music allows the actors to move easily across the set as the camera follows their movement. Lily enters, speaks to "the baron" while standing still, and then rushes dramatically to a chair while the music covers her move; after another move to the window (more music), "the baron" joins her, and they again speak to each other. All the dialogue is spoken with both actors stationary, and all movement, both of actors and camera, is covered by music, which was recorded later and inserted into the film. A number of scenes follow this strategy: the characters move freely around the set, and the camera follows, but the lines of dialogue are spoken only when there is no movement, and music or sound effects fill in while the camera and the people are moving.

Despite this purely technical function, the music in the film, although often deliberately overstated for humorous effect, always fits the tone and dramatic situation of the scene in which it occurs; it never seems arbitrarily inserted for the sole function of transition. In fact, music sometimes conveys information in lieu of dialogue or facial expression. When François finally remembers that he has seen Madame Colet's secretary in Venice, we see him, cigarette in hand, using a gondola-shaped ashtray. As he looks down, and as we see, from his point of view, a close-up of the ashtray, the orchestra suddenly blurts out a short chorus of "O Sole Mio," the musical motif which accompanied the opening scenes of the film in Venice, where he was robbed. With the close-up of the ashtray and the implication of Venice, nothing more is needed to convey what he is thinking.

Several 1932 reviewers commented favorably on the set design by Paramount's Hans Dreier, who created the sets for twelve of Lubitsch's films. His rendition of Madame Colet's residence in particular is a triumph of art deco. The wide, swirling staircase, the shimmer of glass and metal in graceful curves, the slickly styled clocks, the luster of silk drapery, the sparkle of chandeliers— all of these visual details are given sufficient prominence to suggest wealth, style, sophistication, and a touch of fantasy.

The stylistic flourishes in the decor are paralleled by the flourishes of composition and camera movement which give the film's direction an art deco feeling as well. Stylized compositions include the shot of the Major from inside the ladies' shop as he stands outside looking into the display case, his figure framed by a huge circle in the display window. Only when the camera pulls back do we find out where he is and what makes the circle. Several shots portray reflections in mirrors, so that the characters are framed twice. One elaborate mirror shot shows a reflection of the great curving staircase as Mariette and Gaston ascend it.

Each of the camera angles has a smooth, self-consciously graceful quality which calls attention to its style. In an early scene, for example, a view which looks like a single shot is actually a combination of three or four separate ones. The camera floats around the Hotel Venezia, from one balcony, past rooms, walls, and ivy, until it finds the balcony on the opposite side of the hotel where Monescu is standing and glides smoothly through space toward him. Lubitsch lets us know that he realizes that the film is a stylized fantasy. The charming artificiality of his characters is reflected in their dazzling and witty repartee, the decor is exaggeratedly modern, and even the music over-states itself, parodying the role of musical commentary and punctuation. Part of the fun of viewing the film comes in knowing that the film style itself is deliberately exaggerated, as if the director wanted the film to be as stylized, artificial, and comical as the characters and situations it depicts.

The mixture of self-conscious stylization in the direction, the decor, and even in the characters, when considered in relation to the interplay of illusion and reality in the plot, reveals a central structure in the film. There is an opposition between the romantic and glamorous surface illusion of life and the mundane, dingy reality beneath it. Life as we would like it to be opposes life as it is. The opening scene of the film establishes this dominant conflict and prepares us for the many humorous surprises of the rest of the film. We first see a back alley with brick walls, a garbage can, and a dog. As the garbage man enters the frame and carries off the can, we hear no sound except the realistic sounds of steps and clanks. The camera pans as it follows him, revealing very unexpectedly a canal in Venice with a garbage-laden gondola moored at its side. We see and hear the garbage as the man dumps it onto the heap. Then, as he pushes off to continue his rounds, he suddenly bursts into a fervent, heartfelt rendition of "O Sole Mio." Lubitsch plays against our expectations by opening with a drab reality, then surprising us by placing it in Venice, and then making us confront our romantic preconceptions: we had not thought of Venice, with its canals and gondolas, in quite this way before.

The purpose of a comedy is primarily to entertain, however, and enter-tainment means escaping the drab realities, so Lubitsch properly introduces his main characters as "the baron" and "the countess." The viewer is also deceived by their appearances for a time before being made a party to their secrets. They are really thieves, simply trying to make a buck.

For Depression-era audiences, the classy thieves who move in the highest circles of society and manage to make off with a fortune in cash and jewelry are perfect "mythic" figures to arouse audience sympathy. Lily and Gaston reconcile the contradiction between the romantic illusion and the dingy real-ities. They retain their real, lower-class identity as thieves but combine with it an elaborate upper-class masquerade. By merely acting out their own, and possibly the viewer's fantasies of wealth, wit, and elegance, they manage to get rich. Perhaps it is this structure as much as the sparkling dialogue, the sophisticated sexual humor, the fluidity of the camera, the inventiveness of the sound track, and the "Lubitsch touch" that makes the film as appealing for contemporary audiences as it was when it was first released.

William O. Huie, Jr.

TUNES OF GLORY

Released: 1960
Production: Colin Lesslie for Knightsbridge
Direction: Ronald Neame
Screenplay: James Kennaway; based on his novel of the same name
Cinematography: Arthur Ibbetson
Editing: Anne V. Coates
Running time: 105 minutes

Principal characters:
Lieutenant-Colonel
Jock Sinclair, DSO, MC .... Alec Guinness
Lieutenant-Colonel Basil Barrow .... John Mills
Major Charlie Scott, MC .... Dennis Price
Mary Titterington .... Kay Walsh
Corporal Piper Ian Fraser ....John Fraser
Corporal Jimmy Cairns, MC ....Gordon Jackson
Morag Sinclair .... Susannah York
Pipe Major .... Duncan Macrae

There is a certain kind of confrontation at which the British cinema has always excelled: that between two men, preferably from different social backgrounds, probably soldiers or ex-soldiers, over some notion of traditional values, such as honor, responsibility, or decency. They are isolated from the rest of the world, often in a German or Japanese prisoner-of-war camp, which justifies the absence of women and makes the identification of class differences unmistakable through the distinction between officers and "other ranks." The key factor in the conflict, however, is that it generally moves *inside*. Whereas conflicts in the American cinema tend to be worked out in action in a landscape, those in the British cinema tend to be worked *through* (rarely *out*) in words in a room.

If the above interpretation, applied to *Tunes of Glory*, rather reduces the film to a formula, it is partly because that formula accounts for much of its appeal and also because *Tunes of Glory* is a very fine example of it. It shows a conflict between two men, soldiers, over a question of tradition (the proper way to run a regiment) in a closed environment (a Scottish castle in the dead of winter). It is a class conflict: one of the men has risen from the ranks, the other is "officer class," directly descended from previous Colonels of the regiment. Women are incidental, almost added as an afterthought. The risen-from-the-ranks officer has a liaison with an actress at the local theater, and his daughter is having an affair with a noncommissioned officer; the other man is a widower. The scene is set for one of those slow-burn conflicts between two great actors (Alec Guinness and John Mills) in which the clash is not so much on the surface as in glances, gestures, and brief, barbed comments.

Jock Sinclair, DSO, MC (Alec Guinness), a career soldier from the Glasgow slums, rose to his position as acting commander as a result of war service. He is a hard-drinking, forthright officer loved by his men; his officers are equally loyal to him, knowing him to be a fine soldier, although some of them—notably Major Charlie Scott (Dennis Price)—think the regiment could do with a more disciplined, efficient commander. They are all taken aback, however, when, in the middle of a party in the Officers' Mess, he tells them that a new man is on his way up from London to take over. Right on cue into the midst of the slightly maudlin drunkenness of the party comes the new Colonel, Basil Barrow (John Mills) dressed in a neat civilian tweed suit. Barrow is a desk officer with a lot of administrative experience but little battle experience. He spent much of the war in a prison camp, an experience which has left its mark on his nerves. He is determined to reestablish order and discipline in the regiment, a move which earns him the dislike of the other officers, who had grown used to Jock's free and easy ways. Barrow and Jock dislike each other instinctively, because of their backgrounds, and professionally, because of their attitudes toward command. The conflict comes to a head over an almost ridiculous issue. Barrow decides that the officers do not dance like gentlemen: Scottish dancing is an important part of the regiment's tradition, and he is determined that they shall abandon their wild whoops and flings. To make his point he orders them to turn out every morning before breakfast for dancing lessons.

Reassured about the dancing, he decides to revive the tradition of a cocktail party for the local civilian dignitaries, but the party is ruined when, surreptitiously encouraged by Jock, the officers resort to their old dancing habits. Barrow, almost beside himself with fury, stops the party. This is probably Mills's finest moment, as the strains of prison camp life and the present situation break through his veneer of military self-control and well-bred politeness. Realizing, however, that he has made a fool of himself, he drives off in his jeep—a scene which, by contrast with the preceding one, seems melodramatic and contrived.

In the meantime, Jock goes out on a drinking spree, meets some of his NCO's in a pub, then suddenly catches sight of Morag (Susannah York), his daughter, with Corporal Ian Fraser (John Fraser) the piper. He loses his temper and strikes Fraser, a serious offense, since they are both in uniform. Jock finally agrees to plead with Barrow not to start court martial proceedings, and, to his surprise, Barrow agrees. It turns out to be a fatal decision, however; the other officers see the change of mind as an instance of Barrow's weakness when faced with Jock. Realizing that he will never have their respect and that his command of the regiment is, therefore, impossible, he shoots himself. Jock is filled with remorse; he summons the other officers, upbraids them for "murdering" Barrow and tells them of his plans for a special funeral. As he expands on his ideas for the ceremony, the other officers realize that Jock's mind is beginning to go under the strain of recent events. Quietly, they escort him home.

Although it is difficult to see how else screenwriter James Kennaway and director Ronald Neame could have ended *Tunes of Glory*, the final scenes nevertheless register as a miscalculation, tipping the film into melodrama as imaginary bagpipes begin to swirl in Jock's head. Up to that point Kennaway's script has followed a strikingly effective curve from high comedy (the first encounter between Barrow and the regiment) through mounting hysteria (the dance; Jock striking Fraser in the pub) to tragedy (Barrow's suicide). Indeed, at almost every level the movie is an exemplary piece of smooth, professional crafting. Kennaway's screenplay is admirably constructed and acutely written. He has established a shifting framework of conflict with Jock and Barrow at opposite ends of the spectrum, and Charlie Scott and Jimmy Cairns (Gordon Jackson) mediating between them, the latter honestly, the former dishonestly. In terms of social class—an essential element in British postwar cinema which frequently renders it puzzling to outsiders—the screenplay is equally carefully constructed, with Jock's behavior distasteful to Barrow for other than military reasons, and Jock frankly contemptuous of a man whom he believes has only got to where he is because of his birth. The class conflict is neatly—perhaps too neatly—echoed in Morag's affair with Fraser, which reverses the situation for Jock: an officer's daughter with an enlisted man.

The art direction is exceptionally fine, with the castle dominating the snow-covered town. The interiors of the Officers' Mess are heavy and colorful with paneling, trophies, and, above all, tradition. *Tunes of Glory* has an unmistakable Scottish mood to it, obviously helped by the sound of the pipes, but contained too in the way in which such sounds hang in the cold air, as in the credit sequence when Morag approaches the castle, or the more important one as Barrow draws up outside to the sound of Jock's "farewell" party taking place inside. Above all, however, *Tunes of Glory* is memorable for its performances—not only the principals but also the whole range of Scottish character actors (above all Jackson and the inevitable Duncan Macrae as the Pipe Major) who give life to what could so easily have been a schematic screenplay. Under Neame's skillful and restrained direction, Mills and Guinness carry the film, the former with the less rewarding part bringing a real sense of history to Barrow's tormented calmness, the latter bristling beneath a slightly improbable red crew cut which, one critic remarked, made him look like Stan Laurel. Guinness gives a skillful though perhaps slightly technical performance; it is difficult to believe that he had much feeling for Jock or, ultimately, much belief in the character. He got the better reviews, but it was Mills who won the Volpi prize at the Venice Film Festival, which, ironically, Guinness had won the previous year for his part in *The Horse's Mouth*.

Made with some initial opposition from the British War Office (as it was still called in those days), *Tunes of Glory* was warmly, although not rapturously, received in Britain, since many critics had their doubts about the concluding suicide and madness. In New York it was welcomed with a great deal more enthusiasm and broke records in its first week at the Little Carnegie Theater on 57th Street. Since then, it has tended to merge back into the formula from which it emerged and to be remembered as an actor's showcase or as one of those rare films which treat Scotland as something other than a music-hall joke. It deserves better. Coming as it did just as the French "New Wave" broke across the world's cinema screens, *Tunes of Glory* is Old Wave at its finest.

Nick Roddick

TWO FOR THE ROAD

Released: 1967
Production: Stanley Donen for Twentieth Century-Fox
Direction: Stanley Donen
Screenplay: Frederic Raphael
Cinematography: Christopher Challis
Editing: Richard Marden
Running time: 112 minutes

Principal characters:
Mark Wallace	Albert Finney
Joanna Wallace	Audrey Hepburn
Howard Manchester	William Daniels
Kathy Manchester	Eleanor Brown
Maurice Dalbret	Claude Dauphin
Jackie	Jacqueline Bisset
Ruth Manch	Gabrielle Middleton
David	Georges Descrieres

Two for the Road is a glib tour of marriage, a cinematic and literal trip through the representative joys and crises of coupling. Like all quick tours, however, it provides quick delights and a desire for longer stays. It is evocative rather than provocative, and therein lies its strengths and weaknesses. While not an original story, perhaps, *Two for the Road* is an original and clever handling of an old story. Tidy and effective, it is the saga of courtship and marriage, this time the marriage of Mark (Albert Finney), and Joanna Wallace (Audrey Hepburn). He is a "just arrived" successful thirty-five-year-old British architect, and she is his glibly humorous, long-suffering—but not quietly so—wife. We follow them through their intensely romantic courtship, their still tactile first year of marriage, the joys and frictions emanating from the birth of their daughter, and finally to the actions and infidelities which raise major questions about the future of their marriage.

The evolution of their relationship is captured in a series of vignettes juggled back and forth in time, punctuating this twentieth century marriage. Their first meeting is a case in point. Mark is a vagabond architectural student hitchhiking through France compiling a photographic collection of significant Gallic buildings. His first night's lodging finds him in the company of six female British singers on tour through France. Mark, playing the *roué*, proves to be as interested in female forms as he is in architectural ones. He makes a play for the most voluptuous member, Jackie (Jacqueline Bissett), only to be thwarted when she and four of the other girls contract chicken pox. Conveniently, Joanna is immune, so she and Mark head toward southern France. Mark, contemptuous of his apparently unprofessional colleague, patronizingly professes interest only in buildings, yet within three days he is in love. Their love is simple and uncomplicatedly romantic, as idyllic as their hitchhiking mode of travel; and, like hitchhikers everywhere, they effuse optimism.

The second detailed vignette focuses on the couple's first car, an old MG in which they are again touring France. Vacationing after one year of marriage, they still radiate the romantic spirit of their earlier meeting. Yet what promises to be a carefree journey is dashed when the car catches fire in the merriest misfortune of the film. The ruined car also proves to be symbolic of a major change in their relationship: Joanna is pregnant. Later, we see the family driving a fender-dented, four-door Ford, again on an excursion, but now squabbling over baby bottles, his long working hours, their infidelities—his several, her one—and topics suggesting significant troubles in their marriage.

Finally, in the final stop on this marriage tour, he is a professional success. This time they travel in an expensive Mercedes en route to a major reception celebrating completion of one of his projects. Now, like two veterans briefly home from the front, their idealistic expectation tempered by their past, Mark and Joanna reflect a realistic understanding of marriage behavior, an understanding tempered with affection for each other.

Both Finney and Hepburn are convincing and engaging as Mark and Joanna. Mark is success-oriented. Hard-working, he views the world as a series of objects awaiting manipulation. His overconfidence, bordering on *hubris*, would make him intolerable if it were not mitigated by both his intentional and unintentional humor, his forgetfulness, and a kind of pudgy, teddy-bear physique. Joanna has a wit equal to Mark's, but is attracted by people rather than objects. Her lean beauty augments her quick gaminery and suggests toughness rather than frailty. Hepburn is no shrinking violet and is a match for Finney.

As satisfying and engaging as Finney and Hepburn are, the success of their characters rests largely with the script. Scriptwriter Frederic Raphael, author of *Darling* (1965), provisions these travelers with an endless stream of gosh-why-didn't-I-think-of-that lines. Raphael's writing is as lean and spare as the plot and his heroine's physique. There are no wasted lines here; it is a script both funny and loaded with accurate if not profound observations about marriage.

Raphael's script also provides a conceptual device which makes the film both unusual and captivating. Rather than chronicling this marriage in a standard narrative fashion, Raphael employs a flashback technique which becomes especially intriguing in this film. There are both flashbacks-within-flashbacks as well as flashforwards, all within the past. Moving through this complicated series of time changes, Raphael is at his literary finest since the spoken words and the photographic device of the highway provide the transition between one time sequence and another. This is an intriguing technique, showing the triumph of the scriptwriter, the cinematographer, and the film editor, one which gives the film its most distinguishing feature.

The subject of the film's humor, marriage, is worth comment. The film describes a marriage without evaluating or judging it. Precisely because the film is descriptive rather than analytical, it misses the real emotional pain involved in all marriages. In place of pain we have irony, and while irony is surely an indicator of a fire below, it is not the fire itself. It serves here as insulation from tragedy, not the tragedy itself. True, there are some bracing moments—Joanna takes a lover and, convincingly professing to love him, briefly leaves Mark—but while ripe for dissection, her affair proves to be little more than a pleasant wrong turn into a lovely *cul-de-sac*. Compared with the powerfully painful postmortem dissection of marriage in Ingmar Bergman's *Scenes from a Marriage* (1973), or even Woody Allen's deceptively poignant story of an affair in *Annie Hall* (1977), the message of *Two for the Road* is spare by comparison. Still, the purpose of the film, like detour signs, is to notify, not analyze. Meant to be read from the fast lanes of marriage, *Two for the Road* is a well-constructed, entertaining tour of marriage.

John G. Tomlinson, Jr.

TWO-LANE BLACKTOP

Released: 1971
Production: Michael S. Laughlin for Universal
Direction: Monte Hellman
Screenplay: Rudolph Wurlitzer and Will Corry; based on an original story by Will Corry
Cinematography: Jack Deerson
Editing: Monte Hellman
Sound: Charles Knight
Running time: 102 minutes

> *Principal characters:*
> The Driver .... James Taylor
> G.T.O. .... Warren Oates
> The Girl .... Laurie Bird
> The Mechanic .... Dennis Wilson

Director Monte Hellman has to date made only eight films in twenty years. As a protégé of Roger Corman, he made his debut in 1959 with a low-budget horror film, *Beast from Haunted Cave*, and subsequently, he made two films back to back in the Philippines in 1964, *Back Door to Hell* and *Flight to Fury*, both involving young actor-writer Jack Nicholson. Although meritorious, these works went unnoticed, but in 1965, Hellman once again directed two films back to back with the participation of Nicholson, and the resulting Westerns, *The Shooting* and *Ride in the Whirlwind*, although never properly distributed, were shown at film festivals to great acclaim. Severe and demanding, the two films are also extremely rewarding, representing one of the few valid stylistic advances for the genre since the 1950's. *The Shooting* introduced Warren Oates as something of a talisman—he has appeared in each of the director's subsequent films—and this exceptionally gifted actor has done his finest work for Hellman, notably in *Two-Lane Blacktop* and the sadly neglected *Cockfighter* (1974). Hellman's latest film is another Western, *China 9, Liberty 37* (1978), which has encountered difficulty in obtaining an American distributor—not surprisingly, as it is the *only* Western of the 1970's to demonstrate what the genre would be like had it continued to develop along traditional lines rather than being subverted by revisionism.

Clearly, Hellman's films are almost laughably obscure when compared to those of many of his contemporaries. Although he has had the opportunity to complete relatively few of the many projects with which he has been involved over the years, and although his realized films have been made on low budgets and have been badly distributed, his work has drawn sufficient attention to earn him a passionate critical following. Hellman deserves this esteem, as he represents values generally absent in contemporary American films. His work tends to be quiet and deliberate, characterized by stable compositions, a minimum of dialogue, great visual fluidity in staging and economy of camera movement, clear and careful cinematography, and rhythmic but unobtrusive editing. He gravitates to a cinema based on traditional narrative forms, which he transforms rather than ridicules through a creative process involving a conscious grasp of modern philosophical thought. Hellman's characters, consistently fascinating and brought expressively to life by an interesting group of players, tend to action rather than reflection. This dramatizes the existential nature of their journeys more movingly than would be the case if Hellman permitted himself to portray them with the passivity of an intellectual. Although he demonstrates an acute sensitivity to the present world, he may ultimately be regarded as the last classicist of the American cinema.

A modern character who remains expressive of the action ethos must be delineated according to new precepts. Hellman recognizes this and deals with it in a number of ways in *Two-Lane Blacktop*. The taciturnity of the traditional hero is reduced to virtual inscrutability. The severity with which emotion is suppressed by the driver (James Taylor) and the mechanic (Dennis Wilson) may be measured by their inability or unwillingness to speak of anything other than cars and car-related matters. Game-playing is another symptom of this willful denial of an integrated self. The driver and the mechanic define their lives by seeking out one drag race after another, and G.T.O. (Warren Oates) copes with existence by assuming a new personality and fabricating a story to go with it every time he meets someone. These patterns of behavior should be susceptible to disruption by the catalytic presence of the female, and *Two-Lane Blacktop* does present this possibility. Thrust into the role of *femme fatale*, however, is a teenage girl (Laurie Bird) who is as rootless as the male characters and no less mystifying. Finally, these characters are never identified by name. This does not mean that they are abstract, but rather that they have been stripped down to essentials. Reinvented from existing prototypes, they are deprived only of detail which would destroy their purity.

This purity is also evident in the narrative, which presents a journey with an illusory destination. The driver and the mechanic are heading east in their custom-built Gray 1955 Chevy when the girl climbs into the back seat while they are having lunch in a diner. They drive on, taking no notice of her. Because they have little money, they need to set up a race, and to this end, they venture forth in Santa Fe. The Chevy wins, and the driver goes out for a quiet drink by himself. Returning to the motel, he hears sounds of lovemaking from inside the room, and realizing that the mechanic and the girl are in bed together, he waits outside. That incident seems to have no effect on either of the partners, but it begins to become evident that the girl has an even greater interest in the driver. At the same time, she gives the impression that she would go to bed with almost anyone, not out of any passionate inclination but because that is what she does, just as her companions are defined by driving and tuning up their car.

Also driving east is G.T.O., so named in the credits for his late model orange Pontiac G.T.O. He is not a drag racer, nor does he appear to be going to any particular place. A friendly and extroverted man approaching middle age, he picks up hitchhikers indiscriminately, plays them tapes of music he guesses will be to their taste, and attempts to regale them with stories of his colorful life. He might say that he had to get out of the straitjacket of middle-class life and answer the call of the open road for a few months, or that he won the Pontiac in a crap game in Las Vegas. Some of his passengers are totally unmoved by his stories, and at other times, his sociability is misconstrued. He picks up an old lady and her granddaughter who are going to a cemetery, but although he is quick to point out that he is heading for Florida to get a house ready for his mother, the old lady can only point out that it was a "city car" like his which killed her child. On another occasion, a homosexual hitchhiker (it is easy to miss Harry Dean Stanton in this bit part as his face is barely glimpsed) makes advances. "I'm not into that," G.T.O. responds brusquely. "I've got no time for side tracks."

What he does have time for is an unusual bet with the driver and mechanic: his car against theirs. The pink slips will be mailed to the Washington D.C., post office, and whoever arrives first is the winner. G.T.O. is susceptible to the challenge partly because of the goading of the two younger men, but more crucially because he is drawn to the girl who, during the first meeting of the quartet, is just seductive enough to encourage him. The greater part of the film finds the four characters interacting as they travel across the country. The bet is almost forgotten as the driver and the mechanic fix G.T.O.'s car when it is on the verge of breaking down. He in turn saves them from being beaten up by some local toughs who have taken them for hippies, the one time when his smoothness in fabricating a story is fortuitous. The four alternate riding together, and at one point, when the driver and G.T.O. are in the Chevy, G.T.O. tells the other what may or may not be the truth about himself—that his wife left him and he lost his job and went to pieces— but the driver is quick to cut him off, declaring that he has no interest in anyone's problems. The driver and the girl finally have a brief romantic liaison, but it does not appear to change his attitude toward her. At a drag race, she gets into G.T.O.'s car and the two drive away, with G.T.O. spinning plans for them as they speed through the night, talking to her even while she sleeps. The next morning, the driver provokes a subtle note of disharmony between himself and the mechanic as a result of the unexpected obsessiveness with which he follows G.T.O. and the girl. Finding them at a diner, he makes a proposal to the girl, telling her that they can drive to Ohio and buy some parts for the car. She coldly turns him down and goes off with a motorcyclist. G.T.O. continues on his undirected way, and the driver and mechanic are soon engaged in another drag race.

As loyal to the "game" principle as its characters, the film keeps things as they were initially. The four characters retain their limited identities and remain true to their individual styles of behavior. There are several emotional climaxes but they are oblique and understated. How deeply they affect the characters is a matter of conjecture. G.T.O. tells the girl, unaware that she has fallen asleep, that he is "crazy" about her and admits that "if I'm not grounded soon, I'm going to go off into orbit." The mechanic, who has spotted G.T.O.'s car at the diner, does not tell the driver this until they have traveled another mile and does so with a strange expression of pain. The driver, asking the girl to ride with him again, is no more articulate about his feelings than usual, but his pathetic words are more heartfelt than one would have ever expected from him. Just before the final drag race, the driver looks out the window of the car and sees a peaceful farm, glimpsing there the distant figures of family members living a settled life. His expression is momentarily rueful, but he immediately closes the window, shutting out both sound and image of the farm. As he puts the car in gear and begins to move forward, there is a simulation of the film catching in the projector and burning. That is the final image, implying that the work can stop but not end. The emotional progression in the film's structure is at once real and transparent.

One might ask if this means that the lives of these characters are meaningless. Their individual capacities for relating to other human beings in a directly emotional way are pathetic in each case. It is perhaps from knowledge of this that they find other ways to live. The girl is practiced in impersonally offering her body. G.T.O. is adept at articulating fantasies. The driver and the mechanic are chillingly professional in the art of drag-racing. The emptiness of their respective existences is shut out by these endlessly repeated affirmations of the poise with which they "ride in the whirlwind." Their actions are at once absurd and not absurd, ignoble and noble, cowardly and brave. Life so deliberately reduced to the gestural is a void which the undaunted characters enter with grim speed.

Hellman spent considerable time preparing *Two-Lane Blacktop*, a project which shifted from one studio to another before it was finally made. At Hellman's insistence, novelist Rudolph Wurlitzer completely rewrote the original screenplay by Will Corry, eloquently transforming a "road" picture influenced by the success of *Easy Rider* (1969) into a serious work no longer bound by an allegiance to fashion. The film was shot entirely on location and is dominated by the realistic intimacy of the extraordinary shots photographed inside the two cars, but Hellman and Gregory Sandor (the latter, contrary to the credits, being solely responsible for the cinematography) have achieved a plasticity of color and texture which gives the locations the artificial expressiveness of studio sets. There is no nervous camerawork, either inside or outside the cars. An appropriately oblique presentation prevails, but the compositions are lucid and calm. Hellman has edited these images almost musically, so that the movements of the gray car and the orange car and the alternations of shots involving the characters have a relentless tension and release quality.

Of the four leading players, only Warren Oates is a professional actor. The others were cast partly for limitations which would correspond to the characters they portray. Laurie Bird incarnates the girl as pretty, graceless, and sullen. It may be precisely this combination of qualities which makes her strangely charismatic. Hellman's heroines have generally tended to be cold and remorseless, especially the one played by Millie Perkins in *The Shooting*, but this does not necessarily make him a misogynist. On the contrary, the Laurie Bird character in *Two-Lane Blacktop*, without being at all sentimentalized, metaphorically embodies the romanticism which Hellman, like his male characters, wishes to keep at a distance. Rock musicians James Taylor and Dennis Wilson are encouraged to give performances similar to those demanded by French director Robert Bresson. No striving for dramatic expressiveness is permitted. Taylor is somewhat uncomfortable delivering dialogue, but his physical attributes are exactly right. Wilson, on the other hand, is perfect. If it is impossible to separate him from the character he portrays, this may reflect his experience with the Beach Boys, a group whose songs—composed by his brother Brian—express in a sunnier mood a philosophy which has striking affinities with that of the film.

The conception of these three roles places extraordinary demands on the actor playing the only colorful character. A certain amount of overplaying might be expected, but there is *none*. Oates immerses himself in G.T.O.'s stories so thoroughly that he himself seems to be musing over actual occurrences. He always speaks clearly but not loudly. G.T.O.'s grinning bravado seems barely to conceal loneliness and despair, and Oates masterfully projects the mixed undercurrents of pathos, uncertainty, and genuine good will in each character's words and physical expressions. Most critics who know the film agree that Oates's performance was one of those most deserving of an Academy Award. Unfortunately, the film was so little seen at the time of its release that Academy members were apparently unaware of Oates's remarkable work until it was too late. That has also been the fate of the film itself. It is spoken of as having a cult following, but this has been true of a number of American classics before they were rediscovered by a wider audience and universally acclaimed. With justice, *Two-Lane Blacktop* will ultimately be considered one of the key artistic statements of the 1970's.

Blake Lucas

THE UGLY AMERICAN

Released: 1962
Production: George Englund for Universal
Direction: George Englund
Screenplay: Stewart Stern; based on the novel of the same name by William J. Lederer and Eugene Burdick
Cinematography: Clifford Stine
Editing: Ted Kent
Running time: 120 minutes

Principal characters:
Harrison Carter MacWhite .... Marlon Brando
Deong .... Eiji Okada
Marion MacWhite .... Sandra Church
Homer Atkins .... Pat Hingle
Emma Atkins .... Jocelyn Brando
Grainger .... Arthur Hill
Bing .... Judson Pratt
Senator Brenner .... Judson Laire
Munsang .... George Shibata

The Ugly American focuses on a personal relationship between two men which mirrors the relationship between their respective countries. The men are Harrison Carter MacWhite (Marlon Brando), an American diplomat, and Deong (Eiji Okada), a Sarkhanese who had participated with MacWhite in guerrilla warfare against the Japanese during World War II. The countries are the United States, still in the throes of the Cold War, and Sarkhan, an emerging Southeast Asian state. The film depicts events almost twenty years after MacWhite and Deong had fought together. Now they are positioned as potential adversaries, with MacWhite as the new American ambassador to Sarkhan and Deong as the leader of Sarkhanese nationalists.

Set in the late 1950's or early 1960's, the atmosphere of the film is definitely that of the Cold War. When MacWhite faces the Senate committee which reviews his appointment as ambassador to Sarkhan, the major concern is his relationship with Deong. Senator Brenner (Judson Laire), MacWhite's most aggressive questioner, hammers away at Deong's nationalist views, which the senator equates with Communism. He perceives that anyone who is not totally committed to the American way, even if that person is not an American himself, must be regarded as the enemy. MacWhite therefore must explain his World War II association with Deong and the development of their relationship during the ensuing years. He must also account for Deong's opposition to the pro-American regime now ruling Sarkhan.

Meanwhile, there is indeed strong anti-American feeling in Sarkhan, and the catalyst for that feeling is Freedom Road, ostensibly built by the Americans to improve the country's economy. The Sarkhanese, however, view the road as a manifestation of American imperialism and regard it as a bribe by the Americans to keep them in the American camp in the Cold War. The Sarkhanese feel trapped, their desire for independence threatened by both American imperialism and pressure from the Communist government of neighboring North Sarkhan. Hostility against the Americans erupts when MacWhite arrives to assume his new diplomatic responsibilities. He is greeted at the airport by a rioting mob who almost cause physical injury to him and his wife Marion (Sandra Church). Although the mob may have been partially aroused by Deong's nationalistic slogans of "Sarkhan for the Sarkhanese," MacWhite realizes that his friend is not responsible for the violence. In fact, he wisely recognizes that members of the embassy staff, especially Grainger (Arthur Hill) and Bing (Judson Pratt), must share part of the blame for not foreseeing possible trouble.

Despite their adversary situation, MacWhite assumes that he and Deong will remain friends. He spends his first evening in Sarkhan with Deong, but the mellow atmosphere degenerates into a bitter argument. The American ambassador overreacts to Deong's nationalistic stance, contending that such sentiments are pro-Communist and anti-American. The two men part in hostility, and MacWhite's misunderstanding of Deong's position forces the Sarkhanese leader to seek support elsewhere. That support comes from Munsang (George Shibata), the leader of the Sarkhanese Communists, who dupes Deong into an alliance with North Sarkhanese military forces. Violence erupts at the dedication ceremony for Freedom Road, attended by MacWhite and the leaders of the pro-American Sarkhanese government. Civil war follows, and the nationalist insurgents allow themselves to be manipulated by the Communists, primarily because the Americans failed to recognize their genuine desire for independence.

Although *The Ugly American* indicts American foreign policy for forcing emerging nations into either-or choices which sometimes result in their accepting Communist intervention in their affairs, some positive aspects of America's involvement in Sarkhan are present in the film. Essentially the film suggests that understanding between the two countries is more plausible on a personal than an institutional level. For example, MacWhite continues to believe in Deong, and when he learns that the Communists intend to assassinate Deong, he risks his life to warn his friend. Although he arrives with the warning too late, Deong's death convinces MacWhite that sincere nationalists need not be pro-American or pro-Communist. In a press conference, he acknowledges his responsibility for the events that have transpired and points out how difficult achieving understanding between nations is when even two individuals who have long been friends cannot maintain a smooth relationship. Ironically, the film ends as MacWhite's remarks are broadcast into an American living

The Ugly American

room and an apathetic viewer switches off the television set.

Another positive aspect in the film's treatment of American foreign policy is the activity of Homer (Pat Hingle) and Emma Atkins (Jocelyn Brando, Marlon's sister). He is an engineer involved in the construction of Freedom Road, but additionally the couple have established a clinic to care for the medical needs of the Sarkhanese peasants. They recognize more clearly than the embassy officials what the people of Sarkhan really need to strengthen their nation, and as a result they have established true rapport with them.

Critical reaction to *The Ugly American* was largely negative, with most reviewers claiming that the film blunted the criticism of American foreign policy in the original novel by Lederer and Burdick. Given the episodic nature of that book and the vestiges of Cold War thinking still lingering in Hollywood when the film was made, however, *The Ugly American* seems fairly perceptive in its treatment of American relationships abroad. For the viewer today, the film's major interest lies in its parallels with events that led to American involvement in Vietnam. It is tempting to consider that the same kinds of errors made by the film's Americans might have been made by the nation's actual leaders and resulted in the tragic consequences of war. This element of hindsight in a post-Vietnam War society lends the film an aura of timelessness and arouses in the viewer an awareness of the need to further our understanding of all peoples.

Frances M. Malpezzi
William M. Clements

ULYSSES

Released: 1967
Production: Walter Reade, Jr., and Joseph Strick for Continental
Direction: Joseph Strick
Screenplay: Joseph Strick and Fred Haines; based on the novel of the same name by James Joyce
Cinematography: Wolfgang Suschitsky
Editing: Reginald Mills
Running time: 132 minutes

Principal characters:
Molly Bloom .... Barbara Jefford
Leopold Bloom .... Milo O'Shea
Stephen Dedalus .... Maurice Roeves
Buck Mulligan .... T. P. McKenna
Simon Dedalus .... Martin Dempsey

The movement of the myth of Ulysses from oral tradition to written epic to twentieth century novel and eventually to film seems natural and unavoidable, and director Joseph Strick's 1967 film version is a succinct and beautiful commingling of all of these literary traditions. An understanding of the literary roots of the film is essential to appreciate what Strick has accomplished. Although there are some literary and film critics who claim that a work of art in any form must stand on its own before it can be judged in the context of all other contributing art forms, in this case, those objections must be dismissed. In his film *Ulysses*, Strick's fabric is the oral and literary traditions behind James Joyce's novel as well as that author's monumental work. To focus solely on the story and its execution within the film is to ignore far too much of what this producer-writer-director has brought before his audience.

The oral tradition and written epic upon which Joyce's book was based are familiar to nearly all readers since the story and themes have been repeated innumerable times throughout all of literature. Ulysses, having spent many long and hard years fighting in and leading other men in the Trojan wars, undergoes countless hardships in his efforts to return to his Greek homeland. Once he is home, he learns that his house is overrun by a large number of suitors who hope to win his wife and wealth in his stead. His wife, Penelope, meanwhile, has told the suitors that she will choose one of them to be her new husband once she finishes weaving a tapestry on which she works all day long. Then, each night when the suitors have all retired, she unravels what she has woven to prolong her waiting period for Ulysses yet another day. Likewise, Penelope's and Ulysses' son, Telemachus, defends his father's memory by refusing to believe that his father has been killed and by attempting to defend his father's house against the greedy suitors.

In 1922, Joyce reworked this familiar tale into a modern-day epic centered upon Irishman Leopold Bloom (played by Milo O'Shea in the film). Bloom is not an extraordinary man, unlike his classical prototype, but he *is* a hero. The hero of the twentieth century is the ordinary man who manages to survive in the face of all the complexities of modern industrial society. Bloom's Penelope is his wife, Molly (played by Barbara Jefford in the film). Molly is a singer and is involved in a longstanding affair with another musician, demonstrating little concern as to whether Bloom is aware of her actions. Bloom and Molly have no son—at least no biological son. Instead, the correlation with the classical epic is completed by Bloom's meeting with young Stephen Dedalus (Maurice Roeves).

Stephen appears twice in the body of Joyce's literary works, once in *Ulysses*, and again when he is the titular hero of *Portrait of the Artist as a Young Man*. An examination of Joyce's notes and letters soon shows that Stephen is fashioned after Joyce in his younger days. He is contemplative, isolated, and without any true models whom he can respect as intellectually and spiritually valid. Although the father-son relationship is never stated overtly, and this is even more true in Strick's film, the bonding is made explicit in actions, particularly when the two are drawn together emotionally while in the company of a number of men, one of whom has just become a father, and who loudly, drunkenly, and jovially expound upon the state of fatherhood.

It is made clear in both Joyce's epic and Strick's film that from Bloom's point of view, his external life is intolerable. He is a Jew living in Ireland in socially intolerant times. His work, although it gives him some definition, is not totally satisfying, and he is too weak to confront his wife with his knowledge of her cuckolding of him. In the face of all this, Bloom has no choice, given his character and the forces confronting him, but to retreat to the purely internal life; and Strick's film is masterful in defining this internal life.

Strick's film may be the most successful blending not only of various artistic genres, but also of the internal and external lives of a character ever to be accomplished in film. What affords the director such great success is the use of a camera that is freed from its usual and traditional role. His is a camera that is willing to be indiscriminate in its recording of the external world versus the internal world. Normally, a camera films solely the external world, and the closest it comes to the internal world is recording the characters' responses to their physical and emotional surroundings. In Bloom's case, the external world has been shown to be intolerable, but the camera will not be satisfied with that. Instead, it reacts in a human way: it retreats to the internal world and superimposes what it finds there onto its impressions of the external world. In this sense, Strick has made the camera more "human" than ever before, and it is doubtful that it has been as human since then.

There are two examples of this use of the human camera. One of the more moving scenes in both Joyce's book and Strick's film concerns Stephen as he walks along the beach. Pondering the thoughts and images that have been bombarding him of late, he gives a soliloquy that affords the audience insight into his private world in a way impossible through any other means. To complete the audience's involvement in Stephen's private thoughts, we hear him say, "Shut your eyes and see. . . ." At this point, we are suddenly faced with only darkness, our eyes have been shut for us, and we are then liberated to experience Stephen's mental wanderings with him.

Another example of the human camera can be found toward the beginning of Bloom's day as he walks along the streets of Dublin. A journalist at heart, he tends to see the world through the eyes of a journalist, and because the camera is now Bloom's, we see the world from his perspective as well. In a few moments reminiscent of Lawrence Sterne's *The Life and Opinions of Tristram Shandy, Gent., 1759-1767*, letters in typeface cross Bloom's mind. At this point, several men carrying sandwich boards over their shoulders march across the screen with the same letters printed one on each of the boards. The scene has not been interrupted. In fact, because it is a fusion of the internal and external worlds and for those few moments the internal world has come to the fore, the camera has taught us that neither one exists to the exclusion of the other. If they are not both aspects of the same reality, then they are at least indistinguishably concomitant.

Strick shows the audience through Jefford's performance as Molly during the closing scene of the film that it is the internal world that defines not only what is important in life but also the very essence of the totality of life. Lying in bed during a rare moment with her sexually frustrated husband, Molly's mind wanders from the immediate situation to examine her true and private responses to her relationship with him. Her thoughts, unembellished by romantic explications, either verbal or visual, come to us clearly. "Yes," she states over and over again, perhaps at first tentatively. This is not the happy ending of a romantic or tragic tale. Instead, it is the only positive ending to any situation that is humanly possible. In the face of all the contorted situations imposed on the individual by human relationships and by an outside world that is both independent and indifferent, Molly's words give affirmation that both she and Bloom, modern-day heroes of the contemporary drama of life, and all the rest of us, are alive.

Bonnie Fraser

UNFAITHFULLY YOURS

Released: 1948
Production: Preston Sturges for Twentieth Century-Fox
Direction: Preston Sturges
Screenplay: Preston Sturges
Cinematography: Victor Milner
Editing: Robert Fritch
Running time: 105 minutes

> *Principal characters:*
> Sir Alfred De Carter .... Rex Harrison
> Daphne De Carter .... Linda Darnell
> Barbara .... Barbara Lawrence
> August .... Rudy Vallee
> Tony .... Kurt Kreuger
> Hugo .... Lionel Stander

Unfaithfully Yours is Preston Sturges' most sophisticated and complex creation. With this film he hit upon the perfect balance and sense of proportion among music, dialogue, and visuals. From the first frame to the last, each of these elements serves to complement the others. The premise of the film is based, simply enough, on the theme of discovery, or at least apparent discovery. Sir Alfred De Carter (Rex Harrison), a noted symphony conductor, comes to believe that his wife Daphne (Linda Darnell) has been unfaithful to him with a young "Adonis" named Tony (Kurt Kreuger). As the time for a concert arrives, Sir Alfred's suspicions have solidified. This night he is to conduct three pieces, Rossini's fiery "Semiramide Overture," Wagner's "Pilgrims' Chorus," and Tchaikovsky's "Francesca da Rimini," in that order. With jealousy and distrust coloring his every thought, Sir Alfred begins the concert. As he raises his baton, the camera tracks past the musicians into his somber face, and then into an astounding extra-close shot of his eyes. The audience has entered into his imagination, his unconscious. In the scenes which follow the viewer sees, through Sir Alfred's mind's eye, the intricate plan and execution of Lady De Carter's murder.

It is a brilliant if somewhat overly complex plan. In his mind, Sir Alfred and Daphne are returning from the concert. Slyly Sir Alfred suggests to his wife that she go out dancing this evening, possibly with Tony. After a bit of hesitation, she agrees. While she is dressing, Sir Alfred takes a bulky recorder from its resting place and carries it to another room. There he makes a recording of his voice, at a higher speed, as he screams, "Help, help, help. Stop, Tony, stop." The result is the sound of a woman's voice. He then puts the record in its place and returns to sharpening his razor. Having finished this chore, he enters his wife's room and, a razor in hand, slashes her to death, gleefully. As he leaves the room, he places a nightstand and phone behind the bedroom door. When Tony arrives Sir Alfred asks him to test the sharpness of his razor (which he has, of course, carefully cleaned)—thereby obtaining Tony's prints on the murder weapon. As Sir Alfred leaves, he informs Tony that his wife will be out presently. Downstairs he establishes his alibi by asking the operator to ring his wife. By this time the record Alfred cut has fallen into place on the turntable and Tony has rushed into the bedroom, knocking over the phone and nightstand in the process. He is aghast at the sight of Daphne's body; the operator hears "Daphne's" cries, and Alfred's revenge is completed. The camera now withdraws from his feverish imagination to a shot of Sir Alfred conducting Rossini's febrile finale.

The second daydream sequence is played to the heavily teutonic chords of Wagner's "Pilgrims' Chorus." The camera once again moves into Sir Alfred's mind's eye and the set of his apartment. He has now decided, magnanimously, to forgive his wife's transgressions. As in the train sequence in *The Lady Eve* (1941), this Wagner piece, with its solemnity and penitential mood, serves to underscore humorously the martyr image Alfred is trying to put across to Daphne and, in so doing, render the martyr ridiculous.

The third and final daydream, again precipitated by the camera's movement, shows all three parties to the love triangle returning from the concert. To Tchaikovsky's explosive and stormy music, Sir Alfred confronts this modern version of the famous medieval Italian lovers Francesca and Paolo. In a moment of reckless bravura he challenges Tony to a game of Russian roulette. Tony balks, but the outraged husband does not. He spins the cartridge and places the gun to his head. As he fires, the kettle drums resound in the background and, with Sir Alfred's "suicide," the music reaches a crescendo. The camera tracks back from the conductor as he rushes out to realize his revenge in, presumably, one of three ways.

In the scenes which follow, Sturges presents Sir Alfred's comic and frustrated attempts to realize his fantasies. He returns to his apartment as it is in the first daydream. There he is greeted by the sound of his music box, which plays "Jingle Bells," minus the final notes. Convinced he can execute the design of his first daydream, Sir Alfred proceeds with the schemes. Like the music box, however, which leaves us "hanging up" just at a climactic musical moment, all of his attempts result in comic anticlimaxes. The result is a series of catastrophes. He crashes through the seats of two straw chairs as he stands on them to reach the recorder, he accidentally heaves the recorder out the window, he cuts his finger on the razor, and he finally ends up making a shambles of his apartment.

Having failed miserably at executing his first scheme, he now confronts his wife and, with much pomposity and self-righteousness, forgives her. He sits down to write her a large check, as he had done in his second fantasy, only to be frustrated by a leaky pen. Finally he resorts to the third and final alternative left him. He is again baffled, this time by a verbal misunderstanding and a gun which becomes tangled in wire. He finally resigns himself to his absurd fate. Sensing his distress, however, Daphne reveals the supposedly innocuous circumstances under which she had visited Tony's room and on which his brother-in-law August (Rudy Vallee) had reported. In immediate relief and belief Sir Alfred embraces his wife, and, in a wonderfully intimate two-shot, he delivers this tribute to a woman he believes to be faithfully his: "A thousand poets dreamed a thousand years and you were born, my love." Like many of the other characters in Sturges' films, Sir Alfred has accepted reassuring appearances rather than risk a deeper and possibly more unsettling exploration of reality.

One of the most perplexing elements of this film is its central ambiguity. As the title suggests, the subject concerns a woman suspected of infidelity. Early in the film, Sir Alfred describes two films he has just seen. He says, "I saw a very long picture about a dog, the moral of which was that a dog is a man's best friend, and a companion feature which questioned the necessity of marriage for eight reels and then concluded it was essential in the ninth." In an exaggerated manner the second film Sturges refers to is his own. Sturges, even if he had desired it, could not realistically, particularly in terms of commercial acceptability, have had the film end with the discovery of Daphne's infidelity. He did, however, manage to plant a number of doubts in the mind of the viewer about her sincerity. There is the sarcastic comment her sister Barbara (Barbara Lawrence) makes about Daphne's oft-stated concern and love for Alfred, "If she wasn't my own sister, I'd have a name for her that'd make. . . ." There is also the extreme solicitousness, innocence, and sentimentality inherent in Daphne's character. Her fawning and sentimentality have no precedence in Sturges' female characters. Consequently she strikes one as being slightly off, possibly false. Could the Daphne of Sir Alfred's imagination be closer to the truth? It is a subtle ambiguity which is never resolved and with which the viewer is left to grapple.

The acting in *Unfaithfully Yours* is dominated by the personality of one character rather than by the ensemble as is common in most of Sturges' films. Sir Alfred De Carter is in and vitally involved with almost every scene. Harrison, who plays De Carter, enthusiastically called his role "a better part than Hamlet." The rapid pace of the dialogue and the frequent changes of mood required a professionalism few actors could supply. Whether enunciating "What happy updraft wafts you hither?" or ripping the clothes off a nosy brother-in-law (both, incidentally, within the same scene), Harrison supplies the energy and ability prerequisite to the part.

James Ursini

THE UNFORGIVEN

Released: 1960
Production: James Hill for Hecht-Hill-Lancaster Productions; released by
United Artists
Direction: John Huston
Screenplay: Ben Maddow; based on the novel of the same name by Alan
LeMay
Cinematography: Franz Planer
Editing: Russell Lloyd
Music: Dmitri Tiomkin
Running time: 125 minutes

Principal characters:

Ben Zachary	Burt Lancaster
Rachel Zachary	Audrey Hepburn
Cash Zachary	Audie Murphy
Mattilda Zachary	Lillian Gish
Andy Zachary	Doug McClure
Zeb Rawlins	Charles Bickford
Abe Kelsey	Joseph Wiseman
Johnny Portugal	John Saxon
Georgia Rawlins	Kipp Hamilton
Charlie Rawlins	Albert Salmi
Lost Bird	Carlos Rivas

By 1960, John Huston was a veteran director. During the first part of his career, he produced such classics as *The Maltese Falcon* (1941), *The Treasure of the Sierra Madre* (1948), *The Asphalt Jungle* (1950), and *The African Queen* (1951). All were notable for their outstanding casts (many of which featured Humphrey Bogart) and great stories. By the late 1950's, however, Huston's career seemed to lose its edge. He continued to work, and his films continued to merit study, but many of them were undeniably flawed in one way or another. Occasionally this could be blamed on studio interference; more often, the failure was attributed to Huston himself.

The Unforgiven is one of these interesting but flawed films. It was Huston's first Western (unless one considers *The Treasure of the Sierra Madre* a Western; Warner Bros. promoted it as such), and critic Andrew Sarris has called it one of the most oddly structured Westerns in the history of the genre. The overall tone of the film is decidedly somber, yet Dmitri Tiomkin's score bubbles along the sound track like Richard Rodgers and Oscar Hammerstein's *Oklahoma*; and Kipp Hamilton's portrayal of Georgia Rawlins, one of the film's major secondary characters, is comical. Another important character, Johnny Portugal, disappears without a trace halfway through the film, while Abe Kelsey, the film's eerie nemesis figure, appears sporadically throughout the film, but his significance is not revealed until very late. Nevertheless, *The Unforgiven* has its virtues. A veteran cast headed by Burt Lancaster and Audrey Hepburn delivers several fine performances; and once Huston gets into the meat of his story—about halfway into the film—he tells it with a brooding intensity that is the mark of a genuine film talent.

The Unforgiven is set in the Texas panhandle, circa 1870, and concerns the rancorous relations between the white ranchers (two families in particular—the Zacharys and the Rawlinses) and the Kiowa Indians. By the film's end, the hatred that the whites have for the Indians will come to be centered on Rachel Zachary (Audrey Hepburn), who is—unbeknown to her and to every other character in the film except her mother Mattilda (Lillian Gish), her older brother Ben (Burt Lancaster), and the mysterious Abe Kelsey (Joseph Wiseman)—a full-blooded Kiowa. When the truth about her parentage is revealed, the corrosive hostility between the two races will (temporarily) divide even the Zachary family itself.

As the film opens, however, the Kiowas' depredations are a distant memory. The ranchers' primary problem seems to be romantic. Georgia (Kipp Hamilton), daughter of patriarch Zeb Rawlins (Charles Bickford), has eyes for Ben Zachary; and young Charlie Rawlins (Albert Salme) is bashfully courting Rachel Zachary. These scenes are played for a comic effect which seems oddly disjointed and uncomfortable in a film which is otherwise somber.

Always hovering in the background is the Zacharys' nemesis, Abe Kelsey, a crippled Civil War veteran who has, for reasons that will go unexplained throughout much of the film, decided to bedevil the Zachary clan. He shows up at odd times, often singing "The Battle Hymn of the Republic"; and the mere mention of his name, let alone his presence, is enough to drive Ben Zachary and his younger brother Cash (Audie Murphy) into a cold fury. They try repeatedly to kill him, but he always slips away.

Another theme that Huston develops during the first half of the film is the curiously erotic relationship between Ben and his adopted sister Rachel. She and everyone else know that she is adopted; few, however, are aware of her Indian blood. A stoical man in his thirties, Ben is clearly jealous of Rachel's beaus—he beats up a young Indian ranch hand for even daring to touch her—but he is also clearly disturbed by the quasi-incestuous nature of his feelings for the beautiful young woman. Rachel, however, harbors no such doubts, and tells Ben frankly that she prefers him to any of her other suitors. A zestful, open, and intelligent woman in her early twenties, Rachel is the most appealing character in the film.

Before this dramatic tension can be resolved, the Zacharys' situation is complicated by the arrival of three Kiowa Indians, one of whom, Lost Bird (Carlos Rivas), is Rachel's natural brother. Kelsey has told Lost Bird about Rachel, and the Kiowas have come to reclaim her. Although Ben denies Kelsey's story, the Kiowas are skeptical. Their initial overtures are peaceful, but they are nevertheless adamant: they want Rachel back. When Ben declines to surrender her, they leave, exacting vengeance by attacking the Rawlins household. Charlie Rawlins dies in the raid. Things begin to come to a head when the Zacharys arrive at the Rawlins ranch to pay their respects. Everything is out in the open now, and a shocked Rachel (who knew nothing of the discussion between Ben and Lost Bird) finds herself accused of being a Kiowa. Ben steadfastly denies everything, and vows to bring Kelsey back and make him recant his charges. He dispatches his best rider/tracker—the Indian, Johnny Portugal (John Saxon)—to bring Kelsey in, and after a lengthy chase, Portugal returns with his man.

Kelsey, however, refuses to recant, and, indeed, elaborates on his charge. The scene is one of the film's most effective. It is nighttime, and Kelsey is mounted on a horse with a noose around his neck. Wild of eye, and in an almost singsong voice, he explains his tortured pursuit of the Zacharys. The effect is eerie, and quite compelling. Kelsey's story is that his son was kidnaped by the Kiowas. In a reprisal raid, Kelsey, Ben's father, and others burned a Kiowa village. Rachel, a baby, was the only survivor. Will Zachary took the baby home, and when the Kiowas offered to trade Kelsey's son for Rachel, Zachary refused. Kelsey thus swore vengeance, and has dogged the Zacharys at every opportunity ever since. The scene, and Kelsey's life, ends when Mattilda Zachary, unable to refute Kelsey's claims, swats his horse, which bolts from under the man, hanging him.

Rachel's accuser is dead, but the relationship between the Zacharys and the Rawlinses is poisoned; and when Ben and Mattilda later admit to the rest of the Zachary clan that Kelsey was telling the truth, Cash Zachary, a vociferous Indian hater, leaves home. The remaining family members—Ben, Mattilda, Rachel, and the teenaged Andy (Doug McClure)—face the Kiowas alone.

It is a traumatic time for Rachel, who, in a gesture that is both defiant and heartrending, uses lampblack to smear a single strip of "warpaint" across her forehead. After staring at her image in a mirror for quite some time, she bolts for the door. She is dissuaded from joining the Kiowas only when Ben confesses his love for her. They embrace, and Ben vows that they will marry when their ordeal is over.

The film's denouement is a mixture of hokum and inspiration. The hokum occurs during the first Kiowa attack. The Indians cannot hit a thing, and the whites—even Rachel, who has never fired a gun before—cannot miss. Every Zachary shot fells a treacherous redskin. Huston's better instincts soon take over, however; the Kiowas regroup, dancing to ceremonial flute music to give themselves magical powers. Ben Zachary retaliates by hauling an old piano outside, whereupon Mattilda plays some Mozart for the Kiowas' benefit. The stunned look on the Indians' faces is priceless. The sublimely surrealistic effect is redoubled when the Kiowas mount their next attack—against the piano. The climactic assault on the ranchhouse soon follows, and it too finds Huston in top form. The carnage—including a herd of cattle stampeded over the top of the house (which was built into a hillside) and a realistic fire—is staged, shot, and edited to perfection. Mattilda is killed, Rachel proves her loyalty by shooting her real brother Lost Bird, Cash rejoins the family at an opportune moment, and what is left of the Zachary clan walks out of the smoldering ruins, stoically ready to face the future.

In addition to Huston's moments of marvelous cinematic poetry—Kelsey's "confession," the scenes involving the piano, and so forth—the highlights in *The Unforgiven* come from the acting of the principals in the cast. Audie Murphy and veteran actress Lillian Gish as Cash and Mattilda Zachary are good in parts that could have used a bit more development; and John Saxon gets off to a fine start as Johnny Portugal, before the character vanishes in midfilm. The highest marks, however, must go to the film's stars. Burt Lancaster as Ben Zachary is solid without being stolid and portrays his struggle with his complex feelings about his adopted sister with a convincing subtlety. Audrey Hepburn is equally impressive in a demanding role. A bright, spontaneous girl when the film opens, Rachel Zachary ages quickly when the truth about her Kiowa ancestry is revealed, and Hepburn shows us every emotional nuance.

The Unforgiven was a commercial failure at the time of its initial release. Several factors undoubtedly contributed to this lack of success. *The Unforgiven* was an unusually somber and unconventional Western, containing a good many moral ambiguities. It was uncompromising in its portrayal of white racism, and the suggestion of incest implicit in the relationship between Rachel and Ben possibly bothered viewers.

Another problem was the matter of the film's choppy editing, which hurt *The Unforgiven* with the critics as well as at the box office. The uncertainties in tone that mar the first half of the film, and the curious disappearance of Johnny Portugal, who had appeared to be an important character in the film, indicate substantial revision in the cutting room. Huston has only himself to blame, however, for these flaws—he abandoned the film shortly after the shooting was completed, leaving it to the studio to fashion *The Unforgiven* into its final form. Despite its flaws, however, *The Unforgiven* remains a film worthy of study. The acting, particularly on the part of Audrey Hepburn and Burt Lancaster, is first-rate; and the last half of the film is quite compelling. *The Unforgiven*, then, is an interesting if flawed film by a major director, and its virtues clearly outweigh its faults.

Robert Mitchell

THE UNHOLY THREE

Released: 1930
Production: Metro-Goldwyn-Mayer
Direction: Jack Conway
Screenplay: J. C. Nugent and Elliott Nugent; based on the novel of the same
   name by Clarence Aaron Robbins
Cinematography: Percy Hilburn
Editing: Frank Sullivan
Running time: 74 minutes

Principal characters:
Echo, the Ventriloquist	Lon Chaney
Rosie O'Grady	Lila Lee
Hector McDonald	Elliott Nugent
Tweedledee	Harry Earles
Prosecuting Attorney	John Miljan
Hercules	Ivan Linow
Regan	Clarence Burton
Defense Attorney	Crauford Kent

By the end of 1929 there were only three of the great stars of the silents
who had not made a talking film debut—Greta Garbo, Charlie Chaplin, and
Lon Chaney. In February, 1930, Garbo's first talkie, *Anna Christie*, was
released, and she was acknowledged to be a greater star than ever. Chaplin
with his own unique talent was able to delay his complete talking feature
debut until 1940 with *The Great Dictator*; but Chaney, whose last three silents,
all released in 1929 (*West of Zanzibar*, *Where East Is East*, and *Thunder*),
had sound effects and were scored musically, decided that he, like Garbo,
must make his first talking picture in 1930.

Irving Thalberg, who had brought Chaney to M-G-M from Universal,
helped him decide what his first talkie would be. In 1925 Chaney had filmed
his third M-G-M silent feature, *The Unholy Three*, and it remained one of
his most memorable pictures, the only one that could be effectively remade
as a talking film. The property was turned over to J. C. Nugent and Elliott
Nugent, his son, and they wrote the screenplay, complete with dialogue.
Elliott Nugent, also an accomplished Broadway actor, was signed to play the
romantic lead of Hector, and Jack Conway was engaged to direct.

Tod Browning had directed the silent version with Chaney, and everything
they did together (eight features) had been an unqualified success. Conway
had made only one previous feature with Chaney, *While the City Sleeps* (1928),
and Chaney liked him. Meanwhile, Browning had gone over to Universal and
was hinting that he would like to borrow Chaney for the title role of *Dracula*,
which he was preparing, but that production was not ready for shooting, and

besides, Thalberg wanted Chaney's first talking film to be an M-G-M production. A remake of *The Unholy Three* was thus the best possible solution.

Rumor around Hollywood persisted that M-G-M was delaying Chaney's sound debut because he suffered from a throat affliction. While filming his final silent, *Thunder*, a piece of artificial snow had presumably lodged in his throat, causing constant irritation. Actually, Thalberg himself had delayed any announcement of Chaney's forthcoming debut in talking films because the studio was negotiating a new term contract, and Thalberg wanted to make certain that it was as profitable to Chaney as possible. When the contract was signed, a statement was issued that Chaney would make his talkie debut in a sound version of *The Unholy Three*.

Chaney had wanted Betty Compson to play the role of Rosie O'Grady, the only important female part, which Mae Busch had created in the silent version. Chaney had always had great affection for Compson, because they had first played together in *The Miracle Man* (1919), and their careers had zoomed simultaneously. They had played together again in *For Those We Love* (1921) and only two years previously in *The Big City* (1928). Compson, however, was already working at two other studios on nonexclusive contract deals and was not available; she suggested her good friend, Lila Lee, for the part, and Chaney was very agreeable.

Chaney had been known as "The Man of a Thousand Faces," and now he wanted to be called, as well, "The Man of a Thousand Voices." His role of Echo, the ventriloquist, allowed him to use three other voices in addition to his own and that of the little old lady who sells parrots. Ironically, his throat problems returned as he finished the picture, and he went to New York City, where specialists determined that he was suffering from terminal bronchial cancer. On his return to Hollywood, Thalberg kept alive stories of the properties the studio was preparing for him. Few knew that Chaney was fatally ill, and he himself was not aware that he would not recover his health or make another film. He was only forty-seven; he believed that the future would be bright for him. His voice then went entirely, a bitterly ironic thing to happen to an actor who has just made his debut in a talking film.

The Unholy Three had its premiere in New York, and Chaney was much praised, although most critics noted that the picture was better as a silent. In the summer of 1930, Chaney, hospitalized and in great pain, died of a throat hemorrhage. He was acknowledged as a master of cinema pantomime, but he had proved that he could have gone on, had fate been kinder, as one of the most versatile of the sound screen actors.

The Unholy Three is the story of a trio of crooks from a dime museum—a ventriloquist, a midget, and a strong man—who have it made. The ventriloquist, known as Echo (Lon Chaney), plans the robberies; the midget, Tweedledee (Harry Earles), can gain access through any transom or small aperture; and the strong man, Hercules (Ivan Linow), can force any window or door open. They operate on a three-way split and are helped by Rosie O'Grady (Lila Lee), Echo's moll, who goes through the crowds at the dime museum picking pockets and stealing purses.

The midget precipitates a fight in the museum just as Rosie has turned over to Echo the haul she has made. The police are called, and Echo is barely able to slip the haul back to Rosie. He is pronounced "clean," but he determines that the police will now be watching the museum and it will not be safe to work there any longer. He therefore poses as an old lady who runs a bird shop. The parrots do not really speak; Echo's art as a ventriloquist gives them voices, and customers buy the birds eagerly. When they get the parrots home, however, they no longer talk, so the old lady is called upon and comes into the rich homes, presumably to restore the birds' vocal abilities, but actually to case the places thoroughly and set them up for the midget and Hercules to rob.

The three make a haul, and Echo hires a clerk, Hector MacDonald (Elliott Nugent), to take care of his bird shop while he is out operating. Hector is, of course, ignorant of what is really going on, but he likes Rosie, and she falls in love with him. During one of the robberies, the midget and Hercules commit a murder and cunningly lay the blame on Hector, who is apprehended and held by the police. Rosie tells Echo that if he will save Hector, she will again become Echo's moll. The midget and Hercules are slain, however, by a gorilla they have tormented in its cage. Echo is responsible for whitewashing Hector, but he does not hold Rosie to the agreement they made, knowing that her real love is Hector. Rosie goes off with Hector, the man she really loves, and Echo is left to himself, free, the man of a thousand faces with a thousand voices at his command.

Earles, a real midget, played the role of Tweedledee in both the silent and the talking versions and was very effective in both. Hercules was played in the sound version by the big Russian actor, Linow; the role had been played by Victor McLaglen in the 1925 silent, but in those five years, McLaglen had risen from supporting player to star and was thus not available for this film. The picture was preeminently Chaney's; his is a virtuoso performance if there ever was one. He wanted his audience to believe him capable of playing five roles vocally because he knew that there would always be those who would say that other actors had dubbed lines for his lip synchronization. He therefore had the studio's attorney draw up an affidavit to the effect that he and he alone had acted the role and spoken the lines. It was duly notarized and featured in all publicity above his signature. There was only one Lon Chaney, and he was proud of it.

DeWitt Bodeen

UNION PACIFIC

Released: 1939
Production: Cecil B. De Mille for Paramount
Direction: Cecil B. De Mille
Screenplay: Walter DeLeon, C. Gardner Sullivan, and Jesse L. Lasky, Jr.; based on Jack Cunningham's adaptation of Ernest Haycox's novel *Trouble Shooter*
Cinematography: Victor Milner
Editing: Anne Bauchens
Running time: 135 minutes

> *Principal characters:*
> Mollie Monahan .... Barbara Stanwyck
> Jeff Butler .... Joel McCrea
> Fiesta .... Akim Tamiroff
> Dick Allen .... Robert Preston
> Leach Overmile ....Lynne Overman
> Sid Campeau ....Brian Donlevy
> Monahan .... J. M. Kerrigan
> Asa M. Barrows ....Henry Kolker

The year 1939, a great one for Hollywood, was also an especially good year for the Western. Twentieth Century-Fox released the melodramatic *Jesse James*, with a colorfully incongruous Tyrone Power glowering in the title part; Warners produced the raucous *Dodge City*, dispatching Errol Flynn to scour that unholy town; United Artists released the thrilling *Stagecoach*, John Ford's revolutionary Western that gave the genre its greatest star, John Wayne; and Universal concocted the rowdy *Destry Rides Again*, which resurrected Marlene Dietrich from a career sepulcher and further advanced the soaring popularity of James Stewart. At the same time Paramount produced the melodramatic, raucous, thrilling *Union Pacific*, produced and directed by Cecil B. De Mille as the Western "epic" of 1939.

The longest, biggest-budgeted, most loudly heralded Western of the year, De Mille's *Union Pacific* is not only a colorful account of the onerous laying of the transcontinental railroad, painstakingly researched with the cooperation of the Union Pacific, but it is also a marvelous example of De Mille excesses. More so than any of the director's other works in the genre, such as *The Plainsman* (1936), this film is a *show*, an amalgam of action, sex, and stars, all packaged so that De Mille might demonstrate ". . . his special art of the epic with an action tale on the big canvas of the American West. . . ." as the *Motion Picture Herald* put it.

Union Pacific begins with characteristic De Millean reverence in Washington, where a sober President Ulysses S. Grant (Joseph Crehan) approves the challenge of creating a transcontinental railroad. Soon the train is chugging over the plains, engineered by Irish immigrant Monahan (J. M. Kerrigan), inspired by his spunky daughter Molly (Barbara Stanwyck), and safeguarded by troubleshooter Jeff Butler (Joel McCrea) and his unscrubbed sidekicks Fiesta (Akim Tamiroff) and Leach Overmile (Lynne Overman).

Butler need not look far for trouble. Roosting in one of the coaches, surrounded by lacquered whores and feasting on greasy chicken, is evil Sid Campeau (Brian Donlevy). In the employ of corrupt politician/financier Asa M. Barrows (Henry Kolker), Campeau plots to plague the railroad with various misfortunes. Campeau's chief lieutenant is a marcelled gambler named Dick Allen (Robert Preston). He is an old army pal of Butler, but the two now find themselves on opposite sides in the laying of the railroad and rivals in the courting of Molly.

The railroad war is soon waging. Campeau sends Allen to steal the railroad payroll. Molly persuades Allen to return it, but in the course of her pleading, she becomes his bride, although she really loves Butler. Butler, meanwhile, retaliates against Campeau by leading the railroaders into town and destroying his saloon, while Campeau vows bloody vengeance. Molly, Butler, and Allen then board the train and meet a new menace, Indians. The savages overturn a water tank and derail the train, slaughtering the passengers and, in a typical De Millie touch, engage in buffoonery with ladies' underwear. The whooping heathens are seconds away from victimizing Molly and the men when a train bearing United States Army troops arrives and routs the Indians.

Following this rescue, Allen flees after an amicable parting with Butler. On the historic day at Promontory Point, however, when the railroads meet and the golden spike is to be driven (the real spike itself is used in the film, exhumed from the vault of San Francisco's Wells Fargo Bank), Molly, Butler, and Allen all arrive for the ceremony. So does Campeau, in order to murder Butler. Allen, learning of Campeau's scheme, goes looking for him, and is shot in cold blood by his ex-partner. Butler arrives to hear Allen's dying words(". . . I've drawn the black deuce"), unaware that Campeau is taking aim at his back. Before the villain pulls the trigger, however, Fiesta and Leach arrive and blast him to a much-deserved end. Butler returns to the spike-driving ceremony, where a beaming Molly asks where Allen is. "He'll be waiting for us, Molly," replies the solemn Butler, no doubt fated to wed the widow, "at the end of track." The spike is driven, the crowd cheers, the scene switches to a roaring diesel train, the strains of "Stars and Stripes Forever" swell, and the film races to a triumphant close.

Released on April 28, 1939, *Union Pacific* was sold by Paramount as "The Greatest American Epic of Them All!"; even the premiere in Omaha, Nebraska, where the railroad began, was a spectacle, complete with a Pioneer Ball where De Mille led his costumed stars in the festivities. While there was no Academy Award recognition, the box-office business was enormous, and *Union Pacific* placed, along with *Jesse James*, *Dodge City*, *Stagecoach*, and

Destry Rides Again, among 1939's top-grossing pictures.

A spectacle from start to finish, *Union Pacific* survives nicely today, all the more enjoyable for the De Mille "corn" that sprouts throughout the 135 minutes. The film rolls with such gaudy smoothness that it is impossible to detect that the film actually had *three* directors; De Mille, stricken by overwork and ill health, directed much of the film on a stretcher, while Arthur Rosson and James Hogan supervised some of the location work. The action sequences are superb, especially the desert train wreck. This held such a fascination both to audiences and to De Mille that he later worked a train disaster into 1953's *The Greatest Show on Earth*. There is effective use of location shooting in Iron Springs, Utah, and Canoga Park, California. Best of all, however, is the gallery of performances delivered by excellent actors who are never overwhelmed by the spectacle. As Molly, Stanwyck is not just an Irish-brogued heroine; she personifies the railroad, filled with the dreams and hope that the Union Pacific represents. McCrea is a solidly righteous hero, quiet and credible, while Preston, as the self-sacrificing rascal, reveals sparks of the energy and ebullience he finally allowed to explode nearly two decades later in Broadway's *The Music Man*. Donlevy's sexy villain, complete with top hat, spit curl, and the carnal touch of dipping his cigar into a shot glass, is splendidly vile, while Tamiroff as the whip-cracking Fiesta and Overman as the tobacco-chewing Leach shamelessly battle to scene-steal from each other. The bit players, such as Anthony Quinn, then De Mille's son-in-law, playing a gambler part he considered "embarrassingly small"; Robert Barrat as a bullying railroader who takes on McCrea; and De Mille veteran Julia Faye as an aging prostitute bring just the right touches to the background of the sprawling adventure.

Union Pacific is not considered by historians to be a landmark in the development of the Hollywood Western, but it was never De Mille's objective to revolutionize. He was a showman, and *Union Pacific* is first and foremost stirring entertainment, one of the cinema's most stunning murals of the Old West.

Gregory William Mank

THE UNSUSPECTED

Released: 1947
Production: Charles Hoffman for Warner Bros.
Direction: Michael Curtiz
Screenplay: Ranald MacDougall and Bess Meredyth; based on the novel of the same name by Charlotte Armstrong
Cinematography: Elwood Bredell
Editing: Frederick Richards

Principal characters:
Victor Grandison	Claude Rains
Steven Francis Howard	Michael North
Matilda Frazier	Joan Caulfield
Althea Keane	Audrey Totter
Jane Maynihan	Constance Bennett
Oliver Keane	Hurd Hatfield

The film *The Unsuspected* is a combination of two methods that are common to murder-mystery films. True to the whodunit mystery, the film opens with a murder, and the viewer is neatly tucked between the killer and the victim, unable to identify the evil-doer. The film increasingly alters its approach, however, as it proceeds. The viewer is encouraged to deduce the culprit, Victor Grandison, (Claude Rains), from the rest of the cast, and, soon enough, the audience is privy to the slaying of his next victim. In this way, the film also embraces a second method which exposes the murderer's identity and derives dramatic tension from the factors leading to the moment when he is finally tracked down. Both methods are alternately supported by the highly involved plot, the characters, and their backgrounds.

Victor Grandison is a writer and radio announcer of grisly mystery stories. He becomes a suspect as early as the second scene when, broadcasting in the studio, he reads a story that strikingly resembles the opening murder, which had been disguised as a suicide. By degrees, the plot carefully unravels the backgrounds of the other characters. Althea (Audrey Totter), Victor's penniless niece, lives with him in a large, lavish house but she despises Victor because he favors his ward, the beautiful heiress Matilda Frazier (Joan Caulfield), who at the beginning of the film is thought to have been drowned at sea. Steven Howard (Michael North), an uninvited guest, arrives at a birthday party given in Victor's honor. Although Steven purports to be Matilda's husband and says that he only wants something to remember her by, he has actually come to investigate the mysterious suicide of Victor's secretary. It is then revealed that Matilda has survived the shipwreck. Steven meets her at the airport and takes advantage of her unsettled state of mind. With a falsified certificate and the testimony of a bribed Justice of the Peace, he almost convinces her that they were married only three days before her fateful voyage.

It is further revealed that the house originally belonged to Matilda's father. Victor has apparently been dipping into her inheritance and cannot afford to lose her affection. The secretary, perhaps, knew of Victor's greed and lost her life because of it. Steven, of course, suspects Victor all along, and, similarly, Victor has many reservations about Steven's story, but his uneasiness does not prevent him from committing another murder. Victor is aware of Althea's passionate dislike for him and knows she loves Steven, creating the possibility that she may join him in his attempts to expose Victor's crime. Because it is so easy for Victor to commit murder, when the opportunity arises, he quickly disposes of Althea and her husband, Oliver (Hurd Hatfield). As is true in all of Victor's crimes, he neatly covers his actions. First, he records one of the many arguments between Althea and Oliver; then he severs the brakelines of his car and sends the distraught Oliver off in it. When he is alone with Althea, he records himself shooting her, so that both recordings put together will prove that Oliver murdered his wife before escaping. He also covers himself for the ensuing murder of Matilda, who is also falling in love with Steven. When Matilda offers to help Victor, whom she affectionately calls "Grandy," write a story, he sardonically dictates to her her own suicide note. After drugging her, he lays sleeping pills and the dictated note beside her. Victor then leaves for the broadcasting studio, having also arranged for Steven's death. Both Steven and Matilda survive, however, and finally lead the police to the station where Victor admits to his shivering listeners that this is to be his last broadcast. He tells them a true story this time, his own personal story of the unsuspected man.

Although the viewer suspects Victor to be the culprit from the early moments of the film, our certainty is suspended in the traditional whodunit fashion. Different characters are made to look suspicious at different times. Because the murderer's particular motives are delayed, the audience cannot be sure of Victor's crime until he kills Althea and Oliver. From that point on the real tension centers in the personality of the perfect impostor, the unsuspected man. Victor is a harmonious blend of calm and intensity. While the audience is wondering who and how many are going to die, for Victor, the question never seems to arise. Externally paternal and gentle, he is also extremely methodical. In fact, he is so much so that when he feels the need to kill someone, he is like a person feeling the need to eat something when he is hungry. He simply gets the job done. The audience is continually befuddled by Victor, a man who walks with ease and speaks eloquently and who, at the same time, is a calculating, cold-blooded murderer. Although he seems to be fed-up with his profession, he takes pleasure and secret pride in turning the tools of the trade into a morose hobby. Rains is made for the role. He is an actor who exudes an aura of tremendous confidence, and he gives a splendid performance as the sly impostor.

Neither the whodunit method nor the method which characterizes the murderer is an innovative approach to the murder-mystery film, but there is considerable finesse surrounding the elements of the production. Michael Curtiz's direction, together with Franz Waxman's penetrating musical score, creates the eerie atmosphere of a morgue. The cinematography of Elwood Bredell is both slick and unobtrusive. Throughout the film, there is an overriding sense of quiet that complements the dialogue's dramatic punch.

At the time the film was released, it was generally observed by the critics that *The Unsuspected* was a poor title because it leads the audience to suspect the least likely character, namely Victor Grandison. The singular aim of the film, however, is to afford the viewer an opportunity to follow the antics of a man who is, indeed, above suspicion. The script allows him the luxury of being able to watch the necessary requisites of his schemes fall into place. Conveniently, Althea and Oliver are prone to spirited arguments. Similarly, Victor's ward, Matilda, admires him to such an extent that she offers to take his dictation, ironically playing into the hands of her would-be murderer. Also, the story relies heavily upon the relative novelty of a home recording machine. A decade later, everyone in the Grandison household would have suspected Victor's obsessive preoccupation with the device. Like other mystery films, only the uninvited outsider sees through the household routine to the possible uses of Victor's elaborate toy. It is Steven who catches a glimpse of Victor hiding one of his recordings shortly after shooting Althea.

The film's slick production and understated quality breaks down at the end, when Curtiz feels it necessary to include an anticlimactic car-chase scene. By then, the outcome has become inevitable, and the added dramatic cliché undercuts the obvious fate of Victor Grandison.

Ralph Angel

UP THE DOWN STAIRCASE

Released: 1967
Production: Alan J. Pakula for Warner Bros.
Direction: Robert Mulligan
Screenplay: Tad Mosel; based on the novel of the same name by Bel Kaufman
Cinematography: Joseph Coffey
Editing: Folmar Blangsted
Running time: 124 minutes

Principal characters:
Sylvia Barrett .... Sandy Dennis
Paul Barringer .... Patrick Bedford
Henrietta Pastorfield .... Eileen Heckart
Beatrice Schracter .... Ruth White
Sadie Finch .... Jean Stapleton
Alice Blake .... Ellen O'Mara
Joe Ferone .... Jeff Howard
Doctor Bester .... Sorrell Brooke
McHabe .... Roy Poole
Jose Rodriguez .... Himself

In 1967's *Up the Down Staircase*, Sandy Dennis plays Sylvia Barrett, a schoolteacher in a New York City public school filled with juvenile delinquents. Sylvia is an innocent, if gifted, teacher whose skills work miraculously on the recalcitrant classes that she is given. Although the audience is uplifted by these triumphs, it may strain our credulity a bit to see her successfully teaching *A Tale of Two Cities* to a classroom of unhappy delinquents. Yet it is even more extraordinary to see the rather wispy heroine, fresh out of an ivy-league milieu, manage to apply her liberal intellectual beliefs in a ghetto.

The film is adapted by screenwriter Tad Mosel from Bel Kaufman's novel *Up the Down Staircase*, and some critics seem to feel that the film, by virtue of its screenplay, is more unified than the rather sketchy novel from which it was adapted. Even so, many standard stereotypes have been retained, including teachers who are primarily disciplinarians and have lost faith in the power of teaching; the school nurse who dispenses nothing but tea; and the lovesick student (and teacher too). It is also faithful in reproducing the difficulties of a teacher cutting through the bureaucratic red tape that clogs overcrowded schools.

The film has a number of intertwined stories. In one of the subplots, Patrick Bedford is good as Paul Barringer, an English teacher lost in his own failed dreams of becoming a novelist who in reality becomes a drunk. Critical praises were given to the performance of Ellen O'Mara as the ugly duckling student Alice Blake, who has a crush on him; and there is a classic scene in which he corrects the grammar in her love note to him with disastrous results. Alice, a chunky adolescent, commits suicide by jumping out a window. There is a nice parallel shot later in the film as Sylvia, while teaching, looks out the window to that very spot and forgets for a moment what she has been saying.

Sylvia has her own one-sided flirtation too, as Joe Ferone (Jeff Howard), a student, mistakes her interest in him for romantic attention and attempts to seduce her—an incident which causes Sylvia to attempt to resign. Howard plays the student in a fashion which some criticized for being too close to Marlon Brando, in terms of mannerisms and the like. Eileen Heckart is fine as Henrietta Pastorfield, a somewhat panicky teacher; Sorrell Brooke is good as the solid principal, Doctor Bester, as is Roy Poole in the role of a rather cruel disciplinarian, named McHabe; Ruth White is Beatrice Schracter, Sylvia's older, calmer friend and mentor.

Robert Mulligan, whose previous works include *Baby, the Rain Must Fall* (1965) and *Inside Daisy Clover* (1965), won high praise for his sensitive direction from most critics. Particularly cited is the scene between Barringer and Alice Blake as he cruelly if unwittingly corrects her, and the director has caught poignant details such as her clutching her sleeve while pretending not to be hurt. Some critics felt that Dennis did a good job as the ingenuous teacher, while others complained of her whiney voice and mannerisms. Comparisons were made between *Up the Down Staircase* and *Blackboard Jungle* (1955), although perhaps a 1960's audience was more willing to believe in the problems of the school system and of ghetto kids than an audience of 1955.

Even so, Sylvia is a triumphant figure. Although she hands in her resignation to the principal, near the end of the school year something happens which changes her mind. In a mock trial staged by her class, one student, Jose Rodriguez (played by himself), a shy, almost introverted Puerto Rican student, comes alive when he is selected as the trial judge. His self-confidence and mature approach to the responsibility of being a judge, even if only a make-believe exercise, so moves Sylvia that she decides to stay at the school. She feels that no matter what other failures she has had during the year, if she reaches even one student by her own efforts, then she has been a success.

In the final scene Sylvia triumphantly goes up the "down" staircase at the school, proving her ability to move ahead, even if she has to do it against the mainstream. Her action is a perfect embodiment of the hopeful, liberal tradition maintained throughout the film. Although a fine actress, Dennis has rarely "starred" in a film. Most of her roles have been secondary leads, the most famous of which, perhaps, is her role as the young wife in *Who's Afraid of Virginia Woolf?* (1966), for which she won an Academy Award as Best Supporting Actress. Her best work has undoubtedly been on the Broadway stage, where she has starred in various productions, winning two Tony Awards for her performances.

Marsha McCreadie

VACATION FROM MARRIAGE
(PERFECT STRANGERS)

Released: 1945
Production: Alexander Korda for London Films; released by Metro-Goldwyn-Mayer
Direction: Alexander Korda
Screenplay: Clemence Dane and Anthony Pelissier
Cinematography: George Perinal
Editing: E. B. Jarvis
Running time: 102 minutes

Principal characters:

Robert Wilson	Robert Donat
Catherine Wilson	Deborah Kerr
Dizzy Clayton	Glynis Johns
Elena	Ann Todd
Richard	Roland Culver
Scotty	Caven Watson

Vacation from Marriage, released in England originally as *Perfect Strangers*, came out not long after the end of World War II, and was very familiar, both in theme and locale, to the audience. The story need not be familiar to be enjoyed, however, as the marital relationship under scrutiny could exist at almost any time. The film opens in a dreary section of London in 1940. Robert and Catherine Wilson, splendidly portrayed by Robert Donat and Deborah Kerr, are seen in their equally dreary flat having breakfast, each about to face another routine day. She is in her bathrobe, constantly sneezing into her handkerchief, a dowdy housewife who is frequently plagued with colds. Robert is neatly dressed in a business suit, the proper outfit for a stiff-necked, prim gentleman who works as a bookkeeper for a large trading company. Catherine is depicted as a nurturing housewife, while Robert comes across as a lackluster, namby-pamby company man. Both are nice, but dull.

Robert joins the Navy to aid the war effort, but he is disappointed to find that he is not immediately to be put on a ship. He obviously knows very little about what to expect of Navy life. He is issued a uniform, and his carefully trimmed mustache is shaved off. Meanwhile his wife wonders how he will tolerate military life with his sensitive stomach. Catherine's worries are not totally unfounded. The viewer soon finds Robert on a ship, obviously seasick and unable to tolerate the food. While in this miserable condition, he receives a letter from his wife telling him she has joined the WRENS, a branch of the British women's service.

When Catherine cautiously enters a WRENS' barracks, she is almost immediately informed by Dizzy Clayton (deftly played by Glynis Johns) that she, Catherine, has taken the wrong bunk. Dizzy is a spunky woman who starts taking Catherine in hand, but her efforts are not immediately successful. Catherine initially finds Dizzy rather rude and abrasive. When Dizzy suggests that Catherine put on some lipstick, the mousey ex-housewife informs her new but meddlesome acquaintance that she neither smokes nor uses makeup because her husband does not approve. Once left alone in the barracks, however, Catherine applies some lipstick and adjusts her hat to a more rakish angle. Parallel situations are shown throughout the film. Through the use of this device, the viewer can follow the movements of both Robert and Catherine at almost the same time and can witness the development of each character juxtaposed against that of the other.

As the film continues, eighteen months have passed, and the war is very much in evidence throughout England. One notices immediately that Catherine has not only improved in appearance, but has also immensely gained in self-confidence. Robert has improved as well, but neither person is aware of the changes in the other. Catherine meets a man at a party. The man, Richard (Roland Culver), is a cousin of her friend Dizzy, and Catherine begins to compare Richard to her husband Robert. She muses that she has never danced since she got married, then swiftly adds that her husband is kind. Robert is next seen in a hospital. He has survived the sinking of his ship, but had to row for five days with frozen hands before being rescued. Parallel scenes reveal further complications. The film first flits to a short scene of Catherine on a picnic with Richard, to whom she describes Robert as dependable. Meanwhile, Robert is seen talking with his nurse, Elena (Ann Todd). He begins by telling her how he met his wife at the Polytechnic, but winds up by asking Elena out for an evening before he leaves the hospital. He takes her dancing, and Catherine is also seen dancing at a party somewhere else. Robert describes his rather dreary civilian life to the nurse. He says the war got him out of it, but he is disgruntled when he thinks about going back to his former existence. Elena reveals to Robert that she is a widow whose late husband was a famous explorer, and as she reminisces about him, she tells Robert that ordinary people have done extraordinary things. She kisses him good-bye while the lyrics of a sad, sentimental song are sung in the background.

In the meantime, Catherine's life is becoming complicated. She has received a cable from her husband advising her that he is coming home on leave, but Richard confesses to Catherine that he is in love with her. Confused by this turn of events, she tells Richard that she must go home to see Robert.

In more parallel scenes, the principals are shown on trains. Robert is with his friend Scotty (Caven Watson); Catherine is traveling with Dizzy. At this point, Robert and Catherine have not seen each other in three years. Neither wants to go back to the old life-style, yet it never occurs to either of them that the other person has changed. Both relate what they dislike about their mate, and each one thinks the other cannot function independently. They each believe they will be strangers to each other. Robert does not wish to be like he was before the war; Catherine worries about how she can be intimate with her estranged mate after three years. They are going home out of a sense of duty to each other, but neither feels confident. In fact, Catherine cannot bring herself to go to their apartment, and instead, she proceeds to a phone box to call Robert. She asks him to meet her on neutral ground, as she does not wish to return to the flat nor to him. He is angry and announces that he will not let his wife walk out on him. They finally meet at a bus stop; no kisses, not even handshakes, grace their reunion. Catherine tells Robert the reason she does not wish to return to him. She has been thinking about the life they led before and what it would be like in the future. The couple air their feelings, and she insists on a divorce. He agrees, since that is what he also wants.

Civilized people that they are, they go to a local pub, where Dizzy and Scotty are supposed to meet them. In the light of the pub, the estranged pair get a good look at each other, and both are surprised by what they see. To Robert's astonishment, Catherine asks for a drink, gin, and they begin to discuss their divorce, first going over the old days, then becoming defensive about past behavior. The channels of communication are open more than at any previous time in the marriage. It suddenly begins to strike them that their relationship had been closed, and that each never really understood the other. In the midst of this mutual revelation, a couple celebrating their fiftieth wedding anniversary invites the customers in the pub to help them celebrate. Music plays, and Robert and Catherine start to dance, to their mutual amazement. When Dizzy and Scotty join them and each is surprised by the difference between Catherine's and Robert's descriptions of their spouses and the actual person, Robert and Catherine quarrel and leave the pub.

Joined by Scotty and Dizzy, they try to find a taxi. While waiting, Catherine and Robert reminisce about the neighborhood before the blitz, but they cannot even agree as to where the stores were. This time Robert gets angry, tells his wife what he thinks of her, and storms off into the night. Catherine is having trouble getting used to the new Robert. She tells Dizzy how nice he used to be and that they never quarreled in the past. Since no taxi has come, the women decide to go to the old apartment. At the apartment, Catherine tells Dizzy tales of how she met Robert and about their life together. Robert walks around London pondering his future, and finally arrives at the apartment at daybreak. Catherine is awake, looking out the window, surveying the destruction that the war has brought to London. The couple talk about the damaged city, agreeing that it will have to be rebuilt. Catherine and Robert see a parallel in their own relationship. The war has changed them as it has changed London. Their marriage, like the city, can rise from the rubble and profit from the changes wrought. They have time; both are still young. They kiss, and the viewer is left with the feeling that all will be right for the reunited Wilsons at last.

Vacation from Marriage, although made in the mid-1940's, touches on a theme of contemporary interest—the lack of communication between married people. Through the vehicle of a fine motion picture, not only are the viewers entertained, but there is also a subtle lesson taught as the film traces the growth and evolution of the principal characters: namely, that so much of what is precious in human relationships can be lost when people will not honestly share their thoughts and feelings with one another. The film has excellent acting and clever dialogue and employs splendid use of parallel scenes in the plotting. All in all, it is a gem of a film.

Fern L. Gagné

VERTIGO

Released: 1958
Production: Alfred Hitchcock for Paramount
Direction: Alfred Hitchcock
Screenplay: Alec Coppel and Samuel Taylor; based on the novel *D'Entre les Morts* by Pierre Boileau and Thomas Narcejac
Cinematography: Robert Burks
Editing: George Tomasini
Music: Bernard Herrmann
Running time: 120 minutes

Principal characters:
Scottie Ferguson .... James Stewart
Madeleine/Judy .... Kim Novak
Midge .... Barbara Bel Geddes
Gavin Elster ....Tom Helmore

Alfred Hitchcock's *Vertigo* is a film which functions on multiple levels simultaneously. On a literal level it is a mystery-suspense story of a man hoodwinked into acting as an accomplice in a murder, his discovery of the hoax, and the unraveling of the threads of the murder plot. On a psychological level the film traces the twisted, circuitous routes of a psyche burdened down with guilt, desperately searching for an object on which to concentrate its repressed energy. Finally, on an allegorical or figurative level, it is a retelling of the immemorial tale of a man who has lost his love to death and in hope of redeeming her descends into the underworld, the most famous of these stories being that of Orpheus and Eurydice in Greek Mythology. *Vertigo*'s complexity, however, does not end with this multilevel approach to its tale; the film also succeeds in blurring the already fine line between objectivity and subjectivity. It takes the viewer so far into the mind of the main character (Scottie, played by Hitchcock veteran James Stewart) that the audience's own objectivity, at least initially, is lost and replaced by complete identification with Scottie's fantasies and obsessions.

Scottie is a San Francisco police detective who, during a rooftop chase, nearly plunges to his death. The psychological scars left by this incident and, probably more significantly, by the guilt of having been responsible for the death of a fellow officer who tried to rescue him, induce in Scottie a phobia—vertigo, or fear of high places, the phobia which initially caused his accident.

Throughout the rest of the film Scottie remains psychologically and symbolically suspended from that rooftop. He takes on a job as a private detective for an old college friend named Gavin Elster (Tom Helmore) who is worried about the strange behavior of his wife, Madeleine (Kim Novak), whom Scottie has never met. Madeleine is a wanderer, and in trailing her, Scottie becomes one too. As he follows her through museums, graveyards, and forest haunts he becomes obsessed with this phantom woman who apparently believes herself to be the reincarnation of a turn-of-the-century belle named Carlotta. Visually Hitchcock reinforces this loss of objectivity and descent into obsession by photographing Scottie's wanderings in soft-focus and at a gliding, dreamlike pace. In the scenes of Scottie tailing Madeleine by car through the streets of San Francisco, the vehicle seems to be floating above the pavement. This feeling is enhanced even more by the lilting, musical background of master film composer Bernard Herrmann. With the growth of Scottie's obsession comes an equal and concurrent increase in the credibility of Madeleine's claims. Her appearance, her strange visits to places which Carlotta frequented, and her speech all seem to confirm her belief that she is the reincarnated Carlotta. As noted before, however, Scottie is no longer a logical, detached observer, and because the viewer is given no more information than Scottie, neither is he.

The romance which develops between this obsessive searcher and this half-phantom, half-woman magnificently exploits San Francisco and its environs as a backdrop. Hitchcock's use of landscape and geography is most revealing. The locations chosen are all connected with the past and with time: the Palace of the Legion of Honor Museum, the Portals of the Past, the ancient redwoods. Even the details within scenes are keyed as symbols for the timeless state Scottie has entered: the mirrors (traditional passageways into the underworld) in the flower shop at which Madeleine stops and the elegant restaurant, Ernie's, in which he first sees her, and the fog-enshrouded graveyard of the Mission Dolores.

The central symbol for the film is, however, the mission at San Juan Batista. It is here that Scottie searches for Carlotta's past in hopes of finding verification for Madeleine's claims. Steeped in history, the mission is safely isolated from the everyday world. It is a museum of California's past, a place of religious ritual and retreat. It is to these ancestral roots that Madeleine returns, and it is here that Scottie is forced to confront not only his obsession with her but also his phobia. Madeleine, driven to the site of Carlotta's suicide by some force, ascends the bell tower of the mission, pursued by Scottie. In an agonizingly painful scene, Madeleine jumps from the tower as Scottie, frozen by his acrophobia and unable to climb the staircase, is forced to watch, for a second time, someone fall to his death.

The second half of the film traces Scottie's nervous breakdown and his feeble attempts at recovery, which are halted abruptly with the discovery of a woman named Judy who resembles the lost Madeleine. The confusion of dream and reality is now almost total. The viewer is as perplexed as Scottie as he proceeds to take advantage of this second chance fate has apparently handed him. It is at this moment in the film that Hitchcock makes his most daring move. For the first time he gives the audience access to more information than what is known to Scottie. Judy confesses, in a letter she destroys before sending, that she posed as Elster's wife and that her supposed derangement and suicide were hoaxes concocted by Elster to cover the murder of his wealthy wife.

The tone of the film now changes drastically as the viewer is given back, at least partially, his distance and his objectivity. The mood becomes much more ironic as the audience watches Scottie transform Judy in clothes, makeup, hairstyle, and speech into his image of Madeleine. Perhaps the most powerful visual moment in the film occurs when Judy/Madeleine emerges from the bathroom of her apartment after Scottie has put the final touches on his Galatea. Bathed in an ethereal green light, she embraces Scottie, who is now completely lost in the dream, and the camera begins a series of dizzying 360° tracking shots around the couple. Scottie looks up from the embrace and the apartment has become the mission stables in which he first passionately kissed Madeleine. The scene is a visual externalization of the interior state of Scottie's mind, the dizziness (another form of vertigo), overlapping of fantasy and reality, and obsession becoming madness.

The denouement of the film details Scottie's discovery of the hoax and his painful movement toward a cure. Discovering a piece of Madeleine's jewelry in Judy's dresser, Scottie decides that he must relive the traumatic incident which caused his breakdown. He takes Judy to the mission bell tower and, dragging her behind him, ascends the staircase to the parapet. Elated by his victory, he turns to Judy as if to embrace her. At the moment of his triumph, however, a figure in black appears (a nun literally, figuratively the image of death or moral retribution), and a terrified Judy falls to her death. Scottie walks to the edge of the tower and stares down disconsolately. Instead of breaking the pattern as he intended, he has only succeeded in repeating it. His vertigo has been conquered, but at the price of a second love.

Vertigo is probably one of the most potent influences on a whole generation of filmmakers, particularly the French New Wave, which paid homage to the film again and again. Alain Resnais' *Last Year at Marienbad* (1962) can be seen as an elliptical reworking of the plot of *Vertigo* as well as being filled with details from the film, even down to the musical score. François Truffaut has included an allusion to *Vertigo* in almost all of his own films, but most notably in *The Mississippi Mermaid* (1970), in which a deceptive Catherine Deneuve (in two *personae*, one named Marion, one Julie) leads a maddened Jean-Paul Belmondo on a chase through the corridors of "amour fou."

It is unfortunate that *Vertigo*, which many cinema historians, such as Donald Spots, feel is Hitchcock's masterpiece, as well as one of the greatest films of all time, is unavailable for public screenings in the United States. Along with another masterful Hitchcock/Stewart film, *Rear Window* (1954), litigation makes it difficult, if not impossible, to view. There is so much in *Vertigo*, that a single showing barely opens the door to its understanding. Hopefully the future will provide filmgoers a greater opportunity to view it again—and again.

James Ursini

A VIEW FROM THE BRIDGE

Released: 1961
Production: Paul Graetz for Continental Distributing
Direction: Sidney Lumet
Screenplay: Norman Rosten; based on the play of the same name by Arthur Miller
Cinematography: Michel Kelber
Editing: Françoise Javet
Running time: 110 minutes

Principal characters:
Eddie Carbone .... Raf Vallone
Rodolpho .... Jean Sorel
Beatrice Carbone .... Maureen Stapleton
Catherine .... Carol Lawrence
Marco .... Raymond Pellegrin
Mr. Alfier .... Morris Carnovsky
Mike .... Harvey Lembeck
Lipari .... Vincent Gardenia

Arthur Miller, who is arguably the greatest living American playwright, is the author of such outstanding dramas as *Death of a Salesman*, *All My Sons*, and *The Crucible*. He also wrote the screenplay for *The Misfits* (1961), which contained the final film appearances of his wife Marilyn Monroe and Clark Gable. Other film work included scenes for *Let's Make Love* (1960), starring Monroe and Yves Montand, and the English narrative for Luigi Zampa's *Difficult Years* (1950). *All My Sons*, *Death of a Salesman*, and *The Crucible* were filmed by, respectively, Irving Reis in 1948, Laslo Benedek in 1951, and Raymond Rouleau in 1958. (The latter film is also known as *The Witches of Salem*.) The most faithful screen adaptation of a Miller play, however, is *A View from the Bridge* (1961), directed by Sidney Lumet.

Raf Vallone stars in the film as Eddie Carbone, a hard-working, inarticulate Italian-American longshoreman who labors on the Brooklyn waterfront. He and his wife Beatrice (Maureen Stapleton) are childless, but they have reared their niece Catherine (Carol Lawrence) from birth, and the eighteen-year-old girl is the pride of Eddie's life. The focus of the drama begins when Marco (Raymond Pellegrin) and Rodolpho (Jean Sorel), two of Beatrice's cousins, illegally enter the United States. Eddie hides them in his home and finds them work on the waterfront. Marco, who is married, sends his wages home to his wife and three children, but Rodolpho, who is young, handsome, and single, is attracted to Catherine. She is also attracted to him, angering Eddie, who has sublimated his incestuous feelings for Catherine until he finds a rival for her affections. He rejects his wife, who warns him that his unconscious worship of his niece may result in tragedy, and becomes increasingly jealous of Rodolpho. When he returns home unexpectedly one day and finds the two kissing, he accuses the younger man of wooing Catherine solely to gain American citizenship. When Catherine refuses to believe Eddie's claim, he labels Rodolpho a homosexual and kisses him on the lips in front of her.

Realizing that they must leave Eddie's house as soon as possible, Catherine and Rodolpho are determined to marry. Out of desperation, Eddie betrays Rodolpho and Marco to the immigration authorities, and Marco accuses Eddie of informing on them as they are led away. Marco is set for deportation, but Rodolpho obtains his freedom because he will soon be married to Catherine, an American citizen. Marco is released on bail, however, and forces Eddie to his knees in front of his friends, neighbors, and family. Humiliated, Eddie plunges a dockworker's hook into his chest, and the film ends.

A View from the Bridge, with all its elements of Greek tragedy, was adapted almost word for word by Norman Rosten from Miller's 1955 stage play. The film's tension rests almost entirely on the growing unrest within Eddie Carbone, and his confrontations with Beatrice, Catherine, Rodolpho, and Marco. Sequence after sequence unfolds as Eddie inexorably moves toward his tragic destiny. The film is crisply written, edited, and acted. It is a striking, atmospheric tale about a man who controls his own fate. He perceives whatever he chooses to about a specific situation, and his conscious mind will not admit what exists in his subconscious.

Eddie is an honorable man, which makes his fate even more tragic. He takes in Beatrice's cousins, finds them work, and superficially protects his niece from Rodolpho. In his view of Rodolpho and Catherine's growing love, however, Eddie will not admit his motives, which are more complex than mere feelings of protection. His downfall results not so much from his betrayal of Rodolpho and Marco but from his own self-deception. The final sequence in which Eddie and Marco, each armed with a hook, are set to fight to the death, is particularly horrifying and exciting.

A View from the Bridge, filmed on location in Brooklyn with interiors shot in Paris's Espinay Studios, is only one of a number of New York-oriented films (*The Pawnbroker*, 1965; *Bye Bye Braverman*, 1968; *The Anderson Tapes*, 1971; *Serpico*, 1973; *Dog Day Afternoon*, 1975; *The Wiz*, 1978; *Just Tell Me What You Want*, 1980) directed by Lumet. Lumet, Woody Allen, and Paul Mazursky are the three active directors with the most personalized visions of the city. Allen's New Yorkers are intellectual and neurotic, while Mazursky's are idealistic and searching. The characters in the films of both directors have abandoned the city's outer boroughs for the stylishness and hip ambience of Manhattan's Greenwich Village or Upper East Side.

Lumet's New York is a metropolis of neighborhoods, communities, back alleys, tenements, bars, pool halls, subways, and corner grocery stores. His city dwellers are not writers or art gallery receptionists or aspiring actors but policemen, bank robbers, social workers, and housewives. They are ordinary working-class men and women caught up in the bustle of big-city life, and they are just as likely to live on Flatbush Avenue in Brooklyn as Park Avenue or Riverside Drive. Lumet's New York is also a city of dreams, a potential Land of Oz. His characters, such as Alan King's loud-mouthed tycoon in *Just Tell Me What You Want*, can rise to the upper classes, but usually they do not. On any given day, the one director most likely to be shooting on location somewhere in New York City is Lumet.

A View from the Bridge is cast with actors relatively unknown to American film audiences in 1961. Vallone and Sorel are, respectively, Italian and French-born actors; neither became stars in American films, although Vallone has been cast in numerous Hollywood features. He also starred as Eddie Carbone on the Paris stage, and easily gives the best performance of his career in an English language film. Lawrence, the original Maria in the Broadway production of *West Side Story*, offers a sensitive performance as Catherine, but has had little of a career as a screen actress. Morris Carnovsky, who portrays a lawyer who warns Eddie of the impending disaster and serves as the film's Greek chorus, is a distinguished stage actor who occasionally appears in films.

Stapleton is the only featured performer in the film to have developed a sustained career in American films. *A View from the Bridge* was only the third feature of this versatile character actress, who has performed memorably in *Lonelyhearts* (1959), *Airport* (1970), *Interiors* (1978), and the television film *Queen of the Stardust Ballroom* (1975). Another familiar featured performer cast in a minor role in *A View from the Bridge* is Vincent Gardenia, a fine character actor on television as well as in films who was memorable as the baseball manager in *Bang the Drum Slowly* (1973).

A View from the Bridge is a French/Italian/American production, and was also shot in a French-language version with dialogue by Jean Aurenche. Vallone, who knew no English at the time, spoke his lines phonetically although this in no way detracts from his performance. Lawrence, who spoke no French, learned her lines phonetically for the French version, while Stapleton's dialogue was dubbed in French. The film received good notices. Some critics, however, claimed that it was a bit too theatrical; others felt that Eddie Carbone was a boor, more of a pathetic animal than a tragic hero. Because the film had virtually no visually exciting scenes and little "action" before the last scene, and also because of the lack of big-name stars and studio clout, it did badly at the box office, earning less than one million dollars. It was not on *Variety*'s list of top-grossing films for 1961, and it was televised two years after its release.

Rob Edelman

THE VIRGIN AND THE GYPSY

Released: 1970
Production: Kenneth Harper for Chevron
Direction: Christopher Miles
Screenplay: Alan Plater; based on the novella of the same name by D. H. Lawrence
Cinematography: Robert Huke
Editing: Paul Davies
Running time: 92 minutes

Principal characters:
Yvette	Joanna Shimkus
The Gypsy	Franco Nero
Mrs. Fawcett	Honor Blackman
Major Eastwood	Mark Burns
The Rector	Maurice Denham
Grandma	Fay Compton
Lucille	Harriet Harper
Aunt Cissie	Kay Walsh
The Gypsy's Wife	Imogen Hassall
Uncle Fred	Norman Bird
Leo	Jeremy Bulloch

As the title suggests, *The Virgin and the Gypsy* is a film of contrasts, both subtle and sharp. Based on D. H. Lawrence's final novella of the same name which was discovered in rough draft form after his death and published in 1930, it further explores the Lawrentian themes of the loss of innocence, the revolt against the old order, the hypocrisy of social convention, and the emergence of sexuality.

Appropriately set in the early 1920's, an era heralding great transition, the historical perspective functions as the larger context in which this story of personal change unfolds. At the beginning of the film, two sisters, Lucille (Harriet Harper) and Yvette (Joanna Shimkus), are returning to England after completing their education in France. Their home is a rectory outside the sparsely inhabited village of Colgrave in the North of England, a cold contrast to the warmth of France. When they return home, Lucille intends to find a job, while Yvette merely hopes to fall in love. Harper is well cast as the self-possessed, sensible Lucille, as is Shimkus as the ethereally beautiful Yvette, who is reserved yet full of sexual longing.

Presiding over the gray stone household which has yet to emerge from the nineteenth century is their father (Maurice Denham), an Anglican vicar. Together with his ill-tempered sister, Aunt Cissie (Kay Walsh), his ineffectual brother, Fred (Norman Bird), and his tyrannical mother (Fay Compton), he creates an environment of intolerable self-righteousness from which the girls can only occasionally escape. In order to heighten the absurdity of the family's self-righteous moral stance, there are scenes of gluttony, petty bickering, and, in the case of the milquetoast brother, a penchant for picking up young women. Long absent from the family is the clergyman's wife, of whom he cannot bear to speak, but from whom he fears his daughters, especially Yvette, might have inherited licentious ways. Having come from "bad blood" and "half-depraved stock," the woman, it seems, fled the oppressive life of the vicarage shortly after her daughters were born.

While Lucille settles in and works at her new job, the restless Yvette languishes about the house, fantasizing about a moody, handsome gypsy (Franco Nero) whom she met while on an exciting horseless carriage ride in the country with friends from town. Although she had uncomfortably averted her eyes from his steely gaze while her friends' fortunes were being told by his wife (Imogen Hassall), she now imagines the beginnings of an affair with him. On their third brief and anxious encounter, during which her yearnings are about to be fulfilled inside his tiny, deserted caravan, they are interrupted by the arrival of a chatty, very modern couple wishing to warm themselves at the gypsy's fire. It seems that, while awaiting the woman's divorce, the two have run off together and taken a cottage not far away. Honor Blackman as Mrs. Fawcett, the runaway socialite and newly emancipated woman, is perfect, with the bobbed, marcelled hair and rouged lips typical of the era. As Major Eastwood, her lover, Mark Burns plays a quietly forceful foil to her ebullience.

Recognizing that Yvette is unlike the villagers, who are already censuring their living arrangement, Mrs. Fawcett and the Major provide her with companionship and refuge at their love nest. Yvette's father is scandalized by her association with them, however, and forbids their entrance to a church benefiting "continental revue" that Yvette has produced to relieve her boredom. Denouncing them as "Animals!" when they try to attend the review, he is doubtless reminded of his wife who went away with her lover. He is also highly displeased at Yvette's refusal of marriage to Leo (Jeremy Bulloch), the son of the town's wealthy industrialist, an insipid, freckle-faced boy whom Yvette perceives as being as much of a suffocating influence upon her life as her father was upon her mother's.

Yvette is soon released from her innocence. The circumstances are provided by the bursting of a dam upstream from the rectory. As a metaphor for Yvette's sexuality, the reservoir's stone wall had revealed a disturbing tendency to leak early in the film as the girls passed by it on their way home from France. Damming otherwise freely flowing waters, it preserved the stillness and tranquility of the stream passing by their home. Some superbly orchestrated scenes show its swift and insidious rise as ripples on the surface become waves surging quietly against the shore.

Arriving on horseback only minutes before the deluge reaches the house where Yvette and her grandmother are spending the afternoon, the gypsy attempts to pull the two to safety but fails; the old lady drowns as the lower floor is engulfed. In order to save themselves, Yvette and the gypsy retreat upstairs to a safe room where they remove their soaked clothes to fend off the chill and seek warmth in bed. Yvette awakens alone, the foundations of her father's house in ruins beneath her, the waters crested and spent. Her family waits nervously on the ground outside, below the window where a stepladder waits for her. She descends, but tiptoes past them and past a drowned sheep to join her friends, the lovers on the run, in their car and then drive off. They continue beyond the smoldering fire of the abandoned gypsy camp.

The brother of British actress Sarah Miles, twenty-nine-year-old Christopher Miles has directed this, his first feature film, with control and substance. The use of lush imagery and liberal symbolism reinforces many key scenes and deepens their meaning. An otherwise simple and predictable story thus interpreted involves and challenges the thoughtful viewer. Although probably overemphasizing the lyric beauty of the countryside around Derbyshire and of the Lawrence County estates of Devonshire and Rutland where the film was shot, Miles wisely understates his characters through spare, crisp dialogue, and economy of action. Although critics have labeled his use of symbolism heavy-handed and clichéd, a certain amount of it is vital to the correct interpretation of the story. The frequent appearance of water seems to imply sexual awakening, as do the nude bathing scene and the coital burst of the dam. Yet it also symbolizes a powerfully natural life force. It can also be interpreted as a means of purification or of washing away the old. Other less obscure emblems are the gypsy's black stallion, a caged bird, fire, the stone-cold rectory, its mealtime carnality, the drowned sheep, and the fugitive couple, among others.

In addition to the symbolism, the literary convention of portents adds seasoning to the tale. The cryptic innuendoes uttered by nearly every character, particularly the gypsy and his palm-reading wife, are so subtle that their use, like the symbolism, does not seem contrived. A voguish but effective cinematic device portrays Yvette's lusty reveries. Faded color combined with soundless slow motion re-create the unreality of the scene, which, in one instance, is weakened by the anachronistic untanned bikini line across her bare back. Otherwise richly evocative of the period, social context, and locale, the post-Edwardian settings and costume are faithfully detailed. The only major departure of the film from the novella occurs in the final scene. Lawrence's Yvette does not depart with Mrs. Fawcett and the Major, leaving the reader instead with a much less neatly resolved story and much more to ponder.

Nancy S. Kinney

VOLTAIRE

Released: 1933
Production: Warner Bros.
Direction: John G. Adolfi
Screenplay: Paul Green and Maude T. Howell; based on an unproduced play
  by George Gibbs and E. Lawrence Dudley
Cinematography: Tony Gaudio
Editing: Owen Marks
Running time: 72 minutes

Principal characters:
Voltaire	George Arliss
Madame de Pompadour	Doris Kenyon
Nanette Calas	Margaret Lindsay
François	Theodore Newton
King Louis XV	Reginald Owen
Count de Sarnac	Alan Mowbray
Doctor	David Torrence

The filming of *Voltaire* fulfilled a longtime ambition of its star, George Arliss. Arliss had a long and successful career on the stage before he began appearing in films in the 1920's and had often expressed his wish to play the great eighteenth century French philosopher and author on the stage, but he was never able to find a satisfactory vehicle. At one time George Gibbs, a friend of Arliss, even collaborated with the novelist E. Lawrence Dudley to write a play on Voltaire especially for Arliss. Arliss liked the play and worked with the two on rewriting and polishing it for a stage production, but the project was dropped. Much later, however, when Arliss was at Warner Bros., he again brought up the idea of his playing Voltaire and, somewhat to his surprise, found it accepted. The unproduced play was dusted off and revised by Maude T. Howell and Paul Green, Arliss finally got his chance to portray Voltaire.

Arliss, who was consulted frequently by the studio during the preproduction planning, was sensitive to the problems of presenting an intellectual on the screen. Voltaire's importance and influence rest on his writings, but a man sitting at a desk writing is not especially interesting to watch. In addition, the studio was somewhat dubious about the popularity of such a "highbrow" subject. The solution to all these problems, and one which fit well the populist leanings of Warner Bros., was to present Voltaire chiefly as a precursor of the French Revolution.

Although one of the other characters does call Voltaire "a poet, a dramatist, a philosopher—the greatest France has ever produced," the story told in this film is of a court wit who defies King Louis XV (Reginald Owen). At the opening, a title states that Voltaire "attacked intolerance and injustice" and "educated the masses to think and act." This puts the audience in a sympathetic frame of mind for seeing the eccentric old man who is taken care of by his niece and a servant.

Voltaire's skirmishes with the King are at first seen by the monarch as only the activities of an amusing scoundrel. When he takes the side of Nanette Calas (Margaret Lindsay), the daughter of an unjustly executed man, however, Voltaire is taken more seriously. In this battle Voltaire proves that he is crafty enough to win full redress for the young woman. He uses Madame de Pompadour (Doris Kenyon) to influence the King, and to further his point he writes a play in which Nanette plays the principal role. In addition Voltaire bests Count de Sarnac (Alan Mowbray) in a contest for power. All this makes him so popular with the people that crowds gather to cheer him, and the King orders his writings burned.

When Voltaire warns the King of "gathering clouds of revolution," he is asked to "make us laugh—give us your wit, but keep your wisdom." At the end of the film Voltaire says "I have no scepter, but I have my pen," and then we see shots of revolutionary crowds with words such as *justice* and *tolerance* superimposed over them. *Voltaire* is the portrait of the intellectual as freedom fighter and popular hero.

The first scene in which we see Voltaire sets up the entire characterization. He is wearing an old dressing gown and a scarf wrapped around his head and is oblivious to his appearance and his health. Totally involved in writing a letter of protest to the King, he is ignoring the orders of his doctor (David Torrence) to rest and eat. His food remains uneaten while he drinks cup after cup of coffee, a beverage his doctor has forbidden. When the doctor arrives to check up on him, Voltaire suddenly shifts his attention from the evils of the King to trying to conceal his transgressions from his doctor. To protest that he is ruining his health, Voltaire says, "I haven't time to die while there are thousands of people oppressed, tortured, starving." Thus is established his passionate concern for the people, his eccentricity, and his humanity. The script is characterized by a mixture of ringing speeches such as the one above, many contrasts between the rich and the poor and between Voltaire and the members of the court, and a few telling devices, such as a chess game during which Voltaire suddenly declares that he does not want to protect his king.

Like many other Hollywood historical or biographical films, no matter how well-intentioned its makers, *Voltaire* has more accuracy in its sets than in its plot. Several of the scenes are fictional, but the terrace of the Petit Trianon was so carefully reproduced on the Warner Bros. lot that, Arliss said, he almost spoke his lines when he visited the actual spot the next summer after the filming. It is, of course, not for an exact depiction of history that *Voltaire* is notable but for a vivid and well-acted interpretation of a great man and his influence. Arliss believably portrays Voltaire as a many-faceted man who can be obsessed with his work at the expense of his health at one time and almost foppishly concerned about his appearance at another.

Arliss is ably supported by Kenyon as Madame de Pompadour, Lindsay as Nanette Calas, Mowbray as de Sarnac, and Owen as the King. John Adolfi's direction is simple and straightforward.

Judith A. Williams

WAGONMASTER

Released: 1950
Production: John Ford and Merian C. Cooper for Argosy; released by RKO/
  Radio
Direction: John Ford
Screenplay: Frank S. Nugent and Patrick Ford; based on an original story by
  John Ford
Cinematography: Bert Glennon
Editing: Jack Murray
Running time: 86 minutes

  Principal characters:
  Travis Blue .... Ben Johnson
  Sandy Owens .... Harry Carey, Jr.
  Denver ....Joanne Dru
  Elder Wiggs .... Ward Bond
  Sister Ledeyard .... Jane Darwell
  Prudence .... Kathleen O'Malley
  Uncle Shiloh Clegg ....Charles Kemper
  Floyd Clegg .... James Arness
  Luke Clegg .... Hank Worden
  Reese Clegg .... Fred Libbey
  Jesse Clegg .... Mickey Simpson
  Indian Girl .... Movita Castaneda

  Wagonmaster uses the conventional elements of the Western genre to tell
a very modern story of intolerance. John Ford, who wrote the original story,
told director Peter Bogdanovich, "Along with *The Fugitive* and *The Sun Shines
Bright*, I think *Wagonmaster* came closest to being what I had wanted to
achieve." That these three films all deal with the intolerance of a social group
toward its unconventional but perhaps most valued members is not accidental,
and is further illuminated by an incident recorded by Bogdanovich. During
the Blacklist years in Hollywood, Joseph L. Mankiewicz's Americanism was
questioned by some pro-McCarthy members of the Director's Guild. Ford
stood up, confronted the right-wing spokesman Cecil B. De Mille, and moved
that the Guild give Mankiewicz a vote of confidence, which it promptly did.
This was a more courageous move than it might seem in days when a single
whispered accusation, substantiated or not, could end a career and when
"guilt by association" was the rule of the day.
  Set in the 1870's, *Wagonmaster* is about a group of Mormons who are
traveling West through uncharted country to their "promised land." They ask
Travis Blue (Ben Johnson), a young horse trader, to lead them, and he
reluctantly agrees. *Wagonmaster* is very rich in gentle and nostalgic emotion,
underscored by comedy. This deceptively unpretentious film is in many ways

the high point of Ford's Westerns; in it, the director's optimism and pessimism are in perfect balance. The darker side of his vision gives an emotional depth lacking in earlier films such as *Stagecoach* (1939) and *Drums Along the Mohawk* (1939), but the optimism prevails and renders this film essentially undisturbing and only gentle in its nostalgia, not bitter like later Westerns.

Wagonmaster has a great deal in common with the more famous *Stagecoach*. Both tell stories of a group of people traveling together who are menaced by hostile forces that threaten them with destruction. Travis and *Stagecoach*'s Ringo are similar types—very gentle and kind, silent but strong-willed and capable. Johnson was a minor actor who had worked often for Ford, just as John Wayne at the time of *Stagecoach* was a member of Ford's "stock company." The two are even dressed similarly in black shirts, dark hats, and suspenders. The Dallas character (Claire Trevor) of *Stagecoach* is similar to the Denver character (Joanne Dru) of *Wagonmaster*—a girl with a "shady" background whom the hero nevertheless treats with great respect.

Wagonmaster, however, lacks the structural problems of *Stagecoach*. The film moves by its own energy and not from the necessities of script. The action sequences, far from working at odds with character development, function as expressions of internal tensions being worked out by the characters. Significantly, the Mormons are extricated from a danger far less abstract and alien to them than Indians, not by an equally remote force such as the cavalry, but through their own collective efforts.

The wagon train meets a broken-down company of show people stranded in the desert who function as a challenge to the snobbery and complacency of the Mormons. Their reaction is certainly not Christian—one young Mormon, who later battles with Sandy Owens (Harry Carey, Jr.) over Prudence (Kathleen O'Malley), is in favor of giving them a wagon and sending them off; he does not want that kind of people in their train. The Mormon women are shown looking dark and cloistered, protecting their values from these intruders, and the men only grudgingly agree to give them one of their wagons. Even this "Christian" act is only the Mormons' way of getting rid of them without putting their fates on the Mormons' consciences. It is Travis who insists that the show people go along with them. He insists calmly and Elder Wiggs (Ward Bond) acts as peacemaker, saying that the Lord put them here for a purpose, and they had better not interfere with the Lord's plans.

The audience's own moral assumptions are also held up for scrutiny. For example, when we first see the show people, Denver is lounging in her entertainment dress, very drunk and looking disrespectable in her sexually suggestive pose. Travis is the only one who does not make moral judgment, even going so far as to offer Denver the drink for which he thinks she has asked. Only then do we, and Travis, learn that she wants water and that the show people are drunk because they have had to drink the "elixir" they sell to keep from dying of thirst. They maintain a false dignity that sets them apart from the others, even when they are accepted into the wagon train.

The Denver-Travis relationship is balanced by one between Sandy and Prudence. When Sandy first sees Prudence walking up to the horses with her father, he takes off his hat and bows to her. This action is repeated every time he sees her; even when they are dancing he takes off his hat and bows to her every time she comes around to him in the square dance. Their "romance" is simple and uncomplicated compared to that of Travis and Denver, who have various tensions to overcome before they can come together. In Ford's most bittersweet stories, these problems are too much for the lovers and they never do become a couple, as in *The Searchers* (1956) and *The Man Who Shot Liberty Valance* (1962). The love story is not the most important narrative element, but the eventual union of Travis and Denver reflects the resolution of the Mormon community's tensions.

The dance on the fresh-laid boards is the high point of the first half of the film and seems to be an expression of the community's solidarity. When we look more closely, however, it is apparent that the four couples dancing the Texas Star (Travis and Denver, Sandy and Prudence, the Elder and the older woman from the show troupe, and Sandy's rival with another girl) represent all the unresolved sexual tensions of the film. The apparent unity is false, easily interrupted and exposed as artificial when the outlaw Cleggs walk into the Mormon camp.

Immediately, everything changes. The music stops, the lighting becomes sinister and threatening, and the long, secure shots of the busy community give way to frightened and frightening close-ups. The Cleggs are shot individually in close-up with more backlight than front- or sidelight, which makes them seem even larger and more maniacal. The Elder, Travis, and Sandy are shown in similarly expressive light, making them seem frightened and impotent. The Cleggs not only have interrupted the happy community dance, but they have also denuded it. Even members of the community now are shot in this high-contrast, isolating style, as if they had had their veneer of civilization stripped from them.

A very few scenes later, this dance is parodied in the Indian dance, which is lighted and shot much like the end of the white dance after the Cleggs have interrupted it. Although the two dances constitute essentially the same ritual for their societies, the Indian dance is far more savage, less melodic, and lacking the grace and movement of the more "civilized" ritual. The white women cluster together in fear during the Indian dance, shot in dark, shadowy light. They are threatened by the dance, and they recede into the background much as they did at the appearance of the Cleggs.

In this caricature of the earlier dance in which its civilized veneer has been stripped away, the sexual tensions of the Mormon community are made explicit. Thus, this dance is also interrupted, by the Indian girl (Movita Castaneda) who has been molested by one of the Clegg boys. In the less inhibited society of the Indians, the degenerate, perverted sexuality the Cleggs represent breaks open in a way that it could not in the repressed society of the Mormons. The Cleggs represent perversion brought about by the kind of repression the Mormons practice, and their appearance forces the Mormons to come to terms with that repression.

The first shots in the film are of the Cleggs during their robbery. In this sequence, the lighting is different from that of the rest of the film until the Cleggs come to the wagon train; it is very high contrast, expressionistically claustrophobic and chaotic. Then we see the flight of the Cleggs, intercut with shots of Sandy and Travis and the wagon train, linking the journey of the Cleggs's escape closely with the journey of the Mormons. The Cleggs are thus like the Mormons and like the horse traders in being run or edged out of town. (The card player links them in the dialogue when he refers to "Indians, Mormons, show people . . . and horse traders.")

Uncle Shiloh (Charles Kemper) is presumably the boys' father; he refers to them as "my boys" and to Luke (Hank Worden) as "my oldest boy." He is called "Uncle," however, and this perverts the family relationship in both a real and symbolic way. The Mormons also call him Uncle Shiloh, further acknowledging their own relationship to the evil family and making of him a perverted father figure that they must all repudiate before they can cross the mountain. This situation is apparent from the Cleggs's intrusion into the community. Uncle Shiloh first takes over a bed, leering at the women and rendering the men impotent. The demand for the Mormons' guns symbolically robs them of their virility. The Clegg boys all represent some form of perversion. Floyd (James Arness) carries Denver off repeatedly while Luke voyeuristically leers and laughs maniacally, and Reese (Fred Libbey) lusts after every woman there and eventually rapes the Indian girl. The Cleggs are the physical expression of the Mormons' darker side.

The show people also represent to the Mormons eroticism of an unacceptable, although much less perverted, form. They expose the community's prejudice by their very existence and their refusal to be hypocritical. Denver never tries to act prim and proper while she is with them, and the old woman never accepts less than the truth about her nonlegitimatized relationship with the "doctor." It is Denver's shameless bath that precipitates a fight between Sandy and a Mormon boy over Prudence. Not until the Mormons have overcome these tensions can they reach their goal; then they become free from the threat of the Cleggs and incorporate the old show couple into their group. This further frees Travis and Denver from their own isolation, and they, too, become a couple.

We never see the San Juan Valley of the Mormons, but we feel their sense of destination through the visual style, and we see their faces when they look upon it. This new land exists only in Ford's mind and in theirs, never visually in the film; it remains a dream, more haunting and more emotionally real because of its lack of physical expression.

The last shots are of the journey again, expressing the transcendent unity of those on the wagon train. Now that the Cleggs have been defeated, a unity is possible that could not exist when their presence was poisoning the wagon train and when its own interior tensions were unsettled. The reprise of the journey is not really a reprise; some shots in this sequence did not exist in the body of the film. Sandy and Prudence, Travis and Denver together in wagons, and the elder, Sandy, and Travis singing together—these shots are not in the film, but they belong emotionally in the reprise because they express the emotional unity that now exists.

The primary drive in *Wagonmaster* is thus toward assimilation, toward a creation of a whole from the various parts of the film. The reprise ending, although confusing in time and space, is right because these shots of all the characters, unified into one harmonious and cohesive community, express perfectly the emotional climax of the film.

The concept of such a reprise leads one to examine the nature of the work itself. If its central purpose were merely to tell a story, falsifying that story in the last scenes would be tantamount to a betrayal of the work. If the film is the creation of an artistic sensibility, however, in which emotional validity takes precedence over any other concern, the reprise is exactly right. It becomes the reaffirmation of a work whose value lies above all in its power to move people emotionally.

Janey Place

WAIT UNTIL DARK

Released: 1967
Production: Mel Ferrer for Warner Bros.
Direction: Terence Young
Screenplay: Robert Carrington and Jane Howard Carrington; based on the
  play of the same name by Frederick Knott
Cinematography: Charles Lang
Editing: Gene Milford
Music: Henry Mancini
Running time: 107 minutes

Principal characters:
Susie Hendrix .... Audrey Hepburn
Harry Roat, Jr. .... Alan Arkin
Mike Talman .... Richard Crenna
Sam Hendrix .... Efrem Zimbalist, Jr.
Carlino ....Jack Weston
Lisa .... Samantha Jones
Gloria .... Julie Herrod
Shatner .... Frank O'Brien
Boy .... Gary Morgan

Wait Until Dark, a pulse-quickening mystery thriller about a blind woman
who is hounded by three vicious dope peddlers, was adapted from the 1966
Broadway play directed by theater and film director Arthur Penn. In the role
of the tortured sightless wife, Audrey Hepburn plays the part filled by Lee
Remick on the stage as the vulnerable female victim. *The Spiral Staircase*
(1946) with Dorothy McGuire, *Sorry Wrong Number* (1948) with Barbara
Stanwyck, and *Gaslight* (1944) with Ingrid Bergman are well-known examples
of the "woman alone" film in which terror is derived from the attempt of a
woman to free herself from a menace which no one else knows about or can
help her with.

Taking place in the claustrophobic confines of a Greenwich Village basement apartment, the melodrama concerns a blind woman named Susie Hendrix (Audrey Hepburn), whose blindness was caused by an accident less than
one year ago. She has to fend for herself one afternoon when her commercial
artist and high-fashion photographer husband Sam (Efrem Zimbalist, Jr.) is
summoned to attend to a job in New Jersey. The audience soon learns,
however, that her husband has been called away on a hoax so that three
sinister thugs can search the apartment for a heroin-filled antique musical doll
foisted onto an unwitting, innocent Sam by a double-crossing fashion model
named Lisa (Samantha Jones).

When the terrified Susie insists she does not know where the doll is, the criminals, led by the most malevolent one, Harry Roat, Jr. (Alan Arkin), concoct an elaborate series of disguises in order to gain entrance to her apartment and thus break down her story. Pretending to be a cop, for example, the crooked Carlino (Jack Weston) insinuates that Sam is somehow involved with Lisa's murder.

Although she suspects that Roat and Carlino are impostors, the still-gullible Susie believes that the third hoodlum, Mike (Richard Crenna), is Sam's old Marine Corps buddy. Soon, horrified to realize that the three are in cahoots, Susie sends Gloria (Julie Herrod), her willful young neighbor, to meet the returning Sam at the station. As it turns out, Gloria had been playing with the doll in her family's adjacent apartment all along. Susie soon finds herself trapped, sightless, and vulnerable in her apartment with the telephone lines cut. The intruders force their way into the room, and Susie is a blind witness to the psychopathic killer Roat's murder of Mike and Carlino.

Frantically wielding a knife, Susie smashes all the lights in the apartment so that the menacing man is as sightless as she. Hiding behind the refrigerator, Susie is paralyzed with fright as the diabolical Roat circles in the dark, taps an ominous-sounding cane, and flicks matches in the gasoline drenched and ill-lighted room. In the film's electrifying climax, the mentally deranged man cunningly fixes his attention on a possible source of illumination: with a wicked sneer and quick thrust, he opens the refrigerator door.

As do most films in the "shocker" genre, *Wait Until Dark*, ends with the heroine being rescued in time and the villain being killed. The plot points of the film, however, are not as important as the tension created by the director and actors which make the story believable to the audience. *Wait Until Dark* was quite successful on this level, even to the point of producing screams from the audience whenever it was shown. In some ways the film is in the Alfred Hitchcock mode; in fact, playwright Frederick Knott wrote Hitchcock's 1954 suspense drama *Dial M for Murder*, also notable for a famous "woman alone" scene in which the heroine is terrorized by an intruder. The hidden themes of these films and others of the type play on man's primal fear of the unknown and irrational and the desperate need to turn for help when there is seemingly none available. Henry Mancini's musical score, with the music-box theme introduced in the movie's precredit sequence, helps to create the tense mood, and the use of the dissonant bass provides the appropriate foreboding tones.

Although the film has severe script problems (for example, Susie never even attempts to contact the police or leave her apartment to look for help), Terence Young directs the story to produce considerable suspense. Responsible for such James Bond pictures as *Dr. No* (1962), *From Russia with Love* (1964), and *Thunderball* (1965), Young's technique produces a spine-tingling pace. Produced by Mel Ferrer (Hepburn's husband at the time), the acting in *Wait Until Dark* is excellent. Earning her a nomination for Best Actress by the Motion Picture Academy, Hepburn's performance is believable and honest. The heavies are more than adequately villainous, although Crenna and Arkin had not previously played screen villains. In his first straight dramatic role, Arkin brings his own innate charm to the devilish part. Although known primarily as a wry comedian in such films as *The Russians Are Coming, the Russians Are Coming* (1966) and *The In-Laws* (1977), Arkin proves himself to be a very versatile performer in *Wait Until Dark*. His chilling performance is reminiscent of the late Peter Lorre in some of his better melodramas of the 1930's and 1940's.

The film was a financial success, because of its properly tense script and also because of the personal popularity of star Hepburn. *Wait Until Dark* was made at a period in her career when she was at the height of her popularity at the box office; she made *Two for the Road*, another successful film, in that same year. Just after these two films were released, however, Hepburn and Ferrer were divorced, and Hepburn moved to Europe, remarried, and retired from films for almost ten years. Her next film was *Robin and Marian* (1976); she has made only a few films, and none of them very successful, since that time. Although still beautiful, slim, and elegant in her fifties, Hepburn's recent films have lacked the overall production values which made many of her films of the 1950's and 1960's successes.

Leslie Taubman

WALKABOUT

Released: 1971
Production: Si Litvinoff for Max L. Raab-Si Litvinoff; released by Twentieth Century-Fox
Direction: Nicolas Roeg
Screenplay: Edward Bond; based on the novel of the same name by James Vance Marshall
Cinematography: Nicolas Roeg
Editing: Antony Gibbs and Alan Patillo
Music: John Barry
Running time: 95 minutes

Principal characters:
Man	John Meillon
Girl	Jenny Agutter
Brother	Jucien John
Aborigine	Gulpilil
Young Man	John Illingworth

Walkabout is an atmospheric, stylized film that depends for its effect upon impressions given as much as upon explicit statement of themes or details of plot development. It is visually striking and frequently puzzling. Neither of these qualities is surprising, however, since director Nicolas Roeg first established his reputation as a cinematographer (in such films as *Fahrenheit 451*, 1966, *Far from the Madding Crowd*, 1967, and *Petulia*, 1968) and the script-writer, British playwright Edward Bond, also collaborated on the script of *Blow-Up* (1966). Although the film is based upon a novel by James Vance Marshall that is very popular in Australia, several changes were made in the plot and the overall tone so that the finished film reflects the sensibilities of Roeg and Bond more than those of Marshall.

The plot itself is actually quite simple, even though it has several perplexing elements. A man (John Meillon) takes his two children into the desert in Australia and suddenly begins shooting at them. When they escape, he sets fire to his car and then shoots himself. The two children, a teenage girl (Jenny Agutter) and a boy about six-years-old (Jucien John), are faced with the seemingly impossible task of trying to survive in the desert with no equipment and no preparation. Just when their situation seems most bleak—a waterhole they have found dries up in the morning sun—an Aborigine boy (Gulpilil) finds and saves them. (Incidentally, none of the three is ever given a name.) One evening the Abo boy decorates his body with paint and feathers and dances for the girl, but she reacts only with fear and confusion. The next morning she and her brother find that the Abo has hanged himself, but by that time they have found a road and soon are back in civilization.

There is, of course, much more to the film than this simple plot. The title refers to the Aborigine practice of sending a boy out to live off the land by himself when he is about sixteen. Originally this fact was not explained in the film itself, but later a forty-eight-word explanation was inserted at the beginning of the film. The explanation concludes with this statement: "This is the story of a 'Walkabout.'"

The film is actually the story of more than one walkabout, for the girl's experience as well as the Abo's is an education and a test. She begins by trying to keep up appearances and her brother's spirits. She tells him that he should take care of his clothes because they do not want people to think they are tramps. "What people?" he responds. Then when the Abo appears, she is unable to deal with the fact that he does not know English. She says the word *water* to him several times, finally exclaiming, "You must understand—anyone can understand that!" It takes her little brother, who mimes the act of drinking, to communicate with the Abo. Eventually his sister is able to unbend as the three play together on a tree, and later she swims in the nude as the Abo hunts and fishes.

Indeed, clothing is very much an emblem of civilized life in this film. The brother and sister are both dressed in proper school uniforms at the beginning of the film, but under the influence of the harsh environment and the Abo boy (who wears a minimum of clothing), they become less fastidious about their appearance. On the last day, however, they again put their clothing in perfect order—or as nearly perfect as possible after their days in the outback.

The opening and closing sequences form a frame for the story that emphasizes its contrast of civilized and natural life. In the opening scene the father walks through the city streets and then into an apartment where his wife works in the kitchen while listening to the radio. In the last sequence a younger man (John Illingworth) walks through the city streets and enters an apartment where a young woman works in the kitchen while listening to the radio. When she turns to him, we see it is the girl who experienced the outback. As the man talks to her of his advancement at his office and his raise in salary, a flashback shows that she is not listening; she is remembering a carefree time with the Abo and her little brother. There is one slight change, however. Originally we saw her swimming alone in the nude, but in the flashback all three are swimming together. An offscreen voice reads a lyric from A. E. Housman's *A Shropshire Lad* about "the land of lost content" as the film ends.

The cinematography, the music, and the sounds of the film give it a powerful and distinctive tone. The harsh and exotic qualities of the environment are conveyed through many shots of the strange desert animals, often in close-up, shots of the fiery sun, and long shots of the landscape that emphasize the insignificance of the people within it. The same qualities are accented by the sound track, which contains such noises as the amplified sound of a lizard scurrying across the sand, and the music, which is frequently electronic and often is an outgrowth of the amplified desert sounds. It is as if the audience can hear the sun and sand as well as see them. The cinematography is by the director, Nicolas Roeg, and the music is by John Barry, with significant contributions from the use of the electronic music of Karlheinz Stockhausen and an electronic pop number by Billy Mitchell.

The acting of all three principals—Agutter, John, and Gulpilil—is excellent. John is the son of the director, and Gulpilil is an authentic Aborigine. Aborigines are shy and dislike performing, but Gulpilil was a tribal dancer and thus had some ability and experience as a performer. He was told through an interpreter the situation in each scene and then he improvised his lines in his Aboriginal dialect. In the film he speaks only one word of English.

Overall *Walkabout* is a fine achievement despite a few unnecessary scenes showing scientists and hunters as further contrast between nature and civilization. The film is so visually powerful that some of its images linger in the mind as long as its story does.

Timothy W. Johnson

WAR AND PEACE

Released: 1956
Production: Dino de Laurentiis for Paramount
Direction: King Vidor
Screenplay: Bridget Boland, King Vidor, Robert Westerby, Mario Camerini, Ennio De Concini, and Ivo Perilli; based on the novel of the same name by Count Leo Tolstoy
Cinematography: Jack Cardiff and Aldo Tonti
Editing: Stuart Gilmore and Leo Cattozzo
Running time: 206 minutes

Principal characters:

Natasha Rostov	Audrey Hepburn
Pierre	Henry Fonda
Andrey	Mel Ferrer
Anatole	Vittorio Gassman
Platon	John Mills
Napoleon	Herbert Lom
General Kutuzov	Oscar Homolka
Nicholas Rostov	Jeremy Brett
Helene	Anita Ekberg
Sonya	May Britt

War and Peace is a classic example of a historical epic brought to the film screen via Hollywood. The events of Count Leo Tolstoy's novel are carefully reproduced, but they are seen through the modern, rose-colored glasses of Technicolor and VistaVision. The mid-1950's, when it was produced, saw the film industry trying to grab audiences away from television sets by creating effects on film not possible on the small screen. Although *War and Peace* contains some excellent moments, the problems of the new wide screen were not solved within it. There are many great visuals, in the clash of French and Russian armies, for example, but more intimate scenes are lost in the expanses of the larger frame. The result, of course, is that the battle scenes come off very well, but the viewer remains at a distance from the characters. This is an important flaw in an otherwise well-made and competently acted film.

Despite the fact that the plot is long and intricate, it is easily followed. It concerns, in the main, three characters: Natasha, Pierre, and Andrey. The film follows events in the lives of each, as Napoleon advances into Russia and brings war with him. The film opens with a map showing the French sweep across Europe, then cuts to a shot of the red-uniformed Czarist troops prancing their white horses through the streets of Moscow.

The Rostov family is then introduced; they are a middle-class clan whose reaction to the war is excitement tinged with apprehension. The teenaged daughter, Natasha (Audrey Hepburn), is a sparkling ingenue who cannot always control her budding emotions. Quiet, introspective Pierre (Henry Fonda), close friend of the Rostovs, introduces her to the coolly handsome Prince Andrey (Mel Ferrer). From then on, the actions of one affect the other two, and the events of war change the fates of all three. Early in the film, Natasha and Andrey, a recent widower, become engaged, on the night of Natasha's first ball. The ballroom is resplendent with elegant dancers and bright crystal chandeliers, rivaled only by Natasha's glittering eyes. The entire company seems filled with the joy radiated by their mutual infatuation. War and infidelity interfere, however: Andrey is away and Natasha is wooed by the aggressively passionate cad, Anatole (Vittorio Gassman). On the stormy night of her planned elopement with Anatole, Pierre tells her the truth of Anatole's less than honorable intentions, and she is crushed. Since she has already written Andrey of her new involvement, she has lost both loves.

It is here that the visuals betray the content of the scene: Natasha is despairing and her face is covered with shadows and flickering firelight. This visual cliché does little to enhance the feeling of overpowering sadness that should have been conveyed. Another problem is Hepburn's acting. Throughout the film, she comes across exceptionally well as a joyous child-woman, but when she tries to portray deeply felt emotion, she does not entirely succeed.

Natasha eventually comes to understand herself when she comes face to face with the destruction of war. Napoleon is approaching Moscow, and the Rostovs are packing up to join the exodus from the city. Natasha convinces her family to leave their belongings and instead carry the wounded out to safety. Among them she finds Andrey. They are reconciled, but Andrey dies. Natasha takes this blow with grace, thankful for their last few moments together. She has become a woman. When the French have left in defeat, the Rostovs return to their half-destroyed city.

Pierre, meanwhile, has joined the fighting to try to understand what war is. He looks incongruous in his city clothes and top hat as he ambles down a country lane toward the fray. A galloping Russian cavalry detachment forces him to scramble off the road and up a hill. There he picks a sweet blossom and takes a few steps to a point from which he can see all that happens in the heat of battle. The cinematography is beautifully executed: the picking of the flower to the overview of the battle is seen in one shot that involves tracking to follow Pierre and craning upward behind him to end in a wide shot of a meadow filled with soldiers, horses, and cannon. The end of the shot, with Pierre as a tiny, still figure in the foreground, and the moving masses beyond, expresses the futility he experiences in trying to act on his feelings in such a situation. King Vidor's direction (he also cowrote the script) of these scenes is full of vitality and emotion. Pierre's idealistic search for truth in war is foiled by Andrey. The latter is a cynical soldier, despite (or perhaps because of) the glory he receives for his bravery. It is the philosophical Pierre who proves to be made of sturdier stuff than the soldier-aristocrat Andrey. Natasha is forgiven for her mistake by Andrey only on his deathbed, while Pierre confesses his love to her at the height of her despair. Also, Pierre, not Andrey, survives the war.

It is from a peasant, Platon (John Mills), that Pierre learns the cheerful stoicism and faith that helps him to survive. While the French are occupying Moscow, Pierre returns to the city and is taken prisoner. He becomes friendly with a fellow prisoner, Platon. They and other prisoners are forced to march through the snow and suffer along with the daunted, retreating French. These scenes of white snow, black trees, and gray-faced, dying men are visually among the best in the film. Pierre sees his friend act out his creed, and he takes the peasant's lessons to heart. Although Platon dies, Pierre overcomes all hardships and in the end returns to Moscow and Natasha. The final shot is of Pierre and Natasha walking hand in hand away from the shell of the Rostov house and toward the future.

Historically, American audiences were thought to lack the ability to sit through very long movies. *War and Peace*'s three-and-a-half hours proved that, although not of the calibre of a *Gone with the Wind* (1939), this overlong film could survive at the box office. The box-office test might not have been necessary, however, if the film had dropped a few of its clutter of characters. Besides the war and the three main characters, we are offered glimpses of many of their friends, relatives, and lovers as well as several scenes with Napoleon himself and a few with a cunning Russian general named Kutuzov (concisely played by Oscar Homolka). An example of some completely extraneous material is an on-and-off romance between Natasha's dashing brother Nicholas (Jeremy Brett) and her quiet cousin Sonya (May Britt). It is of little interest and is lamely resolved.

War and Peace was a good attempt at ironing out the difficulties of translating a time-honored classic from the page to film, although it won no major critical awards. The makers of the film went a route which seems to have been inspired by fear of criticism: they tried to put everything in. The pitfalls of this method are as great as those of a freer, less "faithful" adaptation would be. The overwhelming volume of action and turns of plot leave the viewer with a feeling of satiation from quantity rather than quality. Nevertheless, *War and Peace* achieves a good sense of the history and sociology of its events and is one of the more noble attempts of its kind. While not as critically successful as the marathon seven-hour 1964 Russian version of the classic, King Vidor's *War and Peace* is still worth seeing, although late-night television outings are considerably cut.

Stephanie Kreps

THE WAR OF THE WORLDS

Released: 1953
Production: George Pal for Paramount
Direction: Byron Haskin
Screenplay: Barre Lyndon; based on the novel of the same name by H. G. Wells
Cinematography: George Barnes
Editing: Everett Douglas
Special effects: Gordon Jennings
Running time: 85 minutes

> *Principal characters:*
> Clayton Forrester ....Gene Barry
> Sylvia Van Buren ....Ann Robinson
> General Mann .... Les Tremayne
> Pastor Matthew Collins ....Lewis Martin
> Narrator ....Sir Cedric Hardwicke

The publication in 1898 of H. G. Wells's novel *The War of the Worlds* was a result of the author's fascination with the idea of an earthly invasion from outer space. Drawing upon widespread popular interest in Mars, newly aroused by the 1877 discovery of what was thought to be canals on its surface, Wells conjured up a story of a terrifying visit to his native Victorian London by inhabitants of that planet. He also tapped his college-bred knowledge of biology in climaxing the tale by the bacterial plunder of the Martians.

In 1938, actor Orson Welles translated the story into a radio thriller, updating the setting to modern-day New Jersey. Posing as a news broadcaster, Welles recounted the story as if reporting it, complete with bulletins and on-the-scene interviews. Fear seized the radio audience which had tuned in too late to hear the announcement of the fictional drama. Hundreds of panicked listeners swarmed the countryside in search of places to hide from the invaders.

In its 1953 cinematic reincarnation, science-fiction veteran George Pal lent immediacy if not credibility to the story by setting it in up-to-date Southern California. The picture starred the special effects of Gordon Jennings, who had previously won six Academy Awards for his imaginative work, the most recent of which had been for *When Worlds Collide* in 1951. Its sound effects received the first annual award made by the Motion Picture Sound Editors. The five months and $1,600,000 spent in production were devoted almost entirely to the bizarre effects.

The story begins as Sir Cedric Hardwicke intones the opening lines of Wells's novel while the visually splendid planetary worlds of astronomical artist Chesley Bonestell drift by. The hellish glow of alien worlds gives way to a fireball streaking through black space toward the familiar blue ball of earth. As it lands in the wilderness just outside a town, the forest rangers who sight it reel off the azimuth readings of the suspected "comet" or "meteor" in the first of much persuasive scientific jargon which pervades the film's dialogue. Rowdy townspeople come to gape and conjecture at the buried phenomenon, as do a group of scientists from nearby Pacific Tech who coincidentally happen to be camping overnight in the area.

The cool and handsome astronuclear physicist Clayton Forrester (Gene Barry) wears scientist's glasses only long enough to assure us of his brilliance. Sylvia Van Buren (Ann Robinson), a clergyman's niece and library science teacher, has long known of the man's wide repute. Playing the coy and demure heroine, her fawning attentions upon him herald the love story obligatory in films of the era.

While librarian and physicist dance at a square dance in town, a painfully out-of-character pastime written in for the scientist, farmers miles away peer at a stirring mass. A rock-covered hatch unscrews revealing a steaming interior from which emerges, periscopelike, a cobra head seeing red with a single, faceted-lens eye. A shower of lightning from the eye reduces the men to white ash. Fully levitated from the hot hole, the creature shows itself to be a kind of surreal archaeopteryx—a gooseneck lamp atop a saucer-shaped body with green-glowing breast and wingtips. The gigantic specter was actually created out of a three-foot-wide copper dish dressed up with lights operated electrically offstage and propelled by fifteen fine wires suspended from an overhead track. The eerie shriek of its death ray was achieved by reverberating chords of three guitars, played backward.

Clever repetitive use of only three copper models gives the impression of numerous invaders arriving as reinforcements for the initial scout. The first counterattack upon the advancing ranks is made by Sylvia's uncle, the pastor (Lewis Martin). Personifying religion, he bears toward them a symbol of the cross but is summarily returned to ashes and dust by the death ray. Religious faith is the first instrument of man's salvation to fail in the face of the onslaught. Governments, embodied by their military forces, are next unable to deliver mankind from the now global raid. World War II footage is well used here to convey the vastness of the Martian assault and the futility of armaments in defense against it.

Science, as the final savior of humanity, is incarnate in Clayton Forrester. Having escaped with Sylvia from the initial attackers thanks to his light plane which was luckily tied down nearby, he flies her to an abandoned farmhouse where she sets about fixing his breakfast. Use of models and miniatures recreates an impressive demolition of the house by Martian hardware. In reconnaissance of the rubble, a kind of helmeted electronic eye at the end of a hose is extruded by the Martian. Forrester hacks off the head as its neck is quickly reeled in. Sylvia, meanwhile, is stalked by the unseen. Skillfully mounted suspense is shattered at the sight of a suction-toed hand upon her shoulder placed there by a scaly, one-eyed being of pulsating lungs and veins. It flees, leaving Forrester's benign embraces to calm Sylvia's feminine hysteria. Some confusion arises for the viewer at this point as to the nature of the Martians. What was supposed to be creatures of metal which emitted heat rays of death are now understood to be merely the Martian ships, while the bipedal lizard with one eye is the inhabitant.

In its clash with Forrester, the thing has left bloodstains on a scarf which the scientist examines, along with the decapitated hose, back at the Pacific Tech labs. Mingling science with religion, he observes that the demons "must have mortal weaknesses" and that they can conquer the earth in six days, the same duration in which it was made. The cause of their demise is only hinted at in his reference to their anemic blood. Science, as man's last hope in the war of the worlds, fails when the astronuclear physicist's supreme weapon, the "A-bomb," does not stop the global destruction.

The inability of man's institutions to sustain him in a crisis results in the panicked evacuation of Los Angeles, during which scientist and librarian become separated. On this sixth day of warfare, the Martians had evidently circled the globe and returned near their original landing site for a final pass at the city. The ships crash out of control before Los Angeles is fully leveled, however, stopping short of a church where the masses are huddled and where the clergyman's niece is miraculously and at long last located by the exhausted scientist. The camera pans to the open door of a destroyed ship out of which creeps a three-toed hand blistering over with infection from the microscopic invasion of its blood by bacteria.

The infusion of Christian elements into the film version of his story, inconsistent though they are, would not have pleased the atheistic Wells. The triumph of religious faith in resolution of the screen tale goes counter to the film's early implication of the futility of spiritual belief. The strength of the Pal portrayal of *The War of the Worlds* does not, however, lie in Barre Lyndon's screenplay or in Barry's or Robinson's characterizations or performances. As a vehicle for the then state-of-the-art in special effects, the feature's high technical skill puts it across. It is also the forerunner of a genre well received by the filmgoing public in the 1970's—the disaster film.

Nancy S. Kinney

WATERLOO BRIDGE

Released: 1940
Production: Sidney Franklin for Metro-Goldwyn-Mayer
Direction: Mervyn LeRoy
Screenplay: S. N. Behrman, Hans Rameau, and George Froeschel; based on
the play of the same name by Robert E. Sherwood
Cinematography: Joseph Ruttenberg
Editing: George Boemler
Music: Herbert Stothart
Running time: 103 minutes

Principal characters:
Myra .... Vivien Leigh
Roy Cronin .... Robert Taylor
Lady Margaret Cronin .... Lucile Watson
Kitty .... Virginia Field
Madame Olga Kirowa ..... Mme. Maria Ouspenskaya
The Duke .... C. Aubrey Smith

The story of how Vivien Leigh, a twenty-five-year-old British actress with only a handful of screen credits, triumphantly stepped into the coveted role of Scarlett O'Hara is one of Hollywood's most enduring legends. While she garnered an Oscar for her portrayal of Scarlett, cynics and skeptics of the era wondered if her work in *Gone with the Wind* (1939) was a fluke—a situation similar to the doubt in the late 1970's over the status of Sylvester Stallone, the creator of *Rocky* (1977). Unlike Stallone, with his failures with *F.I.S.T.* (1978) and *Paradise Alley* (1979), however, Leigh proved that she was a fine actress with *Waterloo Bridge*, her next film after her *Gone with the Wind* success.

Waterloo Bridge was based on a 1930 play of the same name by Robert E. Sherwood, a melancholy account of a Canadian soldier who falls in love with a London prostitute during World War I. It was first filmed by James Whale in 1931 with Kent Douglass (Douglass Montgomery), Mae Clarke, and Bette Davis in a bit part, and was remade by Curtis Bernhardt in 1956 as *Gaby*, with Leslie Caron and John Kerr. While the latter film even had a happy ending, the 1940 version was considerably more sentimentalized than its predecessor. It is a bittersweet romantic tale, a four-hankie "woman's picture," and the range and scope of Leigh's role was ideally suited for the actress.

The time is still World War I, and Leigh portrays Myra, a young ballet dancer who meets Roy Cronin (Robert Taylor), a British army officer, on London's Waterloo Bridge during an air raid. They dance to "Auld Lang Syne" at the Candlelight Club, fall passionately in love, and plan to marry; but Cronin is unexpectedly called off to the front. Myra is dismissed from the ballet school. She reads in the newspaper that Roy has been killed, becomes distraught, and is forced by both poverty and despair into a life of prostitution. The report of Cronin's death is erroneous, however; he returns and they accidentally meet. She cannot tell him what she has become and reluctantly agrees to let him take her to his mother's castle in Scotland. Because she is no longer an innocent and is unable to forget her "past," she leaves the castle and commits suicide at Waterloo Bridge. A prologue and epilogue projected the story into the time of the film's release. The film opens with a gray-haired Robert Taylor at the bridge, and a British Broadcasting Corporation announcer proclaiming that England was in yet another war with Germany.

The plot of *Waterloo Bridge* is ancient: two lovers are torn apart by the ills of the world, and an unnecessary, silly misunderstanding results in tragedy. In this film, however, under the auspices of Sidney Franklin, the story received a typically lush and glossy M-G-M production. Herbert Stothart's score, dominated by muted violins, perfectly accentuates the mood. Lighting and cinematography are expert; particularly notable is the fade-in, filmed by Joseph Ruttenberg, who had won an Academy Award the previous year for his work on *The Great Waltz*. The opening credits appear on a murky screen, with a foglike effect creating the feeling of depth. After the titles, the screen goes empty and a brief period of silence follows. The voice of the British Broadcasting Corporation announcer is faintly heard; the pitch soon rises and becomes blaringly loud as Taylor appears on the bridge. The sequence was shot under the lowest-key lighting utilized on screen up to that time, the result of a new and more sensitive film stock.

Scenarists S. N. Behrman, Hans Rameau, and George Froeschel's dialogue avoids banality; Myra's prostitution is tastefully depicted, which steered the subject away from any violation of the Hays office Production Code. Director Mervyn LeRoy has glutted his work with strikingly intimate, romantic close-ups of the lovers, thus creating an appropriate feeling for both passion and sentiment. Of the three versions of *Waterloo Bridge*, LeRoy's works best because of the ensuing war and the essential ingredient in all love stories: the chemistry between the lovers. While Myra and Cronin are idealized in all three versions by the script and the casting, here they are most believable.

Ultimately, Leigh's performance is the core of *Waterloo Bridge*; she is as brilliant as she is beautiful. Leigh's transformation of Myra from a naïve, fragile dancer into an empty shell of a woman defeated by fate is intelligent, natural, and eloquent. Her role here is a world apart from that of Scarlett O'Hara. In that role, which made her a star, Leigh portrays an individual who, despite the myriad changes which occur around her, is essentially the same from start to finish: a vixen, a fetching, scheming Southern belle who toys with Rhett Butler and does whatever she deems necessary in order to get what she wants. In the role that affirmed her talent, in *Waterloo Bridge* she undergoes a metamorphosis. In the first scenes, Myra is delicate, virginal, and romantic; by the last reel, she has been broken. She is forever lost, a pitiful, pessimistic woman who is willing to end her own life rather than taint the life of her beloved. Because of its complexity, the role of Myra is probably more demanding of Leigh's resources as an actress than that of Scarlett.

Taylor, who appeared with Leigh in 1938 in the British *A Yank at Oxford*, is surprisingly effective as Cronin. He is not as hammy or one-dimensional as he was opposite Margaret Sullavan in *Three Comrades* (1938) or, most notably, Greta Garbo in *Camille* (1936). His performance here was his best to date, and ranks among the best in his career. Of all his films, *Waterloo Bridge* remained Taylor's personal favorite. The supporting cast is stellar. Lucile Watson as Cronin's aristocratic mother, C. Aubrey Smith as Cronin's compassionate uncle and superior officer, Maria Ouspenskaya as Myra's tyrannical ballet impresario, and Virginia Field as Myra's loyal prostitute/roommate and friend are all solid. Even so, a performance lacking the depth of Leigh's would have destroyed the credibility of the character and the mood of the film.

Although *Waterloo Bridge* was well received by the critics, with Leigh's acting singled out as its outstanding feature, neither film nor star were nominated for Academy Awards. 1940 was a banner year in Hollywood, and no less than ten films vied for Oscars in the major categories: *Rebecca* (the eventual winner), *The Letter*, *Foreign Correspondent*, *The Grapes of Wrath*, *The Great Dictator*, *The Long Voyage Home*, *The Philadelphia Story*, *Kitty Foyle*, *All This and Heaven Too*, and *Our Town*. Superior performances by Ginger Rogers, Joan Fontaine, Martha Scott, Bette Davis, and Katharine Hepburn were in the running for Best Actress, with Rogers coming out on top for her fine work as *Kitty Foyle*. Nevertheless, Leigh's Myra in *Waterloo Bridge* affirmed her talent as an actress, and she later won a second Academy Award for her portrayal of Blanche DuBois in *A Streetcar Named Desire* (1951).

Ronald Bowers

WESTERN UNION

Released: 1941
Production: Harry Joe Brown for Twentieth Century-Fox
Direction: Fritz Lang
Screenplay: Robert Carson; based on the novel of the same name by Zane
  Grey
Cinematography: Edward Cronjager
Editing: Robert Biscoff
Running time: 94 minutes

Principal characters:
Vance Shaw	Randolph Scott
Richard Blake	Robert Young
Edward Creighton	Dean Jagger
Sue Creighton	Virginia Gilmore
Homer	Chill Wills
Herman	Slim Summerville
Jack Slade	Barton MacLane

While the theme of Fritz Lang's *Western Union* is struggle, history tells us that Western Union's expansion of its telegraph service from Omaha to Salt Lake City in the 1860's was remarkably uneventful. The company's biggest headaches were caused by buffalo, who were fond of rubbing against the telegraph poles to scratch their backs, usually knocking the poles down in the process. This, obviously, is not the stuff of an epic Western film. To compensate, director Lang and writer Robert Carson took a novel by Zane Grey (or his ghost writer—there is, in fact, some dispute about whether the film was based on the novel, or vice versa) and revised it liberally. The result is a film full of struggle: Western Union's struggle to bring modern technology to the frontier; the struggle between right and wrong that takes place within the film's protagonist, Vance Shaw; and, last but not least, the struggle of Lang himself to tell his story without interference from the censorious Hays Office, Hollywood's official guardian of public morals.

The Hays Office, in addition to its fairly explicit taboos about sexual matters, had a more general dictum: virtue must be rewarded and vice punished. Lang had a more realistic view of the world, and he worked as much of this view as possible into the film. Vance Shaw is an outlaw, albeit one with a good heart. He commits misdeeds, but he is also capable of heroism.

Lang opens the film with several gorgeous Technicolor shots of classic Western scenery: crested buttes overlooking a boundless prairie, upon which grazes a vast herd of buffalo. The audience's view is shared by a lone horseman who appears onscreen. It soon develops that Vance Shaw (Randolph Scott), the horseman, is being hotly pursued by a posse. He eludes them via a frantic ride down steep hills and, ultimately, through the buffalo herd. His escape exacts a price, however; his horse pulls up lame shortly thereafter.

Shaw soon stumbles upon Edward Creighton (Dean Jagger), a Western Union surveyor who has sustained broken ribs in a fall from his horse. Shaw relieves the man of his mount and is about to ride off when he notices that Creighton is seriously hurt. He returns, administers first aid, and then takes Creighton with him as far as the nearest stage depot, where he drops him off to recuperate. Thus Lang first reveals the two sides of Vance Shaw's character. He is a frontier badman, wanted by the law, but he is also capable of genuine compassion. These two warring facets of Shaw's personality will form the basis of *Western Union*'s plot.

The scene shifts to Omaha, where Western Union is recruiting for its drive to Salt Lake City. Those hired include Herman (Slim Summerville), a cook (the news that he knows enough to remove the wool from a sheep before cooking it brings paroxysms of joy from the other members of the expedition, who are evidently used to cruder chefs), and his assistant, Homer (Chill Wills), a grizzled survivor of a scalping by unfriendly Indians. Homer's bizarre sense of humor, coupled with Herman's penchant for falling into his own cooking pots at critical moments, provides *Western Union* with its comic relief. Also signing aboard are Richard Blake (Robert Young), a tenderfoot dude from the East, and Vance Shaw, as Western Union's main scout. Inevitably, Edward Creighton turns out to be the boss of the expedition. His sister Sue (Virginia Gilmore), herself an expert telegrapher, completes the principals among the Western Union team.

Two important developments occur before the group leaves Omaha. Shaw, realizing that Creighton has recognized him, offers to withdraw from the wagon train: "You don't owe me nothing," he avers. Creighton looks him straight in the eye and replies "How could I? I never saw you before." He is saying, in effect, that although he knows that Shaw has a past, he is willing to give him a fresh start.

Sue Creighton is the film's love interest, and Shaw and Richard Blake are rivals for her affection. Lang constructs two parallel scenes to illustrate their rivalry. In the first, before the expedition leaves Omaha, Blake, the tenderfoot, walks into the Western Union office to pay court to Miss Creighton, only to find that Vance Shaw has arrived ahead of him. Later on in the film, Shaw rides back from the wagon train to see Sue, only to discover that Blake has beaten him to the Western Union office. The three members of the gentle romantic triangle share a laugh over the situation, and Shaw and Blake return to camp. Later, however, Sue commits herself when she gives her prized brooch to Vance Shaw, indicating her preference for him. "I should have known you years ago," he says. "Since then I've made some mistakes." "Mistakes can be corrected," she replies. "Not always," he responds grimly.

Soon after the wagon train leaves Omaha, it is beset by troubles: their cattle are rustled, leaving them short of food. Suspecting Indians, Shaw rides off to investigate. He discovers instead a band of white men in Indian regalia who turn out to be members of Shaw's old gang. Led by one Jack Slade (Barton MacLane), they claim to be Confederate guerrillas out to harass the Yankee telegraph company. Clearly, however, they are more interested in the money they obtain from their raids than in any political cause. Shaw leaves them unharmed. Lang and Carson have given Vance Shaw a second moral test, and this one he fails. He returns to the Western Union camp and advises Edward Creighton that it was indeed Indians who stole his cattle. The filmmakers have shown that Shaw's loyalties are still divided, and that he has not yet completely put aside his outlaw past.

Not long thereafter, the workers at the head of the line are "attacked" by a band of drunken Indians—real ones this time. All they really want is whiskey, but when one of them tries to get away with a surveying instrument, Blake shoots him. The Indians are driven off, but word comes over the telegraph that the base camp is also under attack. When this attack is repelled, one of the marauders' casualties is discovered to be a white man in disguise.

Creighton begins to wonder about Shaw, and his misgivings increase when, as he and his scout ride into town, Jack Slade's gang of unsavory toughs greets Shaw familiarly. "We were both raised in the same corner of Missouri," is the laconic Shaw's only comment, but he is clearly disturbed by the incident.

Following a comic scene in which Creighton, Shaw, and Blake persuade a reluctant Sioux chieftain to permit Western Union to string its wire across Indian territory by nearly electrocuting half of his braves with an electric generator, the film moves swiftly towards its conclusion. Slade lures Shaw out of the camp and asks him to rejoin the gang. The viewer is by now more than curious about the mutual solicitude that Slade and Shaw show each other, particularly since they do not appear to be especially friendly. When Shaw refuses to rejoin Slade, he is not shot. Instead, he is tied up and left behind while the gang sets off for one last attempt to halt work on the telegraph. They intend to burn out the Western Union camp.

Indeed, fire will play a prominent part in the rest of the film. Shaw fans the embers of the gang's dormant campfire, and when the blaze gets going, he stoically holds his hands over the flames until his bonds are burned through. He then rides back to Western Union headquarters, where the base camp is the site of a holocaust. Slade's gang is ultimately repelled, but at a great cost, both in men and property. An angry Creighton demands an explanation for Shaw's absence during the bulk of the fray, and when none is forthcoming, his patience runs out and he fires Shaw.

On his way out of camp, Shaw runs into Blake and tells him what he could not tell Creighton: "Tell Mr. Creighton Jack Slade's my brother." Ominously, he adds, "Tell Mr. Creighton Jack Slade won't bother Western Union no more." Thus much of the mystery is cleared up, both for Blake and for the audience. The scene ends with a stunned Blake watching as Shaw rides off towards a showdown with his brother.

The film's denouement takes place in the town of Elkville. Slade and his gang are in the barbershop, where Slade is getting a shave. Warned of his brother's approach, Slade draws his pistol and places it out of sight under the protective apron he is wearing. When Shaw comes through the door, Slade opens fire, hitting his brother in the shoulder. Everyone begins shooting, and Shaw kills all of the gang, except Slade, before succumbing to his wounds. As Slade prepares to leave the barbershop, he sees a grim Richard Blake striding down the street, ready to take up the battle for his fallen rival and comrade. Both men commence firing, and both are hit. Blake runs out of ammunition and stands helplessly as Slade takes aim. Before he can fire, however, Slade slumps to the ground, dead of his wounds.

The film ends as Edward and Sue Creighton are celebrating the completion of the telegraphic connection between Omaha and Salt Lake City. As the telegraph taps out its message, Sue says, "I wish Shaw could hear it." Her brother replies, "It's a long way from Salt Lake City to Boot Hill in Elkville, but I think he can hear it." Thus the film's three struggles are resolved. Western Union has built its telegraph, Vance Shaw has wrestled with his demons and won, and Lang has managed to make a hero out of a killer and a thief.

Scott, next to John Wayne perhaps the quintessential film Western hero, gives one of his best performances as Vance Shaw. Shaw is a man of few words, but Scott makes the most of his spare dialogue; his silences, too, are eloquent. Jagger's Edward Creighton and Gilmore's Sue Creighton are little more than stock Western characters, but Young as Richard Blake, the dude who becomes one of the company's mainstays, turns in a fine performance, and Wills and Summerville (as Homer and Herman, respectively) work effectively together as the film's comic relief. Ultimately, however, *Western Union* belongs to Lang. The director who rose to greatness via *M* (1931) and other cinematic excursions into the realm of paranoia has created a Western classic.

James P. Girard

WHAT EVER HAPPENED TO BABY JANE?

Released: 1962
Production: Robert Aldrich for Associates and Aldrich Co./Seven Arts;
   released by Warner Bros.
Direction: Robert Aldrich
Screenplay: Lukas Heller; based on the novel of the same name by Henry
   Farrell
Cinematography: Ernest Haller
Editing: Michael Luciano
Music: Frank DeVol
Running time: 132 minutes

   Principal characters:
   Jane Hudson ....Bette Davis
   Blanche Hudson .... Joan Crawford
   Edwin Flagg .... Victor Buono
   Mrs. Bates .... Anna Lee
   Elvira Stitt .... Maidie Norman
   Mrs. Flagg .... Marjorie Bennett
   Baby Jane Hudson .... Julie Allred
   Blanche (younger) .... Gina Gillespie

One of Hollywood's favorite subjects has always been itself. In earlier days, with rare exceptions such as *What Price Hollywood?* (1932) and its descendant *A Star Is Born* (1937), the tone of the film industry's self-portraits was genial and light-hearted. With the decline of the "old Hollywood," however (marked and hastened by the advent of television), these films began to take on a darker cast. Beginning with Billy Wilder's *Sunset Boulevard* and Nicholas Ray's *In a Lonely Place* (both 1950), Hollywood increasingly portrayed itself as the dead-end (or at least wrong-way) street of failed dreams. By the time *A Star Is Born* was remade in 1954, its sentiments were no longer exceptional. This trend produced one of the most fascinating character types in the American cinema: the former film queen obsessed with past glories as she slips into obscurity, unglamorous middle age, and even insanity. This character, definitively incarnated by Gloria Swanson in *Sunset Boulevard*, was a potent symbol for the decay of Hollywood, and lent itself well to emotional extravaganzas on a scale with the egos of these self-deluding creatures. The hysterical peak was reached in *What Ever Happened to Baby Jane?* (1962), which had not one, but two of these specimens on exhibit.

The film appropriately opens with a two-part prologue that is mockingly nostalgic. The first part, set in 1917, establishes vaudeville child star Baby Jane Hudson (Julie Allred) as a spoiled, manipulative brat who inspires adulation from audiences and helpless, self-effacing jealousy from her older sister Blanche (Gina Gillespie). The second part of the prologue takes place in Hollywood in 1935; in the interim, the situation has reversed itself: now Blanche (Joan Crawford) has become a beloved movie star, while Jane (Bette Davis) has developed a drinking problem. Jane's own film career has foundered, although sustained by the studio at Blanche's insistence. Blanche's stardom is cut short, however, when she is crippled in a car accident in which both sisters were involved (in deliberately unspecified roles).

The body of the film is dated "Yesterday" and reveals the sisters living in virtual seclusion in a run-down mansion. Jane has become slatternly and grotesque and drinks heavily; Blanche is confined to a wheelchair in her upstairs bedroom, and is almost totally dependent on Jane, who tends to her grudgingly. We learn from the conversation of a neighbor, Mrs. Bates (Anna Lee), that Jane is considered responsible for the accident that crippled her sister; despite this, Blanche seems to hold no bitterness toward Jane. Jane, on the other hand, makes no effort to conceal her loathing for Blanche, and takes great pleasure in mistreating her.

An emotional crisis is precipitated by a local television station's broadcasting of old Blanche Hudson films; Jane, intensely jealous of Blanche's former stardom, rebuffs inquiries and withholds appreciative fan mail. The only person who is even partially aware of Jane's alcoholism and her increasingly erratic and antagonistic behavior, is their maid Elvira (Maidie Norman). Blanche, unbeknown to Jane, plans to sell their house, and Elvira urges her to have Jane committed; Blanche finds it difficult, but finally promises to take the necessary steps. Jane becomes suspicious and leaves the phone off the hook when she goes out, thus preventing Blanche from using her upstairs extension to call their doctor. Before long, Jane begins to slip into the past; fantasizing a revival of her childhood "Baby Jane" act, she places a newspaper ad for an accompanist. Her behavior toward her sister also becomes more ominous; seeing her as a possible threat to her comeback, she increases Blanche's isolation by removing the upstairs telephone extension completely, and begins starving her by serving repulsive "meals"—first Blanche's pet parakeet, later a cooked rat. Blanche, in desperation, tries to attract the attention of Mrs. Bates by throwing a note from her window, but Jane finds it, confirming her suspicions about Blanche's plans. On Elvira's next visit, Jane gives her the day off, assuring her absence until the following week.

Meanwhile, Jane has hired Edwin Flagg (Victor Buono), an obese, mother-dominated musician, as her accompanist, promising but not delivering a month's advance salary. Their first meeting is interrupted by Blanche's insistent ringing of the buzzer which she uses to summon Jane, and Jane furiously rips it out. When she and Edwin go out, Blanche, ravenously hungry, finds some chocolate in a drawer in Jane's room; she also finds evidence that Jane has been forging her signature on checks, and perhaps intends to eliminate her. Panic-stricken, she makes her way painfully down the stairway to the telephone and calls their doctor, who promises to come right over. Jane, however, returns and overhears the call; after beating Blanche brutally, she calls the doctor back and, imitating Blanche's voice, prevents him from coming. Jane is going out again when Elvira shows up unexpectedly, and Jane discharges her; Elvira pretends to leave, but returns to the house after Jane has gone. She discovers the door to Blanche's room locked and, receiving no response to her frantic knocking, begins to remove the hinges. Jane returns home and confronts her, but Elvira manages to get into the room, where she discovers Blanche bound and gagged; Jane panics and kills Elvira with a hammer, then hides her body in the trunk of their car. When the police make inquiries, Jane, by this time completely insane, begins to make plans for herself and Blanche "to go live at the seashore, like we used to do."

That evening, Edwin is brought to the door, drunk, by the police, who mistake him for a prowler; on Jane's approval, he comes into the house and demands his money. Upstairs, Blanche has partially freed herself and manages to tip over a bedside table; hearing the noise, Edwin investigates, discovers Blanche, and runs away in fear. Jane moves Blanche to the car and drives to the beach, where she frolics on the sand as Blanche lies immobile, dying of starvation. In a final, desperate moment, Blanche confesses that she had accidentally crippled herself trying to run down Jane in the long-ago car accident, but that she had let Jane suffer the burden of guilt for all these years. Jane, enlightened and suddenly feeling kindness toward her sister, goes to buy her an ice-cream cone, when she is spotted by the police, who follow her looking for Blanche. A curious crowd gathers, and Jane, imagining they are an audience from her vaudeville days, begins to do one of her old dance numbers; she is still dancing as the film ends.

One would be missing much of the essence of *What Ever Happened to Baby Jane?* if it were taken altogether seriously. It is, of course, a gripping drama, but on another, equally important, level, it is a brilliantly macabre black comedy. The film cuts with a double-edged sword, playing its melodrama to the hilt and achieving both intense emotional involvement and frequent laughter through a remarkable blend of script, direction, and acting. Many of Jane's actions—such as her perfect imitation of Blanche's voice, employed both for taunting her helpless sister and for deceiving others—are simultaneously blood-chilling and grotesquely funny. Another example is the scene in which Jane brings Blanche her supper, casually remarks that "there are rats in the cellar," then leaves the room; Blanche has earlier been served a parakeet, and she looks with terrified anticipation at the covered dish. Her agonized scream when she uncovers the cooked rat is greeted by Jane with hideous laughter; the viewer vicariously shares both Blanche's horror and Jane's sadistic delight.

Admittedly, the film's plot is highly contrived, contributing to the overall impression that *What Ever Happened to Baby Jane?* is heavy-handed and manipulative. The *Grand Guignol* fireworks certainly command the viewer's attention, but they tend to obscure several interesting themes, perhaps the most intriguing of which is the complex pattern of stunted sexual and familial relationships. This is set up in the prologue, with Baby Jane indulged by her father (and her later fixation on him parodied by her maudlin theme song, "I'm Writing a Letter to Daddy"), while young Blanche is quietly consoled by her mother. As critic Richard Combs has noted, we are presented with "a divided family in which Blanche must have grown up hating her father, and Jane hating her mother." Significantly, most of the main characters in the film are women, and there is a complete absence of "normal" relationships. Jane's past problems include difficulties with men, and the only major male character in her present life is the almost sexless Edwin Flagg, a sort of grotesque parody of a gigolo; in turn, Flagg's only other relationship is with his doting mother (Marjorie Bennett), another in the film's gallery of oddballs. Some critics have complained that the final twist (Blanche's confession) cheapens and falsifies much of what has come before; on a strictly narrative level, this may be true (it is a cheap melodramatic device), but seen in the context of the guilt/jealousy/family themes, it provides an effective ironic counterpoint and adds a further measure of ambiguity to what appears at a casual glance to be a fairly straightforward melodrama.

Director Robert Aldrich, working for the first time with his frequent collaborator Lukas Heller, who later wrote or cowrote five more films for Aldrich, including *Hush . . . Hush, Sweet Charlotte* (1965) and *The Dirty Dozen* (1967), coordinates the various creative elements to maximum effect. Aided by Ernest Haller's expressive black-and-white cinematography, Aldrich emphasizes the film's themes by visually stressing the confining nature of the sisters' house, where much of the action takes place, and the general tackiness of the outside world, from the exterior of the house itself to the seedy Hollywood locations and the littered beach. Frank DeVol's music, consisting primarily of variations on "I'm Writing a Letter to Daddy," strongly underscores both the action of the film and the volatility of Jane's mental state. The editing by Michael Luciano is effective both in overall pacing (no mean feat for a 132-minute film) and in providing the periodic shocks for the viewer. Some of the cross-cutting for suspense purposes seems crude and simplistic, but this is in keeping with the generally blunt, unsubtle surface of the entire film.

A film like *What Ever Happened to Baby Jane?*, however, ultimately stands or falls largely on the strength of its performances. The casting of Crawford and Davis (in their first and only film appearance together) was a stroke of genius. Both were in their fifties at the time, and their film careers had been in the doldrums for several years; they rose to the occasion magnificently, delivering a pair of superior star turns which revitalized their sagging fortunes (although they were both rather unfairly type-cast in "horror" roles for many years thereafter). The role of Jane Hudson virtually demands an emotional *tour-de-force*, and Davis is up to the challenge; her performance, although broad and exaggerated, is affecting on a level much deeper than mere melodrama. A lesser actress might have simply engaged in the requisite scenery-chewing (which Davis certainly does not neglect), but Davis evokes the sad and comic aspects of Jane's existence as well; it is indicative of her success that Jane remains a sympathetic figure despite her generally despicable behavior. Davis' careful modulation of Jane's gradual descent into madness is one of her finest achievements, for which she justly received her tenth Academy Award nomination. Given a considerably less showy role, Crawford wisely chooses to underplay; simply by not challenging Davis on her own level, she easily avoids being completely overshadowed by the latter's histrionics. Crawford is the eye of Davis' emotional storm, and together they dominate the film. Only Buono, in an auspicious film debut, manages to steal any thunder from either actress; he, too, was nominated for an Academy Award (as Best Supporting Actor).

Obviously, the filmmakers were aware that only a pair of real-life aging stars could effectively bring their fictional counterparts to life on the screen. The casting of Crawford and Davis was obviously good box office, further enhanced by the exaggerated publicity surrounding the supposed "feud" between the two temperamental stars; as Aldrich has remarked, this works in favor of the film because "the audience feels that they are privy to real-life secrets" about the pair. Fortunately for the artistic merits of the film, however, Crawford's and Davis' "movie star" images are used for more than mere commercial fodder; it is the filmmakers' shrewd manipulation of their "real" film pasts that makes the casting more than merely a cheap gimmick. One of the most important parts of the film is the "introduction" of the adult Jane and Blanche through the use of clips from their early pictures. Short scenes from the early (1933) Davis features *Ex-Lady* and *Parachute Jumper* are used in the prologue to illustrate Jane Hudson's lack of talent; indeed, the young Davis' acting seems unpromising, but her beauty is undeniable and provides a striking contrast with her later appearance. The film's most wonderful moment, however, is the introduction of the present-day Blanche: the Hudsons' next-door neighbors are shown watching an old "Blanche Hudson" film (Crawford in *Sadie McKee*, 1934), followed by a direct cut from their television screen to a close-up of Blanche watching the same film, rapt with attention, her eyes shining as she beholds the glory of her faded past. This simple and beautiful juxtaposition of images, in its remarkable blending of reality and fantasy, character and performer, sets the tone for *What Ever Happened to Baby Jane?*, a memorable cinematic achievement which is both entertaining and thought-provoking, grandly theatrical and emotionally moving.

Howard H. Prouty

THE WHISPERERS

Released: 1966
Production: Michael S. Laughlin and Ronald Shedlo for Seven Pines; released
  by United Artists
Direction: Bryan Forbes
Screenplay: Bryan Forbes; based on the novel *Mrs. Ross* by Robert Nicolson
Cinematography: Gerry Turpin
Editing: Anthony Harvey
Running time: 105 minutes

Principal characters:
Mrs. Ross	Dame Edith Evans
Archie	Eric Portman
Girl upstairs	Nanette Newman
Charlie	Ronald Fraser
Mrs. Noonan	Avis Bunnage
Conrad	Gerald Sim
National Assistance Officer	Leonard Rossiter
Mr. Weaver	Kenneth Griffith
Earl	Harry Baird
Almoner	Margaret Tyzack
Prostitute	Clare Kelly
Mrs. Ross (younger)	Sarah Forbes

In today's speech, the word "great" is often bandied about so as to dilute its meaning. In the case of Dame Edith Evans' performance in *The Whisperers*, however, one can use any number of superlatives and not be guilty of exaggeration. Dame Edith took a demanding role and made it her own; for her performance, she won the New York Film Critics' Award and was also nominated for an Academy Award.

The Whisperers is not an upbeat film. Through strong performances and excellent cinematography, writer-director Brian Forbes examines the plight of the elderly poor. Evans vividly portrays an impoverished, lonely woman who still manages to maintain her sense of pride and dignity even though she must live on charity and protect herself with layers of fantasy to survive. From the very beginning, as the film credits are superimposed over a bleak English neighborhood, Forbes sets the tone of his work. The viewer first encounters Mrs. Ross (Dame Edith Evans) in her dingy flat, as the camera pans around the premises cluttered with the old lady's memorabilia. The faucet over the kitchen sink drips incessantly. Mrs. Ross is having a snack, and she begins to address the imaginary voices she hears. In a fit of pique, she turns up the volume on her radio to drown out the voices and pounds on the ceiling with a broom. She then turns her attention to writing a letter to the National

Assistance Office. She tells them she will soon come into money, at which time she will repay the government, but in the meantime, she asks for a raise in benefits in order to take care of her bills and buy some shoes.

Later, the old lady's son, Charlie (Ronald Fraser), pays her a visit. She has not seen him for a long time and does not let him in right away. When he does enter the flat, he is very condescending and sarcastic to his mother. He gives her a little money and asks for a cup of tea. While she is making it, he goes into another room and hides a parcel he has been carrying. He returns to the kitchen, but then refuses his tea, as he is suddenly in a hurry to leave. His mother asks him where his parcel is, and he replies that he has left it in the flat and will come back in about a week. As she goes to bed that night she tells her invisible people that Charlie gave her money, but adds that she never asked for it.

The following day, a man (Leonard Rossiter) from the National Assistance Office comes to the flat. He is not Mrs. Ross's usual social worker, and she is obviously uncomfortable with him and most reluctant to show him her other room. The man finds the room full of old newspapers. He tells the old lady that the papers are a fire hazard, but she retorts that she needs them for reference. The social worker eventually checks her shoes. They have holes on the bottoms, which she excuses by saying she caught them on something.

After the man leaves, Mrs. Ross decides to tidy up her flat, and while putting some things away in a cupboard, she comes across Charlie's hidden parcel. She does not recognize it, so she opens the package and finds it full of money. At first she appears frightened, but her mood quickly changes to one of elation. She stuffs the money into a drawer, then writes a rambling letter to her social worker telling him that her inheritance has arrived and she will no longer need charity. She also adds a complaint about the man who came to her flat.

At the National Assistance Office the next day, Mrs. Ross is engaged in conversation by a Mrs. Noonan (Avis Bunnage), a middle-aged housewife who is tough, slightly unscrupulous, and wise enough to size up an opportunity for simple exploitation. Mrs. Ross has been boasting about her inheritance. She allows herself to be taken by Mrs. Noonan to a local pub for sausages and port, and soon becomes tipsy. Mrs. Noonan takes Mrs. Ross to her own flat and gives the old lady another drink. By now, Mrs. Ross is quite drunk, and she rambles on about how things were when she lived in the palace, and finally passes out. Mrs. Noonan takes the opportunity to remove most of the money in Mrs. Ross's purse. When her husband and children return, Mrs. Noonan gives him ten pounds, having secreted the bulk of the money elsewhere. Eventually, Mrs. Noonan hauls Mrs. Ross home in a handcart and dumps her on the doorstep. When a neighbor (Nanette Newman) discovers Mrs. Ross several hours later, the old woman must be taken to the hospital.

Mrs. Ross has pneumonia and is lying under an oxygen tent. Her social worker comes to see her, and there he learns that the police have found her son Charlie, who has confessed to stealing the money. It is now clear to the social worker how the old lady got so much money. Eventually Mrs. Ross is discharged, but is taken to a psychiatric hospital. The social worker comes to visit again, and the doctors explain that an attempt is being made to strip off the fictitious layers of identity that Mrs. Ross has so carefully built up, hoping to force her to face reality.

A decision is made that it would be better for Mrs. Ross not to live alone any more, and the National Assistance Office tracks down the old lady's husband, Archie (Eric Portman), from whom she has been estranged for twenty years. The social worker tells Archie that his wife has been ill and that their son, Charlie, is in jail for armed robbery. Archie has not had contact with his family for years and displays only mild interest in what has happened. The social worker, however, convinces Archie to return to his wife by promising to buy him things if he will go, and he finally agrees. At the psychiatric hospital, the doctor tells Archie that much of his wife's recovery will depend on him.

The couple returns to Mrs. Ross's flat. Much of the clutter is gone; the newspapers have been thrown away, and even the faucet has been fixed. Archie tries to make conversation, but his wife has little to say. He decides to go out and explore the neighborhood, and on his sojourn, he is solicited by a prostitute. When he returns home, his wife is asleep in bed. The next day the old lady looks in her purse and finds most of her money gone. Archie says that she should write a note to the welfare office saying the money was lost. He takes the note to the office, where he is reimbursed, but the social worker says he will send someone around to talk to Mrs. Ross. The social worker offers to get Archie a job as doorman at a movie theater, but the latter does not appear elated at the opportunity. Instead, he goes to a local bookmaker and accepts a day job as chauffeur to the owner, even though he no longer possesses a driver's license.

Archie continues to chauffeur the bookmaker until one day when he is accompanying one of the bookmaker's collectors the man is attacked by thugs. Archie does not stay around to help, but gets in the car and drives away. There is a briefcase full of money in the car, which Archie takes. He leaves town for good with the parting remark, "Poor old bitch, you're on your own again." The bookmaker's thugs then go to Mrs. Ross's flat and tell her that their boss wants to see her husband, but she has no idea what it is all about.

Bit by bit, the flat is becoming cluttered again. Eventually the old lady ventures out. She goes to her social worker and advises him that Archie has not come home in a long time and she has no money. She also tells him about the men who came looking for her husband. The social worker does not believe her story, however, attributing it to the old lady's imagination. She next heads for her old spot at the public library and then on to the mission, resuming her old patterns. She returns home, and the faucet is dripping again. As she enters her flat, she calls out to the invisible occupants, "Are you there?" and smiles. The story has come full circle. The layers which the psychiatrist so carefully peeled away have grown back, but one is left with the impression that underneath it all, she realizes that she has invented her own world, but it is preferable to reality.

Evans was one of Britain's greatest actresses and had a career which spanned more than fifty years of stage and film successes. She appeared in two unmemorable British silent films, *A Welsh Singer* (1915) and *East Is East* (1916), then confined herself to stage work until 1949, when she appeared in *The Queen of Spades*. From this point until shortly before her death in 1976 at the age of eighty-eight, she appeared frequently in both mediums. Perhaps her most memorable film roles were as Lady Bracknell in *The Importance of Being Earnest* (1952) and the aunt in *Tom Jones* (1963). One of her last roles was again for Forbes in his financially unsuccessful reworking of the Cinderella fairy tale, *The Slipper and the Rose* (1976). Her screen roles were always of a supporting nature, but even in the less than successful films in which she played, she was always singled out for critical praise. Her professional association with Forbes was a happy one for both parties. The two were close friends, and she allowed Forbes to write her biography, a privilege which he lovingly accepted. The book, titled *Rose's Girl*, was published shortly after her death.

Fern L. Gagné

WHISTLE DOWN THE WIND

Released: 1961
Production: Richard Attenborough for Rank/Allied Film Makers
Direction: Bryan Forbes
Screenplay: Keith Waterhouse and Willis Hall; based on the novel of the same
name by Mary Hayley Bell
Cinematography: Arthur Ibbetson
Editing: Max Benedict
Music: Malcolm Arnold
Running time: 99 minutes

Principal characters:
Kathy Bostock .... Hayley Mills
The Man .... Alan Bates
Mr. Bostock .... Bernard Lee
Nan Bostock .... Diane Holgate
Charles Bostock .... Alan Barnes
Auntie Dorothy .... Elsie Wagstaff
Jackie .... Roy Holder

Whistle Down the Wind begins when Kathy (Hayley Mills), Charley (Alan
Barnes), and Nan Bostock (Diane Holgate), farm children in Lancashire,
England, rescue a litter of kittens from being drowned and hide them in their
father's barn. That night, Kathy goes to visit the kittens and discovers a
bearded man (Alan Bates) asleep in the hay. When she awakens the man to
ask who he is, he barely wakes up, but whispers "Jesus" before falling back
into a deep sleep. Kathy takes him literally. This introductory scene is the
most difficult in the film for the audience to accept. Kathy appears to be
bright and intelligent, and at least twelve years old, yet she cannot accurately
discern the meaning in the man's statement. We learn later her acceptance
of the man's proclamation is taken literally because she was told by her Sunday
School teacher that Christ would make a second coming and that he is "always
with us." Kathy and her siblings are delighted that He is really with them.
The audience must make a virtual "leap of faith" of their own in order to
accept the motion picture's notion that all of the children are able to believe
that the man is truly Jesus.

Whistle Down the Wind holds its audience during this crucial introduction
scene and throughout the remainder of the film because its reality is presented
exclusively through the children's point of view. This reality is unsympathetic
to the adults in the film, including the man who is mistakenly identified as
"Jesus." The film tries to show events from an innocent perspective known
only to children. The children's point of view, while unsympathetic, does not
appear particularly hostile or rebellious to adults. It merely reflects an accep-

tance of their presence and of their authority as if they were beings from an alien culture who live side by side with the natives but are not like them. Child and adult seem simply to tolerate each other.

Whistle Down the Wind's plot sets these two "cultures" on a collision course beginning with the instance when the children disobey authority and rescue the kittens that their father had condemned. Next, they must steal food from their dinner plates for the animals and let Charley take the blame for creating a disturbance at the table. Auntie Dorothy (Elsie Wagstaff) threatens to cancel Charley's birthday party because she is not satisfied with their responses to her questions. It is obvious that Charley is her perennial scapegoat, and he seethes with frustration because of his lack of power. The weakness of the children is further underscored when Auntie Dorothy tries to belittle Charley's father (Bernard Lee). The man confronts her and wins, because adults do not have to submit to tyranny.

Whistle Down the Wind is filmed in a hard-edged documentary style with black-and-white cinematography by Arthur Ibbetson. Everything is in deep, sharp focus and clearly lit. Even the interior and exterior night sequences are lit for clarity, which creates a crispness in the visual images that contrasts with the lilting musical score of high-pitched woodwinds and triangles by Malcolm Arnold. The main theme is intermingled with variations on the Christmas carol "We Three Kings," and the lightness of the music offsets the visual style, coloring its simplistic and literal reality.

The rolling farmlands of Lancashire provide a naturalistic setting which reinforces this simplistic approach to reality and also echoes the point of view of the children, which is quite literal. Often this means that their perceptions are incisive because their minds are uncluttered. Charley often comments with a childish but world-weary brand of cynicism on the adults who surround him. He is the first to perceive that their "Jesus" is "just a fella." Charley is also the one who realizes that the double-talk of the vicar means, "He don't know, does he?"

At the same time, a child's quickness can mean that he can comprehend things at face value. Kathy thinks that the man she finds in the hay has told her that he is "Jesus." She also thinks he resembles the watercolor postcard of Jesus that she was given in Sunday School. When Kathy gives the man this picture of "himself," she explains, "It was taken a long time ago," to explain that the resemblance is minimal. The man never directly admits that he is Jesus; but he never denies it either. At first the man is confused and does not realize that the children believe him to be Christ. Once he does understand and realizes that he is safe with them, however, he exploits their innocence to secure his hiding place from the police who are trying to apprehend him.

There are, of course, many allegorical moments in the film. For example, the end titles refer to the children as "apostles." More significantly, however, a school bully makes a child betray "Jesus" three times while a nearby train's whistle shrieks like a modern-day cock's crow. The fugitive is finally arrested by the police at the top of a hill and frisked with his arms held outstretched as if he were on a cross. The children arrive as if by magic from all around the surrounding countryside to watch the arrest and are held back by uniformed policemen. They are a silent mob, and their small faces are photographed poignantly. After the man has been driven away, two small girls stop Kathy and ask where "Jesus" is. Kathy tells them that they missed him this time but that he promised to return, because he told her, "you'll be hearing of me again." These scenes are underplayed and staged in a naturalistic manner to offset their awkwardness.

Bates as the man mistaken for Jesus and Mills as Kathy give fine performances. Their acting is casual but sensitive. The children who play Charley and Nan were seven and five years old respectively, and were both amateurs, but Director Bryan Forbes coaches them both excellently. Charley steals several scenes, including the memorable one in which he discovers that his kitten has died. He looks up from the barn floor to where "Jesus" is resting in the hayloft and demands to know if "He" has his cat because Charley had given him the kitten to look after and make well. When Charley finds the little animal dead in some straw on the floor he chastises "Jesus" for his negligence and refuses to accept the explanation that the man has "a lot of things on his mind right now."

Whistle Down the Wind ends inconclusively. The children, except for Kathy and Charley, react passively to the man's arrest. It would have seemed from the emotional attachment that the children bestowed upon the fugitive that his arrest would have been more of a shock to all of them. They believed themselves to be protecting "Jesus" from a second martyrdom, yet they melt back into the countryside after the man is driven away in the police car. Kathy is the most affected by the man's arrest. She makes a complete emotional break from her father when he drags her away to prevent her from helping "Jesus." He is completely baffled by her behavior and cannot understand why she persists in believing that the man is Christ. He cannot make her accept the fact that the man is actually a criminal, because she refuses to forsake her faith for this adult "truth." Her father fails to realize that Kathy is refusing to become disillusioned and in doing so is actually refusing to become an adult. She is adamantly holding onto her innocence and childhood. The film does not resolve its stated conflict between childhood innocence and adult reality. Adults and children alike have been emotionally hurt and continue to be alienated, as exemplified by the relationship between Kathy and her father. Charley's budding cynicism is reinforced as is the shallowness of Auntie Dorothy and Nan.

Whistle Down the Wind is an unusual narrative because it takes children as seriously as they take themselves. There is very little that could be termed precocious or condescending in the film, except perhaps the musical score, which often modulates into a trite and repetitious melody. Forbes, a well-known actor and screenwriter during the 1950's, made his directorial debut with this film, which was one of the first productions completed during his association with prominent actor, director, and producer Richard Attenborough. Together they completed several other fine films, including *The L-Shaped Room* (1963) and *Séance on a Wet Afternoon* (1964). Forbes has also directed *King Rat* (1965), *The Whisperers* (1966), and, more recently, *International Velvet* (1978).

Elizabeth Ward

THE WHOLE TOWN'S TALKING

Released: 1935
Production: Lester Cowan for Columbia
Direction: John Ford
Screenplay: Jo Swerling; based on the novel of the same name by W. R. Burnett
Cinematography: Joseph H. August
Editing: Viola Lawrence
Running time: 95 minutes

> *Principal characters:*
> Arthur Ferguson Jones/
> "Killer" Mannion .... Edward G. Robinson
> Miss "Bill" Clark .... Jean Arthur
> Mr. Healy .... Wallace Ford
> Mr. Hoyt .... Donald Meek
> Detective Sergeant Michael Boyle .... Arthur Hohl

The Whole Town's Talking is a Dr. Jekyll/Mr. Hyde type of story; even though "Killer" Mannion, a notorious criminal whose escape from prison sets the narrative into motion, and Arthur Ferguson Jones, a meek newspaper clerk, are not aspects of the same personality, they are played by the same actor (Edward G. Robinson), and they do switch roles at the end of the film to initiate the happy ending. The unusual twist to this version is its light-hearted mood. There is none of the agonizing introspection or metaphors of good and evil central to most versions of the Faust legend. Indeed, it looks more like *Superman*, with the shy newspaperman pursuing the dynamic girl reporter, unable even to approach her sexually except in his "macho" form.

It is impossible to discuss this film without reference to its production. It looks, feels, and is remembered as if it were a Frank Capra film. With Robert Riskin writing the dialogue, Columbia producing, and Jean Arthur starring as the fast-talking, witty, sarcastic, almost masculine heroine, one would assume it was an assignment marked for Capra which John Ford somehow took over late in production. Actually, Capra had nothing to do with this project at any point, and although Ford is an admirer of Capra, he does not speak of any influence from him and has made no other films that resemble Capra's. The film is charming, but the direction does not suit the project and is definitely not in the finest tradition of Ford. The narrative dynamic rests on comic twists, mistaken identity, and the treatment of police and bureaucrats as incompetent fools, and it possesses a lightness that fits the *Mr. Smith Goes to Washington* (1939)-style comedies of Capra. Nevertheless, the film is a success, perhaps demonstrating that great directors can be fully competent even when they are not being "personal."

The Whole Town's Talking received generally good reviews when it was released, but they were mostly in praise of the acting, the pace, and the humor. Most considered the story trite and old hat, and yet lauded the film for being entertaining to the extent that no one noticed the essential poverty of the script. Robinson was particularly praised for being believable in two roles which depict characters who are decidedly opposite. Robinson says, in his autobiography, *All My Yesterdays*, written with Leonard Spigelgass, that the role was a tremendous opportunity for him. He was "box-office poison" at the time and was frankly surprised when Columbia wanted to borrow him from Warner Bros. for the picture. It sparked a whole new wave of popularity for him, and he had no further difficulty getting parts after his success in this film.

A central theme of *The Whole Town's Talking* is that two totally different personalities can exist in the same person. Arthur Jones and "Killer" Mannion are not the same character, but finding himself the double of an escaped killer brings out a whole new side to Jones's character. He and Mannion merge closer as the film progresses until their ultimate confrontation instigates a comic switch in identities—first planned by Mannion to help him escape his pursuers, but then trapping him as Jones finds the man of action within himself.

Early in the film, Jones is the shy, tender poet whose love for his "Cymbe-line," his romantic name for the definitely unethereal Miss "Bill" Clark (Jean Arthur), girl reporter and star of the paper, does not give him the courage to approach her, so he steals her picture and sends her poems which she finds mushy and offensive. "Bill" herself resembles a Howard Hawks heroine. She is sarcastic, dynamic, witty, and a match for any man. The viewer's visual introduction to her is a tracking shot which leads her as she enters the office, tossing her cigarette away on the floor and bursting through the door on a wave of assurance and confidence. She becomes excited by the idea of a man like the killer, Mannion, but when she realizes that she is with him in Jones's apartment, she is terrified.

When Jones first learns that he resembles the notorious killer, he looks at himself in the mirror, searching his face for possible clues to a killer character. This presentation of the comic, classic visual motif of a man seeing his "shadow" reflected in a mirror creates the most visually exciting scene in the film. Similarly, when Jones sees Mannion in his apartment and they stand on the opposite sides of the room with light between them and darkness surrounding each one, they are the two sides of a reflection. The two merge closer together when they both write Mannion's life story for the newspaper. When Jones gets drunk, having been somewhat liberated by contact with his "shadow," his repressions leave him and the tiger Miss Clark suspected was in him emerges. He grabs her, kisses her, and then leaves for an unheard-of afternoon off. Finally Jones assumes Mannion's identity in order to save himself, Miss Clark, his aunt (Effie Ellsler), and Mr. Hoyt (Donald Meek). Mannion is killed by his own men, who think that he is Jones, and the real Jones leaves for Shanghai with Miss Clark. Having been reluctantly dragged into heroism by his own double, Jones becomes liberated into a healthy sexuality with aggressive confidence, and is freed from the frightened, careful little man that he was. A glimpse of his "shadow," far from destroying him as it does in the usual versions of the Faust legend simply makes him a complete man. This funny, warm twist—so characteristic of Capra's optimistic Americana comedies—makes *The Whole Town's Talking* a fascinatingly healthy variant on what is generally a depressing theme.

A particularly relevant insight into this film for today's viewers is that it is a burlesque of *film noir. Film noir*, a movement of the late 1940's and early 1950's, was characterized by dark, brooding films in which man struggled with his own—as well as society's—dark side, generally losing and generally finding himself betrayed by a strong, sexy woman as well. Of course, *film noir* heroes are rarely able to control their evil manifestation, master the powerful woman, and cut their ties to the narrow society whose repression caused the explosive character split in the first place, but that warm, comic integration is at the heart of the success of *The Whole Town's Talking*.

Janey Place

WHOOPEE!

Released: 1930
Production: Samuel Goldwyn and Florenz Ziegfeld for Samuel Goldwyn; released by United Artists
Direction: Thornton Freeland
Screenplay: William Counselman; based on the musical comedy of the same name by Walter Donaldson, Gus Kahn, and William Anthony McGuire and on the play *The Nervous Wreck* by Owen Davis
Cinematography: Lee Garmes, Ray Rennahan, and Gregg Toland
Editing: Stuart Heisler
Dance direction: Busby Berkeley
Running time: 85 minutes

Principal characters:
Henry Williams	Eddie Cantor
Sally Morgan	Eleanor Hunt
Wanenis	Paul Gregory
Sheriff Bob Wells	John Rutherford
Mary Custer	Ethel Shutta
Jerome Underwood	Spencer Charters
Black Eagle	Chief Caupolican
Chester Underwood	Albert Hackett
Judd Morgan	Walter Law

Eddie Cantor was one of the great names in vaudeville, revue, and musical comedy from 1910 through the 1920's. His two greatest musical comedy successes, *Kid Boots* and *Whoopee!*, were both produced by Florenz Ziegfeld, in whose *Follies* Cantor had starred for a number of years, and both shows were filmed by Cantor, *Kid Boots* as a silent feature for Paramount in 1926 and *Whoopee!* for Goldwyn in 1930. Cantor's comedy style is chiefly dependent upon two types of ethnic humor, Jewish and black-face, and both of these types are very evident in *Whoopee!* In addition, Cantor specialized in portraying weak, almost effeminate young men, and his hero in *Whoopee!* is an example of that specialty.

The original stage production of *Whoopee!*—the musical was revived somewhat unsuccessfully in New York in the late 1970's—opened at the New Amsterdam Theater on December 4, 1928, and ran for 223 performances. It was based on an earlier play, *The Nervous Wreck* by Owen Davis. With its colorful production numbers, very much in the Ziegfeld tradition, with beautiful chorus girls and lavish sets, and its popular musical score, which included "My Baby Just Cares for Me," "A Friend of a Boy Friend of Mine," and the title song, *Whoopee!* was a natural for the new medium of talking pictures, and for its production Ziegfeld combined forces with the most important of independent producers of the period, Samuel Goldwyn. The film was shot in Technicolor, still something of a novelty for full-length feature film use at the time, and most critics agreed that the production was the best Technicolor film to date. The direction, somewhat surprisingly, was handed to Thornton Freeland, not a major name in film production, who is chiefly remembered today for *Flying Down to Rio* (1933) and a number of British films that he directed in the 1930's and 1940's. Perhaps more importantly, the dance numbers were staged by Busby Berkeley, who here experiments with many of the tricks he was to refine and perfect for the Warner Bros. musicals of the later 1930's. Even allowing for the primitive nature of this early talkie, Berkeley's "Stetson" number is a perfect example of how a musical number should be staged, well-regimented, and timed.

The story of *Whoopee!* is the stuff of which musical comedies are made. It is also by today's standards exceedingly racist. Cantor plays Henry Williams, a total hypochondriac who has gone to a California desert resort for his health, and there he is tended by his faithful, domineering nurse, Mary Custer (Ethel Shutta), who is as masculine as Cantor is feminine. Another resident of the area, Sally Morgan (Eleanor Hunt), is secretly in love with and loved by Wanenis (Paul Gregory), a half-breed Indian; because Wanenis is half-Indian, Sally may not marry him, and her father has planned that she marry the very overbearing Sheriff Bob Wells (John Rutherford). After singing "Whoopee!" in his own inimitable style, Cantor helps Sally escape just prior to the wedding ceremony. Sheriff Bob, Sally's father, and Nurse Custer all believe that Henry has eloped with Sally, so they set off in pursuit.

In the meantime, Sally and Henry Williams have stolen gasoline from a car belonging to Jerome Underwood (Spencer Charters) and have reached a ranch, which, unbeknown to them, belongs to Underwood. When Sheriff Bob and company arrive at the ranch, he orders his men to stop any white man they see, whereupon Cantor dons black-face and sings "My Baby Just Cares for Me," dancing around, clapping his hands, and popping his eyes in a style that is uniquely his. Henry and Sally escape again, this time to the Indian reservation of Wanenis' father Black Eagle (Chief Caupolican). Here they are joined by Sheriff Bob, Sally's father, and Nurse Custer just in time to learn that Wanenis is not a half-breed, a surprise for everyone except the audience. The Indian chief had found the boy abandoned at birth by his white American parents. All ends happily with a true Ziegfeldian finale of beautiful showgirls in the sort of Indian regalia in which Indians would never have dreamed of parading across the screen as if the screen were the stage of a theater.

Whoopee! is Cantor's film pure and simple, and so it matters little that the production is almost nothing more than a filmed stageplay. Cantor dominates every scene, except for the aforementioned Berkeley "Stetson" number. He is outrageous and very funny. When Wanenis proudly tells Sally that he went to "your schools," Cantor replies, "Oh, you went to Hebrew school." In one embarrassingly awful sequence, Cantor and the plump, middle-aged actor playing Jerome Underwood roll around on the floor together, pulling down trousers and pulling up shirts to display their operation scars to each other.

Aside from Cantor, several other members of the film cast were also in the original stage production: Shutta, Rutherford, Gregory, Hackett, Charters, and Chief Caupolican. The last is perhaps the most stereotyped American Indian ever recorded on film, with practically a two-word vocabulary consisting of "How" and "Ugh." Hackett, of course, was later to become a prominent Hollywood scriptwriter, working with his wife, Frances Goodrich, on "The Thin Man" series, and also writing the stage and screen versions of *The Diary of Anne Frank*. In the chorus line were at least two stars-to-be, Betty Grable and Virginia Bruce.

Produced at a publicized, and probably inflated, cost of one-and-a-half million dollars, *Whoopee!* was released at a bad time, just as the public was tiring of screen musicals, and yet the film was popular—thanks, of course, largely to Cantor—and was well received by the critics. *The New York Times* (October 1, 1930) reported, "Mr. Cantor's clowning transcends even Mr. Ziegfeld's shining beauties, the clever direction and the tuneful melodies." *Photoplay* (October, 1930) commented, "This is the new type of screen musical. There is no attempt at realism. It's simply a rollicking, roistering, beautiful production that will make you forget Hoover's advice to sit tight because better times are coming. Heck! They are here!" *Variety* (October 8, 1930) announced, "*Whoopee!* has everything a laughable high class musical comedy should have."

Whoopee! proved Cantor to be a major screen comedian, and he went on to star in *Palmy Days* (1931), *The Kid from Spain* (1932), *Roman Scandals* (1933), and *Kid Millions* (1934), among others. Hollywood filmed his life story in 1953, with Keefe Brasselle as the unlikely choice to play the comedian, and in 1956 Cantor received an Honorary Academy Award "for distinguished service to the film industry." Before his death in 1964, he had deplored the fact that his type of ethnic humor had become unacceptable to modern audiences, arguing that there was nothing hateful or offensively insulting in his type of comedy. *Whoopee!* proves the comedian's point, and audiences today are missing much because this variety of humor has been banished from our film and television screens.

Anthony Slide

THE WILD ONE

Released: 1954
Production: Stanley Kramer for Columbia
Direction: Laslo Benedek
Screenplay: John Paxton; based on the short story "The Cyclists' Raid" by
  Frank Rooney
Cinematography: Hal Mohr
Editing: Al Clark
Running time: 79 minutes

Principal characters:
Johnny	Marlon Brando
Kathie	Mary Murphy
Harry Bleeker	Robert Keith
Chino	Lee Marvin
Sheriff Singer	Jay C. Flippen

Underneath the Eisenhower "normalcy" of the early 1950's, something unusual was happening in the United States: early signs of the American youth subculture were beginning to surface. The generations that would soon spawn the rock-and-roll era and the Beat Generation were gradually taking shape, generations characterized by a vague and usually inarticulate dissatisfaction with the traditional American way of life. *The Wild One* deals with one branch of this subculture: the outlaw motorcycle gang.

The film is based on an actual incident in which a gang of motorcycle toughs vandalized the town of Hollister, California, on the Fourth of July, 1947. Producer Stanley Kramer and director Laslo Benedek took the bare bones of this incident and constructed a film that examined both the frightening actions of the gang members and the equally frightening response of the townspeople. The filmmakers decry both the alienation and the repression it provokes.

The Wild One's opening sequence is deservedly famous. The film begins with a ground level shot of a deserted highway. As the camera follows the white median stripe into the horizon, a voice intones "It began for me here on this road. How the whole mess happened I'll never know. . . . Mostly, I remember the girl." A low rumble on the sound track gradually turns into a roar, and a horde of black-jacketed motorcyclists surge into view and past the camera. The Black Rebel Motorcycle Club has arrived.

The gang crashes through a roadblock and into the town of Carbonville, where a legitimate motorcycle race is being held. Intent on disrupting the race, they stroll calmly onto the track behind Johnny (Marlon Brando), their swaggering leader. Sheriff Singer (Jay C. Flippen), a tough lawman, stands up to the gang and faces them down. They leave town, but not until one gang member steals a race trophy and gives it to Johnny. Kramer and Benedek use the stolen trophy as an ironic symbol throughout the film. Despite having done nothing to earn it, Johnny becomes fiercely attached to the trophy; when he gives it away at the film's conclusion, the act seems to signify his possible redemption.

The Rebels descend on the next town down the road, and it soon becomes apparent that the gang has found a fertile ground for its mischief. A combination of venality (the owner of the bar thinks only of the money the gang will spend on his beer) and ineffectuality bordering on cowardice (the local chief of police, Harry Bleeker, played by Robert Keith, is a weak man who proves to be no match for the swaggering Johnny) on the part of the townsfolk give the gang a foothold, and, once their "right" to stay in town is established, it is not long before they begin to take over.

The Rebels stage motorcycle races in the town square and taunt the locals. One of their favorite targets is Jimmy, the elderly bartender whose square attitudes both delight and infuriate the members of the gang. Johnny, meanwhile, is interested in the other bartender, a pretty young girl named Kathie (Mary Murphy). He comes on tough and cool, playing jazz on the jukebox and snapping his fingers in time to the beat.

Much of the Rebels' psychology is revealed in the conversations between Johnny and Kathie. Kramer and Benedek do not so much try to explain Johnny and the Rebels as they let the gang members express their own alienation. Much of Johnny's dialogue is taken verbatim from the interviews that Benedek did with real outlaw motorcyclists in preparing to film *The Wild One*. When Kathie asks Johnny where he will go next, he scoffs incredulously at the idea of a preset destination: "Oh, man, we just *go*." When someone else asks him what he is rebelling against, "What have you got?" is his classic retort.

Johnny and Kathie make an oddly affecting couple. Each is simultaneously attracted to and repelled by facets of the other's life-style. Johnny despises the square life Kathie leads (especially when he discovers her father is the town cop), but he finds himself attracted against his will to her freshness and innocence. For her part, Kathie has little use for Johnny's swaggering bluster—she is unimpressed by his hipster act—but finds herself envying his freedom to pick up and move on when the mood strikes him. She finds small-town life stultifying, although she lacks the courage to leave home.

Confused by his feelings for Kathie, Johnny resolves to lead the Rebels out of town before he gets more involved with her. His plans are changed, however, by the arrival of another group of outlaw cyclists, the Beetles. Led by a man named Chino (Lee Marvin), the Beetles were once affiliated with the Rebels; now, however, the two gangs are rivals.

If Johnny, with his shades, black leather jacket, and existential angst, represents the cool, hipster side of the outlaw consciousness, Chino is precisely the opposite. Where Johnny leads the Rebels with an air of quiet authority, Chino is loudmouthed and crude. Johnny is a smoldering volcano, all the more menacing because the violence beneath the surface is only hinted at. By comparison, Chino is a mere lout, albeit a dangerous one. Dirty and unshaven, he carries himself with none of Johnny's feline grace. In short, he lacks class.

Chino steals Johnny's trophy, and the two stage a running fistfight over the ownership of the award that neither one of them earned. The brawl soon spreads, and a car belonging to one of the locals is overturned. Chino is arrested and jailed, throwing all of the cyclists, Rebels and Beetles alike, into a rage. Whatever their differences, they form a united front when threatened by the straight world. Johnny no longer has the option of leaving town; events have spread beyond his control, and he is locked into a chain of events that will lead to disaster.

When night falls, the cyclists go on a rampage, as neither of the nominal authority figures in the town—Sheriff Bleeker and Johnny—can muster sufficient authority to bring the proceedings to a halt. The filmmakers underscore the irony of the mutual helplessness of these two very dissimilar men by showing them both alone (Bleeker at his home and Johnny at the end of the bar), nursing their drinks.

Johnny seeks out Kathie one last time, rescuing her from a pack of cyclists. They ride to a park, where he kisses her violently. Frightened, she slaps him and runs away crying. She turns around in time to see Johnny being grabbed and savagely beaten by a group of townspeople. Kathie runs to her father and shames him into rescuing Johnny. Pistol in hand, he stands up to his friends and forces them to release the Rebels' leader, who staggers, sobbing, to his cycle, resolved to leave town at last. Riding through town, however, he runs into a trap. Someone throws a tire iron at him; it hits his cycle, and he is thrown off. The cycle plunges into the crowd, killing Jimmy, the elderly bartender.

Johnny is taken into custody, and only the arrival of Sheriff Singer and his men prevent the townspeople from lynching him. Under Singer's patient questioning, the truth about the incident is revealed. Singer lets the silent and sullen Johnny go, remarking caustically that Johnny could "at least say 'thank you.'" Kathie replies "It's all right. He doesn't know how."

The Wild One ends at the café. Johnny walks in, attempting to find a way to say good-bye to Kathie. He sighs, rubs his head, and tries to speak, but he cannot find the words. Finally he slides his beloved trophy over to her. She accepts it with a smile. Johnny, for the first time in the film, smiles back—a significant breakthrough.

Released in 1954, *The Wild One* created an instant furor. The film was banned in England for fourteen years after its release, and had sporadic distribution difficulties in the United States, as guardians of the public morality feared that impressionable audiences would leap to emulate what they saw on the screen. These fears proved to be substantially groundless. What *The Wild One* did inspire was more films. There is a linear progression between Brando's Johnny and the misunderstood youth of James Dean's *Rebel Without a Cause* (1956) and Elvis Presley's *Jailhouse Rock* (1957). The films effects were still being felt more than a decade later, since *Easy Rider* (1969) as well as the Hell's Angels-type motorpsycho exploitation film can trace their origins back to *The Wild One*.

Much of the film's impact can be traced to Brando's stunning portrayal of Johnny, the outlaw with the heart of gold. The performance is vintage early Brando, ranking with his Stanley Kowalski (from *A Streetcar Named Desire*, 1951) and Terry Malloy (from *On the Waterfont*, 1954). No actor has ever been more effective at portraying a man in the grip of emotions so powerful that they render him speechless. Johnny's confused, barely suppressed rage leaves him in this inarticulate state for the duration of the film, as Brando uses gestures, posture, and facial expressions to communicate Johnny's thoughts and feelings. The remainder of the cast works effectively, albeit under Brando's huge shadow. Only Marvin as Chino, who is probably closer to the real outlaw cyclist than Brando's idealized Johnny, really stands out.

The film is also a triumph for its director, Benedek; indeed, it is the only film of note on which he ever worked. While the basic concept and design of the film must be credited to producer Kramer, Benedek's direction of *The Wild One* is unfailingly surehanded. He fleshes out a very simple plot by filling the film with little touches of realism (Benedek's eye and ear for detail are exceptional) that add to the story nicely. Add to this some interesting cinematography—the opening scene is only one of several instances of Benedek's effective use of ground-level camera angles—and Brando's superb acting, and the result is an utterly convincing film that had a major impact, both on cinema and on society.

Robert Mitchell

WILD RIVER

Released: 1960
Production: Elia Kazan for Twentieth Century-Fox
Direction: Elia Kazan
Screenplay: Paul Osborn; based on the novels *Mud on the Stars* by William Bradford Huie and *Dunbar's Cove* by Borden Deal
Cinematography: Ellsworth Fredericks
Editing: William Reynolds
Music: Kenyon Hopkins
Running time: 109 minutes

> *Principal characters:*
> Chuck Glover .... Montgomery Clift
> Carol Baldwin .... Lee Remick
> Ella Garth .... Jo Van Fleet
> Hank Bailey .... Albert Salmi
> Walter Clark .... Frank Overton

Elia Kazan's *Wild River* deals with the policies of the New Deal—specifically with the Tennessee Valley Authority, a federal agency created in the 1930's under President Franklin D. Roosevelt. In 1933, through an act of Congress, the TVA was ordered to purchase large tracts of land in the 780 miles along the Tennessee River and to build sixteen dams for the purpose of flood prevention. Construction of the dams inevitably displaced many people living along the river, and *Wild River* examines problems created by this policy of "greatest good for the greatest number," which allowed a federal agency to destroy or displace local ways of life, property, and community identity. Those who had lived on the river all their lives were ordered to move from soon-to-be-inundated land because, in the long run, the dams would benefit a greater number of people; but the question of what provision was to be made for the destruction of small communities and the identity of river dwellers uprooted from their land remained. Kazan's film broaches the problem of American progress versus the American past by examining the conflicts between intellectuals and the uneducated, city values and country values, bureaucrats and poor farmers.

Nostalgia and mourning for a lost, simpler American community which lives close to the land and gives its members a security of meaningful values is a recurring theme in American films and mythology. Very often, community progress and entrance into a technologically modern era is seen as requiring the sacrifice of individuals who cannot adapt themselves to homogenous social blueprints, and who are appealing because of their strongly individualistic self-sufficiency. *Wild River* creates a tranquil and appealing image of a past which is about to be displaced. The score by Kenyon Hopkins adds considerably to the sense of American tradition in the film. Using simple arrangements for American folk tunes, Hopkins keeps his music unobtrusively winding through the background of the film.

The past is especially represented by one poor farmer living on the river, eighty-year-old Ella Garth (Jo Van Fleet), who tries to prevent the federal government from buying the small island farm on which she has lived for sixty years. The figure who carries the news of progress to Ella and other farmers is a neurotic bureaucrat, Chuck Glover (Montgomery Clift). Glover is at times unsure of his right to uproot small farmers from the land which seems to be their life, but he is certain that the coming of the dams cannot be challenged and should ultimately be championed.

Kazan had the idea for a film about the TVA for many years before *Wild River* was made. In 1934-1935, the approximate period in which the film is set, Kazan had visited the Tennessee Valley and observed the dams being built. In the 1940's, when he worked for the Department of Agriculture, he came into contact with others interested in the TVA: liberal bureaucrats working in the Department of Agriculture. Kazan worked on a script which eventually became the script for the film, but not before it had passed through the hands of additional scriptwriters, including Ben Maddow, Calder Willingham, and Paul Osborn.

The story is about a woman living on an island which is about to be flooded; she resists, but ultimately fails to halt the flow of events. In Ella Garth's case, the conflict is created by a New Deal agency and by her own intractable attachment to her spot of land, the site of her back country life. She orders Glover off her island, telling him, "I don't sell land that I poured my heart's blood into." Trying to get Ella to see reason, Glover makes a visit to her granddaughter, Carol (Lee Remick), a widow with two small children, to enlist her support. Carol is an unusually strong, well-balanced character, something of a rarity for women's roles in Kazan's films. She has lost her husband, but is coping with that loss. She has learned how to make a living, and she also cares for her children and grandmother. She has a boyfriend at the time she meets Glover, a local man, Walter Clark (Frank Overton), who is soon Chuck's rival for Carol. Chuck breaks up Walter and Carol's relationship, and eventually moves her grandmother to a new house on the mainland. Ella dies the day after she moves, her spirit broken. She and the past she embodies literally have no place in the new Tennessee Valley. With no life apart from the identity she had on her land, the TVA's progress kills her. At the film's conclusion the Valley is flooded, altering topographies, economies, and communities, and Chuck leaves with Carol and her children to live in Washington, D.C.

Thus the issue of public versus private interest is set within the context of loss of the past and those who represent some of its most appealing, strong-willed values. Individual need is set against social need, with dams pitted against dirt farmers. The side issue of Southern racism inevitably arises, as black farmers working for the TVA face local small-town prejudice, thus enabling Kazan to add an unnecessary vigilante scene to the film.

Kazan has said that he wanted *Wild River* to be a lyric film rather than a taut social drama. His earlier films, such as *On the Waterfront* (1954), depend to a great extent on editing technique to create symbolic and emotional impact, but the widescreen CinemaScope format of *Wild River* does not permit quick edits as easily as standard format. Every edit becomes more obtrusive, and devices such as close-ups must be used sparingly to avoid jarring the viewer. Kazan uses the widescreen size to create frames within frames, blocking off portions of the screen. One frequent composition in the film has the major characters placed in the background of the shot in focus, while out-of-focus objects or minor characters occupy the foreground of the frame. The style contrasts with the deep-focus work of such directors as William Wyler and Orson Welles, who maintain both foreground and background objects in focus. Kazan's composition leaves the viewer no doubt about which of the items in the shot should command attention. Although the background characters may be overwhelmed in size by a prominent foreground object, they are the characters on which the film is literally focused. As a means of visually presenting social conflict, the use of selective focus indicates that some aspects, people, or effects of a conflict should receive more attention than those the camera has not selected for focus.

Wild River is a film which, unlike other Kazan films on social issues, is not often screened in revival houses; unlike *On the Waterfront* or *East of Eden* (1955), this Kazan film is relatively unknown. As a drama of New Deal policies set within problems of Americana motifs of tradition, however, as well as a film which allows an unusually strong, well-balanced female lead, the movie is of great interest.

Leslie Donaldson

WILL PENNY

Released: 1968
Production: Fred Engel and Walter Seltzer for Paramount
Direction: Tom Gries
Screenplay: Tom Gries
Cinematography: Lucien Ballard
Editing: Warren Low
Music: David Raksin
Running time: 108 minutes

Principal characters:
Will Penny	Charlton Heston
Catherine Allen	Joan Hackett
Preacher Quint	Donald Pleasence
Blue	Lee Majors
Rafe Quint	Bruce Dern
Dutchy	Anthony Zerbe
Alex	Ben Johnson
Horace Greeley Allen	Jon Francis
Doctor Fraker	William Schallert

Will Penny is a film that hardly anyone seems to have heard of, much less seen. Although it received critical praise when it first appeared in 1968, the rather quiet, sensitive approach to the Western that *Will Penny* represented was completely overlooked by audiences.

Will Penny approaches the Western with simplicity, directness, and an eye for the authentic details of frontier life that are often forgotten in a genre that tends to emphasize action at the expense of characterization. Although the film loses the center of its focus and begins to depend upon clichéd Western formula about halfway through its narrative, for the most part, *Will Penny* offers an unusual character study of a cowboy who is not a creature of leisure, not a graceful man with a sixgun, but a lonely, illiterate, aging man with few comforting memories and even fewer hopes for the future.

The opening scene establishes what will be two of the film's main strengths—the evocation of the frontier West through the cinematography of Lucien Ballard, and an uncommonly sensitive portrayal of the title character by Charlton Heston. Against an early morning, cold, blue landscape in the Sierra, Will Penny, a grizzled cowboy, rides herd on some cattle. He emerges as a man who is good at his job, but who is fighting the onslaught of age in a changing world. The cattle drive reaches its destination in Montana, but that destination is not even a town as the men expect, but a railhead that literally stops in the middle of nowhere. The cowboys on the drive are paid, but the boss offers Will the job of bull nurse and the opportunity to ride the train to

Kansas City. Will gives the job to another hand and sets off for the nearest town with two younger cowboys, Blue (Lee Majors) and Dutchy (Anthony Zerbe).

With such an opening, the film begins as an exercise in nonheroics that centers on the aimless life of the cowboys—the boredom of riding herd, the pointless fighting among themselves, the passive acceptance of hardship and even death. Death occurs not as the glorious finale to heroic deeds, but as an everyday, cruel, meaningless occurrence. Will's friend Dutchy is horribly wounded when the three men defend an elk that Blue has found against a motley family of scavengers headed by Preacher Quint (Donald Pleasence) who also claim the kill. Dutchy is shot accidentally by himself when he attempts to pull his gun from his coat pocket. Blue and Will take him to a doctor, but en route they leave Dutchy lying in the freezing cold of an open wagon while they stop for a little fortifying drink at a roadside bar. At another point in the film, Will happens upon a dead cowboy lying beside the trail. Will takes the body back to the ranch where the cowboy had worked, but he does not do so to assure the man a Christian burial. Will hopes to get the dead man's job. *Will Penny* shows that on the frontier, the necessities of survival take precedence over the comforts of sentiment.

The doctor (William Schallert) who finally does take care of Dutchy calls his patient and his two companions "dangerous children." This is an important commentary on director Tom Gries's vision of men who are like children, men whose lives reflect their lack of preparedness for, and refusal to accept, responsibility. Essential losers, these cowboys are caught up in a transient existence that requires little responsibility and offers little fulfillment in return.

Unfortunately, the plot of *Will Penny* seems to reflect Gries's discomfort with maintaining the narrative of the film at this sort of picaresque level. He introduces a refined woman, Catherine Allen (Joan Hackett), and her son (Jon Francis) who are en route to California to join her husband. They briefly meet Will and his two friends when the latter stop at the roadside bar. Later Mrs. Allen and her son "happen" to be squatters in the cabin that Will is supposed to occupy as he rides as the line man in his new job at Flatiron Ranch. Will tries to evict Mrs. Allen, but as he is looking for strays he is viciously attacked by the Quint family, who seek revenge against Will for killing one of the Quints in the fight over the elk. Will crawls back to the cabin and is nursed back to health by Mrs. Allen.

Their growing affection for each other, and Will's adaptation to the first home life he has ever known, are handled with great tenderness by Gries, but the obvious contrivance embodied in the situation is difficult to overcome. The performances by Heston and Hackett are almost enough to rid the material of its overfamiliarity, but the softening of the Will Penny character and the plot contrivance are difficult to accept. Heston's own intelligence begins to steal through his portrayal of Penny and results in robbing the character of some of the depth of ignorance and crudity that initially make him such an unusual and fascinating protagonist. The abrupt redirection of the plot from the wanderings of the cowboys to Will's domestication is nevertheless given some preparation in the earlier scenes of the film. Will's shame at not being able to read or write and his embarrassment at letting a man with a hard luck story have his bull nurse job establish the more sensitive side of the man that Gries chooses to emphasize in the second half of the film.

Gratefully, even when the plot turns to the relationship between Will and Catherine, the necessities of survival on the frontier are not forgotten. The Quints interrupt Will and Catherine's domestic tranquility on Christmas Eve, and screenwriter Gries inserts the *deus ex machina* of Blue and Dutchy to rescue Will and his surrogate family. Catherine wants Will to marry her, but the difficulties of survival are what Will uses as his excuse for the impossibility of starting a new life with her. He tells her they would starve if he were ranching and happened to get hurt. Catherine suggests farming, but Will protests that it would not work, that he is too old and knows nothing but cowboying. Will rides off with his buddies rather than take a chance for something better. What is especially right about this ending is that it confirms the image of the man that was established in the beginning, but which has become clouded by the workings of the plot. Will's age and the difficult prospects of starting life over with a wife and child are not the main issues. Will is incapable of accepting the demands and responsibilities of commitment. He has spent his life passively accepting what comes to him rather than risking what he has in order to achieve something more than mere survival.

Will Penny is not an unflawed work, but it does offer a fresh viewpoint in a well-worn genre. In attempting to balance the realism of frontier life with the expectations of the Western formula, *Will Penny* offers an enticing glimpse of promising aspects of the Western that have yet to be fully exploited.

Gay Studlar

WILL SUCCESS SPOIL ROCK HUNTER?

Released: 1957
Production: Frank Tashlin for Twentieth Century-Fox
Direction: Frank Tashlin
Screenplay: Frank Tashlin; based on his original story and on the play of the same name by George Axelrod
Cinematography: Joe MacDonald
Editing: Hugh S. Fowler
Art direction: Lyle R. Wheeler and Leland Fuller
Running time: 95 minutes

Principal characters:
Rockwell Hunter .... Tony Randall
Rita Marlowe .... Jayne Mansfield
Jenny .... Betsy Drake
Violet .... Joan Blondell
Rufus .... Henry Jones
LaSalle Junior .... John Williams
April .... Lili Gentle
Bobo Branigansky .... Mickey Hargitay
George Schmidlap .... Groucho Marx

The eight films which director Frank Tashlin made with Jerry Lewis are of major significance in the careers of both men, but it is important to remember that Tashlin had already established himself as a writer and director of comedy before he encountered Lewis and that he made many successful films in which Lewis was in no way involved. These films tend to be just as funny as the Lewis vehicles but less farce-oriented. On the whole, they are less frenetic and have more emotional texture. Through these flms, Tashlin's comic vision matured. *Artists and Models* (1955), the first of his Lewis films and one of the last films to pair the comedian with Dean Martin, is arguably Tashlin's most richly imaginative work, but *The Disorderly Orderly* (1964), the last Tashlin-Lewis film, is a more integrated and satisfying work, being more attuned to character development and dramatic substance.

The two Tashlin films which display the best balance of humor and coherence are *The Girl Can't Help It* (1956) and *Will Success Spoil Rock Hunter?*. The glossy CinemaScope and color surfaces of these two films serve stories which demonstrate a charming affection for certain obsessions of the 1950's and which have convincing situations as well. Both films feature Jayne Mansfield, an underrated comedienne whom no director other than Tashlin seems to have fully appreciated. Moving through the worlds of rock and roll in *The Girl Can't Help It* and television advertising in *Will Success Spoil Rock Hunter?* with a body that is almost a caricature of 1950's fantasy, Mansfield gets plenty of laughs but is ultimately revealed to be playing characters who are intelligent human beings with tender feelings and who are at once sensible and somewhat bemused by their roles as sexual icons.

In *Will Success Spoil Rock Hunter?*, Mansfield plays Rita Marlowe, a movie queen and the star of Mansfield's own films (the title of *The Girl Can't Help It* is amusingly evoked a number of times in the screenplay). Mansfield is therefore required to self-consciously project her own image, which she accomplishes with singular grace and without mocking the material. Mansfield might be profitably compared to Marilyn Monroe, also an excellent comedienne but one far more prone to derisive self-parody which is sometimes at odds with her films. In contrast to Monroe, whose more dramatic efforts are sometimes embarrassingly inadequate (especially *The Misfits*, 1961), Mansfield acquitted herself very honorably in such somber works as *The Burglar* and *The Wayward Bus* (both 1957). Mansfield's essentially healthy attitude about herself is admirably evident in her performance in *Will Success Spoil Rock Hunter?*. As a result of this attitude, she has never become a cult figure like Monroe and may be more fairly regarded as an adept performer.

The hero of *Will Success Spoil Rock Hunter?* is the title character (Tony Randall), a copywriter in a large New York advertising agency. The head of the agency is LaSalle Junior (John Williams), who remains aloof from its workings but nevertheless has the power to fire Rock and his boss Rufus (Henry Jones) who are struggling to hold onto the important Stay-Put lipstick account. It is at this point that Rita Marlowe enters the story. Rock happens to see his niece April (Lili Gentle) on television leading the Rita Marlowe fan club in welcoming the star at the airport. He approaches Rita for an endorsement while she is quarreling with her boyfriend Bobo Branigansky, the famed Jungle Man of television (played by Mickey Hargitay, Manfield's real-life husband at the time). As a scheme to make him jealous, she agrees to the endorsement if Rock will pose as her lover. Before he knows it, Rock has become famous as Rita's "Lover Doll" and is suffering romantic reversals with his fiancée Jenny (Betsy Drake). He becomes managing director of the agency after LaSalle Junior retires to the country to grow roses, the latter's true avocation. Ultimately, Rock rebels, reconciles with and marries Jenny, and settles down on a farm; Rufus, who loves the advertising world, takes over the agency; and Rita is reunited with her true love, George Schmidlap (Groucho Marx).

Much of the film's comedy is derived from the pairing of Randall and Mansfield. Randall, a consummate comic actor, has a singular ability to project a bravado born of insecurity. The sequences in which the self-assured Rita teaches Rock to convey the Lover Doll image possess an abundance of sight gags (Rock's elevator shoes and padded shoulders) and double entendres ("I'll never be up to it"). Randall is also the center of a scene that is one of the classic moments of screen comedy. When Rock is promoted, Rufus presents him with his key to the executive men's room. Rock reacts as though the key were the Holy Grail and weeps unashamedly. Billy Wilder, whose own comic talent is prodigious enough to require no outside help, was apparently so impressed by the idea of this scene that he stole it for *The Apartment* (1960), although he did not do as much with it.

In addition to Randall and Mansfield, Tashlin benefits from the comic presences of others in the cast, including Joan Blondell, still in possession of the comic timing she learned at Warner Bros. in the 1930's, as Rita's secretary. The film's greatest appeal, however, is not in the charms of the cast but in Tashlin's flair for satire. As with his presentation of the numerous rock-and-roll acts in *The Girl Can't Help It*, this satire is strangely ambivalent. Tashlin seems to have a perverse fondness for the very things of which he makes fun. The opening gag satirizes the ostentatious Fox CinemaScope logo of the 1950's, with Randall playing all of the instruments as the CinemaScope theme is heard. The film is playfully introduced in a manner reminiscent of Italian playwright Luigi Pirandello, by Randall standing on a bare sound stage before he assumes his role as Rock Hunter. Biting satires of television advertisements follow during the credits, and later in the film, the size of the image is briefly reduced to that of a television screen, tiny in the midst of the immense CinemaScope blackness so that, as Randall explains, television viewers will feel at home.

The breast fetish responsible for the popularity of Rita Marlowe (and Jayne Mansfield) is the subject of Tashlin's most caustic story angle. In *The Girl Can't Help It*, he had built an entire sequence around gags resulting from the reaction of men to Mansfield. In *Will Success Spoil Rock Hunter?* he emphasizes the reactions of women. Rock's fiancée and niece both engage in strenuous exercises to build up their own busts, with the result that they are found unconscious. "It really is better to go to a store if you know what I mean," a friendly doctor advises. In interviews, Tashlin made it clear that he regarded the American obsession with large breasts to be a subject worthy of ridicule. At the same time, his direction of Mansfield indicates that he enjoys her appearance, perhaps because to him it is like a cartoon (an artistic form for which he never lost his fondness and of which he was a past master). Happily, the plasticity derived from Mansfield's physical presence never confuses Tashlin's evident respect for her as a real woman.

For all of the fun Tashlin has with his material, *Will Success Spoil Rock Hunter?* is a transparently moral work. Scorning material values, its characters end by embracing a simple life. It should be emphasized that the film is in actuality an original subject, owing almost nothing beyond its title to George Axelrod's play; therefore, the values it gently encourages derive directly from Tashlin's own sensibility. The film was Tashlin's own favorite of his works, and it is generally considered to be his best.

Unfortunately, it is difficult to regard *Will Success Spoil Rock Hunter?* as a masterpiece. The films most apt to be named as great comedies of the 1950's are by such directors as George Cukor, Howard Hawks, and Vincente Minnelli, who possessed less original comic visions than Tashlin. In many ways, their 1950's comedies do not differ significantly from American comedies of the 1930's and 1940's. The sensibilities of the individual artists provide inflections in material which follows classic models, and that is precisely the reason why those films wear so well. By contrast, Tashlin's satire is somewhat dated; his films seem more like artifacts of the period. He brought comic definition to the 1950's in the same way that Preston Sturges did to the 1940's. Yet the fact that Tashlin's films are so easy to place within their time is also their strength. In showing us an era with humor and style, Tashlin provokes an amused nostalgia. No other artist of comparable talent made this kind of contribution to cinema in the era of *Will Success Spoil Rock Hunter?*

Blake Lucas

WILSON

Released: 1944
Production: Darryl F. Zanuck for Twentieth Century-Fox
Direction: Henry King
Screenplay: Lamar Trotti (AA)
Cinematography: Leon Shamroy (AA)
Editing: Barbara McLean (AA)
Art direction: Wiard Ihnen and James Basevi (AA)
Interior decoration: Thomas Little (AA)
Sound: E. H. Hansen (AA)
Running time: 154 minutes

Principal characters:
Woodrow Wilson .... Alexander Knox
Professor Henry Holmes .... Charles Coburn
Edith Bolling Wilson .... Geraldine Fitzgerald
Joseph Tumulty .... Thomas Mitchell
Ellen Wilson .... Ruth Nelson
Henry Cabot Lodge ....Sir Cedric Hardwicke
William Gibbs McAdoo .... Vincent Price
George Felton .... William Eythe
Dr. Cary Grayson .... Stanley Ridges
Colonel House .... Charles Halton
Senator E. H. ("Big Ed") Jones ....Thurston Hall
Clemenceau .... Marcel Dalio

From the time he organized his own production company, Twentieth Century Pictures, in 1933, Darryl F. Zanuck had been drawn to stories based on the personalities and events of the last two hundred years of Anglo-American history, such as *The House of Rothschild* (1934), *Lloyds of London* (1937), *In Old Chicago* (1938), *Young Mr. Lincoln* (1939), and *Drums Along the Mohawk* (1939). Many of the films dealing with American subjects were written by Lamar Trotti, who late in 1942 began work on an original screenplay called *The Woodrow Wilson Story*. Trotti's first draft was enthusiastically praised by Twentieth Century-Fox story editor Julian Johnson, who thought that with very few changes it could go into production that spring for release in the fall of 1943. In the meantime, however, Zanuck returned from active duty with the Signal Corps, for whom he had produced a documentary on the North African campaign against Rommel, and took over *Wilson* as his and the studio's major contribution to the war effort.

The twenty-eighth President had been a boyhood hero of Zanuck; moreover, his unsuccessful effort to insure American participation in the League of Nations had anticipated the new spirit of internationalism that former Republican Presidential candidate (and Fox board chairman) Wendell Willkie described in his visionary best-seller *One World*. Zanuck proposed, in fact, that if *Wilson* was successful, the studio follow up with a film version of *One World*, with Spencer Tracy starring as Willkie on his around-the-world journey. If *Wilson* flopped, Zanuck is supposed to have promised, in one of the most quoted lines in Hollywood history, "I'll never again make a picture without Betty Grable."

Wilson was budgeted to cost $3,500,000—an astronomical sum in an era when *Gone with the Wind* had cost only $4,000,000 five years before. Zanuck prided himself on his ability as a showman, however; and, as he wrote Fox producer Kenneth Macgowan, "I will not start shooting . . . until I am completely satisfied that I have the opportunity of making [*Wilson*] a popular entertainment." Trotti's original screenplay went through three major revisions before a final shooting script was approved in November, 1943; and director Henry King was still shooting new pages of material (much of it written by Zanuck himself) as late as May, 1944. King was probably Fox's best-known director after John Ford, and had been assigned by Zanuck to some of the studio's most important productions, among them *In Old Chicago*, *Alexander's Ragtime Band* (1938), *Jesse James* (1939), and *The Song of Bernadette* (1943). King has been quoted as saying that *Wilson* was the first film for which Zanuck paid regular visits to the set during production.

In his zeal to do right by his hero, Zanuck deliberately bypassed many of the usual Hollywood economies. In his first draft screenplay, Trotti had helpfully noted that Wilson's appearance before a joint session of Congress to ask for a Declaration of War in 1917 could be re-created by building just as much of the House chamber as was necessary to show the speaker's platform and to pick up reaction shots from the floor and visitor's gallery. In his final revision, however, Trotti called for a long shot (probably at Zanuck's insistence), which meant that the House of Representatives chamber had to be duplicated full-scale for a sequence that ran less than two minutes in the completed film. No sound stage in Hollywood was big enough to contain Zanuck's conception of the Baltimore convention hall where Wilson was nominated the Democratic Party's candidate for President in 1912, so the cavernous Los Angeles Shrine Auditorium had to be draped with bunting and lit with enough electricity for a city of eighty thousand people to provide the right degree of spectacle for Leon Shamroy's Technicolor camera. A million dollars was set aside for advertising, and *Wilson* was ready for release at a total cost of $5,200,000, making it the most expensive film produced anywhere in the world up to that time.

For all Zanuck's tinkering, *Wilson* as released was recognizably the same film that Trotti had written in his screenplay for *The Woodrow Wilson Story* almost two years before. In all of his revisions, Trotti had kept the same opening: Woodrow Wilson (Alexander Knox), then president of Princeton, and his family sitting in the grandstand at a Princeton-Yale football game in

1909. At this point, the viewer naturally expects to see a dramatization of the unsuccessful fight to abolish the Princeton undergraduate eating clubs that first brought Wilson into national prominence as a spokesman for democratic ideals (and which, as Edmund Wilson and other have pointed out, tragically foreshadowed Wilson's unsuccessful battle with the United States Senate over the League of Nations). Instead, the film jumps abruptly to the proposal by New Jersey Democratic Party boss Ed Jones (Thurston Hall) to Wilson that he run as a reform candidate for governor. (In Trotti's first draft, Jones was called by his correct name, James E. Smith.) Trotti had, of course, written a treatment of the eating club controversy, but it was either not shot or more likely cut by Zanuck in an effort to shorten the film's considerable running time.

After this somewhat jerky start, the film does a reasonably thorough job of tracing the major events in Wilson's life until he left the Presidency in 1921: his repudiation of the political bosses after his election as governor; his victory in a close race for the Democratic Presidential nomination in 1912 and his defeat of the Republican William Howard Taft and the "Bull Moose" Teddy Roosevelt that fall; the death of Mrs. Wilson and the marriages of two of his three daughters during his first term; the outbreak of World War I in Europe and Wilson's desperate struggle to maintain American neutrality; his transformation from a grief-stricken widower to an ardent suitor and bridegroom after he met Edith Bolling Galt (Geraldine Fitzgerald) in 1915; the reelection campaign of 1916, when Wilson, running as "the man who kept us out of war," narrowly defeated Republican candidate Charles Evans Hughes; his reluctant acceptance of the necessity for a Declaration of War after Germany resumed unrestricted submarine warfare in 1917; his promulgation of the famous Fourteen Points—including the establishment of a League of Nations to prevent wasteful future wars—and his disappointment when many of the Points were brushed aside by the victorious Allies at the Versailles Treaty conference of 1919; his struggle with Senator Henry Cabot Lodge (Sir Cedric Hardwicke) over ratification of the Treaty and his decision to take the case for the League to "the people"; his desperate railroad journey across the United States, in which he made speeches defending the League in seventeen states in twenty-two days; his breakdown and the stroke that incapacitated him for the rest of his presidency; and the defeat of Democratic candidate James Cox by the Republican Warren G. Harding in the presidential election of 1920, which insured that the United States did not become a member of the League of Nations (and thereby, from Zanuck's and Willkie's internationalist perspective, made a second world war inevitable).

To Zanuck's credit, he resisted any pressure he may have been under to protect the studio's expensive investment by filling *Wilson* with established stars. He rightly perceived that the presence of recognized screen "personalities" in the cast would detract from the audience's acceptance of the actors as reasonable facsimiles of people many of them had seen in the flesh. (It should be remembered that the events of Wilson's presidency were only twenty-three to thirty-one years in the past in 1944. A producer today would encounter the same difficulty casting a film biography of Harry Truman or Dwight Eisenhower.) Alexander Knox, who played Wilson, was a Scottish-Canadian actor whose most notable previous role had been as Edward G. Robinson's educated antagonist in *The Sea Wolf* (1941). Knox was still in his thirties, and he was a more full-bodied man than Wilson had been; but with the aid of a good makeup he managed a convincing impersonation of the President from the ages of forty-four to sixty-six. Fitzgerald was too young and too beautiful in the wrong way to be equally as convincing as Edith Galt (Fitzgerald's beauty was more suggestive of Hollywood than of the mature charms of the attractive but matronly second Mrs. Wilson); but she conveyed the womanly grace that had captivated the lonely widower. Sir Cedric Hardwicke's icy portrayal of Senator Lodge suited Zanuck's and Trotti's conception of *Wilson* as a liberal morality play, although it seems a bit much for a man who was, after all, a professional politician. (The Canadian Knox, the Irish Fitzgerald, and the very British Hardwicke all made no effort to imitate any sort of American accent; and it comes as something of a shock when Knox asks Fitzgerald, on the occasion of their first meeting, if she comes from the South.

The many, many other historical figures with whom Trotti crowded his script (some of them, like Lloyd George, reduced to the briefest of walk-ons) were all carefully cast to type from Hollywood's 1940's pool of dependable character actors. When a very familiar face does turn up, such as Thomas Mitchell (playing Wilson's secretary Joseph Tumulty) or Vincent Price (as Wilson's son-in-law, William Gibbs McAdoo), we accept him as completely as we do the lesser-known actors such as Stanley Ridges (Dr. Grayson) or Charles Halton (Colonel House). To be sure, Charles Coburn is unmistakably Charles Coburn—Hollywood's favorite foxy grandpa—and nobody else in his role as Wilson's friend and Princeton colleague, Professor Holmes. The role is a composite, however, with no question of historical impersonation involved, as is William Eythe's role as Felton, who represents the generation of young men Wilson inspired at Princeton and during the war.

Wilson opened to the respectful notices that a million-dollar advertising budget might have been expected to produce (in his *The New York Times* review, Bosley Crowther called it "a commanding screen biography"); but Zanuck's experience when he personally accompanied a print to his hometown of Omaha for the Nebraska premiere was typical of audience response to the film in most cities where it played. The first night, with State dignitaries and Hollywood celebrities in attendance, was, of course, sold out; but Zanuck was dismayed to learn that only seventy-five seats were sold at the next day's matinee. Some part of this low attendance may have been due to the controversy that still surrounded Wilson's presidency. (When Zanuck met his former family doctor and complained about the film's disappointing Omaha reception, the old man reminded him that Nebraska was a Republican stronghold. "Why should you expect people to pay seventy-five cents to see a movie about Wilson when they wouldn't give ten cents to see him alive?") It seems likelier, however, that the greater part of the 1944 audience was put off by the same thing that makes *Wilson* (even in the shortened, 119-minute television version) such an endurance test today: in his anxiety to be faithful to the historical record, Trotti tried to cram in more information than can be easily absorbed. Perhaps if he had begun his script with America's entry into the war, or even with the armistice, he could have dramatized the complicated negotiations over the Versailles Treaty and American participation in the League of Nations in a manner that would have made audiences understand the differing points of view of Wilson and his two principal antagonists, Clemenceau and Lodge. Instead, Wilson's confrontations with the two men were reduced, in critic James Agee's words, "to one firmly written tizzy and one softly written one," and Lodge's opposition to the League emerges as largely a matter of personal pique. Concentrating the action would probably not have solved Trotti's other great difficulty, which was that he never achieved the imaginative sympathy with Wilson that might have made his character come to life in the way Abraham Lincoln came to life in Trotti's screenplay for *Young Mr. Lincoln*; but the treatment of the isolationist-internationalist controversy in *Wilson* might at least have been intellectually respectable.

In the end *Wilson* lost two million dollars, and Zanuck did not even have the satisfaction of being rewarded for his effort by the members of his own industry. *Wilson* was nominated for Academy Awards in almost every category for which it was eligible, including Best Picture, Best Actor, Best Director, Best Special Effects, and Best Musical Score (Alfred Newman), but won only for Trotti's screenplay and in the technical categories listed at the head of this article. The big winner of 1944 was Leo McCarey's *Going My Way*, which swept most of the major awards. Zanuck did, as it turned out, make many pictures in the years that followed starring Betty Grable; but he also produced many pictures at least as mature and intelligent as *Wilson*—among them, *Boomerang* (1947), *The Snake Pit* (1948), and *Pinky* (1949). One of them, *Gentleman's Agreement* (1947), about anti-Semitism, was voted Best Picture of 1947. Zanuck accepted the Oscar, but, as he pointedly told the Academy Awards audience, he still thought he should have won for *Wilson*.

Charles Hopkins

WIND ACROSS THE EVERGLADES

Released: 1958
Production: Stuart Schulberg for Schulberg Productions; released by Warner Bros.
Direction: Nicholas Ray
Screenplay: Budd Schulberg
Cinematography: Joseph Brun
Editing: George Klotz and Joseph Zigman
Running time: 93 minutes

Principal characters:
Cottonmouth .... Burl Ives
Walt Murdock .... Christopher Plummer
Naomi .... Chana Eden
Mrs. Bradford .... Gypsy Rose Lee
Aaron Nathanson .... George Voskovec
Sawdust .... Pat Henning
Billy One-Arm .... Cory Osceola
Suzy Billy .... Mary Osceola
George Leggett .... Howard I. Smith
Judge Harris .... MacKinlay Kantor

Shortly after the turn of the century, the ecology of the Florida Everglades was violated by a feather craze originating in the growing city of Miami. The Everglades were a sanctuary for the birds which inhabited them, but the feathered hats worn by the fashionable ladies of Miami society were covertly valued more highly than was the law. As a result, while respectable citizens would not invade the sanctuary, gangs of feather pirates, who lived in the glades and subsisted outside the law, were permitted to wipe out, with shotguns, thriving rookeries of snowy egrets and blue herons. The birds suffered this cruel fate solely to be stripped of their beautiful plumes, which were smuggled into Miami for lucrative trade. The twentieth century had arrived. Civilization demanded progress, not the protection of birds. It would take a quixotic figure, a bird lover as entranced by the graceful flights of the winged creatures as he is alienated by the society in which he exists, to attempt a restoration of the natural order of things. Nicholas Ray's *Wind Across the Everglades* creates this man and becomes both his myth and an elegy for the birds with whom he is explicitly identified. The myth describes a madly romantic quest and the elegy evokes the Creation.

The bird lover is Walt Murdock (Christopher Plummer), a member of the Audubon Society, who arrives in Miami on a train which comes to the end of its track in front of a sign reading, "Welcome to Fairyland." Stepping down from the train, he plucks a plume out of a woman's hat and asks her, "How would you like it if this bird wore you for a decoration?" The woman is only symbolic of his real enemy, a red-bearded larger-than-life king of a corner of the "fairyland." Murdock, the handsome prince of the tale, will soon have his first meeting with this formidable adversary, Cottonmouth (Burl Ives), leader of the feather pirates and as much in harmony with snakes as Murdock is with the birds. Having established himself as a rebel with a cause, Murdock becomes a bird warden for the glades. As if to send him forth under a good spell, Naomi Nathanson (Chana Eden), a Jewish shopkeeper's daughter, watches him from her window for a moment, an intimation that she will become his princess. He ventures forth on the first of three journeys, each of which will lead him more deeply into the Everglades and into his own unsettled and ambivalent soul. He travels through a pristine landscape at once serene and cruel, in which God's creatures devour one another to survive. Taking photographs, he sees a man who has materialized as if out of nowhere to appear upside down before him through the camera lens. It is Cottonmouth, but Murdock does not know it until the other rejoins his men, who begin to fire on the birds. Murdock returns to Miami, and in his description of that first impression of the Everglades, he compares it to the world as it must have looked during Creation and describes Cottonmouth and his men as the brothers of Cain.

Murdock is a man transfixed. Aaron Nathanson (George Voskovec), the shopkeeper, is more sympathetic to him than merchant George Leggett (Howard I. Smith), who is in league with the feather pirates, but Nathanson too expresses a belief in progress. "Progress and I never got along very well," replies Murdock, looking rueful in the twilight. What he does not know is that Cottonmouth shares his primitivism and is more expressive of it. The man, unwilling to move into the twentieth century, will ultimately have to acknowledge an uneasy moral alliance with an antagonist who is destroying that which the protagonist wishes to preserve. That is only one of the ambiguities of *Wind Across the Everglades*. If Murdock is so resistant to a world spoiled by its scorn for nature, why does he find romance with a woman, Naomi, who is of that world? The understandable giddiness with which he experiences the beginning of that love affair is not unlike the delirium of his adventures in the glades. It is Murdock's nature to be always restless, to seek the beauty and grace so perfectly captured when "the sun catches their wings," as he says of the birds. Embracing that abstraction so earnestly, he is no less passionate in his embraces of Naomi. In this context, it may seem perverse that he will later drink and laugh and sing with Cottonmouth, for that is like a bird embracing a snake.

The narrative traces Murdock's initially fitful and increasingly obsessive efforts to rid the glades of Cottonmouth. After the brief first meeting of the two men, they do not encounter each other again until Murdock's third journey. In the meantime, Cottonmouth is established as a considerable presence in the film through scenes which describe his domain and present his strange band of men. An early episode finds him laying down the laws of his society. Violence is the ritual of this world. Each member of the gang must be willing to fight to protect his lot. Newcomers are permitted to join the gang if they are able to overcome forcibly established members and take over their dwellings. Cottonmouth himself remains undeposed because he is the strongest and most intimidating member of his domain. Named after a cottonmouth snake he keeps as a pet and considers his friend, he lives by his own gospel: "Eat or be et!"

In Miami, Murdock reveals himself to be a formidable adversary, unintimidated by Cottonmouth's reputation. Smoking cigars and drinking whiskey at the local brothel run by Mrs. Bradford (Gypsy Rose Lee), he looks rugged enough to take on any member of Cottonmouth's gang. He is tricked, however, by one of the outlaws, Sawdust (Pat Henning), who poses as a friend. This initiates the second journey, which finds Murdock guided into the Everglades by Billy One-Arm (Cory Osceola). The one-armed Seminole is an outcast of his tribe and is not even permitted to speak to his wife Suzy Billy (Mary Osceola) whom he glimpses on the riverbank. Aligned with Cottonmouth, Billy has been assigned to kill Murdock but has a change of heart after the other befriends him and elucidates the similarities between the birds and the Seminoles. Cottonmouth punishes Billy by tying him to a poisonous Machinell tree ("the only tree that can carve its initials in you" as one character describes it), and Murdock is left to die in the glades. Suzy Billy dares to bury her dead husband the Seminole way and rescues Murdock, who returns from his journey a very ill man. Recovering, he turns his thoughts away from the treachery within the heart of the glades and warms to the affections of Naomi during a sunlit Independence Day celebration at the beach.

Although Murdock has been established as an idealistic and sympathetic hero and Cottonmouth has revealed himself to be a ruthless, murderous villain, curious affinities of personality and behavior have already begun to undermine the conflict between them. Each respects nature from his own perspective, and each experiences life passionately. Early in the film, Cottonmouth has one of his men sing a plaintive folk song, and later, Murdock listens to a black piano player sing blues at Mrs. Bradford's. This mutual enjoyment of music finally culminates during the bizarre meeting at Cottonmouth Key when the drunken Murdock himself sings one of the outlaws' songs. The Independence Day sequences at the center of the film explicitly link the pleasures of the two characters. Naomi and Murdock begin their love affair with joyful abandon under a bandstand. Elsewhere, Cottonmouth and his men visit some prostitutes with whom they share succulent melons, and the outlaw leader is prompted to voice another of his credos: "Ah! The sweet tasting joys of this world!"

Roused to action by more smuggling of plumes, Murdock obtains a warrant

from Judge Harris (MacKinlay Kantor) to arrest Cottonmouth. He hitches
a ride on a boat and makes his final journey into the Everglades, this time
traveling all the way to Cottonmouth Key, where he is easily overcome by
the outlaws, then hosted by his genial foe during a storm that lasts through
the night. Drinking, singing, laughing, and eating the leg of a roasted bird,
Murdock readily accepts the harmony he feels with the man that he is bent
on bringing down. "This is the best night of jugin' and jawin' I ever seed,"
he tells the other as they sit at opposite sides of a table, their mutual wariness
dissolved. Although this is only an interlude, Cottonmouth has his own sense
of justice. Rather than killing Murdock, he offers the other a chance to take
him to Miami if Murdock can find the way. On the second day of their canoe
journey, it appears that they are far from civilization and that Cottonmouth
has won. Murdock is delirious with fever as he pushes the little boat through
a swamp. Mistaking a tree branch for a snake, he fires his rifle, and Cottonmouth, believing the other was shooting at him, retaliates with his oar, beating
Murdock senseless. The two men realize they have misjudged each other, but
Cottonmouth is bitten by a poisonous snake as he reaches for his hat. Dying,
he gazes at the sky and realizes that Murdock was right about the beauty of
the birds. At the same time, Murdock pleads with Cottonmouth to live,
unwilling to believe that any creature of the glades is strong enough to kill
the outlaw. Cottonmouth sends Murdock on his way, confirming that the bird
lover had been heading in the right direction after all. Oblivious to the struggle's end, the birds take flight once more.

Murdock's destiny is unsettling and mysterious. A primal myth describes
the battle between a bird and a snake which was won by the bird, and *Wind
Across the Everglades* appears to re-create this myth in modern terms. Significantly, while Murdock does prevail, he does not do so by his own efforts
or in the way that he wishes. Cottonmouth, bitten by a snake, metaphorically
destroys himself, forcing Murdock to become a guilty witness. In a sense,
each man has ultimately taken the other's point of view without giving up his
own, and this has rendered the conflict between them unresolvable at a human
level. It is therefore left to nature to choose a survivor, as the conflict has
already been set in motion and cannot be abandoned. Murdock's quest is
fulfilled at the moment when it no longer has meaning for him. The final
frames of film find him between two worlds, wounded and despairing. His
futile victory over Cottonmouth leaves him immersed in the desolation and
aloneness brought by this loss of innocence, unable to gaze untroubled on
paradise.

The fact that author Budd Schulberg initiated the project and nurtured it
for a number of years before writing the final screenplay once production was
finally commenced might lead us to expect a broad and unambiguous social
statement similar to those of *On the Waterfront* (1954) and *A Face in the
Crowd* (1957). Such a statement is resisted, and the film is permitted to be

unemphatic and complex in meaning. Murdock is an unstable and unpredictable hero. His point of view, which is that of both an ecologist and an aesthete, is honored; but so is the opposing one of the barbarous Cottonmouth. Scorn of archetype and convention extends to every aspect of the film's presentation. In this sense, *Wind Across the Everglades* is itself infected with the same madness and folly as its hero. Its shots constitute a rush of fragmented moments, each imbued with a sense of detail treated almost offhandedly and never lingered upon. Miami at the turn of the century is imaginatively re-created by art director Richard Sylbert and actually built on location near the Everglades. The setting of the Everglades itself had not become less perilous with the years, so that shooting sequences there involved hazards similar to those encountered by the characters. Murdock becomes delirious with fever in the story; the same thing happened to director Ray during the making of the film.

Schulberg and Ray were not content to present an unusual treatment of an offbeat subject. As if deliberately to provoke the bewilderment of audiences and critics, they cast the film as strangely as possible. The players include clown Emmett Kelly, jockey Sammy Renick, and figher Tony Galento as members of Cottonmouth's gang, as well as famed stripper Gypsy Rose Lee and celebrated novelist MacKinlay Kantor in other roles. Osceola and his wife Mary were real Seminole Indians with no dramatic experience. In spite of the songs which adorn the work, neither Israeli folksinger Eden nor troubadour Ives sing a note. Plummer was at the time known as a stage actor and was chosen to play the leading role for reasons which are still obscure. In retrospect, the casting of the key roles seems inspired. Plummer is consistently fascinating and attractive as a protagonist who is at once a dreamer and an adventurer, and his air of reflectiveness contrasts effectively with the direct and forceful playing of Ives. The remarkable Osceola makes the stuttering and uncertain Billy One-Arm the antithesis of an Indian stereotype. Eden, who leaves a ravishing impression as the heroine, possesses a natural and unconventional beauty ignored by the cinema both before and after this film. Partly for this reason, Naomi is one of the most startling female characters in any film, being at once brazen and ladylike in her initiation and conduct of a love affair.

Wind Across the Everglades benefits from dazzling contributions to decor, costumes, cinematography, and sound by every member of its creative staff, and Schulberg's screenplay is distinguished both by the singularity of the story and the richly imaginative writing of a kind not elsewhere associated with him. The participation of Ray appears to have been crucial, although he directed part of the film while he was ill and finally had to leave before shooting had been completed. He was not replaced; Schulberg, Plummer, and cinematographer Joseph Brun followed his preparations for the remaining sequences. There is no discernible break of tone or mood, and Ray's work appears to have been undermined only by his absence during the final stages of editing. A musician's strike prompted the use of "canned" music, but the expansively romantic music which was found suits the film's realization as well as the folk ballads and blues which remain as an indication of the kind of score Ray wanted. The film somehow survived every possible tribulation, emerging as a coherent and well-integrated work, persuasively unified by Ray's *mise-en-scène*.

Cinema is necessarily a collaborative art, and it is therefore difficult to account conclusively for the magic which often pervades every aspect of a Ray film. The consistently eloquent performances he elicits from the gifted and limited alike demonstrate an uncommon sensitivity to performance, and attention to decor and visual organization reflects other talents within a director's province. The subjects of his films vary widely, however, and although he was centrally involved in the writing in some instances, other projects appear to have cast him in the role of interpreter of someone else's vision. Interestingly, the extent to which he imposes his personality seems to be unaffected by the origin of the material. If he is engaged by it, characteristic themes, conflicts, and patterns readily emerge. This still fails to explain why his collaborators, generally associated with him only once or twice, seem so sympathetic to his individual artistic impulse. As an example, how much control can he possibly have had over the diverse musical scores, invariably composed by different men (or by no one in the case of *Wind Across the Everglades*), which so persistently convey his own melancholy and romanticism?

Ray was a troubled man, plagued by emotional and physical illnesses which effectively halted his career after only fifteen years. Nevertheless, of twenty films, eleven are masterpieces. None of these eleven films is a marginal or modest work in any ultimate account of cinema. The aesthetic passion and depth of moral purpose expressed in these works are evidence of a sensibility rare in any art form. Displaying common facets, each has a distinctive character of its own. Documentary and melodramatic narrative blend effortlessly in his accounts of rodeos (*The Lusty Men*, 1952), Eskimos (*The Savage Innocents*, 1959), and the Everglades (*Wind Across the Everglades*). Love scenes may be tender and hesitant—notably the sequence in which Bowie (Farley Granger) gives Keechie (Cathy O'Donnell) a watch in *They Live by Night* (Ray's first film in 1947)—bitter and passionate (*Johnny Guitar*, 1954), fraught with disturbance (*In a Lonely Place*, 1950), kissed with a sweetness and lyricism (the sequences under the bandstand in *Wind Across the Everglades*), or touched by an almost spiritual ecstasy (*Party Girl*, 1958). The psychodrama of the opening police-station sequence in *Rebel Without a Cause* (1956) is matched by such diverse revelations as the return of a disillusioned detective (played by Robert Ryan) to the solitude of his apartment in *On Dangerous Ground* (1951), the emergence of a drug-induced madness in the placidity of a middle-class home in *Bigger than Life* (1956), and the philosophical encounters beneath howling desert winds in *Bitter Victory* (1957). Ray's characters bravely embrace their alienation and the contradictions within themselves without ever settling into a state of passive despair. They are inspiring figures in vivid landscapes, their stories at once mirroring and transcending the realities of the modern world.

The vibrant Technicolor images of *Wind Across the Everglades* are exemplary, bracingly conveying a wondrous fairy tale informed by an immediacy of psychological experience. Like the other great works of Ray, this one solicits no simple or superficial response and sustains innumerable viewings without ceasing to be moving and challenging. Sometimes it will seem feverish and sometimes possessed by calm, but it will eternally radiate the beauty and truth fixed within its mysterious heart.

Blake Lucas

WITH A SONG IN MY HEART

Released: 1952
Production: Lamar Trotti for Twentieth Century-Fox
Direction: Walter Lang
Screenplay: Lamar Trotti
Cinematography: Leon Shamroy
Editing: J. Watson Webb, Jr.
Costume design: Charls LeMaire
Musical direction: Alfred Newman (AA)
Running time: 117 minutes

Principal characters:
Jane Froman .... Susan Hayward
John Burn .... Rory Calhoun
Don Ross .... David Wayne
Clancy .... Thelma Ritter
G.I. Paratrooper .... Robert Wagner

From the dawn of the talkies through the present, Hollywood has churned out autobiographical films concerning personages from Knute Rockne to Abraham Lincoln, George S. Patton to Louis Pasteur, Benjamin Disraeli to Clark Gable and Carole Lombard. A popular subgenre has featured athletes or politicians or performers who were crippled by accident, illness, or personal weakness but who retained their dignity or even successfully resumed their careers through courage, perseverance, and the love of a loyal mate. For example, *Pride of the Yankees* (1942) is the story of the immortal baseball star Lou Gehrig, whose career—and life—was shortened by disease. In *Sunrise at Campobello* (1960), Franklin Delano Roosevelt conquers polio eventually to become President. *The Stratton Story* (1949) is the tale of Monte Stratton, a baseball player who continued participating in competitive sports after losing his leg in a hunting accident. In *The Joker Is Wild* (1957) and *The Gene Krupa Story* (1960), Joe E. Lewis and Gene Krupa respectively overcome addiction to drugs or alcohol.

One of the more entertaining and affecting of these films is *With a Song in My Heart*, an account of the life of singer Jane Froman, who recovered from injuries she received in a 1943 plane crash and came back to continue her career. Although this inspirational story line is perhaps trite and certainly played for tears, it is appealing in that the events depicted are not the concoctions of a dramatist but are based upon actual incidents as they occurred to a public figure. *With a Song in My Heart* is not all hospital beds and airplane wrecks, however; the first half of the film centers on Froman's life prior to the plane crash. The singer, played by Susan Hayward, starts her career in

Cincinnati where she makes a radio spot, and quickly skyrockets to fame and glory while marrying singer Don Ross (David Wayne), who assists her in her ascent to the top. Here the script, with an honesty not usually found in such biographical pictures, does not try to cover up the fact that Froman's first marriage was one of convenience. The film shows Froman's rise to fame, which included a stint with Paul Whiteman's orchestra and a successful career on radio, in recordings, and on Broadway. A great deal of her charm during these war years was based on her own personal chic and a glamorous wardrobe. This aspect of Froman's life is marvelously captured in the film by the gorgeous costumes Charles LeMaire designed for Hayward.

On February 22, 1943, Jane Froman nearly lost her life when a Pan Am plane, on which her U.S.O. troupe was enroute to entertain United States servicemen overseas, crashed in the wintry waters off the coast of Lisbon, Portugal. Both of Froman's legs were damaged, the right leg so seriously that it was almost severed. The film poignantly depicts Froman's long ordeal of recovery through numerous major operations, a thirty-pound cast, a motorized wheel chair and finally crutches. At this point, scriptwriter Lamar Trotti added a fictional character, a Brooklyn nurse named Clancy. As played by Thelma Ritter, Clancy is at once cynical, outwardly cold, and demanding, but underneath she is a warmhearted woman who encourages Froman's fight for recovery. It is a wonderful characterization, and it earned Ritter an Oscar nomination for Best Supporting Actress.

To pay her medical bills, Froman resumes performing in public. A scant two years after the mishap, she travels back overseas as a U.S.O. entertainer. Of course, a new and "permanent" love enters her life after the crash in the person of John Burn (Rory Calhoun), the dashing, understanding pilot who was at the helm of the ill-fated plane. Actually Froman divorced her first husband to marry Burn, but by 1956 they too were divorced. Until her death in 1980, Froman lived in Columbia, Missouri, retired and married to an administrator of the University of Missouri, her alma mater.

The strength and popularity of *With a Song in My Heart* rests in its tear-stained, if-you're-courageous-you-can-beat-the-odds story line, as well as in its dazzling Twentieth Century-Fox production. No less than twenty-six songs are performed, and they are dubbed in by the real Jane Froman. Among them are "Blue Moon," "Tea for Two," "Embraceable You," "They're Either Too Young or Too Old," "It's a Good Day," and the title song. Highlighted is an "American Medley" of ten tunes, sung when Froman returns overseas; included, in the spirit of the patriotic fervor of the era, are "America the Beautiful," "Alabamy Bound," "Dixie," "Indiana," "Give My Regards to Broadway," and "California, Here I Come." The creative force of the film is not the director, Walter Lang, as is usually the case, but Trotti, who produced as well as scripted *With a Song in My Heart*. Trotti had previously written the screenplays for several film biographies, such as *The Story of*

Alexander Graham Bell (1939), *Young Mr. Lincoln* (1939), and *Wilson* (1944), and was adept at stretching the formula for optimum entertainment value. *With a Song in My Heart* is a purely commercial film; no attempt is made to dissect Froman's life and career. Any flaws in her character are conveniently ignored; such unpleasantries as Froman's separation from her first husband or the rigors of reaching the show business pinnacle are lightly treated.

Since *With a Song in My Heart* is hardly original, it received indifferent notices from the critics, but it was a hit nevertheless; it was the eleventh-highest-grossing feature of 1952, taking in $3,250,000 in box-office receipts. It was named Best Musical/Comedy by the Hollywood Foreign Press Association and presented with a Golden Globe award; Alfred Newman won an Oscar for Best Scoring of a musical; and, for both 1952 and 1953, Hayward was ranked ninth in the annual poll of top-ten box-office stars. *With a Song in My Heart*, along with Hayward's other 1952 releases—*The Lusty Men* and *The Snows of Kilimanjaro*—totaled more than ten million dollars in earnings. (Trotti was unaware of the film's success, as he died several months after its release.) The film also made a star out of a young actor named Robert Wagner. Early in the film Froman is seen singing to a young, handsome, boyish paratrooper in a nightclub scene. Later in the story, when Froman is on her comeback trail, she meets him once again—this time in a military hospital where he is a shell-shocked veteran. The scene is very touching and had audiences across the country in tears. Twentieth Century-Fox received so much fan mail inquiring about this newcomer that it started him on the road to stardom.

Red-haired, hazel-eyed Hayward was adept at playing emotional, intense women in a crisis, and *With a Song in My Heart* is representative of her career. Although she received her first two Academy Award nominations in 1947 for *Smash Up, The Story of a Woman* and in 1949 for *My Foolish Heart*, she did her most creative and acclaimed screen work in the 1950's. She was nominated for Oscars three additional times during the decade—for *With a Song in My Heart*, *I'll Cry Tomorrow* (1955), and *I Want to Live!* (1958). In the latter, she played Barbara Graham, the real-life convicted murderess who died in the gas chamber, and she finally won an Oscar.

Hayward first came to Hollywood during the late 1930's as a losing candidate for the role of Scarlett O'Hara in *Gone with the Wind* (1939). Her best roles were unlike Froman: women who were essentially weak, who were dominated by their emotions, and who eventually sought refuge in alcohol. In *Smash Up, The Story of a Woman*, she plays the wife of a successful singer who becomes an alcoholic when she feels neglected; in *My Foolish Heart*, based on a J. D. Salinger short story, she is a college girl who marries one man while pregnant by another and begins to drink; in *I'll Cry Tomorrow*, she portrays the tragically alcoholic singer/actress Lillian Roth. The role of Jane Froman requires a projection of inner strength during a struggle to conquer adversity. The film is entertaining Hollywood schmaltz, much uplifted by the earnest performance of its star.

Ronald Bowers

THE WOLF MAN

Released: 1941
Production: George Waggner for Universal
Direction: George Waggner
Screenplay: Curt Siodmak
Cinematography: Joseph A. Valentine
Editing: Ted Kent
Makeup: Jack Pierce
Running time: 70 minutes

Principal characters:
Larry Talbot (the Wolf Man) ....Lon Chaney, Jr.
Sir John Talbot .... Claude Rains
Doctor Lloyd .... Warren William
Captain Paul Montford .... Ralph Bellamy
Frank Andrews .... Patric Knowles
Bela .... Bela Lugosi
Maleva .... Mme. Maria Ouspenskaya
Gwen Conliffe ....Evelyn Ankers
Jenny Williams .... Fay Helm

The high point of horror films, which began in the early 1900's, can be directly attributed to the influx of European filmmakers and actors who immigrated to this country and brought their ancient superstitions and folklore with them, translating them into the classic horror films that chill and thrill American audiences to this day. *The Wolf Man*, released in 1941, was just such a film, and it firmly launched the career of Lon Chaney, Jr., who, refusing to trade on the great name and reputation of his father, had started in films the hard way, playing extras and bit parts, finally receiving his first break as Lennie in the screen version of *Of Mice and Men* (1939).

The Wolf Man is produced and directed by George Waggner, who had previously directed Chaney in the Western hit, *Badlands of Dakota* (1941). Waggner had made a number of horror films for Universal, but *The Wolf Man*, with its original screenplay by Curt Siodmak, was his most ambitious horror drama to date. Filmed in black and white at Universal Studios, *The Wolf Man* has a cast which is composed of horror film veterans, and Waggner and assistant producer Vernon Keays surround their cast with all of the trappings of the classic horror film. The setting is a small, sparsely populated village surrounded by eerie swamps and wild virgin forests. Looming out of the mist, casting its formidable shadow over the village, is the forbidding stone façade of Talbot castle. Here, in this tiny, isolated village, cut off for centuries from the flow of civilization, folklore and legend are a way of life.

As the film opens, a hand extracts a dusty encyclopedia from a bookshelf and opens it to the definition of "Werewolf": "A person who, according to medieval superstition, was changed into a wolf, or was able to assume the form of a wolf at will. An acknowledgment of the beast in man—the dual nature of mankind." Meanwhile, a black limousine winds its way along the lonely road leading up to Talbot castle. Larry Talbot (Lon Chaney, Jr.) is returning home after receiving news of the accidental death of his older brother, John. He is met by his father, Sir John Talbot (Claude Rains), head of the seventh generation of Talbot men and a noted scientist. Rains, a distinguished British-born actor of stage and screen, had made his American film debut in Universal's *The Invisible Man* (1933). Also on hand to welcome Larry home is an old family friend and chief constable of the village, Captain Paul Montford (Ralph Bellamy).

Later that day, Larry enters a small antique store where Gwen Conliffe (Evelyn Ankers), daughter of the proprietor, brings forth a selection of unique artifacts for his perusal. Larry's attention is caught by one item: a cane with a silver head, which upon closer scrutiny reveals the figure of a wolf framed by a pentagram. Observing his interest, Gwen explains that it is the figure of a werewolf, a legendary creature, firmly ensconced in the folklore of the region. "Even a man who is pure in heart and says his prayers at night can turn into a werewolf when the wolf's bane blooms and the autumn moon is bright," she warns.

The following evening, Larry, with his new walking stick in hand, accompanies Gwen Conliffe and her friend, Jenny Williams (Fay Helm), to a gypsy camp where they look forward to having their fortunes told. Bela, the old gypsy fortune teller, is played most effectively by Bela Lugosi, a veteran of horror films who had acted in the stage version as well as the film of *Dracula* (1931). While Jenny has her fortune told, Larry and Gwen stroll companionably through the peaceful camp. Suddenly a scream shatters the tranquillity of the night, holding Larry and Gwen transfixed with horror for one awful moment. Upon recovering his senses, Larry rushes off in the direction of the scream. A dark shape looms up before him, a demonic apparition with slanting eyes that glow red in the light of the full moon. Struggling valiantly to defend himself, Larry strikes out repeatedly with the silver-headed cane until the creature crumbles at his feet. Barely conscious and scarcely aware that he has been bitten by the wolf, Larry staggers off in the direction of Talbot castle.

The following morning, Larry is confronted by his father, Captain Montford, and Dr. Lloyd (Warren William), who bring unsettling news. Jenny Williams has been killed by a wolf. It also seems that Bela, the old gypsy, was found dead with the silver-headed cane lying beside his body. No trace was found of the huge wolf that had torn Jenny Williams apart, and the mystery deepens when Larry attempts to show them the bite he sustained, and it is no longer there.

Larry seeks out the old gypsy woman, Meleva (Maria Ouspenskaya), whom he had seen saying an incantation over the body of Bela. Meleva confirms Larry's worst fears. Bela, her son, had been a werewolf, a demonic creature whose bite has transferred the werewolf curse to Larry. Later, as darkness creeps closer to the edge of this fateful day and the full moon casts its monochromatic shadows, Larry's body begins to change. Silent and menacing, he slips off into the fog-wreathed swamp, seeking a victim. Waggner and his cast have, bit by bit, constructed a high degree of suspense in the audience which culminates in Larry's visual transformation into a werewolf. Jack Pierce, the veteran makeup man who had created such memorable monsters as Frankenstein's and Dracula, is responsible for the creation of the image of the "Wolf Man." The creature that creeps forth under the cover of night to commit unspeakable horrors, however, although frightening, is not the terrifying, bloodlusting beast the audience has expected.

Morning finds Sir John Talbot, Captain Montford, and Dr. Lloyd discussing the death of Richardson, the gravedigger. This is the third bizarre death in as many days. Has the legend of the werewolf become a reality? Can such a horrible creature exist? These are the questions they ask themselves. There is, they admit, a pathological condition known as Lycanthropy in which the sufferer believes himself to be a wild beast and, consequently, develops a taste for raw or putrid meat and a desire to howl and run naked through the woods.

As evening again draws to a close, Frank Andrews (Patric Knowles), a young gamekeeper, assisted by the bravest of the villagers, is setting traps to capture the creature. Larry realizes that he is the wolf man and that he must seek help, but Sir John Talbot, is appalled and skeptical when Larry confesses to being the werewolf. He convinces Larry, however, to allow himself to be incarcerated in his room. If the wolf is caught while Larry is confined, then his wild self-incriminations will be proven unfounded. As Sir John plans to join the villagers in their search for the creature, Larry convinces him to take the silver-headed cane with him as some small measure of protection.

In the final climactic scene, director Waggner brings all of his principal stars together in the fog-shrouded woods surrounding Talbot castle. We see the wolf man slipping stealthily through the silent, waiting night, seeking prey. Meanwhile, Gwen, determined to find Larry, has entered the woods and now stands alone near the edge of a small clearing. Paralyzed with fear, she watches the wolf man rush towards her. Suddenly Sir John is there, beating back the creature with repeated blows of the silver-headed cane. No werewolf can survive an attack by a weapon of pure silver, and, as the creature slips gradually into the shadowy vale of death, it gives up its control of the body and soul it had invaded. Sir John watches in horror as the wolf man changes back into the shape of his son, Larry.

Although *The Wolf Man* is not in itself a classic horror film, it is important as the vehicle which launched the career of Lon Chaney, Jr. As his father, Lon Chaney, Sr., was before him, Lon Chaney, Jr., became a master of disguise, a "Man of a Thousand Faces," in his own right. Following his debut as the wolf man, he went on to become one of the great character actors of American horror films. In addition to a number of other films, Chaney, Jr., starred in no less than thirteen horror films, including such notables as *Calling Dr. Death* (1943), *The Mummy's Curse* (1944), several wolf man films and, in 1971, two years before his death, *The Night of the Werewolf*.

D. Gail Huskins

THE WOMAN IN THE WINDOW

Released: 1944
Production: Nunnally Johnson for RKO/Radio
Direction: Fritz Lang
Screenplay: Nunnally Johnson; based on the novel *Once Off Guard* by J. H. Wallis
Cinematography: Milton Krasner
Editing: Marjorie Johnson
Special effects: Vernon Walker
Running time: 95 minutes

Principal characters:
Professor Richard Wanley .... Edward G. Robinson
Frank Lalor, District Attorney ...... Raymond Massey
Alice Reed .... Joan Bennett
Doctor Barkstane .... Edmund Breon
Heidt .... Dan Duryea
Police Inspector .... Thomas Jackson

Fritz Lang's *Woman in the Window* opened in 1944 to mixed critical reviews. This was primarily because of the film's unexpected ending that violated moral tenets of accountability and what some critics saw as a growing cynicism toward murder and the law in contemporary American films. Despite the ending, which reveals the murder to have been a dream, thus vitiating the "murderer," the film remains a psychological and visual classic, incorporating Lang's earlier thematic preoccupations with the fallibility of man's nature, the arbitrariness of fate. It also illustrated his interest in the idea of a *femme fatale* and her victim with the elegant framing and composition that move the film economically and resolutely along. Although *Woman in the Window* has been compared to *Suspicion* (1942) and other early Alfred Hitchcock films, it is not a thriller in the same sense since the only unknown is how and when the murderer will be revealed.

The film opens slowly, with Professor Richard Wanley (Edward G. Robinson) lecturing his class on criminal psychology and the difference between intentional homicide and self-defense. Next we see him on a train platform as his wife and two children leave New York for the summer without him, and subsequently he joins two friends, Frank Lalor, a District Attorney (Raymond Massey), and Doctor Barkstane (Edmund Breon) at a quiet and decorous men's club to discuss the social possibilities presented by his summer bachelorhood.

In these three compact scenes the professor is established as a responsible, law-respecting, family-obligated man. If he is not infallible, he is at least well-intentioned and not a likely prey to the moral deviations that disrupt the lives of less stable citizens. As he leaves the club alone, he stops to admire the painting of an enigmatic-looking woman in a shop window next door. In a beautifully framed shot reminiscent of the scene in Lang's earlier film *M* (1931), in which the murderer and the child he will later kill stand reflected in a display of knives in a shop window, the model for the painting steps up behind the professor and is herself reflected in the painting. Some intrusive elements of melodrama color the remainder of the film. The woman, whose name is Alice Reed (Joan Bennett) invites the professor to her apartment to see other drawings of her by the same artist. He protests, but ends up drawn to the woman's apartment anyway, and when her lover arrives unexpectedly and attacks him in inexplicable jealousy, the professor stabs and kills him in self-defense.

From the moment the woman stands reflected in the painting until the abrupt moment of the murder, the film has a fantasylike quality, but a sense of urgent reality dominates the remainder of the film as the professor tries to cover up the murder and cope with a blackmailer; he finally collapses into his own destruction rather than go to the police. The professor swears the woman to secrecy and anonymity, and she agrees to let him leave alone to pick up his car on condition that he leave an item that will guarantee his return: a monogrammed lighter. This is the first of an increasing number of incidents that prefigure his vulnerability and inevitable disclosure and create in the audience a sense of identification with and fear for this very ordinary man in an irrevocable crisis. Wanley sets out to dispose of the body and commits one blunder after another. With the body bundled under a blanket in the back of the car, he is almost arrested for going through a red light. Then at a tollgate entrance in a rainstorm, he drops a dime onto the road and has a toll keeper searching around the car in efforts to locate it. When he arrives back at his club, to an atmosphere of security and tradition, reflected in the dim interiors and somber lighting, Lalor attempts to entertain him with the details of the sensational murder the professor has just been attempting to cover up. Lang's sense of fate comes through the rest of the film. It is in the arbitrary accumulation of details—the tire prints in the mud, the imprints in the path, and the scrap of cloth in the barbed-wire fence—that the climax is fixed. Neither the psychology of the man or the woman nor the relationship between the two is ever considered to be the deciding factor of their fate.

With an almost fey sense of self-destruction, the professor goes with Lalor to see where the body was found. He finds himself at the head of the party, leading them to the site, although presumably he has no knowledge of where the body was found. Even so, his respectability leaves him free from suspicion. It is only when Heidt (Dan Duryea), the murdered man's bodyguard who had followed him to the woman's apartment, attempts blackmail that the trap begins to close. The professor manages to get a prescription for sleeping powder from Dr. Barkstane that is a poison when taken in large doses and gives some to the woman who tries to give it to Heidt in a drink. When Heidt becomes suspicious and leaves without taking the drink, she calls and tells the professor of her failure. Believing that his life and reputation have been ruined, Wanley takes an overdose of the powder himself, unaware that as he is doing so the police have just killed Heidt in a gunfight. Several critics have suggested this as the logical ending for the film. It would, in fact, coalesce with Lang's statement that "evil in its many forms—the evil of crime, of weakness, of deceit—must reap some sort of physical or mental punishment."

Instead, what happens is that as Wanley begins to collapse from the effects of the poison, a hand moves into the frame and awakens him. As the camera pulls back, we see the footman at the club waking him and reminding him of the hour. As he leaves the club, we see that the hatcheck man is the man he thought he had murdered and the doorman is Heidt. He again passes the photograph of the woman in the window, but when a streetwalker approaches him, he runs away, having no further interest in that avenue of fantasy.

It may have been a less than satisfying ending for some critics, but the device has been used successfully in a number of films, most notably in *The Wizard of Oz* (1939) and Luis Bunuel's *The Discreet Charm of the Bourgeoisie* (1972). Occasionally the device is intended to be a portent of the future, as in *Dead of Night* (1946). In this film there is no hint of the future, and, even if emotionally unsatisfying to some, it does not detract from the overall merits of the film; in fact, it is more a reflection of the unfinished quality of most dreams. The melodramatics of the murder and the subsequent details also reinforce the dreamlike quality of the bulk of the action. The events seem so farfetched that when they are revealed to have existed only in a dream, they make more sense.

For those who dislike the ending, however, Lang's next film, *Scarlet Street* (1945), is perhaps more satisfying. In this film Robinson, Bennett, and Duryea are again the three stars, playing similar roles as members of a romantic triangle. This film again involves a murder, but in this case Robinson is not dreaming, and the horrible events surrounding the affair are real. The parallel can go even farther, as paintings are significantly featured in the progression of the story.

Joyce Olin

WOMAN OF THE YEAR

Released: 1942
Production: Joseph L. Mankiewicz for Metro-Goldwyn-Mayer
Direction: George Stevens
Screenplay: Ring Lardner, Jr., and Michael Kanin (AA)
Cinematography: Joseph Ruttenberg
Editing: Frank Sullivan
Running time: 112 minutes

Principal characters:
Sam Craig .... Spencer Tracy
Tess Harding .... Katharine Hepburn
Clayton .... Reginald Owen
Ellen Whitcomb .... Fay Bainter
Pinkie Peters .... William Bendix
Flo Peters .... Gladys Blake
Chris .... George Kezas
Matron at orphanage .... Sara Haden

Hollywood legend says that when Katharine Hepburn met Spencer Tracy for the very first time, the actress said "I'm afraid I am a little too tall for you, Mr. Tracy." "Don't worry, Miss Hepburn," the actor reportedly answered, "I'll cut you down to my size." Although some credit producer Joseph L. Mankiewicz as the person who said to Hepburn "Don't worry, Tracy will cut you down to his size," the statement does comment beautifully on the salty chemistry between two of the screen's most brilliant actors and delightfully foreshadows the cinematic battle-of-the-sexes which would characterize their nine films together over the next twenty-five years.

Woman of the Year marked their first appearance together on the screen. Hepburn was responsible for initiating the production, which was based on an idea by Garson Kanin, whose brother Michael had co-authored the screenplay along with Ring Lardner, Jr. Hepburn took the script to M-G-M's studio head Louis B. Mayer and personally acted as agent for the two screenwriters, bringing them an almost unprecedented $100,000 for their script. Fresh from her success in 1940's *The Philadelphia Story*, Hepburn was beginning to exert considerable control over all of the properties in which she was to star. In keeping with this control, Hepburn demanded and received one of M-G-M's top male stars, Spencer Tracy, as her leading man, and George Stevens as her director. Actually, Hepburn had initially wanted George Cukor, who had directed her in *The Philadelphia Story* and *Holiday* (1938), but since Cukor then had other commitments, she decided upon Stevens, who had directed her critically acclaimed performance in *Alice Adams* (1935).

Woman of the Year is an amusing comedy-drama concerning two competitive newspaper columnists who feud in print, fall in love when they finally meet, feud, get married, feud, and finally reconcile. The progression of the story may be fairly predictable, but the blending of the main characters, in addition to a witty and satirical script, make the film one of the classics of the battle-of-the-sexes genre.

Tracy plays Sam Craig, a tough, craggy, down-to-earth sportswriter for *The New York Chronicle* and author of the column "Man About Sports," a popular feature of the newspaper. In the beginning of the film, while Sam is in a bar listening to a radio broadcast of the popular program *Information Please*, he accurately answers a question concerning the most frequently traveled distance, which is ninety feet, the distance between the bases on a baseball diamond. When the show's guest, celebrated woman journalist Tess Harding (Katharine Hepburn), suggests that baseball be abolished for the duration of the war, Sam becomes enraged. Tess writes a column in *The New York Chronicle* dealing with international affairs, but Sam disregards the fact that she is a colleague and lambasts her in his column, going so far as to call her "the Calamity Jane of the fast, international set." Tess responds in her own column, calling Sam "an ostrich with amnesia."

When Tess and Sam are called into the office of the paper's managing editor, Clayton (Reginald Owen), they are both set for a battle, but instead they are immediately impressed and attracted by each other. As something of a peace overture, Sam even invites Tess to a baseball game—her first. At the beginning of the game Tess does not know a strike from the outfield, and as Sam explains that a good pitch must pass between the batter's shoulders and knees, Tess responds, "If the batter were smart, he'd stoop down and fool the pitcher." By the end of the game, however, Sam is impressed by Tess's ability to absorb the rudiments of the game so quickly, and equally impressed with her womanly qualities.

After a quick courtship frequently interrupted by Tess's work, Sam and Tess, who have absolutely nothing in common except physical attraction, decide to get married. They spend a disastrous wedding night in Tess's apartment. There are interruptions by a famous war refugee and all of his friends and a contingency of Sam's more earthy friends, whom he invites in retaliation. Finally, one of Sam's friends, Flo Peters (Gladys Blake), realizes that it is Sam and Tess's honeymoon and hurries everyone out of the apartment so that the couple will finally be able to be alone. The honeymoon is merely a portent of some of the problems which will confront Tess and Sam in their marriage. From the beginning it is obvious that Tess's career and the disparity between Tess's and Sam's personalities will make their relationship difficult. In order to accommodate Tess's more complicated life style, Sam agrees to live in Tess's sumptuous apartment. Tess soon becomes so busy with her column, conferences with world leaders, lectures, and trips around the country, that

Sam begins to feel left out and resentful.

One morning, however, as Tess has sweetly brought Sam breakfast in bed, she begins to discuss the possibility that a child might enrich their lives. Thinking that Tess is pregnant, Sam is elated and says, "I hope it's a boy." "It *is* a boy," she replies. It seems that as part of her war work, she has decided to set a good example for others and adopt a six-year-old Greek war orphan named Chris (George Kezas). As for having her own baby, Tess assures Sam that that would be "impractical."

Bringing the boy into their home brings their relationship to a breaking point. Sam does not want the boy initially, but he softheartedly takes an interest in the child and chastizes Tess for her lack of sensitivity and affection as a mother. The final break occurs when Tess is named "America's Outstanding Woman" and is scheduled to appear at a banquet in her honor. As usual, she is oblivious to Sam and Chris and starts to leave for the banquet without having arranged for a babysitter, feeling that the elevator operator in the apartment building would be there in an emergency. Sam is outraged and refuses to go with Tess to the banquet. When she leaves, Sam decides to pack up the lonely Chris and take him back to the orphanage.

When they arrive at the orphanage and Chris runs happily to his other Greek orphan friends, Sam realizes that he has made the right decision about returning him. Ironically, as he is waiting in the living room of the orphanage matron (Sara Haden), Sam hears the banquet where Tess is receiving her award playing on the radio. The scene is an ironic juxtaposition of the first sequence, in which Sam hears Tess on *Information Please*. While Tess receives her award as the woman of the year, the film audience realizes that in Sam's eyes at this moment, Tess is a total failure as a woman.

Later that night when Tess discovers that Sam has taken Chris back to the orphanage, she goes to get the boy, but is shocked to find that he does not want to come back to her. She leaves, and again the irony of the award is felt. Tess also feels that she is a failure. Sam has left her, but after some introspection, she decides to go after him. She goes to the house where he is staying in the early morning and sneaks in, planning to make him breakfast, her first overt attempt at domesticity. The scene develops subtly, but grows hilarious as Tess makes a shambles of the breakfast. She cannot fix the coffee or the eggs properly, and even the waffles are ruined because she has too much leavening in the batter, making them expand like balloons in the waffle iron. Most of Tess's disastrous cooking is observed by an awakened Sam who finally takes pity on her and stops the disaster. She tearfully says that she wants to be a good wife to him, cooking and cleaning and doing the usual domestic chores, but surprisingly Sam does not want this. The film ends, in a very original vein for the time, with Sam telling Tess that he does not want her to turn into something she is not. What he really wants, and what the conclusion promises, is that their marriage will be the most important thing in both their lives, leaving careers and other differences between them in secondary roles.

The chemistry between Tracy and Hepburn in this film and their subsequent ventures made their films prototypes of later man versus woman comedies. Hepburn was beautiful, intelligent, and accomplished in those films, an equal match for the tough, more down-to-earth Tracy. If the plots of their films, like that of *Woman of the Year*, seem to end with the traditional happy ending of marital bliss with the wife subjugated to the husband, it is only so superficially. Hepburn never lost her femininity or her feminism in these films, which is due as much to her acting and offscreen personality as to the scripts. The dialogue in *Woman of the Year* is first rate, and Lardner and Kanin won an Oscar for their efforts. The jibes that Tracy and Hepburn throw at each other are equally matched by the tender moments of affection between them. Additionally, some of the scenes reminiscent of the 1930's-style screwball comedies, such as the wedding night and the breakfast preparations, are hilarious.

Tracy and Hepburn went through various stages in their onscreen relationships, gradually progressing to their last film together, *Guess Who's Coming to Dinner?* (1967). Hepburn won an Oscar for her performance in that film, which was Tracy's last before his death. Despite other themes explored in that film, the relationship between Tracy and Hepburn remained as beautifully portrayed there as it had been in *Woman of the Year*. The strength of the two characters in the later film, matched by their long-lasting devotion to each other, seems to be a fitting end to the relationship established on the screen twenty-five years before. Considering the Tracy and Hepburn characters in these two films side by side, it is not difficult to see that each had retained his own personality and his own interests, but after twenty-five years they had both softened and become closer together. This seems to be what Sam is asking in the last scene of *Woman of the Year*, and *Guess Who's Coming to Dinner?* is a good companion piece to the earlier film, if only for that reason.

Janet St. Claire

A WOMAN REBELS

Released: 1936
Production: Pandro S. Berman for RKO/Radio
Direction: Mark Sandrich
Screenplay: Anthony Veiller and Ernest Vajda; based on the novel *Portrait of a Rebel* by Netta Syrett
Cinematography: Robert de Grasse
Editing: Jane Loring
Costume design: Walter Plunkett
Running time: 88 minutes

Principal characters:

Pamela Thistlewaite	Katharine Hepburn
Thomas Lane	Herbert Marshall
Judge Thistlewaite	Donald Crisp
Flora Thistlewaite	Elizabeth Allan
Young Flora	Doris Dudley
Gerald	Van Heflin
Betty Bumble	Lucile Watson

The 1936 film *A Woman Rebels* seems particularly important today for two reasons: the very fine performance by Katharine Hepburn and the incorporation of many feminist ideals, given voice to in both the plot line and in numerous speeches by Hepburn. This film, adapted from Netta Syrett's novel *Portrait of a Rebel*, deals with a woman's struggle for emancipation during the Victorian era. Although the film is couched in the familiar mode of the costume melodrama (Hepburn wears no less than twenty-two costumes throughout the film) and was advertised as a sentimental drama involving "dreams—sacrifices—heroism," the plot line presents a woman attempting to discard the shackles of Victorian morality in an effort to live her life as she likes.

Hepburn plays Pamela Thistlewaite, a young upper-middle-class woman in Great Britain during the 1870's who refuses to follow the dictates of her stern and autocratic father, Judge Thistlewaite, played with a proper repressiveness by veteran character actor Donald Crisp. Pamela insists upon living alone, picking the men with whom she wants to spend time, and even earning her living as the crusading editor of a woman's magazine. This clear feminist line is undercut, in part, by the fact that she has been "seduced and abandoned" by an early suitor, Gerald (Van Heflin), who has left her with their child, "Young Flora" (Doris Dudley). Much of the story line involves the gradual falling away of Pamela's defenses after this unfortunate early experience.

A faithful suitor, Thomas Lane, is played with fitting stalwartness by Herbert Marshall, and a portion of the film is given over to watching Pamela as she comes to the realization that she does after all love Lane, the suitor waiting patiently in the wings. Although the excuse provided for her initial rejection of Lane is that she is devoted to her career, the real explanation seems to be that Pamela is ashamed of her status as an unwed mother. Also undercutting what we might see as a strong feminist statement is the fact that Pamela passes her child off as her niece. Her sister, Flora Thistlewaite (Elizabeth Allan), dies during the course of the film, thus paving the way for this deception.

Even so, we do see Pamela determine her own path. The film covers a twenty-year span (some reviewers have remarked that the maturation of mother and daughter often appears out-of-synch even though four different actresses portray Young Flora at various ages). Throughout *A Woman Rebels*, Pamela is counseled by her nurse, chaperone, and confidante, Betty Bumble (Lucile Watson). When the young Pamela challenges her strict Victorian father for sending her to bed as a punishment for reading forbidden books, she defiantly goes off to live alone and work, and—after ultimately dropping her fear of men—she chooses her own mate. Hepburn is particularly fine, as only she can be, in giving speeches and striking stances which assert her independence and individual integrity.

Although RKO/Radio clearly hoped to cash in on the success of Hepburn's Victorian series and to add yet another entry in the costume picture wave, *A Woman Rebels* was not a box-office success, and it ushered in the period of "box-office poison" (as she was labeled) for Hepburn. It is clear that the strong feminist statements and portrayal were too much for the 1930's audience and that even a happy marital ending was not enough to placate a public unused to seeing a heroine thrive as both career woman and single parent.

No major awards were given to anyone connected with the film, although most reviewers praised the direction of Mark Sandrich, who shot it in only fifty-four days. It was Hepburn, who always exercised much artistic control or influence in her films, who recommended both Dudley to play her daughter as an adult and Heflin for the part of the early, dashing lover. After Hepburn had seen them both in Ina Claire's play *End of Summer*, she wanted them for this film. Although Dudley only made a few more films, Heflin went on to become a well-established actor, later appearing with Hepburn in *The Philadelphia Story* on stage, and in 1941 winning an Oscar as Best Supporting Actor of the year as *Johnny Eager*. He had a long and successful career as a character actor, being equally good as a villain or sympathetic hero. He rose to the ranks of male star—usually opposite better-known female costars—in such films as *The Strange Love of Martha Ivers* (1946) with Barbara Stanwyck and *Madame Bovary* (1949) with Jennifer Jones. His last film was *Airport* (1970), in which he played the bomber, released several months before his death of a heart attack in 1971.

Marsha McCreadie

A WOMAN UNDER THE INFLUENCE

Released: 1974
Production: Sam Shaw for Faces International Films
Direction: John Cassavetes
Screenplay: John Cassavetes
Cinematography: Caleb Deschanel
Editing: Tom Cornwell
Running time: 146 minutes

Principal characters:
Nick Longhetti	Peter Falk
Mabel Longhetti	Gena Rowlands
Garson Cross	O. G. Dunn
Doctor Zepp	Eddie Shaw
Mama Longhetti	Katherine Cassavetes
Martha Mortensen	Lady Rowlands

It is not an accident that John Cassavetes chose to title his first independent commercial production *Faces* (1968). No director since Carl Dreyer has been more fascinated with the expressive possibilities of the human physiognomy, or used the close-up more consummately and consistently to explore shifts and fluctuations of feeling between his characters. Yet, if the extreme close-up has become a kind of trade-mark of Cassavetes' work and one of his most powerful expressive devices, it, like any other technical device, has important moral and psychological ramifications. Cassavetes has said that the most important fact about his characters is that they are social beings, but his close-ups in his early films tell us just the opposite. In *Shadows* (1961), *Too Late Blues* (1962), *A Child Is Waiting* (1963), and *Faces*, his first four films, Cassavetes' close-ups communicate the insulation, isolation, and estrangement of his characters from one another. In spite of his inordinate effort to emphasize the social nature of their experiences, Cassavetes' characters seem radically alone and separated from each other. Even when they are communicating, the signals that they send out (their glances, eye movements, and microscopic gestures) are too delicate to be broadcast over longer distances undistorted and too weak to be received by any instrument less sensitive and attentive than Cassavetes' camera. His close-ups become, in effect, our only way of communicating with these characters, as well as their only means of reaching each other.

The close-up becomes an aesthetic problem with which Cassavetes must wrestle in all of the later films. It is in this context that one must view the increasing withdrawal of his camera in *Husbands* (1970), *Minnie and Moskowitz* (1971), and his masterpiece, *A Woman Under the Influence* (1974). In these films he attempts to enlarge his vision, to free his characters from the tyranny of the frame, and to imagine them in authentic communication and contact with a larger, sustaining environment. *A Woman Under the Influence* has its share of emotional and visual close-ups, but for the first time in his career Cassavetes is able to imagine his characters in a vital matrix of personal, familial, and social relations.

A Woman Under the Influence is the relatively simple and uncomplicated story of six months in the lives of an ordinary American family—a construction worker, Nick Longhetti (Peter Falk), his wife Mabel (Gena Rowlands), and their three children—trying to understand the meaning of their love for one another as the mother goes through a nervous breakdown, confinement in a hospital, and the return home. Like most of Cassavetes' films, this one is really little more than a series of anecdotes from a few days in their lives together. There is an afternoon and night when Nick fails to show up for a special evening he had promised Mabel; Mabel's going to bed with another man; a touching scene at the end of which Mabel is committed to a hospital; and the evening of Mabel's return home to her family and relatives. In between these points there are simply a series of social gatherings and encounters between characters. Within this simple and unmelodramatic plot, however, Peter Falk and Gena Rowlands give the performances of their lives, and Cassavetes makes one of the supreme examinations of the triumphs and tragedies of domestic life and love ever filmed.

A Woman Under the Influence is about "influences," and no film more subtly and responsively captures the personal influences to which an individual is subjected in ordinary family life. The drama of the film is precisely this tug and pull between the individual personality and all of the influences to which he is responsible and responsive in this world. In the central scene of the film, one of the most moving performances ever photographed, Mabel Longhetti is not even allowed the luxury of having her own private nervous breakdown. Her husband, her mother-in-law (played wonderfully by Cassavetes' own mother Katherine), and the family physician, Dr. Zepp (Eddie Shaw), all jockey for positions and roles in her "scene." Just at the moments that our sympathies go out most poignantly to Mabel, Cassavetes crosscuts to their reactions, to their parts of the room, and to their preparations for their next appearances beside Mabel. In place of the close-ups and extreme close-ups that would have showed us Mabel's decline under a microscope in an earlier film, Cassavetes deliberately holds his camera low and away from her throughout to keep reminding us of the sheer space around her, and to allow other characters to appear in the borders of her frame, in front of her, or behind her. With an insistence that some audiences have mistaken for technical incompetence, he keeps pulling focus from foreground to middleground to background and back again, making slices through yards of space, and each slice is never more than three or four inches deep at one time. Omniscience is as impossible as objectivity in this world. Cassavetes' slides of focus and shifts of perspective juggle five or ten vantage points in each scene, no one of which is more definitive or authoritative than the rest.

Pulling focus and changing perspectives might be metaphors for the experience of the entire film. What Cassavetes provides is an unending series of "refocusings"—an experience of all the competing, shifting, and overlapping planes of relationship surrounding and ultimately connecting Nick and Mabel in love. No one perspective can command our attention or summarize their relationship for more than a moment in this world of connections without absolutes. Even the home provides no absolute protection or shelter for this family. Nick and Mabel throughout the film keep talking about their house as a sanctuary from the cares and confusions of the world, but Cassavetes denies Nick and Mabel any place of refuge or escape from the influences around them. There is a knock at the front door; the telephone rings; a mother-in-law intrudes unexpectedly; a neighbor visits; or the children suddenly arrive home to remind them of obligations incurred, and responsibilities to fulfill. No moment is exonerated from the hazards of interruption, intrusion, or the complications of a larger context. Nick brings ten coworkers home for breakfast the morning after Mabel's night with another man; the children and Mabel's mother (played by Rowlands' own mother Lady Rowlands) break in on Nick and Mabel alone in bed together; and the whole cast of family and friends gathers to greet Mabel's return from the hospital at the end of the film to ensure that she cannot have even this poignant moment of love and readjustment to herself.

"Be yourself" is the advice that characters give Mabel all through the film. "We're on your side," they argue, but the very strength of *A Woman Under the Influence* is the extent to which (despite each character's limitations) it moves us beyond all such simple definitions of "selfhood" and all the easy demarcations of opposite "sides," opponents, or obstacles. Cassavetes helps us to see the mixed-up selves and roles that are present in any one "self" and the tangled web of influences, connections, and relationships that carry us beyond any possible formulation of "us" versus "them."

In place of melodramatic clarifications, Cassavetes' aesthetic offers us only muddlements of mixed-up caring and entanglements of love. In place of resolutions and solutions, it suggests only that we will negotiate a course of events and confusions that teach us the necessity of ever larger acts of inclusion and awareness. In place of fashionable escapism and the glorification of the individual, it shows circles of responsibility and allegiance that make personal freedom all the more difficult to achieve. It is significant that *A Woman Under the Influence*, although chronologically the most recent, is actually the middle installment of Cassavetes' marriage trilogy. *Minnie and Moskowitz*, the narration of a whirlwind courtship and the beginning of a marriage, is all fantasy, dreams, and idealism. *Faces*, Cassavetes' story of the end of a marriage, is all despair, disillusion, and failures of communication. In this story of a couple in the middle of their marriage, however, Cassavetes manages to combine both extremes, to include wild idealism and harsh realities. The operatic scoring of *A Woman Under the Influence* at certain key moments in the film dangles the possibilities of unlimited personal expansions as grand as any in *Minnie and Moskowitz*, even as the telephones and nervous neighbors remind us of the burnt-out suburban dreams of *Faces*.

What, then, are we to make of Cassavetes' choice of the middle years of a marriage for the conclusion of his trilogy, after the "failures" of healthy ongoing relationships in the two previous films? *Faces* is all cynicism and paralysis; *Minnie and Moskowitz* all callowness and idealism. *A Woman Under the Influence* is in some ways about a waste of personal consciousness that the individual is powerless to control. Yet, like the greatest tragic drama, it is also exhilarating to experience. *A Woman Under the Influence* offers no morals, lessons, or portable doctrines about family life. It offers no resolution, progress, or hope for the end of its characters' struggles. The extraordinary final ten minutes of the film, in fact, suggest how little anything has changed between Nick and Mabel from beginning to end. Nothing is made, affirmed, or achieved by the end of the film except Nick's and Mabel's and the audience's having lived through all that has happened. All any of us gets out of it, like all that Nick and Mabel get from it, is a richer consciousness, richer to the extent that we have suffered together and been forced to see more and respond to more than we would have ever guessed we were capable of doing. We are no wiser, no more hopeful, no more resigned to Nick's and Mabel's relationship than they are themselves. We have simply succeeded with them in negotiating a course of events, a series of influences and interruptions, and managed to keep alive the possibilities of love, generosity, and sensitivity through it all. That may not be much by the standards of success in the world, but in Cassavetes' cinematic universe it is everything and sufficient reason for him to celebrate this very great tragedy as, in his own sincere opinion, his "most optimistic film."

Raymond Carney

WOMEN IN LOVE

Released: 1970
Production: Larry Kramer and Martin Rosen for United Artists
Direction: Ken Russell
Screenplay: Larry Kramer; based on the novel of the same name by D. H. Lawrence
Cinematography: Billy Williams
Editing: Michael Bradsell
Costume design: Shirley Russell
Running time: 132 minutes

Principal characters:
Rupert Birkin	Alan Bates
Gerald Crich	Oliver Reed
Gudrun Brangwen	Glenda Jackson (AA)
Ursula Brangwen	Jennie Linden
Hermione Roddice	Eleanor Bron
Loerke	Vladek Sheybal
Laura Crich	Sharon Gurney

Seldom does a film of great visual distinction give much attention to language, ideas, and characterization. *Women in Love*, however, encompasses all these facets brilliantly. Director Ken Russell and screenwriter Larry Kramer give us a sensitive interpretation of the novel by D. H. Lawrence in which the lush visual style is a splendid cinematic equivalent of Lawrence's writing, and the necessary condensation of the book is well done. The result is a dense but not overburdened example of film art on many levels.

In the Midlands of England in 1920, two sisters, Ursula (Jennie Linden) and Gudrun Brangwen (Glenda Jackson), discuss marriage on their way to watch the wedding of Laura Crich (Sharon Gurney), daughter of the town's wealthy mineowner. Each is especially fascinated by a particular member of the wedding party—Gudrun by Laura's brother Gerald (Oliver Reed) and Ursula by his friend Rupert Birkin (Alan Bates). Ursula is a schoolteacher and Rupert a school inspector; she remembers his coming to her classroom and interrupting her botany lesson to discourse on the sexual nature of the catkin.

The four are later brought together at a house party at the estate of Hermione Roddice (Eleanor Bron), a rich woman whose relationship with Rupert is disintegrating. When Hermione devises as an entertainment for the guests a dance in the style of the Russian ballet, Rupert becomes impatient with her pretensions and tells the pianist to play some ragtime. This sets off spontaneous dancing among the whole group and angers Hermione. When Birkin follows her into the next room, she smashes a paperweight against his head, and he staggers outside, where he discards his clothes and wanders through the woods.

Later, at the Criches' annual picnic, to which most of the town is invited, Ursula and Gudrun find a secluded spot, and Gudrun dances before some longhorn cattle while Ursula sings "I'm Forever Blowing Bubbles." When Gerald and Rupert appear, Gerald calls Gudrun's behavior impossible and ridiculous, then says he loves her. "That's one way of putting it," she replies. After Laura and her new husband drown while swimming in the lake, Ursula and Birkin wander away discussing death and love and end up making love. The sequence ends with a quick, shocking cut from the intertwined bodies of the live lovers to the bodies of the drowned ones.

During one of Gerald and Rupert's discussions, Rupert suggests Japanese-style wrestling, and they strip off their clothes and wrestle in the firelight in a stunningly photographed scene. Rupert enjoys their closeness and says they should swear to love each other implicitly, but Gerald cannot understand Rupert's idea of wanting to have an emotional union with a man as well as an emotional and physical union with a woman.

Ursula and Birkin decide to marry while Gudrun and Gerald continue to see each other. One evening, emotionally exhausted after his father's illness and death, Gerald sneaks into the Brangwen house to spend the night with Gudrun and leaves at dawn. Later, after Ursula and Birkin's marriage, Gerald suggests that the four of them go to the Alps for Christmas. At their inn in the Alps, Gudrun irritates Gerald with her interest in Loerke (Vladek Shey-bal), a homosexual German artist. An artist herself, Gudrun is fascinated with Loerke's idea that brutality is necessary to create art. While Gerald grows increasingly jealous and angry, Gudrun only derides and ridicules him. Finally he can endure it no longer, tries to strangle her, and then trudges off into the snow to die. The film ends with Ursula and Rupert in their cottage in England discussing love: "You can't have two kinds of love. Why should you?" Ursula says. "It seems as if I can't," Rupert responds. "Yet I wanted it."

On one level *Women in Love* is the story of the four main characters trying out their philosophies of love. Rupert Birkin is the most self-aware and analytical of the group, with his own definite ideas of what love should be. He turns away from Hermione, at least in part, because she cannot be spontaneous and instead wants everything to be mental and in her power. With Ursula he wants something more than the conventional idea of love. "We can go one better," he says. He also believes that in addition to a man's love of a woman he can have an equally important, creative, and sacred relationship with a man. Neither Ursula nor Gerald is able to accept or understand this idea. After their nude wrestling, when Rupert says to Gerald that they should swear to love each other implicitly, Gerald can only reply that he must wait until he understands the idea better. Ursula's ideas on love are conventional.

Rather than finding something "better" than love with Rupert she simply wants him to say "my love" to her, and she thinks his wanting to have two kinds of love, one for her and one for a man, is impossible. Except when she has a fit of jealousy over Hermione, however, her conventional love is presented quite favorably so that Birkin's marriage to her is not seen as a compromise. Gudrun, on the other hand, is more emancipated than her sister, but her relationships with men are exercises of power rather than of feeling. Early in the film she goes walking in a rough section of the town at night. When a man approaches her, she both mocks and provokes him and then tries to fight him off. With Gerald she becomes cruel. When he comes to her room after his father's funeral, she gives herself to him without emotion. Their relationship continues until in Austria she torments him with her attentions to Loerke. Later, in their room, she goads him into saying he loves her, then mocks him for saying it, and finally drives him to suicide.

It is the achievement of *Women in Love* that it conveys a coherent plot about fully developed characters yet is also visually stunning. It is aimed not only at the mind and the emotions but also at the eye. From the smallest detail of the costumes and settings to such striking sequences as the nude wrestling and Gudrun's dance before the cattle, the style of the film is opulent but controlled. Except for one scene, in which a sideways camera and slow motion are used to convey the moods of Rupert and Ursula in love, the visual treatment enhances one's appreciation rather than distracts from it.

A justly famous scene epitomizes the style and manner of the film. At an outdoor gathering including Hermione, Rupert, Gerald, Ursula, and Gudrun, all are sitting on white chairs around a white table. Their summer clothes are predominantly white, but are set off by the bright colors of Ursula's dress and Gerald's jacket as well as the green of the grass and trees behind them. In this carefully composed setting Hermione begins to eat a fig, inspiring Rupert to deliver a poetic discourse on the fig, dwelling on its sexual implications. Director Russell uses many close-ups to concentrate on Rupert's speech and the silent reactions of those around the table. The scene is compelling to both the eye and the ear as well as appropriate to the character of Rupert and the eroticism of the film. (Although not in the novel, Rupert's speech is taken from a poem by Lawrence.)

Russell was fortunate to have such fine actors to realize his complex conception of *Women in Love*. Especially noteworthy are Bates, Jackson, and Reed in the most vivid roles—Birkin, Brangwen, and Crich. Rupert's eloquence is made especially convincing by Bates, and Jackson won an Academy Award for her portrayal of the malevolent but fascinating Gudrun. In short, *Women in Love* is not only a masterpiece of visual stylization but also a fully realized dramatic narrative.

Timothy W. Johnson

THE WRONG BOX

Released: 1966
Production: Bryan Forbes for Salamander Films; released by Columbia
Direction: Bryan Forbes
Screenplay: Larry Gelbart and Burt Shevelove; based on the novel of the same name by Robert Louis Stevenson and Lloyd Osbourne
Cinematography: Gerry Turpin
Editing: Alan Osbitson
Running time: 105 minutes

    Principal characters:

Masterman Finsbury	John Mills
Joseph Finsbury	Ralph Richardson
Michael	Michael Caine
Morris	Peter Cook
John	Dudley Moore
Julia	Nanette Newman
Doctor Pratt	Peter Sellers

If awards were given to films on the basis of their outlandishness, *The Wrong Box* would be in contention for top honors. Seldom in the history of film has there been a more outrageously funny farce, led by the delightful writing of Larry Gelbart and Burt Shevelove (adapted from the novel by Robert Louis Stevenson and Lloyd Osbourne), acted with extraordinary vigor by a sterling cast headed by John Mills and Ralph Richardson, and directed with Keystone Kops style pacing by Bryan Forbes. To outline fully the outrageous sequence of events and gags would take entirely too long, and add little to the discussion of the film, but a brief synopsis can convey the basic story line.

In Victorian London, two aged brothers, Masterman (John Mills) and Joseph Finsbury (Ralph Richardson), are bound together not so much by blood as by a Tontine, a form of trust fund lottery in which the last surviving member of a group inherits a considerable fortune. Rapidly declining in both health and wealth, Masterman decides to dispose of his brother so that the money will go to his grandson Michael (Michael Caine), an unpromising medical student. Although they live next door to each other, they have not met for years. Masterman makes several ineffectual attempts on Joseph's life but the latter is too absorbed in his avocation—collecting useless bits of information—to notice.

Also plotting to obtain the inheritance are Joseph's two avaricious nephews, Morris (Peter Cook) and John (Dudley Moore). Wrongly believing that Masterman has died, that Michael is concealing the fact, and that their own uncle has been killed in a train wreck, they crate up what they believe to be Joseph's corpse and ship it back home, hoping to cover up the death. The crate, however, which actually contains the body of the notorious Bournemouth Strangler, is mistakenly delivered to Masterman's house. While the confused Michael is frantically trying to dispose of the body, the two nephews persuade the disreputable Dr. Pratt (Peter Sellers) to sign a post dated death certificate for Joseph.

This only *begins* the confusion and complications; the police begin their own manhunt for the body of the strangler, and the two greedy nephews get their hands on the money. A wild chase takes place (involving nearly everybody in the cast), finally coming to an abrupt halt in the middle of a cemetery, where a funeral is already in progress. The complicated situation is apparently resolved when both Masterman and Joseph appear, alive, and well. The villainy of the cousins is exposed, and the Tontine appears destined for Michael and Julia (Nanette Newman), Joseph's ward, who have fallen in love.

Coscenarists Gelbart and Shevelove wrote *The Wrong Box* to match the pacing of their earlier successful plays, *A Funny Thing Happened on the Way to the Forum*, and the film succeeds admirably in capturing the same frenetic atmosphere, literally racing the audience along from one hilarious situation to the next and giving equal and ample opportunities for its delightful cast.

Critical reaction to the film was, for the most part, quite favorable. *Time* magazine reported: "In this slice of Victorian gingerbread, Director Bryan Forbes [usually noted for somber dramas] reveals an unexpected gift for utter nonsense, using every period cliché and corny camera trick that might be imaginably fermented into vintage black comedy." Bosley Crowther, writing for *The New York Times*, seemed even more ecstatic: "Robert Louis Stevenson and Lloyd Osbourne must be whirling in their graves, convulsed with astonishment and laughter at what a bunch of British actors have done in turning their humorous tale, *The Wrong Box*, into an outlandish film."

Forbes, a British actor, director, and writer, is best known for the stark dramas he directed, such as *The L-Shaped Room* (1963) and *King Rat* (1965). He returned to this type of film with *The Whisperers* (1966), a highly praised film starring Dame Edith Evans. His career has taken many turns in the years since *The Wrong Box*, but he has never produced another successful comedy. His latest film, *Sunday Lovers* (1981), of which he directed the segment starring Roger Moore, was a comedy, but a complete failure, both critically and commercially. It is unfortunate that his flair here has not been utilized more often.

It was the acting, however, so vital to this type of enterprise, which made *The Wrong Box* so successful. Mills as the delightfully wacky Masterman is complemented by the casting of Richardson as an old, scholarly charlatan. Caine as the befuddled medical student is quite good, although not quite as natural a comic as the others. The team of Cook and Moore (in one of their earliest film appearances) provide many of the most lunatic moments of the film as the two bumbling cousins so eager to get hold of the inheritance, reprising the essence of much of their successful comedy routine. Veteran comedy actor Sellers as the slightly absent-minded Dr. Pratt makes the most of his scenes, fumbling around and muttering to himself; he has some of the funniest moments in the film. As a doctor of colored reputation, Pratt lives in a seamy room surrounded by dozens of cats. In one scene he blots the ink on the bogus death certificate by rolling a kitten's bottom over the paper, having found the kitten in his desk drawer while he was looking for some blotting paper. Sellers does this with the nonchalance of a comic genius. Newman, Forbes's wife, appearing as Joseph's ward, is suitably appealing and rounds out the cast of the principals. The rich comic sense of these actors, coupled with Forbes's neat directorial touches, makes for an enjoyable romp.

This type of film, the black comedy, is very difficult to adapt for the screen with any degree of effectiveness, but Forbes expertly blends the more macabre elements of the source with the stunning visual comedy aspects of the treatment to come up with a perfect mixture; no subsequent film of this type has been as fruitful, either artistically or commercially. Different from *The Loved One* (1965) or, more to the point, *M*A*S*H* (1970), *The Wrong Box* is a black comedy which manages to be funny while not being offensive to anyone. For this reason it is arguably the best of the genre.

Ed Hulse

THE YEARLING

Released: 1946
Production: Sidney Franklin for Metro-Goldwyn-Mayer
Direction: Clarence Brown
Screenplay: Paul Osborn; based on the novel of the same name by Marjorie Kinnan Rawlings
Cinematography: Charles Rosher, Leonard Smith, and Arthur E. Arling (AA)
Editing: Harold F. Kress
Art direction: Cedric Gibbons and Paul Groesse (AA)
Interior decoration: Edwin B. Willis (AA)
Running time: 127 minutes

Principal characters:
Penny Baxter	Gregory Peck
Ma Baxter	Jane Wyman
Jody Baxter	Claude Jarman, Jr.
	(AA Special Award)
Buck Forrester	Chill Wills
Pa Forrester	Clem Bevans
Mr. Boyles	Henry Travers
Lem Forrester	Forrest Tucker

The Yearling is based on Marjorie Kinnan Rawlings' Pulitzer Prize-winning novel about a pioneer family who lived in Florida's wild scrub country toward the end of the nineteenth century. The film captures with warmth and restraint the struggle of the Baxter family to scrape together a meager living off the land. Gregory Peck and Jane Wyman play solid, decent people, Penny and Ma Baxter. The father is still hopeful that life can be good, but the mother is embittered over the loss of several children. Their one remaining son, Jody (Claude Jarman, Jr.), enjoys a tender relationship with his father, but in many ways must become a man before he is ready. The film follows Jody's difficult passage through childhood and chronicles the harsh fight against nature that families such as the Baxters endure every day of their lives. Directed by Clarence Brown, a veteran M-G-M director, *The Yearling* is a visually beautiful film. The semitropical country where the Baxters live is lush and green and, like everything about this film, seems natural.

The Yearling is in the same tradition as such motion pictures as John Ford's classic *The Grapes of Wrath* (1940) or Jean Renoir's *The Southerner* (1945), both of which also deal with poor farming people who toil endlessly, but continue working and hoping in the face of continual disasters. On a deeper level, it is about complicated relationships among parents and children. Because of Ma Baxter's inability to love either her husband or her child, Jody grows up emotionally starved. Except for his warm relationship with his father, he has no one to whom he can turn. Thus, when, halfway through the film, he adopts a yearling fawn, the deer is more than a pet to him—it is a friend and fills his days with a richness that previously was missing. As Jody, Jarman gives a performance of the first rank, especially considering the fact that he had never acted before. Brown found him in a schoolroom in rural Tennessee and felt that he was absolutely right for the part of Jody. What the boy lacks in professionalism he makes up for in naturalness and innate ability. Jarman is thin, rather gawky, and has a lilting Southern accent. His scenes reach a great emotional intensity: there is no harder task for a boy than that of murdering a pet he loves or facing starvation, and Jarman handles such tasks with great assuredness.

The Yearling is not merely made up of a series of emotional moments; it contains a great deal of vitality and adventure. There are many vivid sequences, such as the bear hunt, the dog swap, and Pa Baxter's snakebite, which are played with zest and with a great richness of graphic detail. Brown's direction is controlled and intelligent, and thus *The Yearling* always remains simple and believable, despite M-G-M's reputation for more lavish productions.

The story begins as young Jody is working in the corn fields, clearly restless. He leaves his hoe and falls asleep in a quiet glen, but is awakened by Ma Baxter's harsh call. He then runs breathlessly for home, meeting his father on the way. It is established in this scene that father and son understand each other and are bound together by a deep affection. The next morning Penny discovers that Slewfoot, a marauding bear of the brush, has killed the family's calf and shoat; Penny and Jody go after the bear, but it escapes as Penny's gun backfires. Later, the boy and his father go into town and meet their neighbors, the Forresters with whom they get into a fierce argument. When the two families leave, there is bad blood between them. When Ma's hogs are stolen, Penny thinks that the Forresters have trapped them, and on the way to get them back, accompanied by Jody, he is bitten by a rattlesnake. He kills a doe, using its heart and liver to draw the poison out, but leaves the doe's fawn alone in the woods. He struggles to get home and, although near death, survives. Jody must now take over his father's work, for Penny's recovery will be slow.

Jody remembers the fawn left alone in the woods and gets permission to take it home and to bring it up as a pet because Penny feels that its company will make Jody less lonely working in the fields. The boy names the fawn Flag, and together they have glorious times. Jody plants the corn and is delighted to see the first green shoots finally start to come up, but one morning he finds them chewed to the roots—Flag has gotten loose. Jody builds a fence around the corn and ties Flag up, but to no avail; the fawn simply jumps the fence. After several unsuccessful attempts to keep Flag out of the field, Ma Baxter finally insists that Flag must go. Penny wants to wait since he sees how much Flag means to Jody, but when Penny again injures himself working, Ma demands that Jody take the fawn back into the woods before they all starve. Tearfully, Jody walks Flag into the scrub, but the next morning the deer is back into the corn, and Ma cannot be controlled. She shoots at Flag, wounding the yearling. Jody brokenheartedly puts the deer out of its misery and runs away, embittered. When he returns home shortly after and relates his feelings to his father, Penny tells the boy that life is hard, but that he must fight against it. Jody is more serious now and has taken his first step toward manhood, and as Penny says to his wife, "He ain't a yearling no longer."

The Yearling was one of the most critically acclaimed films of 1946. It received several Oscar nominations, including one for Best Picture, with Wyman and Peck also nominated for their acting. The film won Academy Awards for Cedric Gibbons and Paul Groesse, for Art Direction, Edwin B. Willis for his interior decoration, and one for Charles Rosher for cinematography. Additionally, Jarman won a special Oscar as outstanding child actor, which is only occasionally given. The film is one of the finest studies of American rural life that Hollywood has ever produced. *The Yearling* was only Peck's fourth film, but it consolidated his position as an actor who was as versatile as he was handsome, equally adept at drama or comedy, at playing urban or rural heroes. Jarman had only a brief career as an actor. He was to play a troubled Southern boy one more time, however, again under the direction of Brown, in the equally acclaimed *Intruder in the Dust* (1949). Now in his late forties, Jarman is active in other areas of the arts and is the manager of the San Francisco Opera House.

Joan Cohen

YELLOW JACK

Released: 1938
Production: Jack Cummings for Metro-Goldwyn-Mayer
Direction: George B. Seitz
Screenplay: Edward Chodorov; based on the play of the same name by Sidney
   Howard and Paul de Kruif and the novel *Microbe Hunters* by Paul de Kruif
Cinematography: Lester White
Editing: Blanche Sewell
Running time: 83 minutes

Principal characters:
John O'Hara	Robert Montgomery
Frances Blake	Virginia Bruce
Major Reed	Lewis Stone
Charlie Spill	Andy Devine
Doctor Jesse Lazear	Henry Hull
Doctor Finlay	Charles Coburn
"Jellybeans"	Buddy Ebsen
Doctor James Carroll	Stanley Ridges
Gorgas	Henry O'Neill
Busch	Sam Levene
Brinkerhof	Alan Curtis
Breen	William Henry
Major General Leonard Wood	Jonathan Hale

It was a puzzle when a studio with the reputation of M-G-M purchased film rights to Sidney Howard and Paul de Kruif's play, *Yellow Jack*. It would have been much more fitting if Warner Bros. had bought it, for it is in the vein of their social film documents such as *The Story of Louis Pasteur* (1936) and *Dr. Ehrlich's Magic Bullet* (1940). It is exactly the kind of film one might expect Louis B. Mayer to despise, and how it ever got made under his aegis is something of a mystery. It remains, however, one of the few really important films M-G-M ever released, and, along with *Intruder in the Dust* (1949), it has a kind of social significance that is missing from most of M-G-M's products. The stories M-G-M filmed were, for the most part, frames for their stars, designed skillfully to show off that star at his or her best. *Yellow Jack* was never conceived of as a star vehicle; it was an absorbing play with at least twelve good roles for men and a single part for an actress.

Yellow Jack is the suspenseful story of how, even when the Spanish-American War was over, the United States Army remained in Cuba, where Major Walter Reed (Lewis Stone) was engaged in a desperate campaign against yellow fever, which had killed more of his men, the Cuban patriots, and the Spanish enemy than all the bullets that had been fired. Reed is working against time, because at any moment he and his men may be pulled out of the island, and the secret experiments being made in tracking down the source of yellow fever (or yellow jack, as it was commonly called) may go by the board.

Dr. Lazear (Henry Hull), Dr. Finlay (Charles Coburn), and Dr. James Carroll (Stanley Ridges) are, like Reed, confident that the disease is carried by the female yellow-fever mosquito and thence transmitted to human beings. There are peculiarities, however, involved in the transmission. The likeliest assumption involves the time factor—how soon after the mosquito becomes a menace does its inoculation of a victim become deadly? All experiments must be carried on secretly, because the medical corps is expressly forbidden to use any of the enlisted men as guinea pigs, nor are any of these men interested in enrolling for what may well be certain death. A soldier is trained to accept death from a bullet, but he is not interested in becoming a martyr by accepting a bite from a deadly insect. No one has considered, however, that the doctors themselves might lend their bodies to such experimentation, yet, when they are fighting for time, that is exactly what they do. Major Reed obtains the yellow-fever mosquito from Dr. Finlay, and he and three other doctors deliberately infect themselves. Almost immediately, Dr. Reed is recalled to the mainland, and the other doctors bungle their attempts at infection because they themselves cannot be isolated, so the experiment becomes a failure.

Meanwhile, Major Reed has confessed their predicament to Major General Leonard Wood (Jonathan Hale), and soon the soldiers stationed in Cuba learn that if they agree to enlist as guinea pigs in this experimental venture, they will be paid three hundred dollars apiece. Even with this incentive, however, there are no takers. Eventually, however, two privates, John O'Hara (Robert Montgomery) and Brinkerhof (Alan Curtis), do volunteer; each is given the dreaded bite and then padlocked in to wait four days within very sterile quarters for the fever signs to show. Shortly thereafter, two more of the company, Private Busch (Sam Levene) and a private known as "Jelly-beans" (Buddy Ebsen), also volunteer, although, unlike O'Hara and Brink-erhof, they do not disdain three-hundred-dollar payment. They are not innoculated with the mosquito virus, but are locked into filthy quarters, where they sleep upon blankets that are unclean, living in dirt, stench, and foul air which is at least free from mosquito infestation.

Brinkerhof is the first to come down with a classic case of yellow fever, and he is immediately hospitalized. Shortly thereafter, Busch and "Jellybeans" emerge from their filth, dirtier and more foul-smelling than ever; but since the mosquito has not gotten through to them, they do not have yellow jack, and are simply sent off to be cleansed. O'Hara alone remains a disappoint-ment. He has not come down with yellow fever, and is either immune (as a few men are) or is slower than usual in developing signs of the fever. For a brief time the medical corps is disheartened; then O'Hara finally comes down with the disease.

The experiment can now be rated a complete success, and it is the beginning of the end of the yellow fever scourge over all the world. The medical men can go after the disease now that it has been proven that the female mosquito carries the infection and can transmit it for only a short time. What has happened in Cuba can lead to a principle of vaccination against the disease. The Panama Canal can become a fact now that men can live and work free from yellow fever.

M-G-M made only two films during 1938 that can be called prestige productions: *Yellow Jack* and *The Citadel*. Both have medical backgrounds, but only the latter went on to become both prestigious and moneymaking. *Yellow Jack*, for all its merits and high-spirited suspenseful drama relieved by natural comedy moments, was not big at the box office. This must have pleased Mayer, who not only disliked this kind of story, but also had no use for contract star Montgomery, who had already told Mayer that if he were a younger man, Montgomery would give him a good thrashing. Mayer could exult that Montgomery's heading the cast had led to the picture's downfall at the box office.

Yellow Jack was not the kind of picture to draw a star's interest, and that Montgomery wanted to play the role of Johnny O'Hara, one of the four guinea pigs who bring on the control of the insidious yellow fever, speaks highly for him. He plays an American soldier with a becoming Irish brogue and is more ingratiating than he had been in anything since *Night Must Fall* (1937), another Montgomery film that had outraged Mayer. *Night Must Fall* had been a smash hit, however, and had brought Montgomery an Academy Award nomination for Best Actor. Surprisingly, there were no nominations in any category for *Yellow Jack*, although the picture was well liked by both public and critics. The trade magazine *Motion Picture Herald* noted of *Yellow Jack* that at its New York trade showing "even professionally hardened picture reviewers were swept away with the dramatic punch and expert screen workmanship of the production."

As a play on Broadway in 1934, *Yellow Jack* had been a distinguished failure, directed by Guthrie McClintic, with James Stewart playing O'Hara and a star-studded cast of Manhattan favorites very much present. Every actor in the M-G-M film production likewise turns in a sterling performance. The added romance which develops between O'Hara and the pretty blonde nurse, Miss Blake (Virginia Bruce), enhances rather than detracts from the film's appeal. Levene as Busch, another guinea pig soldier, is the only member of the original Broadway cast who repeats his role in the film.

Montgomery made an even fifty pictures at M-G-M from 1929 to 1948, and *Yellow Jack* is listed high among them, even though it is not really a starring vehicle and he had become a well-established star by 1931. Although Montgomery gets first billing, it is more important to note that he fits his part perfectly, as does every other actor in the cast. Montgomery was versatile and could adjust his personality to fit any character. *Yellow Jack* is a class motion picture, inspirational in spite of its tragedies, and it should be more frequently revived. It is actually a historical play, a worthy dramatization of a desperate hour in American history, a time for noble heroism when soldiers were not afraid to die painfully away from the battlefield so that all the world might benefit from their sacrifice.

DeWitt Bodeen

YELLOW SUBMARINE

Released: 1968
Production: King Features-Subafilms; released by United Artists
Direction: George Dunning
Screenplay: Lee Minoff, Al Brodax, Jack Mendelsohn, and Erich Segal; based on an original story by Lee Minoff, and on the song "Yellow Submarine" by John Lennon and Paul McCartney
Cinematography: John Williams
Editing: Brian J. Bishop
Character designer: Heinz Edelmann
Animation direction: Jack Stokes and Bob Balser
Special effects: Charles Jenkins
Running time: 85 minutes

Voices of principal characters:

John	John Clive
Paul	Geoffrey Hughes
George	Peter Batten
Ringo/Chief Blue Meanie	Paul Angelus
Lord Mayor/Nowhere Man	Dick Emery
Fred	Lance Percival

When *Yellow Submarine* appeared in 1968, nearly everyone had heard of the "stars" of this animated film, the Beatles, but almost no one had heard of its director, George Dunning. Nevertheless it was the skill, vision, and talent of Dunning and the many other artists who contributed to the film that made *Yellow Submarine* the imaginative masterpiece it is. The Beatles' not inconsiderable contribution was eight previously written songs and three new ones, but the visual interpretation of each song and the overall framework came from a large creative group. Besides Dunning there are credits to four writers, three designers, and two animation directors, as well as a cinematographer, an editor, and a special effects person.

Dunning, who learned his art from the noted animator Norman McLaren at the National Film Board in Canada, had his own studio which worked mainly on commercials and such sponsored films as one on safety for coal miners. For *Yellow Submarine*, which originally was intended to be a children's film, he collected artists he knew either personally or by reputation into what he called "a gathering of talents, an explosion." An early decision was made that the Beatles and other human characters would be drawn in a stylized manner rather than realistically. The German graphic designer Heinz Edelmann was chiefly responsible for the design of the characters. It was also decided that the actors who speak the Beatles' lines would use a moderate version of the singers' Liverpool accents. In addition, artists working on the film were encouraged to experiment if they saw fit. In fact, Dunning thought of *Yellow Submarine* as an experimental film.

It is, perhaps, surprising that such a good film should emerge from such a large number of creators, but *Yellow Submarine* is both unified and enjoyable. There are two keys to this successful combination of talents: one is the episodic, almost picaresque, structure of the overall plot into which the separate parts may fit, and the other is the essential motif of the film—transformation.

Too many animated films do not take advantage of the form. Animation offers the filmmakers many resources not available in the live action film. It is, therefore, unfortunate that so many animated films, especially the feature-length ones, do little more with the form than have anthropomorphic animals as characters. *Yellow Submarine*, on the other hand, uses animation fully, particularly in two ways: in its depiction of such strange creatures as the Snapping Turks, who have sharklike mouths in their mid-sections, and the Dreadful Flying Glove, which has eyes and a mouth and flies about by itself; and in its transformations. An animated drawing can change from one shape into another or even disappear or become something entirely different. This happens continually in *Yellow Submarine*. For example, when confronted with one huge monster, the submarine first opens up and offers the monster a cigar almost as large as the craft itself, then it becomes a lighter and lights the cigar. The monster then puffs on the cigar two or three times, each time exhaling multihued, fancifully patterned smoke. When the submarine is safely out of the way, the cigar explodes.

The plot is just definite enough to provide a structure and some narrative momentum for the actions, events, and effects which take place but is never so limiting that it prevents a digression or flight of fancy. Pepperland is a paradise eighty thousand leagues beneath the sea where music, laughter, and love prevail. One day it is attacked by the Blue Meanies, who hate love and music, and Fred is sent in the yellow submarine for help. He goes to Liverpool where he persuades the Beatles to accompany him back to save Pepperland. After an eventful trip through such realms as the sea of time, the sea of green, and the sea of holes, during which they pick up Jeremy Hilary Boob, an intellectual nowhere man who occasionally proves quite helpful, they not only rout the Blue Meanies but also make them music-loving and nonviolent.

The imagination of the artists who created *Yellow Submarine* is everywhere evident. For example, the attack on Pepperland by the Blue Meanies begins with the firing of jagged blue projectiles and continues with the efforts of the Apple Bonkers, tall creatures that drop large green apples on their antagonists, paralyzing them and draining all color from them. The ultimate weapon, of course, is the Flying Glove, which flies through the air with its index finger pointed toward its target and then becomes a smashing fist when it reaches that target. Much later, in the "Lucy in the Sky with Diamonds" sequence, there is a contrasting delicacy of mood as we see two brightly colored dancers briefly suggesting Fred Astaire and Ginger Rogers dancing to "Cheek to Cheek" in *Top Hat* (1935). At this moment there is also a display of a technique that Dunning liked—the colors briefly break away from the confines of the outline of the figures and become almost impressionistic splashes of paint.

The treatment of the sequences which accompany the Beatle songs is fresh and creative. The "Eleanor Rigby" segment, for example, has little function in the plot except to set the scene in Liverpool. It also does not "illustrate" the song in the sense of showing images of specifics mentioned in the lyrics. Instead, it consists of images which are splendidly evocative of the themes of the song—repetition, emptiness, and loneliness. There is also very little color in this presentation of such pictures as a gravestone, empty streets, a single falling leaf, and a building in which each of the ten windows contains the same image of a cat being repeatedly and mechanically stroked by an anonymous hand.

Yellow Submarine is not, however, all visual and musical. There are many linguistic motifs, including a good number of puns, allusions to Beatle songs, and the use of words as props and scenery. At the beginning of the Blue Meanie attack, for example, the word *know* is standing in the middle of a field in Pepperland. The always negative Meanies destroy the first and last letters, leaving only the word *no*. *Yellow Submarine* is, then, a triumph of animation and a splendid union of music and pictures.

Judith A. Williams

YOLANDA AND THE THIEF

Released: 1945
Production: Arthur Freed for Metro-Goldwyn-Mayer
Direction: Vincente Minnelli
Screenplay: Irving Brecher; based on the story of the same name by Ludwig Bemelmans and Jacques Thery
Cinematography: Charles Rosher
Editing: George White
Choreography: Eugene Loring
Song: Harry Warren and Arthur Freed
Running time: 108 minutes

Principal characters:
Johnny Parkson Riggs .... Fred Astaire
Yolanda Aquaviva .... Lucille Bremer
Victor Budlow Trout .... Frank Morgan
Amarilla Aquaviva .... Mildred Natwick

It is difficult to classify unhesitatingly *Yolanda and the Thief* as a true masterpiece of the cinema. It is an esoteric, even experimental, film which was produced in the "musical factory" at Metro-Goldwyn-Mayer in the mid-1940's. Described as a musical fantasy film, *Yolanda and the Thief* owes more to ballet and the legitimate theater than it does to the cinema. The most significant aspect of this film is its use of dance to express emotions and further the narrative, something which it does better than many great, famous musicals.

The plot is deceptively simple. Fleeing from local authorities, Johnny Riggs (Fred Astaire) and Victor Trout (Frank Morgan), a pair of slick con men, find themselves in the fictitious South American country of Patria. It is a beautiful, almost mythical environment. Ignoring the abundant beauty which surrounds them, the two bunco artists begin looking for an unsuspecting sucker ripe for swindling. They do not have to wait very long. Johnny meets a lovely heiress, Yolanda Aquaviva (Lucille Bremer), who becomes the target for an elaborate confidence game. It seems that Yolanda is confused. She is unable to manage her affairs, and her scatterbrained aunt who lives with her provides little tangible assistance. In steps Johnny. His plan is to convince Yolanda that he is her Guardian Angel. Being informed by Victor of the penalties for impersonating a Guardian Angel, Johnny goes ahead with his plan to cheat this vision of trusting innocence.

The film then becomes a continual struggle between Johnny's lust for other people's money and his growing love for Yolanda. He is unable to express this complex dilemma to Victor. Rather, he is forced to work out his problems in true Hollywood-Freudian fashion through his dreams. Eventually Johnny confesses to Yolanda that he is not her Guardian Angel and has in fact been trying to swindle her out of a great deal of her family fortune. He also explains that he is deeply in love with her. After a brief period of shock and separation, Yolanda and her "thief" pick up their romance where they left off. Victor is disappointed at the loss of all the money, but understands. Yolanda's aunt Amarilla (Mildred Natwick), suspicious from the start, finds Johnny acceptable as a new member of the family. It seems certain that their happiness is assured.

Yolanda and the Thief is delightful enough fluff during the scenes in which the fairy-tale plot is presented. As soon as the music swells, however, and Astaire begins to dance, the film becomes pure magic. Heralded by dance critics at the time as one of the best treatments of dance on film, *Yolanda and the Thief* boasts two impressive dance numbers. The first, called "the dream ballet," is an incredible combination of interpretive dancing and surreal images. Director Vincente Minnelli provides the rich colors and unusual setting, Eugene Loring offers the smooth choreography, and Astaire supplies the powerful and hypnotic focus to the dance. Essentially this dance is a journey. Continually moving forward, Astaire is engulfed in bold colors and exotic situations. He eventually meets the girl of his dreams dressed in a gown of coins. His dance of love ends in marriage and eventual entrapment. It is a device which serves not only as a suggestion of events yet to happen in the film, but also allows for many of the more subtle emotions present in the characters of Johnny and Yolanda to be expressed on the screen.

The other extended dance number is the more traditional "Coffee Time." Using a fiesta to provide the background for courtship, this dance ritualizes Johnny's feelings toward Yolanda. It is lively, fresh, and completely abandoned. The flavor of the South American locale, the "Latin" rhythms, and the broad dancing of Astaire combine in "Coffee Time" to create a totally satisfying dance. It is both a complete opposite and clever complement to the earlier sixteen-minute "dream ballet."

During the 1940's Astaire, under the direction of Minnelli, created some of the finest moments of dance on the screen. His "Limehouse Blues" number in *Ziegfeld Follies* (1944), which was filmed earlier yet released after *Yolanda and the Thief*, was the complete embodiment of style and movement strived for in *Yolanda and the Thief*; that number was also danced with Bremer. Another sequence from *Ziegfeld Follies* entitled "This Heart of Mine" has been mentioned as a possible inspiration for *Yolanda and the Thief*. In any case, this lavish musical remains a milestone in the history of dance.

The image brought most immediately to mind by the film is an oyster, with the dance numbers shining pearls hidden in the pulpy flesh. The film confirms again Astaire's position as a premier interpreter of screen dance. It also gave Minnelli the ability to construct films which could integrate music, plot, and dance. His classic musicals, *Meet Me in St. Louis* (1944), *The Pirate* (1948),

An American in Paris (1951), and *The Band Wagon* (1953), serve to illustrate that point. *Yolanda and the Thief* has remained an obscure film; it is rarely mentioned in discussing the great Hollywood musicals. Perhaps Minnelli best described his film when he called it "a fantasy film that just didn't perfectly come off."

Carl Macek

YOU CAN'T TAKE IT WITH YOU

Released: 1938
Production: Frank Capra for Columbia (AA)
Direction: Frank Capra (AA)
Screenplay: Robert Riskin; based on the play of the same name by George
 S. Kaufman and Moss Hart
Cinematography: Joseph Walker
Editing: Gene Havlick
Running time: 120 minutes

Principal characters:
Alice Sycamore .... Jean Arthur
Grandpa Martin Vanderhof .... Lionel Barrymore
Tony Kirby .... James Stewart
Anthony P. Kirby .... Edward Arnold
Penny Sycamore .... Spring Byington
Essie Sycamore .... Ann Miller

By 1937, Frank Capra had reached a zenith. The first Hollywood director to have his name above the title on a film's credits was the reigning genius of Columbia, and he was almost singlehandedly able to keep the studio financially sound. His cheery film style and forthright morality had, in recent years, gained him Oscars for Best Direction for *It Happened One Night* (1934) and *Mr. Deeds Goes to Town* (1936). It had also seen him through a little "personal" film that had developed some major headaches: *Lost Horizon* (1937). Now he was looking for another property. While theater-hopping in New York one night, he found it, a play "whose witchery was so entrancing wild horses couldn't have dragged me away before the final curtain," according to the director.

The play was *You Can't Take It with You* by George S. Kaufman and Moss Hart. At first sight, its wacky characters, homey atmosphere, and comic peaks must have seemed ideal for Capra. With a contagious exuberance it centered upon the Sycamore family, a definitely offbeat group who insist on doing whatever they like in life with a dedication matched only by their singular lack of talent. Mom writes epic tragedies because somebody delivered a typewriter to the front door by mistake; Pop makes fireworks in the basement; and Sis practices ballet in the living room while her husband accompanies her on the xylophone. There is also an ex-milkman who helps with the fireworks; that staple of 1930's comedies, the wise-cracking maid; a handyman who would not do anything to jeopardize his goal in life, to stay on relief; and one safe, sane, and usually bewildered daughter. The plot involved that daughter's engagement to a nice young man afflicted with wealthy parents, but nobody paid much attention to the plot. Depression audiences were much more amused by such scenes as the grandfather-patriarch explaining to an Internal Revenue Service man why he would not even consider paying income tax, and the wealthy parents arriving for dinner on a night when everyone's eccentricities are in full force.

For the man who had given America new lessons in how to hitch a ride in *It Happened One Night* and how to turn a park trashbasket into a musical instrument in *Mr. Deeds Goes to Town*, the play *You Can't Take It with You* seemed delightful. Capra also saw more in the work than that, however; he was later to write in his autobiography, *The Name Before the Title*, that the play offered "a golden opportunity to dramatize Love Thy Neighbour in living drama. What the world's churches were preaching to apathetic congregations, my universal language of film might say more entertainingly to movie audiences." The problem was that the play was not so much about loving your neighbor as it was about the 1930's equivalent of "doing your own thing." Capra and his favorite screenwriter, Robert Riskin, set about fixing that, throwing out several of the play's minor characters as well as most of the third act and creating an entire new plot structure. Now the juvenile's wealthy father became a millionaire industrialist needing the Sycamore family property to clinch a huge land deal. The conflict between the lovers, instead of being about snobbish conventionality versus spirited self-expression, became one of capitalism versus the little guy, or as Capra put it, "the viability of a lamb when confronted by a lion." It was the director's favorite theme, and it was one that he had found it necessary to practice many times when confronting the studio bosses.

With the added weight of all of this social consciousness, Capra realized that he had to cast the film very carefully. A staunch believer in the theory that the cast is more important than directorial technique, Capra felt that filmmakers should "forget techniques, forget zoom lenses and subliminal cutting. Remember only that you are telling your story not with gimmicks but with actors." Consequently, Capra cast for strength and very much by type. As the folksy patriarch of the Sycamore clan, Grandpa Martin Vanderhof, Capra chose Lionel Barrymore, who was well on his way to becoming a curmudgeonly senior statesman in films. As the other patriarch, Anthony P. Kirby, he selected Edward Arnold, an actor whose deep voice, large girth, and extensive repertoire of scene-stealing tricks made him the epitome of all overextended tycoons. In the romantic leads, parts that had been largely ignored on stage, Capra cast his favorite actress, Jean Arthur, as Alice Sycamore, and a gangly young juvenile from M-G-M whose career was finally on the rise, James Stewart, as Tony Kirby. For Capra, Arthur was the epitome of the 1930's heroine. She was independent, level-headed, and smart but also warm and caring with a no-nonsense charm that was particularly contagious. Stewart's stubborn good sense and rock-ribbed folksiness were to make him the epitome of a Capra hero and to earn him the lead in two other Capra films, *Mr. Smith Goes to Washington* (1939) and *It's a Wonderful Life* (1947).

The resulting film was another Capra triumph. He won another Oscar for directing it, and it won the Oscar as Best Picture of 1938 and did extremely well at the box office. Even today, it is not hard to see why the film was so popular. It is an amalgam of the screwball comedies of earlier years and of the homey "just-folks" type of filmmaking that had propelled M-G-M's Andy Hardy series into the public consciousness at about the same time. It has charm, a sunny wit, and loads of good humor. It also receives from Capra and Riskin some touch-ups and additions that are every bit as good as anything Kaufman and Hart had originally contributed.

One sequence in particular is, in terms of ingenuity and style, one of the best that Capra and Riskin ever devised. In an attempt to get some time alone with Alice, Tony has retreated to Central Park with her, but his ploy is in vain. It is still the Depression, and some industrious kids are roaming around offering to teach a dance called the Big Apple. This being a Capra film, they cannot be gainsayed, and besides they have a nicely wheezy accordion and a sign that says "25¢ a dance" on one side and "Nuts" on the other. Tony fumbles his way through a lesson, looking somewhat like a stork in a rice paddy, dipping and swaying whenever he least expects it. Alice watches with great amusement, her voice breaking into peals of laughter that would inspire a bellringer. Eventually the two give up trying to escape company and adjourn to the fancy restaurant toward which they had been heading.

Seated at a table and murmuring the usual sweet nothings to each other, the pair get a bit carried away. Tony murmurs that every time he thinks how lucky he is, he could just scream. Then, ever the practical businessman, he starts to chart the progress of that scream as it rises from his toes, curls around his pelvis, and so on. At just about the time it has reached his Adam's apple, the bedazzled Alice lets out a shriek of her own. Tony is nothing if not equal to the occasion. "A mouse!" he cries out, pointing down with a gesture worthy of the Moscow Art Theatre. The result, however, is pure Olson and Johnson. Ladies faint into their *décolletage*, waiters writhe, and pandemonium soon reigns. In the midst of it all, Tony and Alice make a very dignified exit unmindful of the fact that on her back is the sign that says "Nuts."

It should be added that in the midst of all this tomfoolery there occurs one of the better little speeches in the film (it is not in the play). For one brief moment Stewart is allowed to grow wistful and contemplative:

> In school another fellow and I had an idea to utilize the energy in grass. Every blade of grass has a kinetic force that's never been used for anything. We used to work on it every spare moment—all night sometimes—got so excited we forgot to sleep. Then we left school. He's selling automobiles and I'm in some mysterious thing called 'Banking.' I saw him last week—got all excited again—wanted to talk of nothing else.

It has been argued that, by today's standards, speeches such as this one and indeed all of the rest of Capra's films have dated badly. Capra's corn, according to this school of thought, is so idealistic, moralistic, and patronizing that it is hardly palatable to the sophisticate of the 1970's and 1980's. This may be so, although Norman Lear's situation comedies on television have a habit of pointing up moral issues in a very similar way. Capra believed deeply in presenting messages with his films. His almost too-innocent idealism and his pure pleasure in the loving foibles of man is seen to its best advantage in *You Can't Take It with You*. The film predates the darker more complex humor of *Meet John Doe* (1941) and the ironic *It's a Wonderful Life* but also avoids the occasional heavy-handedness of *Mr. Deeds Goes to Town* and *Mr. Smith Goes to Washington*. Like Shakespeare's *A Midsummer Night's Dream* and Mozart's *The Marriage of Figaro*, it represents an artist at his most lyrical ease and most luminous joy.

Lewis Archibald

YOUNG CASSIDY

Released: 1965
Production: Robert D. Graff and Robert Emmett Ginna for Metro-Goldwyn-
  Mayer
Direction: Jack Cardiff and John Ford
Screenplay: John Whiting; based on the book *Mirror in My House* by Sean
  O'Casey
Cinematography: Edward Scaife
Editing: Anne V. Coates
Running time: 108 minutes

Principal characters:

John Cassidy	Rod Taylor
Mrs. Cassidy	Flora Robson
Ella	Sian Phillips
W. B. Yeats	Michael Redgrave
Lady Gregory	Dame Edith Evans
Daisy Battles	Julie Christie
Nora	Maggie Smith
Archie	Jack MacGowran
Tom	T. P. McKenna

Sean O'Casey, one of Ireland's most reknowned writers, was a man of passion and commitment to social justice. He was born in the slums of Dublin in 1884 and had little schooling; he toiled as a laborer and became involved in the Irish National and union movements. His plays *The Shadow of a Gunman*, *Juno and the Paycock*, and *The Plough and the Stars* have become staples of the Abbey Theatre in Dublin. He wrote short stories, poems, essays, and six volumes of autobiography (published between 1939 and 1954) in addition to his plays. His early years were re-created by directors John Ford and Jack Cardiff in an earnest but ultimately unsuccessful film, *Young Cassidy* (1965).

Although the title character is named John Cassidy, the film is a biographical drama about the turbulent life of a young Sean O'Casey; its source is his autobiography, published under the title of *Mirror in My House* in 1956, and the film was developed directly from a 1954 *Life* magazine essay, "The World of Sean O'Casey." The film spans a dozen years in O'Casey's life. It opens in 1911, when the Irish were aggressively protesting British rule. "Young" John Cassidy (Rod Taylor), a day laborer, has a loving mother (Flora Robson) and a married and out-of-work sister (Sian Phillips) with two children to support. He is becoming involved with unions and politics; he is a member of the Irish Transport and General Workers Union and the Irish Citizens Army, and is in training for an uprising against the British. He has also written pamphlets, which he distributes in the evening.

When his words incite a riot, Cassidy realizes that he can accomplish more with his writing than with his fists. He has a brief affair with Daisy Battles (Julie Christie), a music-hall dancer/prostitute, and a longer involvement with Nora (Maggie Smith), a shy clerk in a bookstore who encourages his writing. His play, *The Shadow of a Gunman*, is accepted by the Abbey Theatre. Its production is successful, and he is hailed as a promising young dramatist. He then becomes the protégé of the warmhearted Lady Gregory (Dame Edith Evans) and the haughty Willim Butler Yeats (Michael Redgrave). When a subsequent play, *The Plough and the Stars*, causes a riot because of its subject matter (religion, sex, and the Easter Rising of 1916), Cassidy loses many of his supporters. Eventually, he departs for England—and from Nora—to seek his fortune by himself.

Young Cassidy, filmed on location in and around Dublin, is an episodic film. John Whiting's script attempts to cover too many years and events, and the result lacks cohesion. Certain events are without historical perspective, such as a bitter Dublin transport workers strike, Cassidy/O'Casey's withdrawal from the Citizens Army, and the entire Sinn Fein revolution. Others are glossed over and obscured: for example, the strike is reduced to one day of spirited activity. Still others are simply not factual in relationship to O'Casey's life: Cassidy is depicted in the film as an active participant in the Easter Rising, while in reality, O'Casey had quarreled with the leaders of the Citizens Army and took no part. This decision may very well have saved his life.

Individual sequences are quite moving, however, particularly those which detail Cassidy's relationships with Daisy and Nora, the Citizens Army in the streets, and Yeats chastizing the Abbey Theatre audience's reception of *The Plough and the Stars*. The beauty and spirit of Ireland are nicely captured in Edward Scaife's color cinematography. *Young Cassidy* is certainly not a failure, but neither is it a success. It is mostly uneven, and is not the definitive work either on Irish history or Sean O'Casey.

John Cassidy is easily the best role of Taylor's career. The Australia-born actor offers a solid performance; he is as angry and courageous in his "activist" scenes as he is tender in those with Smith. Taylor is supported by a cast of mostly British actors. Robson, Evans, and, particularly, Redgrave are superb, as usual. Christie is exquisitely seductive in one of her early roles as the sensuous Daisy Battles; Smith is delightfully sensitive and supportive as the shy Nora. Both actresses are well cast. Their roles are among the first of their respective film careers. Both have since won Oscars (Christie for *Darling*, 1965; Smith for *The Prime of Miss Jean Brodie*, 1969, and *California Suite*, 1978), and have become stars.

Ford was the original director of *Young Cassidy*. In 1936, he had filmed *The Plough and the Stars*, but the result was theatrical and boring, a rare Ford misfire. The director's other "Irish" films—*The Informer* (1935), *The Quiet*

Man (1952), and *The Rising of the Moon* (1957)—were far more successful. In an earlier day, he might have cast John Wayne as John Cassidy and Maureen O'Hara as Nora, and surrounded them with his "stock" company of Irish players, Victor McLaglen, Ward Bond, Barry Fitzgerald, and Arthur Shields. Unfortunately, Ford became ill shortly after the start of production and was replaced by Jack Cardiff. Cardiff is an outstanding cinematographer who received an Academy Award for his color cinematography in *Black Narcissus* (1947), and nominations for *War and Peace* (1956) and *Fanny* (1961). He also shot *Four Feathers* (1939), *Caesar and Cleopatra* (1945), and *The Red Shoes* (1948). Easily his best film as director is *Sons and Lovers* (1960), based on the D. H. Lawrence novel, for which he received another Oscar nomination. Cardiff was instructed by the producers to follow Ford's design for the film, although Ford had directed only a few scenes, several encounters between Taylor and Christie.

Only Cardiff received directorial credit, but *Young Cassidy* was still billed as "A John Ford Film," his penultimate film before his death in 1973. Also, the script was approved by O'Casey shortly before he died in 1964. *Young Cassidy* received mixed reviews. The film cannot be found on *Variety*'s list of the high-rental films of 1965, having earned less than one million dollars at the box office. It has become a frequent staple of television late-night viewing, however, and remains entertaining, in great part because of the fine performances of some major acting talents in small roles.

Rob Edelman

THE YOUNG LIONS

Released: 1958
Production: Al Lichtman for Twentieth Century-Fox
Direction: Edward Dmytryk
Screenplay: Edward Anhalt; based on the novel of the same name by Irwin Shaw
Cinematography: Joe MacDonald
Editing: Dorothy Spencer
Running time: 170 minutes

Principal characters:

Christian	Marlon Brando
Noah	Montgomery Clift
Michael Whiteacre	Dean Martin
Hope Plowman	Hope Lange
Margaret Freemantle	Barbara Rush
Gretchen Hardenberg	May Britt
Captain Hardenberg	Maximilian Schell
Françoise	Liliane Montevecchi
Plowman	Vaughn Taylor
Captain Colclough	Herbert Rudley
Simone	Dora Doll
Sergeant Brandt	Parley Baer

The Young Lions is the filmed version of Irwin Shaw's best-selling novel about war, its horrors, and its effects on society as seen through the separate but interwoven stories of three soldiers. Edward Dmytryk's direction keeps the film moving from one major character to another, back and forth continuously until the three stories converge at the end of the film. The emphasis is not on combat or action sequences but on the inner beliefs and reactions of the characters.

The film opens at an Alpine ski resort in 1938. Christian Diestl (Marlon Brando) is a young German ski instructor there who supports Hitler because he feels the Führer will bring about a better life for the German people. Christian discusses his feelings at a New Year's Eve party with a young American tourist, Margaret Freemantle (Barbara Rush). He tells her that even though he is behind Hitler, he is not a Nazi. Newsreels then show the coming of the war and the surrender of France. Christian, now a German soldier, travels the road to Paris to meet his new officer, the staunch Nazi Captain Hardenberg (Maximilian Schell).

The American characters, Noah Ackerman (Montgomery Clift) and Michael Whiteacre (Dean Martin), are first seen at a New York draft center where both are being inducted. Michael, a suave, engaging Broadway entertainer and producer, tries to appeal his draft status without much success. He meets the young Jew Noah, an introverted store clerk, and invites him to a party that night. At the party, Noah meets Michael's girl, the lovely socialite Margaret (one of the film's ironies). He is also introduced to a sweet young girl named Hope (Hope Lange), whom he escorts home. After initial misunderstandings, the two are drawn together, and their romance progresses to the point that Hope introduces Noah to her staunch Vermonter father (Vaughn Taylor). Noah's earnest nature and obvious love for Hope overcome her father's initial distrust, and he consents to their marriage.

The episodic style leads back to Paris where Christian's friend Sergeant Brandt (Parley Baer) introduces him to a young French girl, Françoise (Liliane Montevecchi), who tauntingly asks, "How many Frenchmen have you killed?" Although Christian is at first angered by the girl, later he is somewhat mollified by her apology, and they become friends. Françoise recognizes his humane side. At this point in the war, he is still idealistic about the Nazi regime, but he soon begins to have nagging doubts which are initially small ones, but which become stronger as the war continues. One of his duties is to arrest a French youth, drag him from his mother's house over her cries of anguish, and turn him over to the Gestapo for "questioning." When Christian shares his concern over army methods with his superior, Hardenberg tells Christian that the Germany Army is invincible because it obeys orders without question, and suggests that Christian will feel better after his upcoming leave in Berlin. Hardenberg requests that on his leave, Christian deliver a gift of French lace to his wife Gretchen (May Britt), whom Christian finds to be beautiful, but not faithful to her husband. Christian soon becomes her lover, but is just one of many officers with whom she has had an affair. This loveless relationship further disillusions him.

Back in New York, Noah and Michael prepare to leave for basic training. Michael is still fighting his responsibility, saying he is too important on Broadway to be gone, but secretly admitting to himself his basic cowardice. Margaret urges him to act like a man so she can be proud of him. Noah, on the other hand, is ready and willing to fight even though this means leaving behind his new wife, Hope.

During basic training, the theme of the senseless cruelty of anti-Semitism and one Jew's means of dealing with it is portrayed as Noah is taunted by the men and officers of his company. His book, James Joyce's *Ulysses*, is confiscated by Captain Colclough (Herbert Rudley), he is made the barracks scapegoat, and his hidden cache of money is stolen. When Noah demands satisfaction, the four biggest and roughest soldiers respond. Michael acts as Noah's second at the brawls in which Noah is badly beaten, but after the first two fights, Michael asks the Captain to stop the uneven brutality. He tells Michael that if he keeps quiet he will earn a transfer from this combat unit to the Special Services. The transfer papers are sent through even though Michael is still upset by the cruelty. Noah continues the fights and slowly earns the respect of the men because he fights clean and hard and never gives up, even against the most brutal opponent. He actually wins the last fight and then deserts camp.

Soon after his desertion, his conscience returns and he gives himself up. While he is in prison, a pregnant Hope comes to visit him, and with her encouragement Noah decides to return to his company. The prejudiced captain, who cannot change his ways, vows to make him or break him. Michael, however, has brought the situation to the attention of a higher authority, and soon the Captain is facing a court martial. At last, Noah is accepted by the men in his company, and his book and money are returned to him.

During this time the German army is attacking the British in North Africa. After the successful ambush of a British patrol, Captain Hardenberg gives an order to shoot all enemy wounded. When a wounded British soldier stumbles across Christian's path, however, he is unable to shoot, even though he feels the cold gaze of Hardenberg on him. A furious Hardenberg then pulls out his own pistol and shoots the wounded soldier.

Later, in order to escape besieging Allied troops, Christian and Hardenberg take off across the desert on a motorcycle. When a disillusioned Christian moans that he is sick of the great German army and sick of doing his duty, he and Hardenberg argue and the motorcycle runs over a land mine. Christian is spared serious injury, but Hardenberg suffers severe facial injuries. When Christian visits Hardenberg in a German hospital, he is told that Gretchen still loves her husband and wants him home from the hospital as soon as he is discharged. Christian is amazed at the apparent good spirits of the dauntless Hardenberg, whose obvious gangrene sickens him. The Captain asks Christian to visit Gretchen and reassure her that he is all right, and also offhandedly asks him for a bayonet so that he can put a fellow patient out of his misery. Hardenberg tells Christian that the other patient moans in the night and begs to be delivered.

When Christian returns to Berlin, he is further disheartened by the desolate bomb ruins. At Gretchen's apartment, he finds out the truth about her reaction to her husband's wounds. Gretchen tells Christian that she wrote her husband telling him their life together was over and advising him to enter a veteran's hospital. Shocked, Christian asks if the Captain is now at a veteran's hospital, and she replies that the Captain killed himself in the army hospital with a bayonet. Totally revolted by the heartless Gretchen and his own part in Hardenberg's death, Christian shoves her aside and leaves.

At a German inn, Christian runs into his old friend Sergeant Brandt, and they decide to drive back to Paris together. In Paris, Christian is reunited with Françoise and Brandt with his love, Simone (Dora Doll), Françoise's friend. Brandt feels that war changes nothing, and he is planning to desert the army and settle down in France with Simone. When she asks Christian if he will report Brandt, Christian replies that he will not. After Brandt and Simone retire for the evening, Christian describes the insanities of war to Françoise. They spend the night together, but in the morning he leaves her with a note, "I love you. Forgive me, but I am a German soldier." Even though he is disgusted and disillusioned, he is still a prisoner of his sense of duty and plans to return to his unit now that his leave is over.

A sense of duty is also plaguing Michael as he and Margaret suffer through an air raid while in a London bar. Although his desire to be attached to Special Services has been fulfilled, he still feels guilty over not being in combat with the men of his old unit. Margaret, recognizing his ambivalence, tries to make him test himself. Finally, Michael realizes that he cannot escape the consequences any longer, and he requests a transfer back to his old company now fighting in Normandy. He also asks Margaret to marry him when he returns. Now that Michael has rejoined his company, the three characters are drawn together for the climax. In several taut scenes, Noah's company tries to cut through the German lines and rejoin the major American forces. Noah, buoyed by the news of the birth of a daughter, has survived his harrowing days of basic training to become a brave and competent soldier. He even makes a daring rescue of one of his old tormentors. Michael, very impressed with Noah's actions and attitudes, at last admits his own cowardice.

Close to the advancing Americans, Christian wanders alone, separated from his unit who have all run off. He comes across a concentration camp whose purpose and operations are explained to him by the distraught camp commandant. Christian has finally lost all faith in his fatherland. Completely revolted, he stumbles out of the camp and symbolically smashes his rifle against a tree stump. Wearily, but knowingly, he advances toward the American lines and his preordained rendezvous with Michael and Noah.

Shortly after Christian leaves the concentration camp, the Americans discover its existence. The horror of man's inhumanity to man especially affects Noah. He and Michael go for a walk to recover from the shock, and they discuss Noah's father and the war. As the two friends talk, it becomes clear that Noah's character has strengthened and that Michael has matured and become less selfish as a result of all their experiences. Their conversation is interrupted by sounds from the surrounding woods. They look up to see Christian approaching. Quickly, Michael responds to what he thinks is a hostile soldier and shoots the demoralized German. Christian dies, but the two Americans ultimately survive the war and return safely home.

A film that ambitiously tries to depict the horrors of war, the consequences of anti-Semitism and the advancement of man's character through strength and humanity by interweaving three story lines cannot hope to succeed totally. Jumping back and forth from story to story, from Paris to New York to Berlin, makes the plot difficult to follow and does not allow characters to develop fully. The women characters, especially, seem peripheral, but even Michael's and Noah's motivations often appear rather mysterious. Director Dmytryk does succeed in creating a mood of deepening tension by changing from light to very dark as the film progresses. In fact, the black-and-white cinematography of veteran cameraman Joe MacDonald was honored with an Academy Award nomination.

What made the film interesting to critics were the lead performances, especially that of Brando, who dyed his hair blonde and affected a German accent to play Christian. Most critics were impressed with his sensitive portrayal of the optimistic youth whose values undergo tremendous changes during the war. Clift as Noah did not fare as generously at the critics' hands, although he is always interesting, if somewhat mannered. Martin turned in quite an engaging and rounded performance in one of his early dramatic roles. In a supporting role, Schell as Hardenberg received almost unanimous praise for his performance as the ultimate Nazi.

In addition to Brando's and Schell's performances, one scene was constantly singled out by critics as being outstanding: that of the German ambush of the British patrol in North Africa. The validity of Shaw's original themes as interpreted by scriptwriter Edward Anhalt produces a competent and engrossing if not epic war film.

Maria Soule

YOU'RE A BIG BOY NOW

Released: 1967
Production: Phil Feldman for Warner Bros.
Direction: Francis Ford Coppola
Screenplay: Francis Ford Coppola; based on the novel of the same name by
   David Benedictus
Cinematography: Andrew Laszlo
Editing: Aram Avakian
Music: Robert Prince
Running time: 96 minutes

   Principal characters:
   Bernard Chanticleer .... Peter Kastner
   Barbara Darling .... Elizabeth Hartman
   Margery Chanticleer .... Geraldine Page
   Miss Thing .... Julie Harris
   I. H. Chanticleer .... Rip Torn
   Raef .... Tony Bill
   Amy .... Karen Black
   Richard Mudd .... Michael Dunn

You're a Big Boy Now was Francis Ford Coppola's first major directing effort after an entry into the film industry via several "blue" films, a chain of exploitation films for Roger Corman, and screenwriting credits for *This Property Is Condemned* (1966) and *Is Paris Burning?* (1965). It is fundamentally an urban coming-of-age film that explores in a picaresque, whimsical way, with minor forays into the bizarre, what might happen to a virginal young man whose parents are more interested in his maturation rate than he is. Based loosely on the novel with the same title by English writer David Benedictus, *You're a Big Boy Now* follows nineteen-year-old Bernard Chanticleer (Peter Kastner) as he roller skates, rambles, and fantasizes his way through life, largely under the influence of other people. His father, I. H. Chanticleer (Rip Torn), is a New York library curator of incunabula with a private taste for rare erotica as well. He calls Bernard into his office and informs him that it is time for him to leave home and get his own apartment. His very possessive mother Margery (Geraldine Page), who was nominated for an Academy Award for Best Supporting Actress, prefers keeping Bernard at home and show her confused devotion to him by sending him locks of her hair and warning him away from young women. She also tries to rename Bernard's dog "Rover," to which he responds by insistently calling it "Dog." It is the one small margin of self-assertion and control in Bernard's life at this point and one he will not relinquish.

   Of Bernard's two friends at the library, Amy (Karen Black) wants to offer him warmth, affection, and potentially a remedy for his innocence. Raef (Tony Bill) wants to offer him enticements, excitement, and information on sexual initiation. Bernard, however, wants only Barbara Darling (Elizabeth Hartman), an off-Broadway actress/discotheque dancer whom he sees for the first time when she comes into the library where he is a roller-skating book page. Under his father's advice and his mother's solicitous control, Bernard moves to an apartment under the dominion of Miss Thing (Julie Harris), a painfully sublimated widow who maintains a pet rooster trained to attack only young girls, much to Mrs. Chanticleer's satisfaction. From this setting of confused freedom, Bernard ventures into the streets of New York on his own for the first time.

As he wanders around Times Square, the camera picks up some of the images that reflect the imagined freedoms and delights that he does not know how to acquire. He looks through a glass shop window at goods he wants but cannot have, a parallel to the image of Barbara dancing in a glass cage seen later in the film. He approaches a dance hall but is afraid to go in, finally conquers his insecurity, and slips into a porno shop only to be repelled by the crude, loveless sexuality. He leaves the shop for another store-front-operation that offers sexy film strips, and, in a moment of Freudian slapstick, his tie is caught in the rolling mechanism just as the film reaches the climax. Amy, who has been following him, steps in to free him with a handy if incongruous scissors, and Bernard is "saved," foreshadowing the end of the film when he will literally be released from jail by Amy's concern.

Shortly after he moves into his apartment, Bernard sees "Niggers Go Home" scrawled on a subway billboard, makes the associative leap that home is where the heart is, and the heart is in the highlands. His mental acrobatics are reflected in a nice bit of cinematography by Andy Laszlo showing a dancing row of black children following a black bag-piping pied-piper to some mythical homeland. This is, in some measure, what Bernard is trying to find for himself; a definition of self, home, and freedom. As he wanders into the go-go district, where he rediscovers Barbara Darling, the camera ranges around the streets of New York picking up bits of garish 42nd Street life that balances the comic-strip surreality of the plot against the hard edges of the city. Seduced by the seemingly sexual Barbara as he watches her erotic dancing in a psychedelically lighted discotheque, Bernard finds that life in her seraglio is calculated more to confuse than seduce. Having been sexually assaulted as a young girl by an albino hypnotherapist with a wooden leg, which she has captured as a trophy, the vindictive Miss Darling is on a permanent mission against men.

Bernard writes a letter to Barbara. She invites him to her apartment out of curiosity, arouses him just to the point of orgasm, and then crawls into bed claiming a headache and leaving him impotent. Elizabeth Hartman, who had played relatively sedate characters in *A Patch of Blue* (1966) and *The*

Group (1966), was Coppola's choice to play a sexually charged, man-hating seductress, and she does so with skill and intensity.

The day after Bernard's failure with Barbara, Miss Thing, worried about Bernard's overnight absence from the apartment and assuming that he is with Amy, goes to the library to see his father. Mr. Chanticleer, as his name suggests, has something in common with the lusty rooster of the Chaucerian tale. Unlike Miss Thing's rooster, however, the purpose of his attack is to conquer, not to repel, and he inveigles Miss Thing into the rare book vault where he tries to seduce her. When Bernard arrives and sees what is going on, he feels overwhelmed and taken advantage of and rebels by stealing the library's rare Gutenberg Bible. In the last of the film's too-frequent chase scenes, everyone takes out after Bernard, and Barbara catches up with him and knocks him out with her trophy wooden leg. Locked up safely away from all the confusing advisers who have only hindered and undermined his freedom, Bernard reassesses what he wants, is bailed out by the supportive Amy, and romps off down the street with Dog and Amy to the lyricism and optimism of the Lovin' Spoonful sound track.

The film is bright and fast-moving and has some fine location shots of New York streets and the elegant interiors of the New York Public Library, many of them utilizing the *cinéma vérité* effects of a hand-held camera. Altogether, the film works at some unresolvable cross purposes. Coppola could have taken his naïve hero and paraded him through a progression of picaresque misadventures and been successful. What he could not do was add a midget biographer (of Barbara Darling), an albino hypnotherapist-rapist, and a string of Mack Sennett chase scenes and keep the film focused and cohesive. Coppola acknowledged that the chase scenes, particularly Bernard's final sprint through Macy's with the Gutenberg Bible, were redundant and not particularly effective. Although the film lost money despite the range of known performers in the film, it was an evolutionary turning point in Coppola's career. Critical response to Coppola's directing was that it was fresh, exacting, and a welcome sign that the film industry had a new talent, which was later to blossom in *The Godfather* (1972).

Joyce Olin

ZULU

Released: 1964
Production: Stanley Baker and Cy Endfield for Paramount
Direction: Cy Endfield
Screenplay: John Prebble and Cy Endfield; based on an article by John Prebble
Cinematography: Stephen Dade
Editing: John Jympson
Music: John Barry
Running time: 135 minutes

Principal characters:
Lieutenant John Chard .... Stanley Baker
Reverend Otto Witt .... Jack Hawkins
Margaretta Witt .... Ulla Jacobsson
Private Henry Hook .... James Booth
Lieutenant Gonville Bromhead .... Michael Caine
Narrator .... Richard Burton

Zula, a film which glorifies the British Empire, is based on fact. On January 22, 1879, 105 Britons battled with some four thousand Zulu warriors. Eleven of the British defenders survived what seemed insurmountable odds, and each became the recipient of the Victoria Cross, the highest British military decoration awarded for valor. Following in the tradition of adventure films such as *Gunga Din* (1939) and *The Four Feathers* (1939), *Zulu* honors the British colonial spirit by examining valor among men. A common trait of these films, which might be labeled "colonial Westerns," is their focus upon men who must choose between cowardice and courage. What distinguishes *Zulu*, in addition to its real-life story, is the fact that viewers are shown both sides of the war. The Zulus are superb warriors, and their leaders are skilled strategists. The film's story and dialogue pay tribute to their military skills.

From its opening moments, however, we recognize that this film will be an examination of British bravery. There is even a brief narration by Richard Burton behind the opening scenes, introducing the reenactment. News of the impending confrontation is revealed when a missionary and his daughter attend a ceremonial celebration. It is a mass wedding with hundreds of couples participating. The bare-breasted young maidens each carry small spears as proof of their chastity, and they perform a vivid tribal dance opposite the warriors they are to marry. During this African spectacle, the missionary Otto (Jack Hawkins) and his daughter, Margaretta (Ulla Jacobsson), learn that a band of Zulu warriors has wiped out a British detachment. Twelve hundred soldiers were killed, and the Zulus, who have taken the men's rifles, are now headed for Rorke's Drift.

Witt's mission is located at Rorke's Drift, which is also the site of an army outpost. After arriving back at the outpost and revealing plans of the attack, Witt is incensed to learn that the soldiers plan to make a stand. Plans for a stand are marked by a confrontation between the supercilious Lieutenant Bromhead (Michael Caine) and Lieutenant Chard (Stanley Baker). Bromhead, the regimental officer in charge, is angered that Chard, his senior because of two month's additional service, is therefore in command. Arrogant and rather foppish, Bromhead contrasts with the self-made officer Chard. Ultimately, however, the two men must ignore their personal conflicts and different backgrounds in order to prepare for the outpost's defense.

As they go about planning defensive tactics, Witt, who is an alcoholic, tries to persuade Chard to evacuate the garrison. Witt's urgings, including his reminder to the men that they obey the "Thou Shalt Not Kill" biblical commandment, results in his being locked up by the soldiers. His rather frustrated daughter works for a while setting up the station's hospital, preparing if for the battle victims who will soon arrive. Before the attack, however, Chard, who does not want his men to become demoralized, sends Witt and his daughter off in their wagon, presumably to safety. The anticipation of pending battle is heightened when the men hear a noise off in the distance; it is, notes one of the men, like the chugging of an approaching train. The Zulus are attacking the men's nerves by beating their spears on shields.

When the Zulus finally appear, the British are dumbfounded, for the grassy slopes outside the outpost are literally covered with a sea of native warriors. Appearing across the horizon, the Zulus wear animal skins and necklaces made of baboon teeth; they are chanting, "Usuto! Usuto!" ("Kill! Kill!") The warriors begin the assault, attacking in ranks. British firepower mows down the first wave. The Zulus simply regroup, however, and keep on coming. After each assault they come closer to the outpost. The 105 soldiers, armed with Martini-Henry rifles, cannot withstand the more than four thousand warriors bearing spears and shields. Before each attack by the Zulus, the men listen to the ominous war chants. In between attacks, the soldiers assess their losses, which are mounting, and their ammunition supply, which is dwindling.

Eventually, the Zulus reach the station buildings, and hand-to-hand combat ensues between the natives and the soldiers. Private Hook (James Booth) is among the injured men in the infirmary who battle warriors heroically, hand-to-hand. Following this assault on the station, the air is silent. Although the British have successfully turned this last wave of warriors, they know that an endless supply of warriors still waits for battle, and with only eleven men remaining alive, they know that this will be their last stand. The Zulu warriors retreat, however, for the first time in their history. Before doing so they roar a signal of acknowledgment saluting the courage of the incredulous Britons. With their shields raised in tribute, the Zulus withdraw from battle. As the film ends, the narration lists the names of the eleven men of B Company,

2nd Battalion, 24th Regiment of Foot, South Wales Borderers, who received the Victoria Cross.

A lavish production in which the battle scenes comprise more than one hour, *Zulu* succeeds as an epic and as a humanistic tale. For, alongside the grandeur, there are many intimate moments. When the battle has at last ended, a reconciled Chard and Bromhead each confess that they had no prior combat experience, offering a moment of warm camaraderie. Most of the fighting men were Welsh, and the film also pays tribute to their traditions. When the Zulus approach roaring a war chant, a group of the men who worry that fatalities will harm their choral group respond by singing "Men of Harlech."

Zulu examines the horrors of war on both sides of the battle. The outpost hospital is a scene of appalling terror. Signs of carnage are everywhere, and, as the film comes to an end, the camera probes the endless sea of black bodies spread across the fields. The film does not shy away from portraying the reality of war. *Zulu* is not without its share of clichéd moments, however; for example, the battle for command between Chard and Bromhead is carried out in strictly "stiff-upper-lip" tradition, with Bromhead feeling superior because of his aristocracy. Another such moment finds a soldier being chastised for an unbuttoned tunic during the heat of the day. While the screenplay manages to relay crisply a barrage of historical facts and figures, the characterizations are allowed to develop. The film's only superficial characters are Witt and his neurotic daughter, but because they are taken out of the action about halfway through, they do not really deter the story line. They are simply used as tools to bring the message of warring Zulus to the men.

Enhanced by a stirring score by John Barry, *Zulu* marks the screen debut of Caine in the role of Bromhead. It is an auspicious debut, considering that Bromhead is, initially, an unlikable fellow who only gains our respect for his courage near the film's end. It also showed Caine as a gentleman, whereas his later films, such as *Alfie* (1966), usually featured him as a more earthy London cockney, which reflects his actual origin. Starring as Chard is Baker, coproducer of the film. The Welsh actor, who appeared in numerous British and American films, teamed with director Cy Endfield for the historical reenactment. At first, the two ran into difficulty. Messages and antiheroes were prominent 1960's themes—not battles between Zulus and Britons. Joseph E. Levine's participation in the project, however, which marked his entry into British film production, gave the adventure film the necessary impetus it needed.

At Baker's insistence, *Zulu* was filmed on location in Africa, at great expense. Baker even enlisted the aid of the country's Zulus to portray their warrior ancestors. Because of these unique filming conditions, the project drew considerable media interest. Widely reported was the fact that Baker's request for actual Zulu performers caused some initial problems, because the

Zulus had never before seen a film. The only film print Baker could get hold of was an old Gene Autry Western, but after screening it for the Africans, Baker had their enthusiastic support.

Pat H. Broeske

CUMULATIVE

INDEXES

FIRST SERIES

(Numbers shown in lightfaced type)

AND

SECOND SERIES

(Numbers shown in boldfaced type)

TITLE INDEX

(**Bold type** signifies Second Series)

TITLE INDEX

III

TITLE INDEX

DIRECTOR INDEX

ABBABIE D'ARRAST, HARRY D'
Laughter   **III-1333**
Topaze   **VI-2537**

ADOLFI, JOHN G.
Voltaire   **VI-2622**

ALDRICH, ROBERT
Attack!   **I-130**
Big Knife, The   I-159
Dirty Dozen, The   I-448
Kiss Me Deadly   **III-1269**
Longest Yard, The   **III-1431**
What Ever Happened to Baby Jane?   **VI-2649**

ALLEN, IRWIN
Towering Inferno, The   **VI-2550**

ALLEN, LEWIS
Uninvited, The   IV-1801

ALLEN, WOODY
Annie Hall   I-86
Bananas   **I-166**
Interiors   II-844
Love and Death   **III-1449**
Manhattan   III-1069
Sleeper   **V-2199**

ALTMAN, ROBERT
McCabe and Mrs. Miller   **IV-1477**
M*A*S*H   III-1083
Nashville   III-1181
Thieves Like Us   **VI-2478**
3 Women   **VI-2514**

ANDERSON, LINDSAY
If. . . .   **III-1103**
O Lucky Man!   III-1231
This Sporting Life   IV-1726

ANDERSON, MICHAEL
Around the World in 80 Days   I-101
Shake Hands with the Devil   **V-2159**

ANNAKIN, KEN
Longest Day, The   **III-1424**
Those Magnificent Men in Their Flying
Machines   **VI-2490**

ANTHONY, JOSEPH
Rainmaker, The   III-1419

ANTONIONI, MICHELANGELO
Blow-Up   I-191

APTED, MICHAEL
Coal Miner's Daughter   I-365

ARLISS, LESLIE
Man in Grey, The   **IV-1505**

ARMSTRONG, GILLIAN
My Brilliant Career   **IV-1680**

ARNOLD, JACK
Incredible Shrinking Man, The   II-836
Mouse That Roared, The   III-1159

ARZNER, DOROTHY
Craig's Wife   I-397

ASHBY, HAL
Being There   I-145
Coming Home   I-375
Harold and Maude   II-714
Landlord, The   **III-1300**
Last Detail, The   II-942
Shampoo   **V-2163**

ASQUITH, ANTHONY
Browning Version, The   **I-353**
Importance of Being Earnest, The   II-817
Pygmalion   III-1399

ATTENBOROUGH, RICHARD
Oh! What a Lovely War   **IV-1767**

AVAKIAN, ARAM
Cops and Robbers   **II-519**

AVILDSEN, JOHN G.
Rocky   III-1465
Save the Tiger   **V-2096**

BACON, LLOYD
Action in the North Atlantic   **I-14**
Footlight Parade   **II-800**
Larceny, Inc.   **III-1304**
Marked Woman   **IV-1541**
42nd Street   II-561

BADHAM, JOHN
Saturday Night Fever   **V-2089**

BAKER, ROY
Night to Remember, A   III-1203

BEATTY, WARREN
Heaven Can Wait   **II-727**

BEAUMONT, HARRY
Broadway Melody, The   I-243

BECKER, HAROLD
Onion Field, The   **IV-1815**

BENEDEK, LASLO
Death of a Salesman   I-421
Wild One, The   **VI-2668**

BENNETT, COMPTON
King Solomon's Mines   **III-1261**
Seventh Veil, The   IV-1523

BENTON, ROBERT
Kramer vs. Kramer   II-919
Late Show, The   **III-1330**

BERESFORD, BRUCE
Breaker Morant   **I-331**

BERGER, LUDWIG
Thief of Bagdad, The   IV-1703

BERNHARDT, CURTIS
Interrupted Melody   III-1162

BERTOLUCCI, BERNARDO
Last Tango in Paris   **III-1318**

BLYSTONE, JOHN
County Chairman, The   **II-538**

BOGDANOVICH, PETER
Last Picture Show, The   **III-1314**
Paper Moon   **IV-1863**

BOLESLAWSKI, RICHARD
Miserables, Les   III-1114
Rasputin and the Empress   III-1425
Theodora Goes Wild   **V-2454**

BOORMAN, JOHN
Deliverance   I-432
Excalibur   **II-731**
Point Blank   **IV-1913**

BORZAGE, FRANK
Farewell to Arms, A   II-524
Moonrise   **IV-1644**
Mortal Storm, The   **IV-1654**
Secrets   **V-2128**
Three Comrades   IV-1731

BOULTING, JOHN
I'm All Right, Jack   **III-1124**
Magic Box, The   **IV-1485**
Seven Days to Noon   **V-2150**

BOULTING, ROY
Family Way, The   **II-753**

BRAHM, JOHN
Lodger, The   **III-1409**

(**Bold type** signifies Second Series)

BRANDO, MARLON
  One-Eyed Jacks **IV-1795**
BRIDGES, ALAN
  Hireling, The **III-1034**
BRIDGES, JAMES
  Paper Chase, The III-1293
BROCA, PHILIPPE DE
  King of Hearts II-905
BROOK, CLIVE
  On Approval **IV-1781**
BROOK, PETER
  Marat/Sade **IV-1530**
BROOKS, MEL
  Blazing Saddles I-184
  High Anxiety **III-1027**
  Producers, The III-1388
BROOKS, RICHARD
  Blackboard Jungle **I-264**
  Cat on a Hot Tin Roof I-308
  Elmer Gantry II-498
  In Cold Blood **III-1138**
  Professionals, The **IV-1944**
  Sweet Bird of Youth **V-2387**
BROWN, CLARENCE
  Ah, Wilderness! I-26
  Anna Christie **I-92**
  Anna Karenina I-82
  Free Soul, A **II-847**
  Human Comedy, The **III-1073**
  Intruder in the Dust **III-1166**
  National Velvet **IV-1710**
  Yearling, The **VI-2721**
BROWN, MELVILLE
  Check and Double Check **I-446**
BROWNING, TOD
  Dracula I-482
  Freaks **II-842**
BRUCKMAN, CLYDE
  Movie Crazy **IV-1661**
BUCQUET, HAROLD S.
  Dr. Kildare's Strange Case **II-650**
BURGE, STUART
  Othello **IV-1828**
BUTLER, DAVID
  Calamity Jane **I-389**
  Littlest Rebel, The II-992
  Road to Morocco III-1454
BUZZELL, EDWARD
  At the Circus **I-127**

CACOYNNIS, MICHAEL
  Zorba the Greek IV-1904
CAHN, EDWARD L.
  Law and Order **III-1337**
CAMMELL, DONALD
  Performance III-1310
CAPRA, FRANK
  Arsenic and Old Lace I-105
  Bitter Tea of General Yen, The I-172
  It Happened One Night II-852
  It's a Wonderful Life II-856
  Lady for a Day **III-1285**
  Lost Horizon III-1006
  Meet John Doe III-1087
  Mr. Deeds Goes to Town **IV-1613**
  Mr. Smith Goes to Washington III-1128
  State of the Union IV-1627
  You Can't Take It with You **VI-2734**

CARDIFF, JACK
  Sons and Lovers **V-2221**
  Young Cassidy **VI-2738**
CARPENTER, JOHN
  Halloween **II-969**
CASSAVETES, JOHN
  Faces **II-741**
  Husbands **III-1076**
  Minnie and Moskowitz **IV-1594**
  Woman Under the Influence, A **VI-2711**
CATES, GILBERT
  I Never Sang for My Father **III-1086**
CAVALCANTI, ALBERTO
  Dead of Night **II-595**
CHAPLIN, CHARLES
  City Lights I-352
  Great Dictator, The II-678
  Limelight II-978
  Modern Times III-1134
  Monsieur Verdoux **IV-1630**
CIMINO, MICHAEL
  Deer Hunter, The I-427
CLAIR, RENE
  And Then There Were None I-68
  Forever and a Day **II-815**
  I Married a Witch II-806
CLAVELL, JAMES
  To Sir with Love **VI-2530**
CLAYTON, JACK
  Great Gatsby, The II-690
  Innocents, The **III-1151**
  Pumpkin Eater, The **IV-1947**
  Room at the Top III-1469
CLINE, EDWARD
  Bank Dick, The I-129
  Million Dollar Legs III-1101
  My Little Chickadee **IV-1689**
  Never Give a Sucker an Even Break III-1193
  You Can't Cheat an Honest Man IV-1891
CLOUSE, ROBERT
  Enter the Dragon **II-715**
COE, FRED
  Thousand Clowns, A IV-1728
COMFORT, LANCE
  Old Mother Riley Detective **IV-1778**
CONWAY, JACK
  Arsene Lupin **I-113**
  Boom Town **I-305**
  Libeled Lady **III-1358**
  Tale of Two Cities, A IV-1667
  Unholy Three, The **VI-2597**
COOK, FIELDER
  Patterns III-1302
COOPER, MERIAN C.
  King Kong II-900
COPPOLA, FRANCIS FORD
  Apocalypse Now I-94
  Conversation, The **II-515**
  Godfather, The II-638
  Godfather, Part II, The II-644
  Rain People, The **V-1972**
  You're a Big Boy Now **VI-2746**
CORMAN, ROGER
  Little Shop of Horrors, The **III-1396**
CORNELIUS, HENRY
  Genevieve **II-865**
  I Am a Camera II-800
  Passport to Pimlico III-1299

XIV

DIRECTOR INDEX

COWARD, NOEL
   In Which We Serve   II-833
CRICHTON, CHARLES
   Dead of Night   **II-595**
   Lavender Hill Mob, The   II-948
CROMWELL, JOHN
   Abe Lincoln in Illinois   I-1
   Algiers   **I-37**
   Anna and the King of Siam   I-78
   Caged   **I-386**
   Enchanted Cottage, The   II-502
   Goddess, The   **II-896**
   In Name Only   II-822
   Of Human Bondage   III-1237
   Prisoner of Zenda, The   III-1375
   Since You Went Away   **V-2193**
   So Ends Our Night   **V-2208**
CROSLAND, ALAN
   Jazz Singer, The   II-866
CRUZE, JAMES
   Great Gabbo, The   **II-926**
   I Cover the Waterfront   **III-1083**
CUKOR, GEORGE
   Actress, The   **I-18**
   Adam's Rib   I-6
   Bhowani Junction   **I-205**
   Bill of Divorcement, A   **I-239**
   Born Yesterday   I-209
   Camille   I-285
   David Copperfield   **II-574**
   Dinner at Eight   I-444
   Double Life, A   **II-664**
   Gaslight   II-600
   Girls, Les   **II-885**
   Holiday   II-758
   Little Women   II-988
   Marrying Kind, The   **IV-1544**
   My Fair Lady   III-1170
   One Hour with You   III-1268
   Pat and Mike   **IV-1873**
   Philadelphia Story, The   III-1330
   Romeo and Juliet   **V-2053**
   Star Is Born, A   IV-1619
   Sylvia Scarlett   **V-2404**
   What Price Hollywood?   IV-1835
   Women, The   IV-1872
CUMMINGS, IRVING
   In Old Arizona   **III-1142**
   Story of Alexander Graham Bell, The   **V-2281**
CURTIZ, MICHAEL
   Adventures of Robin Hood, The   I-9
   Angels with Dirty Faces   I-72
   Captain Blood   **I-400**
   Casablanca   I-305
   Charge of the Light Brigade, The   **I-427**
   Four Daughters   **II-832**
   Life with Father   **III-1367**
   Mildred Pierce   III-1098
   Night and Day   **IV-1713**
   Private Lives of Elizabeth and Essex, The   III-1383
   Sea Hawk, The   IV-1497
   Sea Wolf, The   **V-2116**
   Unsuspected, The   **VI-2603**
   Yankee Doodle Dandy   IV-1888

DACOSTA, MORTON
   Auntie Mame   **I-134**
   Music Man, The   **IV-1676**
DASSIN, JULES
   Brute Force   **I-360**

   Canterville Ghost, The   **I-396**
   Naked City, The   **IV-1700**
   Topkapi   **VI-2540**
DAVES, DELMER
   Broken Arrow   I-248
   Destination Tokyo   **II-625**
   Hanging Tree, The   **III-975**
   Pride of the Marines   **IV-1924**
   Summer Place, A   **V-2344**
   3:10 to Yuma   **VI-2511**
DAVIS, OSSIE
   Cotton Comes to Harlem   **II-528**
DEAN, BASIL
   Sing as We Go   IV-1557
DEARDEN, BASIL
   Blue Lamp, The   **I-287**
   Dead of Night   **I-595**
   League of Gentlemen, The   **III-1340**
DE MILLE, CECIL B.
   Cleopatra   I-356
   Dynamite   **II-684**
   Greatest Show on Earth, The   II-697
   Plainsman, The   III-1352
   Ten Commandments, The   **V-2430**
   Union Pacific   **VI-2600**
DEPALMA, BRIAN
   Carrie   **I-408**
DIETERLE, WILLIAM
   Devil and Daniel Webster, The   **II-632**
   Dr. Ehrlich's Magic Bullet   I-454
   Hunchback of Notre Dame, The   II-786
   Juarez   **III-1232**
   Life of Émile Zola, The   II-970
   Midsummer Night's Dream, A   **IV-1587**
   Portrait of Jennie   III-1358
   Story of Louis Pasteur, The   **V-2284**
DMYTRYK, EDWARD
   Broken Lance   **I-343**
   Caine Mutiny, The   I-275
   Crossfire   **II-548**
   Murder, My Sweet   III-1164
   Young Lions, The   **VI-2741**
DONEN, STANLEY
   Charade   I-323
   Funny Face   **II-859**
   On the Town   III-1259
   Seven Brides for Seven Brothers   IV-1515
   Singin' in the Rain   IV-1560
   Two for the Road   **VI-2576**
DOUGLAS, GORDON
   Them!   **V-2450**
DOWNEY, ROBERT
   Putney Swope   **V-1955**
DUNNING, GEORGE
   Yellow Submarine   **VI-2728**
DWAN, ALLAN
   Sands of Iwo Jima   **V-2080**

EASTWOOD, CLINT
   Bronco Billy   **I-346**
   Outlaw Josey Wales, The   **IV-1842**
EDWARDS, BLAKE
   Breakfast at Tiffany's   I-215
   Days of Wine and Roses   I-418
   Operation Petticoat   **IV-1818**
   Party, The   **IV-1866**
   Pink Panther, The   III-1343
   10   **V-2426**

DIRECTOR INDEX

GLENVILLE, PETER
  Becket I-138
  Summer and Smoke **V-2339**
GORDON, MICHAEL
  Act of Murder, An **I-11**
  Cyrano de Bergerac I-400
  Pillow Talk III-1339
GORDON, STEVE
  Arthur **I-116**
GOULDING, EDMUND
  Constant Nymph, The **II-511**
  Dark Victory I-409
  Dawn Patrol I-416
  Forever and a Day **II-815**
  Grand Hotel II-672
  Great Lie, The **II-933**
  Nightmare Alley III-1207
  Old Maid, The **IV-1771**
  Razor's Edge, The III-1429
  Trespasser, The **VI-2564**
GRANT, JOE
  Fantasia II-513
GREEN, ALFRED E.
  Dangerous **II-564**
  Jolson Story, The II-877
  Silver Dollar **V-2186**
GREEN, GUY
  Angry Silence, The **I-89**
  Mark, The **IV-1538**
    GRIES TOM
  Will Penny **VI-2675**
GRIFFITH, D. W.
  Struggle, The IV-1645
GUILLERMIN, JOHN
  Towering Inferno, The **VI-2550**

HALEY, JACK, JR.
  That's Entertainment **V-2443**
HALL, ALEXANDER
  Down to Earth **II-667**
  Here Comes Mr. Jordan II-737
  My Sister Eileen **IV-1693**
HAMER, ROBERT
  Dead of Night **II-595**
  Kind Hearts and Coronets II-889
HAMILTON, GUY
  Goldfinger **II-904**
  Inspector Calls, An **III-1155**
HAND, DAVID
  Snow White and the Seven Dwarfs IV-1575
HARDWICKE, SIR CEDRIC
  Forever and a Day **II-815**
HARVEY, ANTHONY
  Lion in Winter, The **III-1382**
HASKIN, BYRON
  War of the Worlds, The **VI-2639**
HATHAWAY, HENRY
  Call Northside 777 I-280
  House on 92nd Street, The **III-1065**
  How the West Was Won **III-1069**
  Lives of a Bengal Lancer **III-1404**
  True Grit IV-1780
HAWKS, HOWARD
  Ball of Fire I-119
  Big Sky, The **I-229**
  Big Sleep, The I-162
  Bringing Up Baby I-237
  Dawn Patrol, The **II-578**

Gentlemen Prefer Blondes II-613
His Girl Friday II-751
I Was a Male War Bride **III-1098**
Monkey Business III-1144
Only Angels Have Wings III-1279
Red River **V-2000**
Rio Bravo **V-2018**
Scarface: The Shame of the Nation III-1490
Sergeant York IV-1509
To Have and Have Not IV-1752
Twentieth Century IV-1791
HECHT, BEN
  Angels over Broadway **I-86**
  Crime Without Passion **II-541**
  Scoundrel, The **V-2113**
HEERMAN, VICTOR
  Animal Crackers I-75
HEISLER, STUART
  Biscuit Eater, The **I-253**
  Star, The **V-2260**
HELLMAN, MONTE
  Two-Lane Blacktop **VI-2579**
HENRY, BUCK
  Heaven Can Wait II-727
HENZELL, PERRY
  Harder They Come, The **III-982**
HICKOX, DOUGLAS
  Entertaining Mr. Sloane **II-724**
  Theatre of Blood IV-1689
HIGGINS, COLIN
  Foul Play **II-823**
HILL, GEORGE ROY
  Butch Cassidy and the Sundance Kid I-264
  Sting, The IV-1634
HILL, GEORGE W.
  Big House, The **I-220**
  Min and Bill II-1107
HILL, JAMES
  Born Free **I-312**
HILLER, ARTHUR
  Americanization of Emily, The I-64
  Hospital, The II-766
HITCHCOCK, ALFRED
  Birds, The **I-249**
  Blackmail I-181
  Dial M for Murder I-440
  Foreign Correspondent II-556
  Frenzy **II-849**
  I Confess **III-1080**
  Lady Vanishes, The II-933
  Lifeboat II-974
  Man Who Knew Too Much, The **IV-1519**
  Marnie III-1076
  Mr. and Mrs. Smith **IV-1604**
  North by Northwest **IV-1742**
  Notorious **IV-1752**
  Psycho III-1391
  Rear Window **V-1983**
  Rebecca III-1434
  Saboteur **V-2076**
  Shadow of a Doubt IV-1526
  Spellbound IV-1597
  Stage Fright **V-2246**
  Strangers on a Train **V-2298**
  Suspicion IV-1663
  39 Steps, The IV-1723
  To Catch a Thief IV-1747
  Trouble with Harry, The IV-1777
  Vertigo **VI-2612**
  Wrong Man, The IV-1880

XVII

DIRECTOR INDEX

Shining, The **V-2175**
Spartacus **V-2231**
2001: A Space Odyssey IV-1798

LA CAVA, GREGORY
My Man Godfrey III-1178
Stage Door **V-2242**
LANDFIELD, SIDNEY
Hound of the Baskervilles, The II-770
LANG, FRITZ
Beyond a Reasonable Doubt **I-202**
Big Heat, The **I-216**
Fury II-596
Ministry of Fear **IV-1590**
Rancho Notorious **V-1976**
Scarlet Street **V-2110**
Western Union **VI-2645**
Woman in the Window, The **VI-2702**
You Only Live Once IV-1894
LANG, WALTER
Desk Set **II-616**
King and I, The II-897
Mother Wore Tights **IV-1658**
Sitting Pretty IV-1564
With a Song in My Heart **VI-2694**
LAUGHLIN, TOM
Billy Jack **I-242**
LAUGHTON, CHARLES
Night of the Hunter, The III-1200
LAUNDER, FRANK
Belles of St. Trinian's, The **I-193**
Happiest Days of Your Life, The **III-978**
I See a Dark Stranger II-809
LEAN, DAVID
Blithe Spirit I-188
Bridge on the River Kwai, The I-225
Brief Encounter I-230
Dr. Zhivago I-468
Great Expectations II-685
Hobson's Choice II-754
In Which We Serve II-833
Lawrence of Arabia II-959
Oliver Twist III-1256
Ryan's Daughter III-1480
Summertime **V-2348**
This Happy Breed **VI-2483**
LEE, ROWLAND V.
Count of Monte Cristo, The **II-531**
LEISEN, MITCHELL
Arise My Love **I-107**
Death Takes a Holiday I-424
Easy Living **II-688**
Lady in the Dark **III-1293**
Midnight **IV-1574**
To Each His Own **VI-2526**
LEONARD, ROBERT Z.
Great Ziegfeld, The **II-936**
In the Good Old Summertime **III-1145**
Pride and Prejudice **IV-1919**
LEROY, MERVYN
Anthony Adverse **I-96**
Bad Seed, The **I-159**
Gold Diggers of 1933 **II-900**
I Am a Fugitive from a Chain Gang II-803
Johnny Eager **III-1224**
Little Caesar **III-1390**
Madame Curie III-1033
Million Dollar Mermaid III-1104
Mister Roberts III-1121
Quo Vadis III-1411

Random Harvest **V-1979**
They Won't Forget **VI-2474**
Waterloo Bridge **VI-2642**
LESTER, RICHARD
Funny Thing Happened on the Way to the
   Forum, A II-592
Hard Day's Night, A II-712
Help! **III-1012**
Knack, The **III-1279**
Petulia III-1314
Robin and Marian **V-2034**
Superman II **V-2371**
LEVIN, HARRY
April Love **I-104**
LEWIN, ALBERT
Moon and Sixpence, The **IV-1638**
Picture of Dorian Gray, The III-1335
LEWIS, JERRY
Nutty Professor, The III-1227
LEWIS, JOSEPH H.
Gun Crazy **II-949**
LITVAK, ANATOLE
All This and Heaven Too **I-65**
Anastasia **I-71**
Blues in the Night **I-294**
Snake Pit, The **V-2202**
Sorry, Wrong Number **V-225**
LLOYD, FRANK
Cavalcade I-316
Forever and a Day **II-815**
If I Were King **III-1107**
Mutiny on the Bounty III-1167
LOGAN, JOSHUA
Bus Stop I-259
Fanny **II-757**
Picnic **IV-1895**
Sayonara **V-2099**
South Pacific IV-1589
LOSEY, JOSEPH
Accident **I-4**
Blind Date **I-270**
Boy with Green Hair, The I-212
Concrete Jungle, The **II-503**
Doll's House, A **II-657**
Go-Between, The II-633
King and Country **III-1257**
Servant, The **V-2138**
LUBIN, ARTHUR
Buck Privates I-252
Francis in the Navy **II-839**
Phantom of the Opera, The III-1322
LUBITSCH, ERNST
Angel **I-82**
Bluebeard's Eighth Wife **I-290**
Cluny Brown **I-480**
Design for Living **II-609**
Heaven Can Wait II-724
Love Parade, The III-1026
Merry Widow, The **IV-1568**
Ninotchka III-1210
One Hour with You III-1268
Shop Around the Corner, The **V-2183**
To Be or Not to Be IV-1743
Trouble in Paradise **VI-2567**
LUCAS, GEORGE
American Graffiti I-56
Star Wars IV-1623
LUMET, SIDNEY
Dog Day Afternoon I-474
Long Day's Journey into Night III-999

Network III-1190
Pawnbroker, The **IV-1880**
Serpico IV-1512
Twelve Angry Men IV-1783
View from the Bridge, A **VI-2616**
LUSKE, HAMILTON
Pinocchio **IV-1902**
LYNCH, DAVID
Elephant Man, The **II-705**

MACARTHUR, CHARLES
Crime Without Passion **II-541**
Scoundrel, The **V-2113**
MCCAREY, LEO
Affair to Remember, An **I-24**
Awful Truth, The I-109
Bells of St. Mary's, The **I-196**
Duck Soup **II-673**
Going My Way II-648
Love Affair **III-1446**
Ruggles of Red Gap **V-2066**
MACKENDRICK, ALEXANDER
Ladykillers, The II-939
Man in the White Suit, The III-1056
Sweet Smell of Success **V-2391**
Tight Little Island IV-1738
MCLAGLEN, ANDREW V.
ffolkes **II-778**
MCLEOD, NORMAN Z.
Horse Feathers **III-1051**
It's a Gift **III-1195**
Monkey Business III-1141
Paleface, The **IV-1850**
Topper IV-1770
MALICK, TERRENCE
Badlands **I-163**
MAMOULIAN, ROUBEN
Applause **I-100**
Blood and Sand **I-280**
Dr. Jekyll and Mr. Hyde I-457
Golden Boy **II-651**
Love Me Tonight III-1022
Mark of Zorro, The III-1070
Queen Christina III-1404
Silk Stockings IV-1553
MANKIEWICZ, JOSEPH L.
All About Eve I-40
Cleopatra **I-466**
Five Fingers **II-784**
Ghost and Mrs. Muir, The **II-877**
Julius Caesar II-881
Letter to Three Wives, A **III-1355**
No Way Out **IV-1735**
Sleuth IV-1567
Suddenly, Last Summer **V-2333**
MANN, ANTHONY
Cid, El **I-458**
Great Flamarion, The **II-923**
Naked Spur, The **IV-1704**
Winchester '73 IV-1848
MANN, DANIEL
Butterfield 8 **I-372**
Come Back, Little Sheba I-370
I'll Cry Tomorrow **III-1117**
Rose Tattoo, The III-1472
MANN, DELBERT
Marty III-1079
Separate Tables IV-1506
MARSHALL, GEORGE
Blue Dahlia, The **I-283**

Destry Rides Again I-436
How the West Was Won **III-1069**
You Can't Cheat an Honest Man IV-1891
MARTON, ANDREW
King Solomon's Mines **III-1261**
Longest Day, The **III-1424**
MATE, RUDOLPH
D.O.A. **II-560**
MAYO, ARCHIE
On Trial **IV-1792**
Petrified Forest, The **IV-1888**
Svengali **V-2384**
MAZURSKY, PAUL
Blume in Love **I-298**
Bob and Carol and Ted and Alice **I-301**
Harry and Tonto **III-989**
Unmarried Woman, An IV-1805
MEDAK, PETER
Ruling Class, The **V-2070**
MEINS, GUS
Babes in Toyland **I-137**
MENZIES, WILLIAM CAMERON
Things to Come IV-1716
MILES, CHRISTOPHER
Virgin and the Gypsy, The **VI-2619**
MILESTONE, LEWIS
All Quiet on the Western Front I-43
Front Page, The **II-586**
Of Mice and Men III-1240
Rain III-1415
Red Pony, The **V-1997**
Strange Love of Martha Ivers, The **V-2290**
Walk in the Sun, A IV-1816
MILLER, DAVID
Captain Newman, M.D. **I-405**
Lonely Are the Brave **III-1417**
Midnight Lace **IV-1582**
MILLER, ROBERT ELLIS
Heart Is a Lonely Hunter, The **III-1002**
MINNELLI, VINCENTE
American in Paris, An I-60
Bad and the Beautiful, The I-112
Band Wagon, The I-123
Brigadoon **I-339**
Cabin in the Sky I-271
Clock, The **I-472**
Designing Woman **II-612**
Father of the Bride **II-770**
Gigi II-621
Lust for Life **IV-1467**
Meet Me in St. Louis III-1091
Pirate, The **IV-1906**
Some Came Running **V-2211**
Tea and Sympathy **V-2419**
Yolanda and the Thief **VI-2731**
MONTGOMERY, ROBERT
Lady in the Lake **III-1297**
MULLIGAN, ROBERT
Fear Strikes Out **II-773**
Love with the Proper Stranger III-1029
Summer of '42 IV-1652
To Kill a Mockingbird IV-1756
Up the Down Staircase **VI-2606**
MURNAU, F. W.
Tabu **V-2408**
MURPHY, DUDLEY
Emperor Jones, The **II-709**

DIRECTOR INDEX

DIRECTOR INDEX

Cactus Flower **I-379**
Odd Couple, The   III-1234
SANDRICH, MARK
Carefree   I-292
Follow the Fleet   **II-549**
Gay Divorcee, The   **II-605**
Shall We Dance   IV-1529
Top Hat   IV-1764
Woman Rebels, A   **VI-2709**
SANTELL, ALFRED
Winterset   IV-1859
SAVILLE, VICTOR
Evergreen   **II-728**
Forever and a Day   **II-815**
SCHAFFNER, FRANKLIN J.
Best Man, The   **I-199**
Islands in the Stream   **III-1189**
Patton   III-1306
Planet of the Apes   III-1355
SCHALTZBERG, JERRY
Panic in Needle Park, The   **IV-1856**
SCHERTZINGER, VICTOR
One Night of Love   III-1275
SCHLESINGER, JOHN
Billy Liar   **I-245**
Darling   I-412
Day of the Locust, The   **II-586**
Far from the Madding Crowd   II-517
Kind of Loving, A   II-894
Midnight Cowboy   III-1095
Sunday, Bloody Sunday   **V-2363**
SCHNEIDER, ALAN
Film   II-531
SCHOEDSACK, ERNEST B.
King Kong   II-900
SCHUMLIN, HERMAN
Watch on the Rhine   IV 1820
SCORSESE, MARTIN
Alice Doesn't Live Here Anymore   **I-44**
Mean Streets   **IV-1554**
Raging Bull   **V-1962**
Taxi Driver   IV-1678
SCOTT, RIDLEY
Alien   I-37
SEATON, GEORGE
Airport   **I-27**
Counterfeit Traitor, The   **II-534**
Country Girl, The   I-390
Miracle on 34th Street   **IV-1597**
Teacher's Pet   IV-1682
SEGAL, ALEX
All the Way Home   **I-62**
SEITER, WILLIAM A.
Roberta   **V-2029**
SEITZ, GEORGE B.
Family Affair, A   **II-749**
Love Finds Andy Hardy   III-1015
Yellow Jack   **VI-2724**
SELWYN, EDGAR
Sin of Madelon Claudet, The   **V-2189**
SHARMAN, JIM
Rocky Horror Picture Show, The   **V-2044**
SHARPSTEEN, BEN
Dumbo   **II-680**
Pinocchio   **IV-1902**
SHERMAN, LOWELL
Morning Glory   III-1150
She Done Him Wrong   IV-1539

SHERMAN, VINCENT
Across the Pacific   **I-8**
Mr. Skeffington   III-1125
Old Acquaintance   III-1249
SHUMLIN, HERMAN
Confidential Agent   **II-507**
SIDNEY, GEORGE
Anchors Aweigh   **I-79**
Bye Bye Birdie   **I-375**
Harvey Girls, The   **III-992**
Kiss Me Kate   **III-1272**
Scaramouche   **V-2102**
Show Boat   IV-1549
Three Musketeers, The   **VI-2505**
SIEGEL, DON
Beguiled, The   **I-141**
Dirty Harry   I-451
Flaming Star   **II-541**
Invasion of the Body Snatchers   II-848
Riot in Cell Block 11   **III-1451**
Shootist, The   IV-1542
SILVER, JOAN MICKLIN
Hester Street   II-741
SILVERSTEIN, ELLIOT
Cat Ballou   **I-412**
SIODMAK, ROBERT
Cobra Woman   **II-485**
Crimson Pirate, The   **II-545**
Dark Mirror, The   **II-567**
Killers, The   **III-1254**
Spiral Staircase, The   IV-1601
SIRK, DOUGLAS
All That Heaven Allows   **I-53**
Imitation of Life   **III-1132**
Magnificent Obsession   **IV-1491**
Tarnished Angels, The   **V-2412**
There's Always Tomorrow   **VI-2457**
Written on the Wind   IV-1876
SMIGHT, JACK
No Way to Treat a Lady   **IV-1738**
SPIELBERG, STEVEN
Close Encounters of the Third Kind   I-362
Jaws   II-863
Sugarland Express, The   **V-2336**
Raiders of the Lost Ark   **V-1966**
STAHL, JOHN M.
Imitation of Life   **III-1128**
Keys of the Kingdom, The   **III-1251**
Leave Her to Heaven   II-963
Magnificent Obsession   **IV-1488**
STALLONE, SYLVESTER
Rocky II   **V-2041**
STEPHANI, FRANK
Flash Gordon   **II-796**
STERNBERG, JOSEF VON
Blonde Venus   **I-273**
Morocco   **IV-1650**
Scarlet Empress, The   **V-2106**
Shanghai Express   **V-2167**
STEVENS, GEORGE
Alice Adams   I-33
Diary of Anne Frank, The   **II-642**
Giant   II-616
Gunga Din   **II-959**
I Remember Mama   **III-1089**
More the Merrier, The   III-1147
Penny Serenade   **IV-1883**
Place in the Sun, A   III-1349
Shane   IV-1534

XXIII

MAGILL'S SURVEY OF CINEMA

Swing Time **V-2398**
Talk of the Town, The IV-1671
Woman of the Year **VI-2705**
STEVENSON, ROBERT
Back Street **I-153**
Forever and a Day II-815
Jane Eyre II-860
Mary Poppins **IV-1550**
STRAYER, FRANK R.
Blondie on a Budget **I-277**
STRICK, JOSEPH
Ulysses **VI-2587**
STUART, MEL
If It's Tuesday, This Must Be Belgium **III-1113**
One Is a Lonely Number **IV-1802**
STURGES, JOHN
Bad Day at Black Rock I-116
Great Escape, The II-684
Gunfight at the O.K. Corral **II-952**
Hour of the Gun **III-1061**
Magnificent Seven, The III-1037
Old Man and the Sea, The **IV-1775**
STURGES, PRESTON
Christmas in July **I-454**
Great McGinty, The II-693
Hail the Conquering Hero **II-963**
Lady Eve, The II-929
Miracle of Morgan's Creek, The III-1111
Palm Beach Story, The **IV-1853**
Sullivan's Travels IV-1648
Unfaithfully Yours **VI-2590**
SWIFT, DAVID
Parent Trap, The III-1296

TASHLIN, FRANK
Artists and Models **I-119**
Will Success Spoil Rock Hunter? **VI-2678**
TAUROG, NORMAN
Adventures of Tom Sawyer, The I-15
Boys' Town **I-325**
Broadway Melody of 1940 I-245
Girl Crazy II-630
Room for One More **V-2059**
Skippy **V-2196**
TAYLOR, SAM
Coquette **II-524**
THOMAS, GERALD
Carry on Nurse I-301
THOMAS, RALPH
Doctor in the House **II-646**
No Love for Johnnie **IV-1732**
THOMPSON, J. LEE
Guns of Navarone, The II-700
Tiger Bay **VI-2519**
THORPE, RICHARD
Ivanhoe **III-1202**
Jailhouse Rock **III-1205**
Night Must Fall **IV-1717**
Three Little Words **VI-2502**
TILL, ERIC
Hot Millions **III-1058**
TOTH, ANDRE DE
House of Wax II-772
TOURNEUR, JACQUES
Cat People I-312
I Walked with a Zombie **III-1093**
Out of the Past III-1287

TRUFFAUT, FRANCOIS
Fahrenheit 451 II-510
TUTTLE, FRANK
This Gun for Hire **VI-2481**

USTINOV, PETER
Billy Budd I-165

VADIM, ROGER
Barbarella **I-170**
VAN DYKE, W. S.
Manhattan Melodrama **IV-1527**
Naughty Marietta III-1186
Prisoner of Zenda, The III-1375
San Francisco III-1487
Trader Horn **VI-2554**
Tarzan, the Ape Man IV-1675
Thin Man, The IV-1709
VARNEL, MARCEL
Let George Do It **III-1348**
VIDOR, CHARLES
Gilda II-627
Ladies in Retirement **III-1282**
Love Me or Leave Me **III-1455**
VIDOR, KING
Champ, The **I-421**
Citadel, The I-343
Duel in the Sun **II-676**
Fountainhead, The **II-828**
Hallelujah! II-704
Northwest Passage IV-1745
Our Daily Bread III-1284
Stella Dallas IV-1631
Street Scene **V-2317**
War and Peace **VI-2636**

WAGGNER, GEORGE
Wolf Man, The **VI-2698**
WALKER, STUART
Mystery of Edwin Drood, The **IV-1696**
WALLACE, RICHARD
It's in the Bag **III-1198**
Little Minister, The **III-1393**
Night to Remember, A **IV-1728**
WALSH, RAOUL
Gentleman Jim **II-868**
High Sierra II-748
In Old Arizona **III-1142**
Lawless Breed, The II-956
Pursued **IV-1950**
Roaring Twenties, The III-1458
Strawberry Blonde, The **V-2310**
They Died with Their Boots On **VI-2461**
White Heat IV-1839
WALTERS, CHARLES
Barkleys of Broadway, The **I-177**
Easter Parade II-491
Good News **II-911**
Lili **III-1371**
Unsinkable Molly Brown, The IV-1808
WEILL, CLAUDIA
Girl Friends **II-882**
WEIR, PETER
Last Wave, The **III-1325**
Picnic at Hanging Rock **IV-1899**
WELLES, ORSON
Citizen Kane I-346
Lady from Shanghai, The **III-1288**
Magnificent Ambersons, The III-1036
Stranger, The **V-2294**

XXIV

DIRECTOR INDEX

SCREENWRITER INDEX

(Bold type signifies Second Series)

BEHM, MARC
  Help! **III-1012**
BEHRMAN, S. N.
  Anna Karenina I-82
  Queen Christina III-1404
  Quo Vadis III-1411
  Tale of Two Cities, A IV-1667
  Waterloo Bridge **VI-2642**
BELLAH, JAMES WARNER
  Man Who Shot Liberty Valance, The III-1059
  Sergeant Rutledge **V-2135**
BELOIN, EDMUND
  Harvey Girls, The **III-992**
BELSON, JERRY
  Smile IV-1572
BENCHLEY, PETER
  Jaws II-863
BENCHLEY, ROBERT
  Foreign Correspondent II-556
BENÉT, STEPHEN VINCENT
  Devil and Daniel Webster, The **II-632**
BENNETT, CHARLES
  Foreign Correspondent II-556
  Forever and a Day **II-815**
  39 Steps, The IV-1723
BENSON, SALLY
  Anna and the King of Siam I-78
  Shadow of a Doubt IV-1526
BENTON, ROBERT
  Bonnie and Clyde I-205
  Kramer vs. Kramer II-919
  Late Show, The III-1330
BERCOVICI, LEONARDO
  Bishop's Wife, The **I-256**
BERESFORD, BRUCE
  Breaker Morant **I-331**
BERGEN, ERIC
  Elephant Man, The **II-705**
BERGMAN, ANDREW
  Blazing Saddles I-184
BERGMAN, HENRY
  City Lights I-352
BERKELEY, REGINALD
  Cavalcade I-316
BERKMAN, TED
  Fear Strikes Out **II-773**
BERMAN, SAM
  Scarlet Pimpernel, The IV-1493
BERNEIS, PETER
  Portrait of Jennie III-1358
BERNSTEIN, WALTER
  Train, The **VI-2558**
BERTOLUCCI, BERNARDO
  Last Tango in Paris III-1318
BEZZERIDES, A. I.
  Action in the North Atlantic **I-14**
  Kiss Me Deadly **III-1269**
  On Dangerous Ground **IV-1784**
BIRO, LAJOS
  Four Feathers II-566
  Private Life of Don Juan, The **IV-1933**
  Private Life of Henry VIII, The III-1379
  Rembrandt **V-2007**
  Scarlet Pimpernel, The IV-1493
BLACK, JOHN D. F.
  Shaft **V-2156**

BLANK, DOROTHY ANN
  Snow White and the Seven Dwarfs IV-1575
BLANKFORT, MICHAEL
  Act of Murder, An **I-11**
  Adam Had Four Sons **I-21**
  Broken Arrow I-248
BLATTY, WILLIAM PETER
  Exorcist, The II-506
BLAU, RAPHAEL
  Fear Strikes Out **II-773**
BLEES, ROBERT
  Magnificent Obsession **IV-1491**
BLOOM, HAROLD JACK
  Naked Spur, The **IV-1704**
BLUM, EDWIN
  Canterville Ghost, The **I-396**
  Down to Earth **II-667**
  Stalag 17 **V-2256**
BOASBERG, AL
  Freaks **II-842**
BODEEN, DEWITT
  Billy Budd I-165
  Cat People I-312
  Enchanted Cottage, The II-502
  I Remember Mama **III-1089**
BOEHM, SYDNEY
  Big Heat, The **I-216**
BOGDANOVICH, PETER
  Last Picture Show, The **III-1314**
BOLAND, BRIDGET
  War and Peace **VI-2636**
BOLOGNA, JOSEPH
  Lovers and Other Strangers **III-1461**
BOLT, ROBERT
  Dr. Zhivago I-468
  Lawrence of Arabia II-959
  Man for All Seasons, A III-1053
  Ryan's Daughter III-1480
BOLTON, GUY
  Love Parade, The III-1026
BOND, EDWARD
  Blow-Up I-191
  Walkabout **VI-2633**
BOORMAN, JOHN
  Excalibur **II-731**
BOOTH, CHARLES G.
  House on 92nd Street, The **III-1065**
BORG, SONIA
  Storm Boy **V-2277**
BOULANGER, DANIEL
  King of Hearts II-905
BOULLE, PIERRE
  Bridge on the River Kwai, The I-225
BOULTING, JOHN
  I'm All Right, Jack **III-1124**
BOULTING, ROY
  Seven Days to Noon **V-2150**
BOWER, DALLAS
  Henry V **III-1019**
BOWERS, WILLIAM
  Gunfighter, The **II-956**
  Night and Day IV-1713
  Support Your Local Sheriff **V-2380**
BOX, MURIEL
  Seventh Veil, The IV-1523

SCREENWRITER INDEX

SCREENWRITER INDEX

L

CINEMATOGRAPHER INDEX

(**Bold type** signifies Second Series)

MARLEY, PEVERELL
Adam Had Four Sons **I-21**
Alexander's Ragtime Band **I-33**
Count of Monte Cristo, The **II-531**
Dynamite **II-684**
Greatest Show on Earth, The II-697
Hound of the Baskervilles, The II-770
In Old Chicago II-825
Life with Father **III-1367**
Night and Day **IV-1713**
Pride of the Marines **IV-1924**
Winterset IV-1859
MARSH, OLIVER T.
Arsene Lupin **I-113**
Broadway Melody of 1940 I-245
David Copperfield **II-574**
Great Ziegfeld, The **II-936**
Rain III-1415
San Francisco III-1487
Sin of Madelon Claudet, The **V-2189**
Tale of Two Cities, A IV-1667
Women, The IV-1872
MARSHALL, WILLIAM
Check and Double Check **I-446**
MARTA, JACK
Cat Ballou **I-412**
Man from Music Mountain, The **IV-1501**
MARTIN, ROBERT
Sing as We Go IV-1557
MATÉ, RUDOLPH
Dodsworth I-471
Down to Earth **II-667**
Foreign Correspondent II-556
Gilda II-627
Love Affair **III-1446**
My Favorite Wife III-1175
Pride of the Yankees **IV-1927**
Stella Dallas IV-1631
That Hamilton Woman IV-1685
To Be or Not to Be IV-1743
MELLOR, WILLIAM C.
Bad Day at Black Rock I-116
Compulsion I-380
Diary of Anne Frank, The **II-642**
Giant II-616
Great McGinty, The II-693
Love in the Afternoon III-1018
Naked Spur, The **IV-1704**
Peyton Place III-1318
Place in the Sun, A III-1349
Road to Morocco III-1454
MESCALL, JOHN J.
Bride of Frankenstein, The I-222
Magnificent Obsession **IV-1488**
One More River **IV-1805**
Show Boat IV-1545
METTY, RUSSELL
All My Sons **I-50**
All That Heaven Allows **I-53**
Bringing Up Baby I-237
Captain Newman, M.D. **I-405**
Forever and a Day **II-815**
Imitation of Life **III-1132**
It's in the Bag **III-1198**
Magnificent Obsession **IV-1491**
Man of a Thousand Faces **IV-1513**
Midnight Lace **IV-1582**
Misfits, The III-1117
Mr. Peabody and the Mermaid **IV-1619**
Spartacus **V-2231**
Story of G.I. Joe, The IV-1638

Stranger, The **V-2294**
That's Entertainment **V-2443**
There's Always Tomorrow **VI-2457**
Touch of Evil **VI-2546**
Written on the Wind IV-1876
MILLER, ARTHUR
Anna and the King of Siam I-78
Gentleman's Agreement II-610
Gunfighter, The **II-956**
How Green Was My Valley II-776
Keys of the Kingdom, The **III-1251**
Letter to Three Wives, A **III-1355**
Mark of Zorro, The III-1070
Ox-Bow Incident, The III-1290
Razor's Edge, The III-1429
Song of Bernadette, The IV-1581
MILLER, ERNEST W.
Steel Helmet, The **V-2271**
MILLER, VIRGIL
Charlie Chan in Panama **I-437**
MILNER, VICTOR
Christmas in July **I-454**
Cleopatra I-356
Design for Living **II-609**
Lady Eve, The II-929
Love Me Tonight III-1022
Love Parade, The III-1026
One Hour with You III-1268
Palm Beach Story, The **IV-1853**
Plainsman, The III-1352
Strange Love of Martha Ivers, The **V-2290**
Trouble in Paradise **VI-2567**
Unfaithfully Yours **VI-2590**
Union Pacific **VI-2600**
MOCKRIDGE, CYRIL J.
Judge Priest **III-1236**
MOHR, HAL
Act of Murder, An **I-11**
County Chairman, The **II-538**
Destry Rides Again I-436
Four Poster, The **II-836**
Jazz Singer, The II-866
Member of the Wedding, The **IV-1561**
Midsummer Night's Dream, A **IV-1587**
Phantom of the Opera, The III-1322
Rancho Notorious **V-1976**
Watch on the Rhine IV-1820
Wild One, The **VI-2668**
MOORE, RICHARD
Life and Times of Judge Roy Bean, The **III-1363**
Reivers, The **V-2004**
Sometimes a Great Notion **V-2217**
MOORE, TED
Dr. No. **II-654**
From Russia with Love II-582
Goldfinger **II-904**
Man for All Seasons, A III-1053
Prime of Miss Jean Brodie, The III-1371
MORGAN, IRA
Great Gabbo, The **II-926**
Modern Times III-1134
MORRIS, OSWALD
Beat the Devil **I-190**
Entertainer, The **II-720**
Fiddler on the Roof II-527
Guns of Navarone, The II-700
Heaven Knows, Mr. Allison **III-1008**
Lolita **II-1413**
Look Back in Anger **III-1435**

CINEMATOGRAPHER INDEX

CINEMATOGRAPHER INDEX

WEST, BRIAN
  Apprenticeship of Duddy Kravitz, The   I-98
WEXLER, HASKELL
  America America   **I-68**
  Best Man, The   **I-199**
  Coming Home   I-374
  In the Heat of the Night   II-829
  Loved One, The   **III-1458**
  Medium Cool   **IV-1557**
  One Flew Over the Cuckoo's Nest   III-1265
  Thomas Crown Affair, The   **VI-2486**
  Who's Afraid of Virginia Woolf?   IV-1842
WHITE, LESTER
  Family Affair, A   **II-749**
  Love Finds Andy Hardy   III-1015
  Yellow Jack   **VI-2724**
WILCOX, JOHN
  Mouse That Roared, The   III-1159
  Outcast of the Islands   **IV-1838**
WILD, HARRY J.
  Gentlemen Prefer Blondes   II-613
  Murder, My Sweet   III-1164
WILLIAMS, BILLY
  Exorcist, The   II-506
  Sunday, Bloody Sunday   **V-2363**
  Women in Love   **VI-2715**
WILLIAMS, JOHN
  Yellow Submarine   **VI-2728**
WILLIS, GORDON
  All the President's Men   I-51
  Annie Hall   I-86
  Godfather, The   II-638
  Godfather, Part II, The   II-644
  Interiors   II-844
  Klute   II-915

Landlord, The   **III-1300**
Manhattan   III-1067
Paper Chase, The   III-1293
WORTH, DAVID
  Bronco Billy   **I-346**
WOTTITZ, WALTER
  Longest Day, The   **III-1424**
WYER, REGINALD H.
  Carry on Nurse   I-301
  Seventh Veil, The   IV-1523
WYNN, MANNY
  Luck of Ginger Coffey, The   **III-1464**

YOUNG, FREDDIE A.
  Bhowani Junction   **I-205**
  Caesar and Cleopatra   **I-383**
  Dr. Zhivago   I-468
  Goodbye, Mr. Chips   II-663
  Ivanhoe   **III-1202**
  Lawrence of Arabia   II-959
  Lust for Life   **IV-1467**
  Mogambo   III-1138
  Ryan's Daughter   III-1480
YOUNG, ROBERT
  Nothing but a Man   **IV-1749**

ZSIGMOND, VILMOS
  Cinderella Liberty   **I-462**
  Close Encounters of the Third Kind   I-362
  Deer Hunter, The   I-427
  Deliverance   I-432
  Hired Hand, The   **III-1031**
  McCabe and Mrs. Miller   **IV-1477**
  Sugarland Express, The   **V-2336**

EDITOR INDEX

(**Bold type** signifies Second Series)

FEHR, RUDI
 Dial M for Murder   I-440
 House of Wax   II-772
 Humoresque   II-782
 I Confess   **III-1080**
 Key Largo   II-885
 Watch on the Rhine   IV-1820
FELD, GEORGE
 Macomber Affair, The   **IV-1481**
FERRIOL, CAROLINE
 Stunt Man, The   **V-2321**
FIELDS, VERNA
 American Graffiti   I-56
 Jaws   II-863
 Medium Cool   **IV-1557**
 Paper Moon   **IV-1863**
 Sugarland Express, The   **V-2336**
FINK, JOHN F.
 Great Flamarian, The   **II-923**
FOWLER, GENE, JR.
 Beyond a Reasonable Doubt   **I-202**
FOWLER, HUGH S.
 Flaming Star   I-541
 Gentlemen Prefer Blondes   II-613
 Hemingway's Adventures of a Young
  Man   **III-1016**
 Life and Times of Judge Roy Bean, The   **III-1363**
 List of Adrian Messinger, The   **III-1386**
 Patton   III-1306
 Planet of the Apes   III-1355
 Seven Year Itch, The   IV-1519
 Will Success Spoil Rock Hunter?   **VI-2678**
FOWLER, MARGE
 Elmer Gantry   II-498
 Mr. Peabody and the Mermaid   **IV-1619**
 Separate Tables   IV-1506
 Three Faces of Eve, The   **VI-2498**
FREND, CHARLES
 Citadel, The   I-343
 Goodbye, Mr. Chips   II-663
 Major Barbara   **IV-1495**
FRIEDGEN, BUD
 That's Entertainment   **V-2443**
 That's Entertainment, Part II   **V-2447**
FRITCH, ROBERT
 One Potato, Two Potato   **IV-1809**
 Unfaithfully Yours   **VI-2590**

GARDNER, CYRIL
 Trespasser, The   **VI-2564**
GAY, NORMAN
 Exorcist, The   II-506
GERSTAD, HARRY
 Champion   **I-424**
 Crossfire   **II-548**
 Cyrano de Bergerac   I-400
 Gun Crazy   **II-949**
 High Noon   II-745
 Home of the Brave   **III-1045**
 Men, The   **IV-1565**
 Spiral Staircase, The   IV-1601
GIBBONS, JIM
 Modern Hero, A   **IV-1626**
GIBBS, ANTONY
 Fiddler on the Roof   II-527
 Jesus Christ Superstar   **III-1216**
 Knack, The   **III-1279**

 Loneliness of the Long Distance Runner,
  The   II-996
 Loved One, The   **III-1458**
 Luck of Ginger Coffey, The   **III-1464**
 Performance   III-1310
 Petulia   III-1314
 Taste of Honey, A   **V-2415**
 Tom Jones   IV-1760
 Walkabout   **VI-2633**
GIBSON, JAMES
 Blessed Event   **I-267**
GILMORE, STUART
 Airport   **I-27**
 Enemy Below, The   **II-712**
 Hail the Conquering Hero   **II-963**
 Lady Eve, The   II-929
 Million Dollar Legs   III-1101
 Miracle of Morgan's Creek, The   III-1111
 Palm Beach Story, The   **IV-1853**
 Sullivan's Travels   IV-1648
 War and Peace   **VI-2636**
GLADWELL, DAVID
 If. . . .   **III-1103**
 O Lucky Man!   III-1231
GLEN, JOHN
 Spy Who Loved Me, The   IV-1608
GOLDEN, ROBERT
 Night of the Hunter, The   III-1200
GOLDMAN, JOHN
 Man of Aran   **IV-1516**
GOLDSTONE, DUKE
 Destination Moon   **II-623**
GRAY, WILLIAM S.
 Great Ziegfeld, The   **II-936**
GREENBERG, JERRY
 Boys in the Band, The   **I-321**
 French Connection, The   II-574
 Kramer vs. Kramer   II-919
GREENBURG, CHRIS
 Muppet Movie, The   **IV-1668**
GREENE, DANFORD
 Blazing Saddles   I-184
 M*A*S*H   III-1083
 Rocky II   **V-2041**
GRIBBLE, BERNARD
 Death Wish   **II-600**
 I'll Never Forget Whatshisname   **III-1121**
 Man in the White Suit, The   III-1056
 Mark, The   **IV-1538**
GROSS, FRANK
 All That Heaven Allows   **I-53**
 Lawless Breed, The   II-956
 Operation Petticoat   **IV-1818**
GROSS, ROLAND
 None but the Lonely Heart   III-1217
 On Dangerous Ground   **IV-1784**
 Set-Up, The   **V-2142**
 Thing, The   IV-1712
GUIDICE, DON
 Three Days of the Condor   **VI-2494**
GUTHRIDGE, JOHN D.
 Browning Version, The   **I-353**
 Importance of Being Earnest, The   II-817
 League of Gentlemen, The   **III-1340**

HACKNEY, JOHN
 Monty Python and the Holy Grail   **IV-1633**

EDITOR INDEX

PERFORMER INDEX

ABASCAL, NATIVIDAD
Bananas **I-166**
ABBOTT, BUD
Buck Privates I-252
ABBOTT, JOHN
Gambit **II-862**
ABBOTT, PHILLIP
Sweet Bird of Youth **V-2387**
ABEL, WALTER
Arise My Love **I-107**
Fury II-596
Mr. Skeffington III-1125
ACOSTA, RUDOLPH
Flaming Star II-541
ADAIR, JEAN
Arsenic and Old Lace I-105
ADAIR, ROBERT
Journey's End **III-1229**
ADAM, RONALD
Seven Days to Noon **V-2150**
ADAMS, CASEY
Summer and Smoke **V-2339**
ADAMS, DOROTHY
Laura II-948
ADAMS, EDIE
Apartment, The I-90
Best Man, The **I-199**
Love with the Proper Stranger III-1029
ADAMS, JOE
Manchurian Candidate, The **IV-1523**
ADAMS, JONATHAN
Rocky Horror Picture Show, The **V-2044**
ADAMS, JULIE
Bright Victory I-234
Lawless Breed, The II-956
ADAMS, LESLIE
Crime Without Passion **II-541**
ADAMS, NICK
Pillow Talk III-1339
Rebel Without a Cause **V-1987**
ADAMS, STANLEY
Breakfast at Tiffany's I-215
Lilies of the Field **III-1374**
Requiem for a Heavyweight III-1444
ADDAMS, DAWN
Moon Is Blue, The **IV-1642**
ADDIE, ROBERT
Excalibur **II-730**
ADDY, WESLEY
Network III-1190
Seconds **V-2124**
ADLER, LUTHER
D.O.A. **II-560**
ADORF, MARIO
Major Dundee **IV-1498**
ADRIAN, IRIS
Roxie Hart **V-2063**
ADRIAN, MAX
Boy Friend, The **I-318**
Henry V **III-1019**
AGUTTER, JENNY
Walkabout **VI-2633**
AGAR, JOHN
Sands of Iwo Jima **V-2080**
She Wore a Yellow Ribbon **V-2171**

AHERNE, BRIAN
Forever and a Day **II-815**
I Confess **III-1080**
Juarez **III-1232**
My Sister Eileen **IV-1693**
Night to Remember, A **IV-1728**
Sylvia Scarlett **V-2404**
Titanic **VI-2522**
AKED, MURIEL
Colonel Blimp **II-489**
Happiest Days of Your Life, The **III-978**
AKINS, CLAUDE
Caine Mutiny, The I-275
Inherit the Wind **III-1148**
Rio Bravo **V-2018**
ALBEE, JOSH
Jeremiah Johnson **III-1209**
ALBERNI, LUIS
Anthony Adverse **I-96**
Count of Monte Cristo, The **II-531**
Easy Living **II-688**
One Night of Love III-1275
Roberta **V-2029**
Svengali **V-2384**
Topaze **VI-2537**
ALBERT, EDDIE
Attack! **I-130**
Brother Rat **I-349**
Captain Newman, M.D. **I-405**
I'll Cry Tomorrow **III-1117**
Longest Yard **III-1431**
Oklahoma! III-1246
Roman Holiday **V-2050**
Sun Also Rises, The **V-2352**
ALBERTSON, FRANK
Bachelor Mother **I-149**
Ah, Wilderness! I-26
Alice Adams I-33
Fury II-596
ALBERTSON, JACK
Poseidon Adventure, The III-1361
ALBRIGHT, LOLA
Champion **I-424**
ALBRIGHT, WALLY
Trespasser, The **VI-2564**
ALDA, ROBERT
Imitation of Life **III-1132**
ALDERSON, ERVILLE
County Chairman, The **II-538**
ALDON, MARI
Summertime **V-2348**
ADREDGE, TOM
Rain People, The **V-1972**
ALEXANDER, JANE
All the President's Men I-51
Brubaker **I-356**
Kramer vs. Kramer II-919
ALEXANDER, JOHN
Arsenic and Old Lace I-105
Jolson Story, The II-877
Marrying Kind, The **IV-1544**
ALEXANDER, KATHERINE
Barretts of Wimpole Street, The **I-181**
Death Takes a Holiday I-424
In Name Only II-822
ALEXANDER, RICHARD
Flash Gordon **II-796**
Law and Order **III-1337**

(**Bold type** signifies Second Series)

PERFORMER INDEX

AXELROD, JACK
  Bananas **I-166**
AYLESWORTH, ARTHUR
  Marked Woman **IV-1541**
AYLMER, FELIX
  Chalk Garden, The **I-418**
  Hamlet II-708
  Henry V **III-1019**
  Ivanhoe **III-1202**
  Separate Tables IV-1506
AYRES, LEW
  Advise and Consent I-18
  All Quiet on the Western Front I-43
  Dark Mirror, The **II-567**
  Dr. Kildare's Strange Case **II-650**
  Holiday II-758
  Johnny Belinda **III-1220**

BABY BIFFIE
  Penny Serenade **IV-1883**
BABY JANE
  Imitation of Life **III-1128**
BACALL, LAUREN
  Big Sleep, The I-162
  Confidential Agent **II-507**
  Designing Woman **II-612**
  Key Largo II-885
  Shootist, The IV-1542
  To Have and Have Not IV-1752
  Written on the Wind IV-1876
BACH, BARBARA
  Spy Who Loved Me, The IV-1608
BACKUS, JIM
  Francis in the Navy **II-839**
  Man of a Thousand Faces IV-1513
  Pat and Mike **IV-1873**
  Rebel Without a Cause **V-1987**
BACLANOVA, OLGA
  Freaks **II-842**
BADDELEY, HERMIONE
  Belles of St. Trinian's, The **I-193**
  Christmas Carol, A I-336
  Passport to Pimlico III-1299
  Unsinkable Molly Brown, The IV-1808
BADEL, ALAN
  This Sporting Life IV-1726
BADHAM, MARY
  To Kill a Mockingbird IV-1756
BAER, BUDDY
  Quo Vadis III-1407
BAER, MAX
  Harder They Fall, The **III-986**
BAER, PARLEY
  Young Lions, The **VI-2741**
BAGGETT, LYNN
  D.O.A. **II-560**
BAILEY, PEARL
  Landlord, The **III-1300**
BAINTER, FAY
  Children's Hour, The I-329
  Human Comedy, The **III-1073**
  Jezebel II-870
  Our Town **IV-1834**
  Woman of the Year **VI-2705**
BAIRD, ANTONY
  Dead of Night **II-595**

BAIRD, HARRY
  Whisperers, The **VI-2654**
BAKER, ART
  Farmer's Daughter, The **II-760**
BAKER, CARROLL
  Baby Doll **I-141**
  Big Country, The **I-212**
  Cheyenne Autumn **I-449**
  Giant II-616
  How the West Was Won **III-1069**
BAKER, DIANE
  Diary of Anne Frank, The **II-642**
  Marnie III-1076
  Prize, The **IV-1941**
BAKER, FAY
  Star, The **V-2260**
BAKER, HYLDA
  Saturday Night and Sunday Morning **V-2086**
BAKER, JOE DON
  Junior Bonner **III-1247**
BAKER, KENNY
  At the Circus **I-127**
BAKER, KENNY
  Star Wars IV-1623
BAKER, STANLEY
  Accident **I-4**
  Alexander the Great **I-30**
  Blind Date **I-270**
  Concrete Jungle, The **II-503**
  Guns of Navarone, The II-700
  Richard III **V-2014**
  Zulu **VI-2749**
BAKEWELL, WILLIAM
  All Quiet on the Western Front I-43
BALABAN, BOB
  Close Encounters of the Third Kind I-362
  Girl Friends **II-882**
BALDWIN, EVELYN
  Struggle, The IV-1645
BALFOUR, BETTY
  Evergreen **II-728**
BALFOUR, KATHARINE
  America America **I-68**
BALKIN, KAREN
  Children's Hour, The I-329
BALL, JANE
  Keys of the Kingdom, The **III-1251**
BALL, LUCILLE
  Follow the Fleet II-549
  Stage Door **V-2242**
BALSAM, MARTIN
  All the President's Men I-51
  Breakfast at Tiffany's I-215
  Little Big Man **II-981**
  Psycho III-1391
  Seven Days in May **V-2144**
  Thousand Clowns, A IV-1728
  Twelve Angry Men IV-1783
BANCROFT, ANNE
  Elephant Man, The **II-705**
  Graduate, The II-667
  Miracle Worker, The **IV-1601**
  Pumpkin Eater, The **IV-1947**
BANCROFT, GEORGE
  Angels with Dirty Faces I-72
  Mr. Deeds Goes to Town **IV-1613**
  Stagecoach IV-1612

LXXXIV

BUCKLER, JOHN
David Copperfield **II-574**
BUCKLEY, BETTY
Carrie **I-408**
BUJOLD, GENEVIEVE
King of Hearts II-905
BUKA, DONALD
Watch on the Rhine IV-1820
BULL, JOHN
Loneliness of the Long Distance Runner, The II-996
BULL, PETER
Dr. Strangelove I-465
BULLOCH, JEREMY
Virgin and the Gypsy, The **VI-2619**
BULOFF, JOSEPH
Silk Stockings IV-1553
Somebody Up There Likes Me **V-2214**
BUNNAGE, AVIS
L-Shaped Room, The II-925
Loneliness of the Long Distance Runner, The II-996
To Sir with Love **VI-2530**
Whisperers, The **VI-2654**
BUNSTON, HERBERT
Last of Mrs. Cheyney, The **III-1310**
BUONO, VICTOR
What Ever Happened to Baby Jane? VI-2649
BUPP, TOM
It's a Gift **III-1195**
BURDEN, HUGH
No Love for Johnnie **IV-1732**
BURGESS, DOROTHY
In Old Arizona **III-1142**
Modern Hero, A **IV-1626**
BURGESS, HELEN
Plainsman, The III-1352
BURGHOFF, GARY
M*A*S*H **III-1083**
BURHAN, TERRY
Imitation of Life **III-1132**
BURKE, ALFRED
Angry Silence, The **I-89**
BURKE, BILLIE
Bill of Divorcement, A **I-239**
Craig's Wife I-397
Dinner at Eight I-444
Father of the Bride **II-770**
Sergeant Rutledge **V-2135**
Topper IV-1770
Wizard of Oz, The IV-1867
BURKE, JAMES
At the Circus I-127
Night to Remember, A **IV-1728**
Ruggles of Red Gap **V-2066**
BURKE, KATHLEEN
Island of Last Souls **III-1185**
Lives of a Bengal Lancer **III-1404**
BURKE, PAUL
Thomas Crown Affair, The **VI-2486**
BURKE, WALTER
All the President's Men **I-57**
President's Analyst, The **IV-1916**
Support Your Local Sheriff **V-2380**
BURNET, DON
Jailhouse Rock **III-1205**

BURNETTE, SMILEY
Man from Music Mountain, The **IV-1501**
BURNS, BART
Fear Strikes Out **II-773**
BURNS, JACK
Night They Raided Minsky's, The **IV-1725**
BURNS, MARK
Virgin and the Gypsy, The **VI-2619**
BURR, RAYMOND
Place in the Sun, A III-1349
Rear Window **V-1983**
BURSTYN, ELLEN
Alice Doesn't Live Here Anymore **I-44**
Exorcist, The II-506
Harry and Tonto **III-989**
Last Picture Show, The **III-1314**
BURTON, CLARENCE
Unholy Three, The **VI-2597**
BURTON, FREDERICK
One Way Passage **IV-1812**
BURTON, NORMAN
Save the Tiger **V-2096**
BURTON, RICHARD
Alexander the Great **I-30**
Becket I-138
Bitter Victory **I-259**
Cleopatra **I-466**
Look Back in Anger **III-1435**
Night of the Iguana, The **IV-1721**
Robe, The **V-2025**
Spy Who Came in from the Cold, The IV-1604
Who's Afraid of Virginia Woolf? IV-1842
Zulu VI-2749
BURTON, ROBERT
Big Heat, The **I-216**
Broken Lance **I-343**
BURTON, WENDELL
Sterile Cuckoo, The **V-2274**
BUSH, BILLY "GREEN"
Alice Doesn't Live Here Anymore **I-44**
Five Easy Pieces **II-538**
BUSH, JAMES
You Can't Cheat an Honest Man IV-1891
BUSHELL, ANTHONY
Journey's End **III-1299**
BUTTERWORTH, CHARLES
Love Me Tonight III-1022
Magnificent Obsession **IV-1488**
BUTTONS, RED
Longest Day, The **III-1424**
Poseidon Adventure, The III-1361
Sayonara **V-2099**
They Shoot Horses Don't They? **VI-2470**
BYINGTON, SPRING
Ah, Wilderness! I-26
Charge of the Light Brigade, The **I-427**
Devil and Miss Jones, The **II-636**
Enchanted Cottage, The II-502
Family Affair, A **II-749**
Heaven Can Wait II-724
In the Good Old Summertime **III-1145**
Little Women II-988
Roxie Hart **V-2063**
You Can't Take It with You **VI-2734**
BYRNE, ANNE
Manhattan III-1067

COTTEN, JOSEPH
  Citizen Kane I-346
  Duel in the Sun **II-676**
  Farmer's Daughter, The **II-760**
  Gaslight II-600
  Magnificent Ambersons, The III-1036
  Petulia III-1314
  Portrait of Jennie III-1358
  Shadow of a Doubt IV-1526
  Since You Went Away **V-2193**
  Third Man, The IV-1719
COUGHLIN, KEVIN
  Defiant Ones, The **II-604**
COULOURIS, GEORGE
  Citizen Kane I-346
  None but the Lonely Heart III-1217
  Outcast of the Islands **IV-1838**
  Watch on the Rhine IV-1820
COURTENAY, TOM
  Billy Liar **I-245**
  Dr. Zhivago I-468
  King and Country **III-1257**
  King Rat II-911
  Loneliness of the Long Distance Runner, The **II-996**
COURTLAND, JEROME
  Battleground **I-184**
COURTNEIDGE, CICELY
  L-Shaped Room, The **II-925**
COWAN, JEROME
  Maltese Falcon, The III-1049
  Miracle on 34th Street **IV-1597**
  Shall We Dance IV-1529
COWARD, NOEL
  In Which We Serve **II-833**
  Our Man in Havana **IV-1831**
  Scoundrel, The **V-2113**
COWLING, BRUCE
  Battleground **I-184**
  Stratton Story, The **V-2303**
COX, RONNY
  Deliverance I-432
  Onion Field, The **IV-1815**
COY, WALTER
  Lusty Men, The **IV-1471**
  Searchers, The IV-1502
  So Big **V-2205**
CRABBE, BUSTER
  Flash Gordon **II-796**
CRAIG, HELEN
  Snake Pit, The **V-2202**
  They Live by Night **VI-2467**
CRAIG, JAMES
  Devil and Daniel Webster, The **II-632**
  Human Comedy, The **III-1073**
  Kitty Foyle **III-1276**
CRAIG, MICHAEL
  Angry Silence, The **I-89**
CRAIG, WENDY
  I'll Never Forget Whatshisname **III-1121**
  Servant, The **V-2138**
CRAIN, JEANNE
  Leave Her to Heaven II-963
  Letter to Three Wives, A **III-1355**
  Margie **IV-1533**
  Pinky III-1346
CRANE, NORMA
  Fiddler on the Roof I-527
  Tea and Sympathy **V-2419**

CRAVAT, NICK
  Crimson Pirate, The **II-545**
CRAVAT, NOEL
  5,000 Fingers of Doctor T., The **II-792**
CRAVEN, FRANK
  Our Town **IV-1834**
CRAVEN, JOHN
  Human Comedy, The **III-1073**
CRAWFORD, BRODERICK
  All the King's Men **I-57**
  Born Yesterday I-209
  Larceny, Inc. **III-1304**
CRAWFORD, JOAN
  Grand Hotel II-672
  Humoresque II-782
  Johnny Guitar II-874
  Mildred Pierce III-1098
  Rain III-1415
  What Ever Happened to Baby Jane? **VI-2649**
  Women, The IV-1872
CRAWFORD, MICHAEL
  Funny Thing Happened on the Way to the Forum, A **II-592**
  Knack, The **III-1279**
CREGAR, LAIRD
  Blood and Sand **I-280**
  Heaven Can Wait **II-724**
  Lodger, The **III-1409**
CRENNA, RICHARD
  Wait Until Dark **VI-2630**
CREWS, LAURA HOPE
  Angel **I-82**
  Camille **I-285**
  One Foot in Heaven **IV-1798**
CRIBBINS, BERNARD
  Frenzy **II-849**
CRINO, ISA
  Lilies of the Field **III-1374**
CRISP, DONALD
  Charge of the Light Brigade, The **I-427**
  Dawn Patrol I-416
  Dr. Jekyll and Mr. Hyde I-461
  How Green Was My Valley II-776
  Jezebel II-870
  Juarez **III-1232**
  Lassie Come Home **III-1307**
  Last Hurrah, The **II-945**
  Life of Émile Zola, The **II-970**
  National Velvet **IV-1710**
  Old Maid, The **IV-1771**
  Private Lives of Elizabeth and Essex, The III-1383
  Red Dust III-1438
  Svengali **V-2384**
  Uninvited, The IV-1801
  Woman Rebels, A **VI-2709**
  Wuthering Heights IV-1884
CROCKER, HENRY
  Gentleman Jim **II-868**
CROMWELL, JOHN
  3 Women **VI-2514**
CROMWELL, RICHARD
  Jezebel II-870
  Lives of a Bengal Lancer **III-1404**
  Young Mr. Lincoln IV-1897
CRONYN, HUME
  Brute Force **I-360**

C

CI

DALE, ESTHER
Awful Truth, The I-109
Crime Without Passion II-541
Egg and I, The II-695
Margie IV-1533
DALIO, MARCEL
To Have and Have Not IV-1752
Wilson VI-2682
DALL, JOHN
Champion I-424
Corn Is Green, The I-387
Gun Crazy II-949
Spartacus V-2231
DALLIMORE, MAURICE
Collector, The II-494
DALTON, AUDREY
Separate Tables IV-1506
Titanic VI-2522
DALTON, TIMOTHY
Lion in Winter, The III-1382
DANA, LEORA
Some Came Running V-2211
3:10 to Yuma VI-2511
DANE, KARL
Big House, The I-220
D'ANGELO, BEVERLY
Coal Miner's Daughter I-365
Hair II-966
DANIELL, HENRY
Body Snatcher, The I-198
Camille I-285
Girls, Les II-885
Great Dictator, The II-678
Jane Eyre II-860
Lust for Life IV-1467
Philadelphia Story, The III-1330
Private Lives of Elizabeth and Essex,
The III-1383
Witness for the Prosecution IV-1862
DANIELS, ANTHONY
Star Wars IV-1623
DANIELS, BEBE
Rio Rita V-2022
Silver Dollar V-2186
42nd Street II-561
DANIELS, HENRY H., JR.
Meet Me in St. Louis III-1091
DANIELS, WILLIAM
Graduate, The II-667
President's Analyst, The IV-1916
Thousand Clowns, A IV-1728
Two for the Road VI-2576
DANIELSON, CLIFF
Johnny Eager III-1224
DANN, ROGER
I Confess III-1080
DANNER, BLYTHE
Hearts of the West III-1005
DANO, ROYAL
Red Badge of Courage, The V-1994
Trouble with Harry, The IV-1777
DANOVA, CESARE
Mean Streets IV-1554
DANQUAH, PAUL
Taste of Honey, A V-2415
DANSON, TED
Onion Field, The IV-1815

DANTINE, HELMUT
Alexander the Great I-30
DANTON, RAY
I'll Cry Tomorrow III-1117
DARBY, KIM
True Grit IV-1780
DARCEL, DENISE
Battleground I-184
D'ARCY, ALEXANDER
Awful Truth, The I-109
DARDEN, SEVERN
Hire Hand, The III-1031
President's Analyst, The IV-1916
DARIN, BOBBY
Captain Newman, M.D. I-405
DARLING, JOAN
President's Analyst, The IV-1916
DARNELL, LINDA
Anna and the King of Siam I-78
Blood and Sand I-280
Letter to Three Wives, A III-1355
Mark of Zorro, The III-1070
My Darling Clementine IV-1685
No Way Out IV-1735
Unfaithfully Yours VI-2590
DARR, VONDELL
On Trial IV-1792
DARREN, JAMES
Guns of Navarone, The II-700
DARRIEUX, DANIELLE
Alexander the Great I-30
Five Fingers II-784
DARROW, JOHN
Hell's Angels II-734
DARWELL, JANE
Caged I-386
Craig's Wife I-397
Devil and Daniel Webster, The II-632
Grapes of Wrath, The II-675
Jesse James III-1212
Last Hurrah, The II-945
Sun Shines Bright, The V-2355
There's Always Tomorrow VI-2457
Wagonmaster VI-2625
DAUPHIN, CLAUDE
Barbarella I-170
Two for the Road VI-2576
DAVALOS, RICHARD
East of Eden I-488
DAVENPORT, DORIS
Westerner, The IV-1830
DAVENPORT, HARRY
Hunchback of Notre Dame, The II-786
King's Row III-1265
Larceny, Inc. III-1304
Meet Me in St. Louis III-1091
One Foot in Heaven IV-1798
Ox-Bow Incident, The III-1290
Princess O'Rourke IV-1930
Scoundrel, The V-2113
DAVENPORT, NIGEL
Man for All Seasons, A III-1053
DAVID, THAYER
Little Big Man II-981
Save the Tiger V-2096
DAVIDSON, WILLIAM B.
Sun Valley Serenade V-2359

ECCLES, JANE
  Look Back in Anger **III-1435**
EDA-YOUNG, BARBARA
  Serpico IV-1512
EDDY, NELSON
  Naughty Marietta III-1186
  Phantom of the Opera, The III-1322
EDEN, BARBARA
  Flaming Star II-541
EDEN, CHANA
  Wind Across the Everglades **VI-2687**
EDEN, MARK
  Séance on a Wet Afternoon **V-2120**
EDESON, ROBERT
  Home Towners, The **III-1048**
EDWARDS, CLIFF
  Dumbo **II-680**
  Pinocchio **IV-1902**
  Sin of Madelon Claudet, The **V-2189**
EDWARDS, OLGA
  Christmas Carol, A I-336
EDWARDS, JAMES
  Bright Victory I-234
  Home of the Brave **III-1045**
  Member of the Wedding, The **IV-1561**
  Steel Helmet, The **V-2271**
EDWARDS, VINCE
  Three Faces of Eve, The **VI-2498**
EGAN, EDDIE
  French Connection, The II-574
EGAN, PETER
  Hireling, The **III-1034**
EGAN, RICHARD
  Summer Place, A **V-2344**
EGGAR, SAMANTHA
  Collector, The **II-494**
  Seven-Per-cent Solution, The **V-2153**
EGLEVSKY, ANDRE
  Limelight II-978
EIKENBERRY, JILL
  Arthur **I-116**
EKBERG, ANITA
  War and Peace **VI-2636**
EKLAND, BRITT
  Night They Raided Minsky's, The **IV-1725**
ELAM, JACK
  Support Your Local Sheriff **V-2380**
ELDREDGE, JOHN
  Dangerous **II-564**
ELCAR, DANA
  Sting, The IV-1634
ELDRIDGE, FLORENCE
  Act of Murder, An **I-11**
  Inherit the Wind **III-1148**
  Mary of Scotland **IV-1547**
  Misérables, Les III-1114
  Modern Hero, A **IV-1626**
ELG, TAINA
  Girls, Les **II-885**
ELLERBY, HARRY
  Desk Set **II-616**
ELLIMAN, YVONNE
  Jesus Christ Superstar **III-1216**
ELLINGTON, DUKE
  Anatomy of a Murder **I-75**
  Check and Double Check I-446

ELLIOT, LAURA
  Strangers on a Train **V-2298**
ELLIOTT, DENHOLM
  Apprenticeship of Duddy Kravitz, The I-98
  Cruel Sea, The **II-551**
  Holly and the Ivy, The **III-1038**
  King Rat II-911
  Night They Raided Minsky's, The **IV-1725**
  Raiders of the Lost Ark **V-1966**
  Robin and Marian **V-2034**
ELLIOTT, JANE
  One Is a Lonely Number **IV-1802**
ELLIS, ANTONIA
  Boy Friend, The **I-318**
ELLIS, DIANE
  Laughter **III-1333**
ELLIS, EDWARD
  Fury II-596
  Thin Man, The IV-1709
  Winterset IV-1859
ELLISON, JAMES
  I Walked with a Zombie **III-1093**
  Plainsman, The III-1352
ELSOM, ISOBEL
  Ladies in Retirement **III-1282**
  Monsieur Verdoux **IV-1630**
ELTON, EDMUND
  Stella Dallas IV-1631
ELZY, RUBY
  Emperor Jones, The **II-709**
EMANUEL, ELZIE
  Intruder in the Dust **III-1166**
  Sun Shines Bright, The **V-2355**
EMERSON, HOPE
  Caged **I-386**
EMERTON, ROY
  Henry V **III-1019**
EMERY, DICK
  Yellow Submarine **VI-2728**
EMERY, GILBERT
  One More River **IV-1805**
EMERY, JOHN
  Here Comes Mr. Jordan II-737
EMHARDT, ROBERT
  3:10 to Yuma **VI-2511**
EMMETT, E. V. H.
  On Approval **IV-1781**
ENGEL, SUSAN
  Butley **I-367**
ENRIQUEZ, RENE
  Bananas **I-166**
ERDMAN, RICHARD
  Men, The **IV-1565**
  Stalag 17 **V-2256**
ERICKSON, JOHN
  Bad Day at Black Rock I-116
ERICKSON, LEIF
  Tea and Sympathy **V-2419**
ERSKINE, EILEEN
  Great Expectations II-685
ESMOND, CARL
  Ministry of Fear **IV-1590**
ETHIER, ALPHONZ
  Law and Order **III-1337**
EUSTREL, ANTHONY
  Caesar and Cleopatra **I-383**

GARLAND, JUDY
  Clock, The **I-472**
  Easter Parade I-491
  Girl Crazy II-630
  Harvey Girls, The **III-992**
  In the Good Old Summertime **III-1145**
  Judgment at Nuremberg **III-1239**
  Love Finds Andy Hardy III-1015
  Meet Me in St. Louis III-1091
  Pirate, The **IV-1906**
  Star Is Born, A IV-1619
  Wizard of Oz, The IV-1864

GARLAND, TIMOTHY
  Charlie Bubbles **I-433**

GARNER, DON
  My Darling Clementine **IV-1685**

GARNER, JAMES
  Americanization of Emily, The I-64
  Children's Hour, The I-329
  Great Escape, The II-682
  Hour of the Gun **III-1061**
  Sayonara **V-2099**
  Support Your Local Sheriff **V-2380**

GARNER, PEGGY ANN
  Jane Eyre II-860
  Tree Grows in Brooklyn, A **VI-2561**

GARR, TERI
  Close Encounters of the Third Kind I-362
  Conversation, The **II-515**

GARRETT, BETTY
  On the Town III-1259

GARSON, GREER
  Goodbye, Mr. Chips II-663
  Julius Caesar II-881
  Madame Curie III-1033
  Mrs. Miniver III-1131
  Pride and Prejudice **IV-1919**
  Random Harvest **V-1979**

GARY, HAROLD
  French Connection, The II-574

GARY, LORRAINE
  Jaws II-863

GASSMAN, VITTORIO
  War and Peace **VI-2636**

GATES, LARRY
  Above and Beyond **I-1**
  In the Heat of the Night II-829
  Invasion of the Body Snatchers II-848

GATLIFF, FRANK
  Ipcress File, The **III-1175**

GAUNT, VALERIE
  Horror of Dracula II-762

GAVIN, JOHN
  Imitation of Life **III-1132**
  Midnight Lace **IV-1582**
  Psycho III-1391
  Spartacus **V-2231**

GAYNOR, JANET
  Star Is Born, A IV-1616

GAYNOR, MITZI
  Girls, Les **II-885**
  South Pacific IV-1589

GAZZARA, BEN
  Anatomy of a Murder **I-75**
  Husbands **III-1076**

GAZZO, MICHAEL
  Godfather, Part II, The II-644

GEAR, LUELLA
  Carefree I-292

GEDDES, BARBARA BEL
  Caught **I-415**
  Panic in the Streets **IV-1860**

GEER, WILL
  Bright Victory I-234
  Broken Arrow I-248
  In Cold Blood **III-1138**
  Intruder in the Dust **III-1166**
  Jeremiah Johnson **III-1209**
  Reivers, The **V-2004**
  Seconds **V-2124**
  Winchester '73 IV-1848

GEESON, JUDY
  To Sir with Love **VI-2530**

GELIN, DANIEL
  Man Who Knew Too Much, The **IV-1519**

GENN, LEO
  Moby Dick **IV-1623**
  Quo Vadis III-1411
  Snake Pit, The **V-2202**

GENTLE, LILI
  Will Success Spoil Rock Hunter? **VI-2678**

GENTRY, RACE
  Lawless Breed, The II-956

GEOFFREY, PAUL
  Excalibur **II-731**

GEORGE, GLADYS
  Maltese Falcon, The III-1049
  Roaring Twenties, The III-1458

GEORGE, SUSAN
  Looking Glass War, The **III-1439**
  Straw Dogs **V-2306**

GEORGES-PICOT, OLGA
  Love and Death **III-1449**

GERAY, STEVEN
  Big Sky, The **I-229**
  Gilda II-627
  In a Lonely Place **III-1135**
  Moon and Sixpence, The **IV-1638**

GERICKE, EUGENE
  I Was a Male War Bride **III-1098**

GERRARD, CHARLES
  Journey's End **III-1229**

GHOSTLEY, ALICE
  Grease **II-918**

GIALLELIS, STATHIS
  America America **I-68**

GIBSON, HENRY
  Nashville III-1181

GIBSON, MIMI
  Wings of Eagles, The IV-1853

GIBSON, RICHARD
  Go-Between, The II-633

GIBSON, VIRGINIA
  Seven Brides for Seven Brothers IV-1515

GIELGUD, JOHN
  Arthur **I-116**
  Becket I-138
  Elephant Man, The **II-705**
  Julius Caesar II-881
  Loved One, The **III-1458**
  Oh! What a Lovely War **IV-1767**
  Richard III **V-2014**

GIERASCH, STEFAN
  Jeremiah Johnson **III-1209**

KANTOR, MACKINLAY
  Wind Across the Everglades **VI-2687**
KAPOOR, S. P.
  Look Back in Anger **III-1435**
KARAM, ELENA
  America America **I-68**
KARLIN, MIRIAM
  Clockwork Orange, A **I-475**
KARLOFF, BORIS
  Body Snatcher, The I-198
  Bride of Frankenstein, The I-222
  Frankenstein II-570
  Lost Patrol, The **III-1443**
  Mummy, The **IV-1664**
  Scarface: The Shame of the Nation III-1490
KARLWEIS, OSCAR
  Five Fingers **II-784**
KARNS, ROSCOE
  It Happened One Night II-852
  Twentieth Century IV-1791
KARRAS, ALEX
  Blazing Saddles I-184
KASTNER, PETER
  You're a Big Boy Now **VI-2746**
KASZNAR, KURT
  Kiss Me Kate **III-1272**
  Lili **III-1371**
KATH, KATHERINE
  Moulin Rouge III-1154
KATZ, WILLIAM
  Carrie **I-408**
KAVANAUGH, DORRIE
  Hester Street II-741
KAYE, DANNY
  Court Jester, The I-393
KAYE, MOIRA
  Taste of Honey, A **V-2415**
KAYE, STUBBY
  Cat Ballou **I-412**
KAZAN, ELIA
  Blues in the Night **I-294**
KEACH, STACY
  Fat City **II-763**
  Heart Is a Lonely Hunter, The **III-1002**
  Life and Times of Judge Roy Bean, The **III-1363**
KEAMS, GERALDINE
  Outlaw Josey Wales, The **IV-1842**
KEAN, MARIE
  Barry Lyndon I-132
KEANE, BASIL
  Harder They Come, The **III-982**
KEARNEY, MICHAEL
  All the Way Home **I-62**
KEATING, LARRY
  Above and Beyond **I-1**
  Daddy Long Legs I-404
KEATON, BUSTER
  Film II-531
  Forever and a Day **II-815**
  Funny Thing Happened on the Way to the Forum, A II-592
  In the Good Old Summertime **III-1145**
  Limelight II-978
KEATON, DIANE
  Annie Hall I-86

Godfather, The II-638
Godfather, Part II, The II-644
Interiors II-844
Love and Death **III-1449**
Lovers and Other Strangers **III-1461**
Manhattan III-1067
Play It Again, Sam **IV-1909**
Sleeper **V-2199**
KEATS, STEVEN
  Death Wish **II-600**
  Hester Street II-741
KEDROVA, LILA
  Zorba the Greek IV-1904
KEEFER, DON
  Riot in Cell Block 11 III-1451
KEEL, HOWARD
  Calamity Jane **I-389**
  Kiss Me Kate **III-1272**
  Seven Brides for Seven Brothers IV-1515
  Show Boat IV-1549
KEELER, LEONARDE
  Call Northside 777 I-280
KEELER, RUBY
  Footlight Parade **II-800**
  42nd Street II-561
  Gold Diggers of 1933 **II-900**
KEEN, GEOFFREY
  Angry Silence, The **I-89**
  Born Free **I-312**
  Cry the Beloved Country **II-554**
  Doctor in the House **II-646**
  Genevieve **II-865**
  No Love for Johnnie **IV-1732**
KEEN, PAT
  Kind of Loving, A II-894
KEENE, TOM
  Our Daily Bread III-1284
KEHOE, JACK
  Serpico IV-1512
KEITEL, HARVEY
  Alice Doesn't Live Here Anymore **I-44**
  Mean Streets **IV-1554**
  Taxi Driver IV-1678
KEITH, BRIAN
  Parent Trap, The III-1296
  Russians Are Coming, The Russians Are Coming, The **V-2073**
KEITH, DAVID
  Brubaker **I-356**
KEITH, IAN
  Cleopatra I-356
  Mary of Scotland **IV-1547**
  Nightmare Alley III-1207
  Queen Christina III-1404
  Three Musketeers, The **VI-2505**
KEITH, ROBERT
  Boomerang! **I-309**
  Love Me or Leave Me **III-1455**
  Wild One, The **VI-2668**
  Written on the Wind IV-1876
KELLAWAY, CECIL
  Guess Who's Coming to Dinner? **II-945**
  Harvey II-720
  I Married a Witch II-806
  Interrupted Melody **III-1162**
  Postman Always Rings Twice, The III-1365
  Wuthering Heights IV-1884

PERFORMER INDEX

KONARSKI, C.
  Christmas Carol, A I-336
KONG, AH
  Tabu **V-2408**
KONSTANTIN, LEOPOLDINE
  Notorious **IV-1752**
KORMAN, HARVEY
  Blazing Saddles I-184
  High Anxiety **III-1027**
KOSHETZ, NINA
  Algiers **I-37**
KOSSOFF, DAVID
  Mouse That Roared, The III-1159
KOTTO, YAPHET
  Alien I-37
  Brubaker **I-356**
  Nothing but a Man **IV-1749**
  Thomas Crown Affair, The **VI-2486**
KOVACS, ERNIE
  Our Man in Havana **IV-1831**
KREUGER, KURT
  Enemy Below, The **II-712**
  Unfaithfully Yours **VI-2590**
KRISTOFFERSON, KRIS
  Alice Doesn't Live Here Anymore **I-44**
  Blume in Love **I-298**
KROEGER, BARRY
  Gun Crazy **II-949**
KRUGER, ALMA
  Craig's Wife I-397
  Dr. Kildare's Strange Case **II-650**
  Saboteur **V-2076**
  These Three **IV-1693**
KRUGER, HARDY
  Barry Lyndon I-132
  Blind Date **I-270**
KRUGER, OTTO
  Dr. Ehrlich's Magic Bullet I-454
  High Noon II-745
  Magnificent Obsession **IV-1491**
  Saboteur **V-2076**
  They Won't Forget **VI-2474**
KRUGMAN, LOU
  I Want to Live! II-813
KRUSCHEN, JACK
  Apartment, The I-90
  Unsinkable Molly Brown, The IV-1808
KUHN, MICKEY
  Red River **V-2000**
  Strange Love of Martha Ivers, The **V-2290**
KULKY, HENRY
  5,000 Fingers of Doctor T., The **II-792**
KUN, MAGDA
  Dead of Night **II-595**
KUNEY, EVA LEE
  Penny Serenade **IV-1883**
KURTZ, MARCIA JEAN
  Dog Day Afternoon I-474
  Panic in Needle Park, The **IV-1856**

LACEY, CATHERINE
  Tight Little Island IV-1738
LACEY, RONALD
  Raiders of the Lost Ark **V-1966**
LACY, JERRY
  Play It Again, Sam **IV-1909**

LADD, ALAN
  Blue Dahlia, The **I-283**
  Great Gatsby, The **II-929**
  Shane IV-1534
  This Gun for Hire **VI-2481**
LADD, DIANE
  Alice Doesn't Live Here Anymore **I-44**
LAFFAN, PATRICIA
  Quo Vadis III-1411
LAHR, BERT
  Night They Raided Minsky's, The **IV-1725**
  Wizard of Oz, The IV-1867
LAING, HUGH
  Brigadoon **I-339**
LAIRE, JUDSON
  Ugly American, The **VI-2584**
LAKE, ARTHUR
  Blondie on a Budget **I-277**
  Topper IV-1770
LAKE, VERONICA
  Blue Dahlia, The **I-283**
  I Married a Witch **II-806**
  Sullivan's Travels IV-1648
  This Gun for Hire **VI-2481**
LALARA, CEDRIC
  Last Wave, The **III-1325**
LALARA, MORRIS
  Last Wave, The **III-1325**
LAMARR, HEDY
  Algiers **I-37**
  Boom Town **I-305**
LAMBERT, ANNE
  Picnic at Hanging Rock **IV-1899**
LAMBERT, JACK
  Killers, The **III-1254**
LAMBRINOS, VASSILI
  Unsinkable Molly Brown, The IV-1808
LAMONT, MOLLY
  Awful Truth, The I-109
  Moon and Sixpence, The **IV-1638**
LAMOUR, DOROTHY
  Greatest Show on Earth, The II-697
  Hurricane, The II-793
  Road to Morocco III-1454
LAMPERT, ZOHRA
  Splendor in the Grass **V-2238**
LANCASTER, BURT
  Airport **I-27**
  All My Sons **I-50**
  Birdman of Alcatraz I-169
  Brute Force **I-360**
  Come Back, Little Sheba I-370
  Crimson Pirate, The **II-545**
  Elmer Gantry II-498
  From Here to Eternity II-577
  Go Tell the Spartans **II-892**
  Gunfight at the O.K. Corral **II-952**
  Judgment at Nuremberg **III-1239**
  Killers, The **III-1254**
  Professionals, The **IV-1944**
  Rainmaker, The III-1419
  Rose Tattoo, The III-1472
  Separate Tables IV-1506
  Seven Days in May **V-2144**
  Sorry, Wrong Number **V-2225**
  Sweet Smell of Success **V-2391**
  Swimmer, The **V-2395**
  Train, The **VI-2558**
  Unforgiven, The **VI-2593**

CXL

MILLER, DENNY
  Party, The **IV-1866**
MILLER, GLENN
  Sun Valley Serenade **V-2359**
MILLER, JASON
  Exorcist, The II-506
MILLER, PEGGY
  Pursued **IV-1950**
MILLER, SUSAN
  Never Give a Sucker an Even Break III-1193
MILLS, HAYLEY
  Chalk Garden, The **I-418**
  Family Way, The **II-753**
  Parent Trap, The III-1296
  Tiger Bay **VI-2519**
  Whistle Down the Wind **VI-2658**
MILLS, JOHN
  Chalk Garden, The **I-418**
  Family Way, The **II-753**
  Goodbye, Mr. Chips II-663
  Great Expectations II-685
  Hobson's Choice II-754
  In Which We Serve II-833
  King Rat II-911
  Oh! What a Lovely War **IV-1767**
  Rocking Horse Winner, The III-1462
  Ryan's Daughter III-1480
  This Happy Breed **VI-2483**
  Tiger Bay **VI-2519**
  Tunes of Glory **VI-2572**
  War and Peace **VI-2636**
  Wrong Box, The **VI-2718**
MILLER, JOHN "SKINS"
  Sun Valley Serenade **V-2359**
MILNER, MARTIN
  Compulsion I-380
  Gunfight at the O.K. Corral **II-952**
  Life with Father **III-1367**
  Sweet Smell of Success **V-2391**
MINCIOTTI, ESTHER
  Marty III-1079
MINEO, SAL
  Cheyenne Autumn **I-449**
  Rebel Without a Cause **V-1987**
  Somebody Up There Likes Me **V-2214**
MINER, JAN
  Lenny **III-1344**
MINNELLI, LIZA
  Arthur **I-116**
  Cabaret I-267
  Charlie Bubbles **I-433**
  Sterile Cuckoo, The **V-2274**
MINORU, NESHIDA
  Shanghai Express **V-2167**
MINOTIS, ALEXIS
  Panic in the Streets **IV-1860**
MIRACLE, IRENE
  Midnight Express **IV-1578**
MIRANDA, ISA
  Summertime **V-2348**
MIRREN, HELEN
  Excalibur **II-731**
  O Lucky Man! III-1231
MISENER, HELEN
  Night to Remember, A III-1203
MITCHELL, CAMERON
  Carousel I-298

Death of a Salesman I-421
  Love Me or Leave Me **III-1455**
MITCHELL, GEORGE
  Unsinkable Molly Brown, The IV-1808
MITCHELL, GRANT
  My Sister Eileen **IV-1693**
MITCHELL, GWEN
  Shaft **V-2156**
MITCHELL, JAMES
  Band Wagon, The I-123
MITCHELL, JOHNNY
  Mr. Skeffington III-1125
MITCHELL, MILLARD
  Foreign Affair, A **II-812**
  Gunfighter, The **II-956**
  Naked Spur, The **IV-1704**
  Singin' in the Rain IV-1560
  Twelve O'Clock High IV-1786
  Winchester '73 IV-1848
MITCHELL, THOMAS
  Alias Nick Beal **I-41**
  Angels over Broadway **I-86**
  Dark Mirror, The **II-567**
  Gone with the Wind II-654
  High Noon II-745
  Hunchback of Notre Dame, The II-786
  Hurricane, The II-793
  It's a Wonderful Life II-856
  Keys of the Kingdom, The **III-1251**
  Long Voyage Home, The III-1003
  Lost Horizon III-1006
  Only Angels Have Wings III-1279
  Our Town **IV-1834**
  Stagecoach IV-1612
  Theodora Goes Wild **V-2454**
  Wilson **VI-2682**
MITCHELL, YVONNE
  Tiger Bay **VI-2519**
MITCHUM, ROBERT
  Crossfire **II-548**
  Enemy Below, The **II-712**
  Farewell, My Lovely I-521
  Heaven Knows, Mr. Allison **III-1008**
  Last Tycoon, The **III-1322**
  Longest Day, The **III-1424**
  Lusty Men, The **IV-1471**
  Night of the Hunter, The III-1200
  Out of the Past III-1287
  Pursued **IV-1950**
  Red Pony, The **V-1997**
  Ryan's Daughter III-1480
  Story of G.I. Joe, The IV-1638
  Sundowners, The **V-2367**
MITROVICH, MARTA
  Dark Mirror, The **II-567**
MODICA, ROBERT
  Rain People, The **V-1972**
MOFFAT, DONALD
  Rachel, Rachel **V-1958**
MOFFETT, SHARYN
  Body Snatcher, The I-198
  Mr. Blandings Builds His Dream House **IV-1609**
MOLLISON, HENRY
  Tight Little Island IV-1738
MOLNAR WALTER
  To Have and Have Not IV-1752
MONAHAN, RICHARD
  Steel Helmet, The **V-2271**

PICKENS, SLIM
  Blazing Saddles   I-184
  Dr. Strangelove   I-465
  One-Eyed Jacks   **IV-1795**
PICKFORD, MARY
  Coquette   **II-524**
  Secrets   **V-2128**
PICKLES, VIVIAN
  Harold and Maude   II-716
  O Lucky Man!   III-1231
  Sunday, Bloody Sunday   **V-2363**
PICKLES, WILFRED
  Billy Liar   **I-245**
  Family Way, The   **II-753**
PICON, MOLLY
  Fiddler on the Roof   II-527
PIDGEON, WALTER
  Advise and Consent   I-18
  Bad and the Beautiful, The   I-112
  Command Decision   **II-498**
  Executive Suite   **II-735**
  Forbidden Planet   **II-805**
  Funny Girl   II-589
  How Green Was My Valley   II-776
  Madame Curie   III-1033
  Million Dollar Mermaid   III-1104
  Mrs. Miniver   III-1131
PIERCE, JAMES
  Flash Gordon   **II-796**
PIGOTT, TEMPE
  One More River   **IV-1805**
PIOUS, MINERVA
  It's in the Bag   **III-1198**
PITCAIRN, JACK
  Journey's End   **III-1229**
PITEOFF, SACHA
  Anastasia   **I-71**
PITHEY, WENSLEY
  Oh! What a Lovely War   **IV-1767**
PITTS, ZASU
  Guardsman, The   **II-942**
  Life with Father   **III-1367**
  Ruggles of Red Gap   **V-2066**
PLACE, MARY KAY
  Starting Over   **V-2267**
PLATT, EDWARD
  Rebel Without a Cause   **V-1987**
PLATT, LOUISE
  Stagecoach   IV-1612
PLATT, MARC
  Down to Earth   **II-667**
  Seven Brides for Seven Brothers   IV-1515
PLEASENCE, DONALD
  Cul-de-Sac   **II-557**
  Great Escape, The   II-682
  Halloween   **II-969**
  Hearts of the West   **III-1005**
  Last Tycoon, The   **III-1322**
  Look Back in Anger   **III-1435**
  No Love for Johnnie   **IV-1732**
  Will Penny   **VI-2675**
PLESHETTE, SUZANNE
  Birds, The   **I-249**
  If It's Tuesday, This Must Be Belgium   **III-1113**
PLOWRIGHT, JOAN
  Entertainer, The   **II-720**

PLUMMER, CHRISTOPHER
  Man Who Would Be King, The   III-1063
  Sound of Music, The   IV-1586
  Wind Across the Everglades   **VI-2687**
POITIER, SIDNEY
  Blackboard Jungle   **I-264**
  Cry the Beloved Country   **II-554**
  Defiant Ones, The   **II-604**
  Edge of the City   **II-692**
  Guess Who's Coming to Dinner?   **II-945**
  In the Heat of the Night   II-829
  Lilies of the Field   **III-1374**
  No Way Out   **IV-1735**
  Raisin in the Sun, A   III-1422
  To Sir with Love   **VI-2530**
POLLARD, MICHAEL J.
  Bonnie and Clyde   I-205
  Russians Are Coming, The Russians Are
    Coming, The   **V-2073**
POLLOCK, NANCY R.
  Pawnbroker, The   **IV-1880**
POOLE, ROY
  Up the Down Staircase   **VI-2606**
POPE, GLORIA
  It's in the Bag   **III-1198**
POPWELL, JOHNNY
  Heart Is a Lonely Hunter, The   **III-1002**
PORTER, DON
  Candidate, The   **I-393**
PORTMAN, ERIC
  Magic Box, The   **IV-1485**
  Whisperers, The   **VI-2654**
POSTA, ADRIENNE
  To Sir with Love   **VI-2530**
POVAH, PHYLLIS
  Pat and Mike   **IV-1873**
POWELL, ADDISON
  Thomas Crown Affair, The   **VI-2486**
  Three Days of the Condor   **VI-2494**
POWELL, DICK
  Bad and the Beautiful, The   **I-112**
  Blessed Event   **I-267**
  Christmas in July   **I-454**
  Footlight Parade   **II-800**
  42nd Street   II-561
  Gold Diggers of 1933   **II-900**
  Midsummer Night's Dream, A   **IV-1587**
  Murder, My Sweet   III-1164
POWELL, ELEANOR
  Broadway Melody of 1940   I-245
POWELL, JANE
  Seven Brides for Seven Brothers   IV-1515
POWELL, LOVELADY
  I Never Sang for My Father   **III-1086**
POWELL, RUSSELL
  Check and Double Check   **I-446**
POWELL, WILLIAM
  Great Ziegfeld, The   **II-936**
  Libeled Lady   **III-1358**
  Life with Father   **III-1367**
  Manhattan Melodrama   **IV-1527**
  Mr. Peabody and the Mermaid   **IV-1619**
  One Way Passage   **IV-1812**
  Mister Roberts   III-1121
  My Man Godfrey   III-1178
  Thin Man, The   IV-1709
POWER, HARTLEY
  Dead of Night   **II-595**

RETTIG, TOMMY
    5,000 Fingers of Doctor T., The   **II-792**
    Panic in the Streets   **IV-1860**
    So Big   **V-2205**
REVERE, ANNE
    Body and Soul   I-195
    Gentleman's Agreement   II-610
    National Velvet   **IV-1710**
    Place in the Sun, A   III-1349
    Song of Bernadette, The   IV-1581
REVILL, CLIVE
    Fine Madness, A   **II-781**
REY, FERNANDO
    French Connection, The   II-574
REYNOLDS, BURT
    Deliverance   I-432
    Longest Yard, The   **III-1431**
    Starting Over   **V-2267**
REYNOLDS, DEBBIE
    How the West Was Won   **III-1069**
    Singin' in the Rain   IV-1560
    Three Little Words   **VI-2502**
    Unsinkable Molly Brown, The   IV-1808
REYNOLDS, GENE
    Boys' Town   **I-325**
    In Old Chicago   II-825
REYNOLDS, JOYCE
    Constant Nymph, The   **II-511**
REYNOLDS, MARJORIE
    Ministry of Fear   **IV-1590**
REYNOLDS, OWEN
    Old Mother Riley Detective   **IV-1778**
REYNOLDS, WILLIAM
    All That Heaven Allows   **I-53**
    There's Always Tomorrow   **VI-2457**
RHOADES, BARBARA
    Goodbye Girl, The   **II-915**
    Harry and Tonto   **III-989**
RHODES, CHRISTOPHER
    Shake Hands with the Devil   **V-2159**
RHODES, ERIK
    Gay Divorcee, The   II-605
    Top Hat   IV-1764
RHODES, MARJORIE
    Family Way, The   **II-753**
    Old Mother Riley Detective   **IV-1778**
    On Approval   **IV-1781**
RHYS-DAVIES, JOHN
    Raiders of the Lost Ark   **V-1966**
RICCIARDI, WILLIAM
    Scoundrel, The   **V-2113**
RICE, FLORENCE
    At the Circus   **I-127**
RICH, ALLAN
    Serpico   IV-1512
RICH, IRENE
    Champ, The   **I-421**
    Check and Double Check   **I-446**
    Mortal Storm, The   **IV-1654**
RICH, RON
    Fortune Cookie, The   **II-818**
RICHARDS, ADDISON
    Boys' Town   **I-325**
    Northwest Passage   **IV-1745**
RICHARDS, ANN
    Sorry, Wrong Number   **V-2225**

RICHARDS, AUBREY
    Ipcress File, The   **III-1175**
RICHARDS, BEATH
    Guess Who's Coming to Dinner?   **II-945**
RICHARDS, FOLEY
    Sergeant Rutledge   **V-2135**
RICHARDS, JEFF
    Seven Brides for Seven Brothers   IV-1515
RICHARDS, KYLE
    Halloween   **II-969**
RICHARDSON, IAN
    Marat/Sade   **IV-1530**
RICHARDSON, RALPH
    Citadel, The   I-343
    Dr. Zhivago   I-468
    Fallen Idol, The   **II-745**
    Four Feathers   II-566
    Heiress, The   II-730
    Holly and the Ivy, The   **III-1038**
    Long Day's Journey into Night   III-999
    Looking Glass War, The   **III-1439**
    O Lucky Man!   III-1231
    Oh! What a Lovely War   **IV-1767**
    Our Man in Havana   **IV-1831**
    Outcast of the Islands   **IV-1838**
    Things to Come   IV-1716
    Richard III   **V-2014**
    Wrong Box, The   **VI-2718**
RICHMAN, MARK
    Friendly Persuasion   **II-852**
RICHMOND, KANE
    Charlie Chan in Panama   **I-437**
RICHTER, DANIEL
    2001: A Space Odyssey   IV-1798
RICKSON, JOE
    Stagecoach   IV-1612
RIDGELY, JOHN
    Big Sleep, The   I-162
    Destination Tokyo   **II-625**
    Pride of the Marines   **IV-1924**
RIDGES, STANLEY
    Act of Murder, An   **I-11**
    Crime Without Passion   **II-541**
    If I Were King   **III-1107**
    Scoundrel, The   **V-2113**
    They Died with Their Boots On   **VI-2461**
    To Be or Not to Be   IV-1743
    Wilson   **VI-2682**
    Winterset   IV-1859
    Yellow Jack   **VI-2724**
RIGBY, EDWARD
    Happiest Days of Your Life, The   **III-978**
    Stars Look Down, The   **V-2263**
RIGG, DIANA
    Hospital, The   II-766
    Theatre of Blood   IV-1689
RILLA, WALTER
    Scarlet Pimpernel, The   IV-1493
RIORDAN, MARJORIE
    Mr. Skeffington   III-1125
RISS, DAN
    Panic in the Streets   **IV-1860**
RITCHARD, CYRIL
    Blackmail   I-181
RITCHIE, JUNE
    Kind of Loving, A   II-894

PERFORMER INDEX

TILBURY, ZEFFIE
  Mystery of Edwin Drood, The **IV-1696**
TILVERN, ALAN
  Bhowani Junction **I-205**
TINDALL, LOREN
  Good News **II-911**
TINDAMA, RIANO
  Trader Horn **VI-2554**
TINGWELL, CHARLES
  Breaker Morant **I-331**
  Murder She Said **IV-1672**
TOBEY, KENNETH
  Candidate, The **I-393**
  I Was a Male War Bride **III-1098**
  Thing, The IV-1712
  Wings of Eagles, The IV-1853
TOBIAS, GEORGE
  Hunchback of Notre Dame, The II-786
  My Sister Eileen **IV-1693**
  Sergeant York IV-1509
  Set-Up, The **V-2142**
  Silk Stockings IV-1553
  Strawberry Blonde, The **V-2310**
TOBIN, GENEVIEVE
  One Hour with You III-1268
  Petrified Forest, The **IV-1888**
TOBY, RUTH
  Our Town **IV-1834**
TODD, ANN
  Intermezzo **III-1159**
  Margie **IV-1533**
  Pride of the Marines **IV-1924**
TODD, ANN
  Seventh Veil, The IV-1523
  Vacation from Marriage **VI-2608**
TODD, ELEANOR
  Lusty Men, The **IV-1471**
TODD, RICHARD
  Stage Fright **V-2246**
TODD, THELMA
  Horse Feathers **III-1051**
  Monkey Business III-1141
TOGNAZZI, UGO
  Barbarella **I-170**
TOLAN, KATHLEEN
  Death Wish **II-600**
TOLAN, MICHAEL
  Hour of the Gun **III-1061**
TOLER, SIDNEY
  Blonde Venus I-273
  Charlie Chan in Panama **I-437**
  If I Were King **III-1107**
  It's in the Bag **III-1198**
  Night to Remember, A **IV-1728**
TOLKAN, JAMES
  Love and Death **III-1449**
TOMLIN, LILY
  Late Show, The **III-1330**
  Nashville III-1181
TOMLINSON, DAVID
  Mary Poppins **IV-1550**
  Tom Jones IV-1760
TONE, FRANCHOT
  Advise and Consent I-18
  Bombshell I-202
  Dangerous **II-564**
  Five Graves to Cairo **II-789**

Lives of a Bengal Lancer **III-1404**
Mickey One **IV-1571**
Mutiny on the Bounty III-1167
Three Comrades IV-1731
TOOMEY, REGIS
  High and the Mighty, The **III-1023**
  Meet John Doe III-1087
TOPOL
  Fiddler on the Roof II-527
TORME, MEL
  Good News **II-911**
TORN, RIP
  King of Kings II-908
  Sweet Bird of Youth **V-2387**
  You're a Big Boy Now **VI-2746**
TORRENCE, DAVID
  Voltaire **VI-2622**
TORRENCE, ERNEST
  I Cover the Waterfront **III-1083**
TORRES, RAQUEL
  Duck Soup **II-673**
TOTTENHAM, MERLE
  Cavalcade I-316
  Night Must Fall **IV-1717**
TOTTER, AUDREY
  Alias Nick Beal **I-41**
  Lady in the Lake **III-1297**
  Set-Up, The **V-2142**
  Unsuspected, The **VI-2603**
TOUBUS, PHILIP
  Jesus Christ Superstar **III-1216**
TOUMANOVA, TAMARA
  Private Life of Sherlock Holmes, The **IV-1936**
TOVAR, LUPITA
  Westerner, The IV-1830
TOWERS, CONSTANCE
  Sergeant Rutledge **V-2135**
TRACY, LEE
  Best Man, The **I-199**
  Blessed Event **I-267**
  Bombshell I-202
  Dinner at Eight I-444
TRACY, SPENCER
  Actress, The **I-18**
  Adam's Rib I 6
  Bad Day at Black Rock I-116
  Boom Town **I-305**
  Boys' Town **I-325**
  Broken Lane **I-343**
  Captains Courageous I-289
  Desk Set **II-616**
  Dr. Jekyll and Mr. Hyde I-461
  Father of the Bride **II-770**
  Fury II-596
  Guess Who's Coming to Dinner? **II-945**
  Inherit the Wind **III-1148**
  Judgment at Nuremberg **III-1239**
  Last Hurrah, The II-945
  Libeled Lady **III-1358**
  Northwest Passage **IV-1745**
  Old Man and the Sea, The **IV-1775**
  Pat and Mike **IV-1873**
  Power and the Glory, The III-1368
  San Francisco III-1487
  State of the Union IV-1627
  Test Pilot **V-2439**
  Woman of the Year **VI-2705**

CHRONOLOGICAL LIST OF TITLES

1927

Jazz Singer, The

1928

Home Towners, The
On Trial
Terror, The

1929

Applause
Blackmail
Broadway Melody, The
Bulldog Drummond
Coquette
Dynamite
Great Gabbo, The
Hallelujah!
In Old Arizona
Last of Mrs. Cheyney, The
Love Parade, The
Rio Rita
Street Girl
Trespasser, The

1930

All Quiet on the Western Front
Animal Crackers
Anna Christie
Big House, The
Check and Double Check
Dawn Patrol, The
Hell's Angels
Journey's End
Laughter
Little Caesar
Min and Bill
Morocco
Unholy Three, The
Whoopee!

1931

Arrowsmith
Champ, The
Cimarron
City Lights
Dracula

Frankenstein
Free Soul, A
Front Page, The
Guardsman, The
Monkey Business
Public Enemy, The
Sin of Madelon Claudet, The
Skippy
Street Scene
Struggle, The
Svengali
Tabu
Trader Horn

1932

Arsene Lupin
Bill of Divorcement, A
Blessed Event
Blonde Venus
Dr. Jekyll and Mr. Hyde
Farewell to Arms, A
Freaks
Grand Hotel
Horse Feathers
I Am a Fugitive from a Chain Gang
Law and Order
Love Me Tonight
Million Dollar Legs
Mummy, The
One Hour with You
One Way Passage
Rain
Rasputin and the Empress
Red Dust
Scarface: The Shame of the Nation
Shanghai Express
Silver Dollar
Tarzan, the Ape Man
Trouble in Paradise
What Price Hollywood?

1933

Bitter Tea of General Yen, The
Bombshell
Cavalcade
Death Takes a Holiday
Design for Living
Dinner at Eight
Duck Soup

(**Bold type** signifies Second Series)

Emperor Jones, The
Flying Down to Rio
Footlight Parade
42nd Street
Gold Diggers of 1933
I Cover the Waterfront
Invisible Man, The
Island of Lost Souls
King Kong
Lady for a Day
Little Women
Morning Glory
Power and the Glory, The
Private Life of Henry VIII, The
Queen Christina
Secrets
She Done Him Wrong
Topaze
Voltaire

1934

Babes in Toyland
Barretts of Wimpole Street, The
Cleopatra
Count of Monte Cristo, The
Crime Without Passion
Evergreen
Gay Divorcee, The
Imitation of Life
It Happened One Night
It's a Gift
Judge Priest
Little Minister, The
Lost Patrol, The
Man of Aran
Manhattan Melodrama
Merry Widow, The
Modern Hero, A
Of Human Bondage
One More River
One Night of Love
Our Daily Bread
Private Life of Don Juan, The
Scarlet Pimpernel, The
Sing as We Go
Thin Man, The
Twentieth Century

1935

Ah, Wilderness!

Alice Adams
Anna Karenina
Bride of Frankenstein, The
Captain Blood
County Chairman, The
Dangerous
David Copperfield
Informer, The
Littlest Rebel, The
Lives of a Bengal Lancer
Magnificent Obsession
Midsummer Night's Dream, A
Miserables, Les
Mutiny on the Bounty
Mystery of Edwin Drood, The
Naughty Marietta
Night at the Opera, A
Roberta
Ruggles of Red Gap
Scoundrel, The
Sylvia Scarlett
Tale of Two Cities, A
39 Steps, The
Top Hat
Whole Town's Talking, The

1936

Anthony Adverse
Camille
Charge of the Light Brigade, The
Craig's Wife
Dodsworth
Flash Gordon
Follow the Fleet
Fury
Great Ziegfeld, The
Hollywood Boulevard
Libeled Lady
Mary of Scotland
Mr. Deeds Goes to Town
Modern Times
My Man Godfrey
Petrified Forest, The
Rembrandt
Romeo and Juliet
San Francisco
Show Boat
Story of Louis Pasteur, The
Swing Time
Theodora Goes Wild

You Can't Cheat an Honest Man
Young Mr. Lincoln

1940

Abe Lincoln in Illinois
All This and Heaven Too
Angels over Broadway
Arise My Love
Bank Dick, The
Biscuit Eater, The
Blondie on a Budget
Boom Town
Broadway Melody of 1940, The
Charlie Chan in Panama
Christmas in July
Dr. Ehrlich's Magic Bullet
Dr. Kildare's Strange Case
Fantasia
Foreign Correspondent
Grapes of Wrath, The
Great Dictator, The
Great McGinty, The
His Girl Friday
Kitty Foyle
Let George Do It
Letter, The
Long Voyage Home, The
Mark of Zorro, The
Mortal Storm, The
My Favorite Wife
My Little Chickadee
Northwest Passage
Our Town
Philadelphia Story, The
Pinocchio
Pride and Prejudice
Rebecca
Sea Hawk, The
Shop Around the Corner, The
Thief of Bagdad, The
Waterloo Bridge
Westerner, The

1941

Adam Had Four Sons
Back Street
Ball of Fire
Blood and Sand
Blues in the Night

Buck Privates
Citizen Kane
Devil and Daniel Webster, The
Devil and Miss Jones, The
Dr. Jekyll and Mr. Hyde
Dumbo
Great Lie, The
Here Comes Mr. Jordan
High Sierra
How Green Was My Valley
Johnny Eager
King's Row
Ladies in Retirement
Lady Eve, The
Little Foxes, The
Major Barbara
Maltese Falcon, The
Meet John Doe
Mr. and Mrs. Smith
Never Give a Sucker an Even Break
One Foot in Heaven
Penny Serenade
Sea Wolf, The
Sergeant York
So Ends Our Night
Strawberry Blonde, The
Sullivan's Travels
Sun Valley Serenade
Suspicion
That Hamilton Woman
They Died with Their Boots On
Western Union
Wolf Man, The

1942

Across the Pacific
Casablanca
Cat People
Gentleman Jim
I Married a Witch
In Which We Serve
Larceny, Inc.
Magnificent Ambersons, The
Major and the Minor, The
Male Animal, The
Mrs. Miniver
Moon and Sixpence, The
My Sister Eileen
Night to Remember, A
Now, Voyager

Ox-Bow Incident, The
Palm Beach Story, The
Pride of the Yankees
Road to Morocco
Roxie Hart
Saboteur
Spitfire
Talk of the Town, The
This Gun for Hire
To Be or Not to Be
Woman of the Year
Yankee Doodle Dandy

1943

Action in the North Atlantic
Cabin in the Sky
Colonel Blimp
Constant Nymph, The
Destination Tokyo
Five Graves to Cairo
For Whom the Bell Tolls
Forever and a Day
Girl Crazy
Heaven Can Wait
Human Comedy, The
I Walked with a Zombie
Lassie Come Home
Madame Curie
Man in Grey, The
Mr. Lucky
More the Merrier, The
Old Acquaintance
Old Mother Riley Detective
Phantom of the Opera, The
Princess O'Rourke
Shadow of a Doubt
Song of Bernadette, The
Watch on the Rhine

1944

Arsenic and Old Lace
Canterville Ghost, The
Cobra Woman
Double Indemnity
Gaslight
Going My Way
Hail the Conquering Hero
Henry V
Jane Eyre

Keys of the Kingdom, The
Lady in the Dark
Laura
Lifeboat
Lodger, The
Meet Me in St. Louis
Ministry of Fear
Miracle of Morgan's Creek, The
Mr. Skeffington
Murder, My Sweet
National Velvet
None but the Lonely Heart
On Approval
Since You Went Away
To Have and Have Not
Uninvited, The
Wilson
Woman in the Window

1945

Anchors Aweigh
And Then There Were None
Bells of St. Mary's, The
Body Snatcher, The
Caesar and Cleopatra
Clock, The
Confidential Agent
Corn Is Green, The
Dead of Night
Enchanted Cottage, The
Great Flamarion, The
House on 92nd Street, The
It's in the Bag
Leave Her to Heaven
Lost Weekend, The
Mildred Pierce
Picture of Dorian Gray, The
Pride of the Marines
Saratoga Trunk
Scarlet Street
Southerner, The
Spellbound
Stairway to Heaven
Story of G.I. Joe, The
They Were Expendable
Tree Grows in Brooklyn, A
Vacation from Marriage
Walk in the Sun, A
Yolanda and the Thief

1946

Anna and the King of Siam
Best Years of Our Lives, The
Big Sleep, The
Blithe Spirit
Blue Dahlia, The
Brief Encounter
Cluny Brown
Dark Mirror, The
Duel in the Sun
Gilda
Harvey Girls, The
Humoresque
It's a Wonderful Life
Jolson Story, The
Killers, The
Margie
My Darling Clementine
Night and Day
Postman Always Rings Twice, The
Razor's Edge, The
Seventh Veil, The
Spiral Staircase, The
Stranger, The
To Each His Own
Yearling, The

1947

Bachelor and the Bobby Soxer, The
Bishop's Wife, The
Black Narcissus
Body and Soul
Boomerang!
Brute Force
Crossfire
Double Life, A
Down to Earth
Egg and I, The
Fugitive, The
Gentleman's Agreement
Ghost and Mrs. Muir, The
Good News
Great Expectations
I See a Dark Stranger
Lady in the Lake
Life with Father
Macomber Affair, The
Miracle on 34th Street
Monsieur Verdoux

Mother Wore Tights
Nightmare Alley
Odd Man Out
Out of the Past
Pursued
Random Harvest
This Happy Breed
Unsuspected, The

1948

Act of Murder, An
All My Sons
Barkleys of Broadway, The
Big Clock, The
Boy with Green Hair, The
Call Northside 777
Caught
Command Decision
Easter Parade
Force of Evil
Foreign Affair, A
Hamlet
I Remember Mama
Johnny Belinda
Key Largo
Lady from Shanghai, The
Letter from an Unknown Woman
Louisiana Story
Mister Blandings Builds His Dream House
Mr. Peabody and the Mermaid
Moonrise
Naked City, The
Paleface, The
Pirate, The
Portrait of Jennie
Red River
Red Shoes, The
Search, The
Sitting Pretty
Snake Pit, The
Sorry, Wrong Number
State of the Union
They Live by Night
Three Godfathers
Three Musketeers, The
Treasure of the Sierra Madre, The
Unfaithfully Yours

Limelight
Lusty Men, The
Man in the White Suit, The
Marrying Kind, The
Member of the Wedding, The
Million Dollar Mermaid
Monkey Business
Moulin Rouge
Naked Spur, The
Outcast of the Islands
Pat and Mike
Quiet Man, The
Rancho Notorious
Room for One More
Scaramouche
Singin' in the Rain
Star, The
Tonight at Eight-Thirty
Viva Zapata!
With a Song in My Heart

1953

Actress, The
Band Wagon, The
Big Heat, The
Calamity Jane
Cruel Sea, The
5,000 Fingers of Doctor T., The
From Here to Eternity
Gentlemen Prefer Blondes
House of Wax
I Confess
Julius Caesar
Kiss Me Kate
Lawless Breed, The
Lili
Mogambo
Moon Is Blue, The
Pickup on South Street
Robe, The
Roman Holiday
Shane
So Big
Stalag 17
Sun Shines Bright, The
Titanic
War of the Worlds

1954

Bad Day at Black Rock

Beat the Devil
Belles of St. Trinian's, The
Bridges at Toko-Ri, The
Brigadoon
Broken Lance
Caine Mutiny, The
Country Girl,The
Dial M for Murder
Doctor in the House
Executive Suite
Genevieve
High and the Mighty, The
Hobson's Choice
Inspector Calls, An
Johnny Guitar
Magnificent Obsession
On the Waterfront
Rear Window
Riot in Cell Block 11
Sabrina
Seven Brides for Seven Brothers
Star Is Born, A
Them!
20,000 Leagues Under the Sea
Wild One, The

1955

All That Heaven Allows
Artists and Models
Big Knife, The
Blackboard Jungle
Daddy Long Legs
Desperate Hours, The
East of Eden
Francis in the Navy
I Am a Camera
I'll Cry Tomorrow
Interrupted Melody
Kiss Me Deadly
Love Is a Many-Splendored Thing
Love Me or Leave Me
Marty
Mister Roberts
Night of the Hunter, The
Oklahoma!
Picnic
Rose Tattoo, The
Seven Year Itch, The
Summertime
To Catch a Thief

Ben-Hur
Blind Date
Compulsion
Diary of Anne Frank, The
Hanging Tree, The
Imitation of Life
League of Gentlemen, The
Look Back in Anger
Mouse That Roared, The
North by Northwest
Nun's Story, The
On the Beach
Operation Petticoat
Pillow Talk
Rio Bravo
Room at the Top
Savage Innocents, The
Shake Hands with the Devil
Some Like It Hot
Suddenly, Last Summer
Summer Place, A
Tiger Bay

1960

Angry Silence, The
Apartment, The
Butterfield 8
Carry on Nurse
Concrete Jungle, The
Elmer Gantry
Entertainer, The
Flaming Star
I'm All Right, Jack
Inherit the Wind
Little Shop of Horrors, The
Magnificent Seven, The
Midnight Lace
Our Man in Havana
Psycho
Saturday Night and Sunday Morning
Sergeant Rutledge
Sons and Lovers
Spartacus
Sundowners, The
Tunes of Glory
Unforgiven,The
Wild River

1961

Breakfast at Tiffany's

Children's Hour, The
Cid, El
Fanny
Guns of Navarone, The
Hustler, The
Innocents, The
Judgment at Nuremberg
Kind of Loving, A
King of Kings
Mark, The
Misfits, The
No Love for Johnnie
One-Eyed Jacks
Parent Trap, The
Raisin in the Sun, A
Splendor in the Grass
Summer and Smoke
Taste of Honey, A
View from the Bridge, A
West Side Story
Whistle Down the Wind

1962

Advise and Consent
Billy Budd
Birdman of Alcatraz
Counterfeit Traitor, The
David and Lisa
Days of Wine and Roses
Dr. No
Hemingway's Adventures of a Young Man
Lawrence of Arabia
Lolita
Loneliness of the Long Distance Runner, The
Lonely Are the Brave
Long Day's Journey into Night
Longest Day, The
Man Who Shot Liberty Valance, The
Manchurian Candidate, The
Miracle Worker, The
Murder She Said
Music Man, The
Phantom of the Opera, The
Requiem for a Heavyweight
Ride the High Country
Sweet Bird of Youth
To Kill a Mockingbird
Ugly American, The

Morgan!
Professionals, The
Russians Are Coming, The Russians
  Are Coming, The
Seconds
Whisperers, The
Who's Afraid of Virginia Woolf?
Wrong Box, The

1967

Accident
Barefoot in the Park
Bonnie and Clyde
Cool Hand Luke
Dirty Dozen, The
Far from the Madding Crowd
Graduate, The
Guess Who's Coming to Dinner?
Hour of the Gun
I'll Never Forget Whatshisname
In Cold Blood
In the Heat of the Night
King of Hearts
Marat/Sade
Point Blank
President's Analyst, The
To Sir with Love
Two for the Road
Ulysses
Up the Down Staircase
Wait Until Dark
You're a Big Boy Now

1968

Barbarella
Boston Strangler, The
Bullitt
Charlie Bubbles
Charly
Faces
Funny Girl
Heart Is a Lonely Hunter, The
Hot Millions
If. . . .
Isadora
Lion in Winter, The
Night They Raided Minsky's, The
No Way to Treat a Lady
Odd Couple, The

Oliver!
Party, The
Petulia
Planet of the Apes
Producers, The
Rachel, Rachel
Rosemary's Baby
Swimmer, The
Thomas Crown Affair, The
2001: A Space Odyssey
Will Penny
Yellow Submarine

1969

Alice's Restaurant
Bob and Carol and Ted and Alice
Butch Cassidy and the Sundance Kid
Cactus Flower
Downhill Racer
Easy Rider
Goodbye Columbus
I Never Sang for My Father
If It's Tuesday, This Must Be Belgium
Lovers and Other Strangers
Medium Cool
Midnight Cowboy
Oh! What a Lovely War
Prime of Miss Jean Brodie, The
Putney Swope
Rain People, The
Reivers, The
Sterile Cuckoo, The
Support Your Local Sheriff
Tell Them Willie Boy Is Here
They Shoot Horses Don't They?
True Grit
Wild Bunch, The

1970

Airport
Boys in the Band, The
Cotton Comes to Harlem
Diary of a Mad Housewife
Entertaining Mr. Sloane
Five Easy Pieces
Husbands
Landlord, The
Little Big Man
Looking Glass War, The

CHRONOLOGICAL LIST OF TITLES

M*A*S*H
Owl and the Pussycat, The
Patton
Performance
Private Life of Sherlock Holmes, The
Ryan's Daughter
Virgin and the Gypsy, The
Women in Love

1971

Bananas
Beguiled, The
Billy Jack
Boy Friend, The
Carnal Knowledge
Clockwork Orange, A
Dirty Harry
Fiddler on the Roof
French Connection, The
Go-Between, The
Harold and Maude
Hired Hand, The
Hospital, The
Klute
Last Picture Show, The
McCabe and Mrs. Miller
Minnie and Moskowitz
Panic in Needle Park, The
Shaft
Sometimes a Great Notion
Straw Dogs
Such Good Friends
Summer of '42
Sunday, Bloody Sunday
Two-Lane Blacktop
Walkabout

1972

Cabaret
Candidate, The
Deliverance
Fat City
Frenzy
Godfather, The
Jeremiah Johnson
Junior Bonner
Last Tango in Paris
Life and Times of Judge Roy Bean, The

One Is a Lonely Number
Play It Again, Sam
Poseidon Adventure, The
Ruling Class, The
Sleuth
Sounder
Super Fly

1973

American Graffiti
Blume in Love
Butley
Cinderella Liberty
Cops and Robbers
Doll's House, A
Don't Look Now
Exorcist, The
Harder They Come, The
Hireling, The
Jesus Christ Superstar
Last Detail, The
Mean Streets
O Lucky Man!
Paper Chase, The
Paper Moon
Save the Tiger
Serpico
Sleeper
Sting, The
Theatre of Blood
Touch of Class, A

1974

Apprenticeship of Duddy Kravitz, The
Badlands
Blazing Saddles
Chinatown
Conversation, The
Death Wish
Godfather, Part II, The
Great Gatsby, The
Harry and Tonto
Lenny
Longest Yard, The
Monty Python and the Holy Grail
Sugarland Express, The
That's Entertainment
Thieves Like Us

CXCV

Towering Inferno, The
Woman Under the Influence, A

1975

Alice Doesn't Live Here Anymore
Barry Lyndon
Day of the Locust
Dog Day Afternoon
Farewell, My Lovely
Hearts of the West
Hester Street
Jaws
Love and Death
Man Who Would Be King, The
Nashville
One Flew Over the Cuckoo's Nest
Rocky Horror Picture Show, The
Shampoo
Smile

1976

All the President's Men
Bad News Bears, The
Carrie
Last Tycoon, The
Network
Outlaw Josey Wales, The
Robin and Marian
Rocky
Seven-Per-cent Solution, The
Shootist, The
Taxi Driver
That's Entertainment, Part II

1977

Annie Hall
Close Encounters of the Third Kind
Goodbye Girl, The
High Anxiety
Islands in the Stream
Julia
Late Show, The
Saturday Night Fever
Spy Who Loved Me, The
Star Wars
3 Women

1978

Coming Home
Deer Hunter, The

Foul Play
Girl Friends
Go Tell the Spartans
Grease
Halloween
Heaven Can Wait
Interiors
Midnight Express
Unmarried Woman, An

1979

Alien
All That Jazz
Apocalypse Now
Being There
Breaking Away
Electric Horseman, The
Hair
Kramer vs. Kramer
Last Wave, The
Manhattan
Muppet Movie, The
Norma Rae
Onion Field, The
Picnic at Hanging Rock
Rocky II
Starting Over
10

1980

Big Red One, The
Breaker Morant
Bronco Billy
Brubaker
Coal Miner's Daughter
Elephant Man, The
ffolkes
My Brilliant Career
Ordinary People
Raging Bull
Shining, The
Storm Boy
Stunt Man, The

1981

Arthur
Excalibur
Raiders of the Lost Ark
Superman II